Penguin Education X55

The Labour Market

Penguin Modern Economics Readings

General Editor

B. J. McCormick

Advisory Board

K. J. W. Alexander
R. W. Clower
J. Spraos
H. Townsend

The Labour Market

Selected Readings

Edited by B. J. McCormick and E. Owen Smith

Penguin Books

Penguin Books Ltd, Harmondsworth,
Middlesex, England
Penguin Books Inc., 7110 Ambassador Court,
Baltimore, Md 21207, U.S.A.
Penguin Books Australia Ltd, Ringwood,
Victoria, Australia

First published by Penguin Books 1968

This selection © B. J. McCormick and E. Owen Smith, 1968
Introduction and notes © B. J. McCormick, 1968

Made and printed in Great Britain by
Richard Clay (The Chaucer Press) Ltd, Bungay, Suffolk
Set in Monotype Times

Contents

Introduction

Since the problems of labour have become a focus for the attention of sociologists, psychologists, and political scientists as well as economists, some demarcation seems to be necessary. The economist who studies the labour market does so with the tools of his profession and within the framework imposed by his discipline; he considers firstly microeconomics (the pricing and allocation of labour between various employments) and secondly macroeconomics (the broad aggregates of employment and wages and their interaction with other aggregates such as the capital, price level, shares in the national income, and economic growth).

In considering these problems the economist often takes for granted features of labour which are the concern of others. Morale, the capacity of the worker, and his scale of preferences are assumed to be given, and institutions are ignored unless they are shown to influence behaviour, wages, and employment. The political allegiances of workers and trade unions and the problems of trade-union democracy are outside his purview, interesting though they may be to others. Nevertheless, the labour economist has often to wander outside his discipline because labour matters: workers cannot be bought and sold, and people cannot be disassociated from their services.

This volume of readings does not seek to be comprehensive. It attempts to reflect the economist's propensity to theorize and his current desire to test his theories by showing, for instance, how abstract models which embody basic features of labour markets yield predictions that have to be checked against the usual results of actual markets. The volume also tries to embrace the current preoccupations of economists with problems that have social and political implications, such as incomes policies, the powers and responsibilities of trade unions, and unemployment, all of which demand the tools of economics for their understanding and appreciation.

The microeconomic theory of labour demand considers the direction and magnitude of changes in the demand for labour as the price of labour varies. The theory consists of two parts: there is first of all the demand for personal services, e.g. taxi drivers and osteopaths, which is really an aspect of the general theory of consumer's behaviour, and there is secondly the indirect demand or derived demand for labour based upon the demand for commodities. The entrepreneur, attempting to maximize his profits, is seen to be guided in his demand for factors of production by a law of diminishing marginal revenue productivity whereby successive units of a factor yield successively smaller additions to receipts from product sales. This theory has been criticized on the grounds that businessmen do not or cannot attempt to maximize profits, and hence there is no justification for a belief in a negatively sloping demand curve for labour.

The supply side of the labour market has always tended to be the Achilles' heel of wage theories and after a long period of neglect it is at last attracting attention. What determines the apparent constancy of the labour force as a proportion of the total population? What accounts for the secular rise in the participation rate of married women? What have been the determinants of the secular fall in hours of work? How do we explain the differential incidence of unemployment? What part do unions play in determining relative wages and their allocation? The break-through in theorizing has occurred by re-examining the theory of household behaviour. The household possesses certain skills and undertakes certain basic activities (domestic production, consumption, market production, and leisure); skills and tastes in conjunction with wages for market jobs determine the division of activities within the household, just as skills and tastes also determine the type of market activity undertaken. Preferences for combination of monetary and non-monetary rewards clash with capacity (skill) to perform certain jobs, so that the theory of labour supply, like the theory of the firm, is witnessing the challenge of two powerful general theories (utility theory and capital theory) for dominance. Capital theory has come to play an increasing role in our understanding of the acquisition of skills (human capital).

The economist who seeks to understand the economic impact of trade unions must study their structure, government, and wage policies. Why do unions organize particular groups of workers? Can they be understood with the traditional tools of economic analysis or is it sometimes the case, as Turner (reading 5) suggests, that unions just do not like to see anyone left unorganized? The problem of trade-union government, i.e. of democracy in trade unions, is of concern to the economist only to the extent that he needs to understand how wage policies emerge, since if there is a divorce of ownership from control, then the behaviour of such unions will presumably differ from that of those unions whose leadership readily responds to rank and file demands.

Do changes in relative wages cause changes in the allocation of labour or do the numbers employed in different occupations result from the availability of jobs *per se*? The answer to this question has political as well as academic implications, because if relative wages do not serve as the means by which labour is allocated, the formulation of a national-incomes policy is so much simpler, there being no need to add qualifications to the general rule that wages should advance in line with productivity increases. Moreover if relative wages perform no economic function, then there exists the possibility that relative wages may themselves be determined by non-economic forces. Wage differentials may be dictated by custom, by unions, or by economic forces and it is the task of the economist to explain their movements.

Causative factors in the movement of money-wage levels play a crucial role in the explanation of inflationary processes and the possible causes and cures of mass unemployment or inflation. Does inflation result from pressures arising on the demand or the supply side of the labour market? Is there any simple universal law relating demand to the movement of money wages or do institutional changes in the labour market over a period of time invalidate simple propositions? What part do different methods of wage payment play in the inflationary process? The articles in the penultimate section are devoted to the analysis of these contemporary problems, problems which affect our attempt to secure full employment, stable prices, and a steady rate of growth.

The final section is devoted to a classic problem. How can we explain the distribution of the national income? Is the macro-distribution simply brought about by the aggregation of the results of microeconomic decisions into which marginal productivity enters or are there more general considerations to be borne in mind?

Part One The Demand for Labour

The profit-maximizing entrepreneur is guided in his demand for factors of production by a law of diminishing marginal (value) productivity. The degree to which demand responds to a change in the price of a factor depends upon the determinants of the elasticity of derived demand. The article by Lester is concerned primarily with whether the demand curve for labour has a negative slope; various methods can be used to test the marginal-productivity doctrine and Lester employs the questionnaire. The selection from Machlup illustrates the dangers of using the questionnaire and also the difficulties of testing the doctrine.

1 R. A. Lester

Shortcomings of Marginal Analysis for Wage-employment Problems

Lester, R. A. (1946) Shortcomings of marginal analysis for wage employment problems. *Amer. Econ. Rev.*, 36, 63–82.

The conventional explanation of the output and employment policies of individual firms runs in terms of maximizing profits by equating marginal revenue and marginal cost. Student protests that their entrepreneural parents claim not to operate on the marginal principle have apparently failed to shake the confidence of the textbook writers in the validity of the marginal analysis. Indeed, the trend over the past decade has been to devote more and more space in elementary textbooks to complicated graphs illustrating marginal relationships and to detailed discussions of marginal analysis under a variety of assumed circumstances.[1]

A gap, however, exists between marginal theory of the firm and general theories concerning employment, money, and the business cycle.[2] Textbooks that spend so much of the students' time on the mathematics of profit maximization according to marginal analysis may not mention that principle at all in chapters dealing with the price level, the business cycle, national income, etc. The respective roles of markets and costs in determining output and employment are not clearly explained. The hiatus exists in Keynes's *General Theory*, despite his efforts to avoid inhabiting two separate theoretical worlds. He fails to reconcile his continued adherence to the marginal-productivity theory with his

1. The minutiae of marginalism consume, for example, approximately half of the pages of K. E. Boulding, *Economic Analysis* (1941), and A. M. McIsaac and J. G. Smith, *Introduction to Economic Analysis* (1937), and about one-third of the pages of M. J. Bowman and G. L. Bach, *Economic Analysis and Public Policy* (1943), and A. L. Myers, *Elements of Modern Economics* (1937).

2. For a similar opinion see Jacob Marschak, 'A cross section of business cycle discussion,' *Amer. Econ. Rev.*, vol. 35, no. 3 (June 1945), pp. 371–2.

new theories of employment determination, based on effective demand.[3]

This paper does not pretend to bridge the gap between individual-firm theory and general theory. In examining the relationship between wages and employment from the point of view of the individual firm and investigating the shortcomings of marginal analysis for wage–employment matters, it does, however, represent a step in that direction. Much more evidence must be accumulated before definitive conclusions can be drawn regarding wage–employment relationships. The tentative conclusions of this paper are based on scattered evidence, including new material collected by the author, partly from discussions with numerous southern business executives but mainly in the form of written replies by fifty-odd concerns to questions concerning the relative role of different factors in determining their employment, alterations in their variable costs per unit with changes in rate of output, and their probable adjustments to an increase in wages relative to those paid by competing producers.[4]

As much of the evidence in the paper rests on the written replies of 58 southern concerns, a brief explanation of the selection and collection procedures used is given at this point. A detailed questionnaire was mailed in June 1945 to the presidents or executive officers of 430 southern manufacturing firms in industries known to have a significant north–south wage differential. Anonymous reply was possible and most answers were not identified. A total of 68 replies were received. However, 10 firms answered that most of the questions were too difficult or would require too much time to answer, so that only 58 of the replies contain answers to two or more of the questions. The 58 replies are distributed as follows by industry: 17 furniture producers, 13 metal-working firms (foundry, machinery and valve producers), 11 cotton-clothing manufacturers (producing work clothes, men's shirts, women's dresses, and cotton underwear), 4 full-fashioned hosiery manufacturers, 3 producers of shoes and leather, 3 paint producers, 4 chemical manufacturers, and 3 stove

3. See *The General Theory of Employment, Interest and Money* (1936), pp. 5, 17–18, and 77.

4. Financial support for this study has been supplied by the General Education Board.

producers.[5] Employment in these 58 firms averaged 600 (range 8[6]–8,200).

I

The relative importance of various factors (market demand, wage rates, non-labor costs, profits, production techniques, etc.) in determining the volume of employment offered by a firm constituted the subject matter of the first set of questions in the questionnaire. The objective was to obtain the judgment or opinion of the business executives, partly because policy decisions in those firms presumably are based largely upon such opinions.

The executives were asked: 'What factors have generally been the most important ones in determining the volume of employment in your firm during peacetime?' They were requested to rate the factors in terms of the percentage of importance of each; the total was not to exceed a rating of 100%, and, if one factor alone was important, it was to be marked 100%. The listing of the factors was as follows:

a. Present and prospective market demand (sales) for your products, including seasonal fluctuations in demand.

b. The level of wage rates or changes in the level of wages.

c. The level of material costs and other non-wage costs and changes in the level of such non-labor costs.

d. Variations in profits or losses of the firm.

e. New techniques, equipment, and production methods.

f. Other factors (please specify).

The answers gave overwhelming emphasis to current and prospective market demand for products of the firm as the im-

5. The 430 companies to which questionnaires were sent were distributed as follows: 103 furniture, 59 metal-working, 146 cotton-clothing, 23 full-fashioned hosiery, 19 shoes and leather, 25 paint and varnish, 17 chemicals, and 30 stoves. Only companies located entirely in the south were selected, and practically all of them were located in only one community. Geographically the replying firms are confined to the following states: Alabama, Arkansas, Florida, Georgia, Louisiana, North Carolina, Tennessee, Texas, and Virginia.

6. The next smallest firms are two with 25 employees each.

portant factor in determining its volume of employment. Out of 56 usable replies, 28 (or one-half) rated factor *a* (market demand) at 100%. Both shoe producers, 3 out of the 4 full-fashioned hosiery firms, and 11 out of the 16 furniture manufacturers were in that category; on the other hand, only 3 out of the 11 cotton clothing concerns and none of the 3 paint companies rated market demand 100%.

The replies of the other 28 firms that rated two or more factors as important are summarized in table 1.

Factor *b* (wages and changes in wage levels) and factor *d* (profits) are rated surprisingly low by the executive officers of these 56 firms in view of the emphasis placed on those two factors by marginal analysis. On the other hand, the relative stress placed on materials and other non-labor costs as a factor in determining

Table 1

Relative Importance of Factors Influencing a Firm's Employment as Indicated by Weighting Given by 28 Firms Rating 2 or More Factors

	a (Market)	*b* (Wages)	*c* (Non-labor costs)	*d* (Profits)	*e* (Technique)	*f* (Others)
Number of times mentioned	28	13	18	11	16	5
Average weight per time mentioned	65%	15%	14%	13%	17%	16%
Average for all 28 replies	65·0%	7·6%	9·5%	5·1%	9·7%	3·1%

the firm's volume of employment is surprisingly high. Non-labor costs are mentioned more frequently than wages, and they are considered more important than wages in determining the volume of employment by the replying firms in the furniture, cotton-clothing, paint, and chemical industries. Indeed, wages are not given a rating at all by any of the replying paint or chemical concerns, and only 1 out of 6 metal-working firms marking two or more factors gave any weight to wage item *b*. Yet labor costs were an important element in the total costs of practically all of these firms.[7]

The relative rating of item *e* (new techniques and changes in production methods) is not unexpected. The other factors mentioned under item *f* included 'competition' and 'management', which might perhaps have been properly included under items *a* and *e*. Replies of at least two firms indicated a realization that the various factors listed were not completely independent. That was, or course, correct.[8]

The failure to lay more stress on wages as a factor in determining the volume of employment is all the more surprising in view of the relatively high ratio of labor to total cost in most of the replying firms. Indeed, the correlation is remarkably low between the stress placed on wages as an employment factor and the percentage that labor costs are of the firm's total costs. True, 5 out of the 11 concerns with labor costs constituting from 40 to 60% of total costs marked wages as an important item in determining the firm's employment,[9] whereas only 1 of the 10 firms with wages from 12 to 20% of total costs did so. However, only one-tenth of the firms with wages ranging from 30 to 39% of the total cost mentioned wages as an important employment factor, whereas one-third of the firms with labor costs ranging from 21 to 29% of total costs marked wages along with one or more other factors.

In qualifying or elaborating their answers regarding the role of present and prospective demand for the firm's product, 8 concerns explained that they manufacture for stock during dull seasons, 3 others said that demand for their products had been stable or steadily increasing before the war, and 2 others replied that the operation of their equipment requires 'just so many men', so that 'during peacetime employment is more or less permanent'.

7. Each firm was requested to state the percentage that labor costs are of its total costs. The average for all replying firms was labor costs 29·3% of total costs (range 12–60%). The average was 23% for shoes and leather, 24% for paint, 25% for furniture, 31% for chemicals, 33% for cotton clothing, full-fashioned hosiery, and stoves, and 39% for metal-working concerns. Judging by census data, the average for all manufacturing is around 20%.

8. For example, wages affect profits and may influence the introduction of new techniques.

9. The top firm, with labor costs at 60% of total cost, was not, however one of the 5.

It is clear from numerous interviews that most business executives do not think of employment as a function of wage rates but as a function of output.[10] When questioned regarding the employment effects of increased or reduced wages they usually end up by stating that orders, not wage changes, are the important factor in output and employment. As explained in section III below, business executives generally do not think of deliberate curtailment of operations and employment as an adjustment to wage increases, partly because some plants and operations require fixed crews under existing techniques of production and partly because, as indicated under section II below, businessmen believe that variable costs per unit of production increase as production and employment are curtailed.

II

In recent years a number of attempts have been made to discover the way costs vary with changes in output. Individual-firm studies by Joel Dean and Theodore O. Yntema indicate that average variable costs (and marginal costs) tend to be constant per unit of product over the usual range of output, which includes up to practically full capacity.[11] Other statistical studies suggest that a

10. That our business men are no different in this regard from business men abroad seems to be indicated by experience in Germany under the 'Papen plan' for economic recovery introduced in September 1932. Through tax subsidies and other concessions, German entrepreneurs were able to hire additional workers, on the average, for about half the existing wage rates. Although such wage reduction for additional employees might have been expected to increase employment, employers hesitated to increase employment and output without an increase in orders, so that unemployment in Germany increased about 20% during the 5 months following introduction of the plan (see Gerhard Colm, 'Why the "Papen plan" for economic recovery failed', *Social Research*, vol. 1, 1934, especially pp. 90–1).

See also E. Ronald Walker's opinion based on Australia's experience during the 1930s in *From Economic Theory to Policy* (University of Chicago Press, Chicago, 1943), pp. 73–4.

11. See Joel Dean, *Statistical Determination of Costs With Special Reference to Marginal Costs* (University of Chicago Press, Chicago, 1936), *Statistical Cost Functions of a Hosiery Mill* (University of Chicago Press, Chicago, 1941), and *The Relation of Cost to Output for a Leather Belt Shop* (Nat. Bur. of Econ. Research, New York, 1941); and United States Steel Corporation, *T.N.E.C. Papers*, vol. 1, pp. 223–302. For criticisms see Hans Staehle, 'Statistical cost functions: appraisal of recent contributions', *Amer. Econ. Rev.*, vol. 32, no. 2 (June 1942), pp. 321–32; Caleb Smith, 'The

great number of American manufacturing firms operate under increasing average variable labor returns, primarily because marginal labor requirements decrease per unit as output rises toward full capacity.[12] Some studies indicate a definite tendency, especially in the durable goods industries, toward decreasing marginal cost of production, at least until almost full capacity is reached.[13]

In the present study a series of questions was asked regarding unit variable costs and profits at various rates of output. In reply to the question, 'At what level of operations are your profits generally greatest under peacetime conditions?' 42 firms answered 100% of plant capacity. The remaining 11 replies ranged from 75 to 95% of capacity.[14] Six of the 11 did not answer succeeding questions that would have supplied substantiating data. Some of them said these succeeding questions were 'too theoretical' or 'too technical', or that 'data were not available for an exact answer'. One simply stated: 'Our cost is based on 90% of capacity'. Of the 5 firms that did offer substantiating material, 3 gave cost estimates and 2 gave the following reasons: 'Assuming that if we were at 100% we would have to pay considerable overtime wages', and 'Theoretical 100% is likely to produce too many strains'.

The executives were also asked how, in peacetime, their factory operating costs (excluding overhead or fixed charges) per unit of output are usually affected by an increase or a decrease in the

---

cost-output relation for the U.S. Steel Corporation', *Rev. Econ. Stat.*, vol. 24 (November, 1942), pp. 166–76; and Everet Straus, 'Cost accounting and statistical cost functions', *Amer. Econ. Rev.*, vol. 35, no. 3 (June 1945) pp. 430–1.

12. See, for example, B. H. Topkis, 'Labor requirements in cement production', *Mo. Lab. Rev.*, vol. 42 (March 1936), p. 575; B. H. Topkis and H.O. Rogers, 'Man-hours of labor per unit of output in steel', *Mo. Lab. Rev.*, vol. 40 (May 1935), p. 1161; and M. Ezekiel, *$2,500 a year* (Harcourt Brace, New York, 1936), pp. 180–2.

13. Henry M. Oliver, Jr., 'The relationship between total output and man-hour output in manufacturing industry', *Quart. Jour. Econ.*, vol. 55 (February 1941), pp. 239–54; and M. Ezekiel and K. H. Wylie, 'Cost Functions for the Steel Industry', *Journ. Amer. Stat. Assoc.*, vol. 36 (March 1941), pp. 91–9.

14. These 11 firms were distributed as follows: 1 in furniture, 3 in cotton clothing, 2 in paint, 1 in chemicals, 1 in stoves, and 3 in metal-working.

company's rate of operations. More specifically they were asked the percentage by which an increase in operations from 95 to 100% (also 90–95%, 80–90%, and 70–80%) would tend to result in a rise or fall in operating or variable costs per unit of output. The answers are summarized in table 2 for 32 firms giving data indicating they have decreasing marginal variable costs up to 100% capacity,[15] along with 3 firms giving data showing increasing marginal costs beginning at 90, 80, and 75% of capacity.[16] Firms reporting decreasing unit costs up to 100% of capacity have also been classified according to the percentage that their labor costs are of total costs, and averages for 4 categories of labor-cost ratios are given.

The table opposite indicates some differences in the slope of the average decreasing unit cost curve for different industries. The decline is especially sharp for the metal-working firms and for others (full-fashioned hosiery, shoes, and chemicals) at operations between 70 and 90% of plant capacity. For furniture firms, on the other hand, the rate of decrease in unit variable costs is reported to be higher from 95 to 100% or from 90 to 95% of capacity than it is from 70 to 80% or 80 to 90% of capacity.

The answers seem to indicate that the percentage of labor to total cost of production has little direct influence upon the slope of the decreasing unit cost curve at operations between 70 and 100% of capacity. The average slope of the unit cost curve for firms with labor-cost ratios from 40 to 60% resembles that of the curve for firms with ratios from 12 to 20%. The peculiar slope of the average curve for firms with labor-cost ratios from 21 to 29%

15. An additional firm stated that its variable costs per unit decreased with increased operations from 70 to 100% of capacity, but it did not offer any percentage figures.

A study by the Oxford economists indicated that 13 firms were operating under conditions of decreasing costs, 4 under conditions of constant cost, and 2 under increasing costs. See R. L. Hall and C. J. Hitch, 'Price theory and business behaviour', *Oxford Economic Papers*, no. 2 (May 1939), p. 20, fn. 1.

16. A total of 17 firms that answered the other questions declined to attempt answers to this one, giving such reasons as 'don't know', 'no accurate figures', 'no exact answers', and 'too much theory'. In addition, 4 firms gave non-numerical answers that roughly indicated the character of their cost–output relations; their answers are referred to in the text.

apparently is largely explained by the fact that furniture firms predominate, representing 9 of the 13 firms in that classification.

Constant unit variable costs between the range of 70 and 100% capacity operations were reported by 3 firms.[17] In addition, 2 concerns[18] reported such constant costs between 90 and 100% of capacity, and 6 others[19] gave figures showing a per unit cost

Table 2

Decline in Unit Variable Cost with Increase in
Scale of Output

	Increase of operations (in % of plant capacity)			
	95 to 100%	90 to 95%	80 to 90%	70 to 80%
Average for 33 firms with maximum profits at 100% capacity	5·5%	5·7%	7·7%	9·5%
14 furniture firms	6·4	5·9	4·6	5·2%
7 cotton-clothing firms	5·6	4·9	6·9	7·5
6 metal-working firms	4·8	7·9	12·5	15·9
6 others	4·7	5·4	9·6	13·9
Average for decreasing cost firms with labor-to-total-cost ratios from				
40–60% (6 firms)	4·1%	4·4%	6·6%	8·1%
30–39% (6 firms)	2·1	2·3	4·3	5·2
21–29% (13 firms)	8·1	7·2	5·8	5·5
12–20% (6 firms)	1·9	2·0	4·2	6·2
3 firms with maximum profits at 90, 80, and 75% of capacity				
1 cotton-clothing firm	1·0% rise	1·0% drop	1·5% drop	4·0% drop
1 paint producer	25·0% rise	25·0% rise	10·0% rise	0·0%
1 chemical concern	10·0% rise	? rise	? rise	0·0%

variation of no more than from 1 to 8% over the whole range from 70 to 100% of capacity. The president of one chemical firm, not included in the above data, replied: 'I am not in a position to estimate exact answers, but believe that operating costs in the brackets you outline would vary little. Of course, costs would fall if we increased our operations from 70 to 100%.

As further checks on the replies of the executives, they were asked: 'Under normal peacetime conditions, is it possible at times to reduce your operating costs per unit of output by lowering

17. Two in furniture and one in clothing. To quote from the explanation of two of them: 'Our unit cost remains the same if you exclude overhead and fixed charges', and 'As long as overhead and fixed charges are excluded, the unit cost would not vary much either way, if any'.

18. One in furniture and one in metal-working.

19. Three in furniture, two in shoes, and one in metal-working.

your rate of operations?' Of 44 replies, 43 were 'no' and 1 was 'yes'. Some replying 'no' qualified their answers. One said, 'By reducing from more than 100% of capacity to 100%, costs are likely to fall.' Another added, 'If we work regular hours 100% capacity is point of greatest efficiency and lowest cost but may not be if that involves a great deal of overtime.' A number remarked that plant efficiency tends to fall as operations are reduced, that payroll costs do not increase in direct proportion to the volume of operations so that operating costs per unit are lower at higher levels of output, or that operating costs per unit always are lower as 100% capacity production is approached. The firm answering 'yes' gave as its explanation of how lowered operations would permit lower unit variable costs: 'Get rid of all incompetent employees, cease selling to chiselers and risky accounts, do more of work instead of paying someone else to do it.'

A few of the answers to this question raise doubts as to the validity of the replies of some firms to previous cost questions, particularly those reporting increasing marginal variable costs beginning at 75–95% of capacity. Two of the replies may also indicate a failure to distinguish clearly between fixed and variable costs. Nine of the firms reporting maximum profits at 75–95% of capacity answered 'no' to this question as to whether it was possible to reduce unit variable costs by lowering the rate of operations.[20] Those 9 included the 3 firms that reported U-shaped cost curves, with rising unit variable costs beginning at 75, 80, and 90% of capacity. Two of them were the only replying firms in their industries that reported such cost curves below 100% of capacity.[21]

The significant conclusion from the data in this section is that most of the manufacturing firms in the industries covered by this survey apparently have decreasing unit variable costs within the range of 70 to 100% of capacity production – or at least their executive officials believe that to be the case, which is the

20. The other 2 of the 11 firms in that category failed to answer this question.

21. Seven other cotton-clothing firms and 3 other chemical concerns definitely reported decreasing unit costs. The two other paint companies gave no detailed cost figures. One reported maximum profits at 100% of capacity and the other at 80% of capacity.

22

important factor in determining company policy, whatever the actual facts may be.[22]

If company output and employment policies are based on the assumption of decreasing marginal variable cost up to full capacity operations, much of the economic reasoning on company employment adjustments to increases or decreases in wage rates is invalid, and a new theory of wage–employment relationships for the individual firm must be developed.

The Oxford economists found that a great majority of the business entrepreneurs they questioned[23] 'were in profound ignorance' regarding the elasticity of demand for their products and that 'answers to questions about increasing or decreasing marginal prime costs were seldom given with confidence'.[24] Their sample 'erred, if at all, by being biased in favor of well-organized and efficiently conducted businesses', and the entrepreneurs convinced the economists that uncertainty concerning elasticities of demand and marginal prime cost were 'due not to any negligence or lack of zeal for knowledge' on the part of the business men 'but to the nature of the case'.[25] The economists concluded that the results of their study 'seem to vitiate any attempts to analyse normal entrepreneurial behaviour in the short period in terms of marginal curves. They also make it impossible to assume that wages in the short run will bear any close relation to the marginal product (or marginal revenue) of the labour employed.'[26]

The present author's interviews with business men indicate that most entrepreneurs do not tend to think in terms of marginal variable cost. The heads of manufacturing concerns hiring, say,

22. The T.N.E.C. study of *Industrial Wage Rates, Labor Costs and Price Policies* (monog. no. 5, 1940) revealed that unit labor costs increased as volume fell and declined as rate of operations expanded in the International Harvester Company's plants and in the plants of two paper companies; operating efficiency was lower when volume was small, partly because of more frequent shifting with shorter runs (see pp. xix, xx, 35–37, and 117–19).

23. Apparently the statements quoted in this paragraph rest primarily on the evidence of 38 of the entrepreneurs interviewed.

24. R. F. Harrod, 'Price and cost in entrepreneurs' policy', *Oxford Economic Papers*, no. 2 (May 1939), pp. 4, 5.

25. ibid., p. 5.

26. R. L. Hall and C. J. Hitch, 'Price theory and business behaviour', *Oxford Economic Papers*, no. 2, p. 32.

50 or more workers consider such a procedure both unnecessary and impractical because: (1) they seem convinced that their profits increase as the rate of operations rises, at least until full plant capacity is reached – they have no faith in the validity of U-shaped marginal variable cost curves unless, perhaps, overtime pay is involved; (2) they consider repeated shifts in the size of a plant's working force, or in its equipment, with changes in the relative costs of different productive factors to be impractical, their adjustments to cost changes taking most frequently the form of product shifts that require little, if any, alteration in equipment; and (3) they see the extreme difficulty of calculating marginal variable costs and the marginal productivity of factors, especially in multiprocess industries and under present accounting methods. In thinking about employment in their firm, therefore, they tend to emphasize current and prospective demand for their products and the full-crew requirements for their existing facilities, rather than the current level of wage rates.

III

The practical and technical difficulties involved in attempting to apply the marginal analysis to wage–employment matters deserve more attention than can be given them here. This discussion only indicates some of the problems involved in shifting the proportion of factors in manufacturing plants or in calculating the marginal contributions of factors, and, at the same time, points to certain disturbing data.

There is a lack of good case material on the redistribution of factors purely in response to increases or decreases in wage rates. The very existence of unused plant capacity indicates that it is not feasible to substitute capital equipment for labor; otherwise that would have been done because the use of such idle equipment is practically 'costless' in view of the fact that fixed charges on it cannot be avoided.

Most industrial plants are designed and equipped for a certain output, requiring a certain work force. Often effective operation of the plant involves a work force of a given size.[27] Certain

27. That, for example, is largely true of automatic-machine tending (such as is characteristic of pulp and paper plants, metal and oil refineries, chemical plants, textile mills, etc.) and of assembly-line operations. It is also

techniques of production, allowing little variation in the use of labor, may be the only practical means of manufacturing the product. Under such circumstances, management does not and cannot think in terms of adding or subtracting increments of labor except perhaps when it is a question of expanding the plant and equipment, changing the equipment, or redesigning the plant. The flexibility of many plants is, however, extremely limited, especially those designed for early stages of manufacturing, such as the smelting, refining, compounding, and rolling of materials.

From much of the literature the reader receives the impression that methods of manufacture readily adjust to changes in the relative costs of productive factors. But the decision to shift a manufacturing plant to a method of production requiring less or more labor per unit of output because of a variation in wages is not one that the management would make frequently or lightly. Such action involves the sale (at a loss?) of existing facilities not usable under the new method and the purchase of new facilities and equipment to replace those discarded, to say nothing of retraining workers and readapting the whole organization.[28] Such new investment presumably would not be undertaken simply to reduce a current and expected net loss, or if there was a likelihood that the wage change would only be temporary or that the cost relationships between factors would be considerably altered again in the near future.[29]

Those who argue for wage reductions on the grounds that a certain relationship exists between wage rates and employment tend to overlook the fact that a shift to less capitalistic or more labor-consuming method may be impractical not only for reasons given above but also because the skilled workers necessary to

true that the size of the work force is largely fixed in service lines like banks, rail and bus transportation, theaters, postal delivery, etc.

28. Not to mention countless other problems like the effect of any lay-offs on the company's unemployment tax under experience rating, possible changes in its property-tax assessment, or resulting changes in employee or community attitudes.

29. The management might also hesitate to take such action if the market value of facilities and equipment to be sold was expected to rise, or if the market value of the equipment to be bought was expected to fall, or if marked improvements in technique were in the offing.

operate the antiquated equipment are no longer available. Indeed, as Randall Hinshaw points out, writers who believe a wage reduction will tend to stimulate new investment often appear to assume that the investment will be in the form of the most up-to-date equipment, which would require less rather than more labor per unit of output.[30] That, of course, would be contrary to what one might expect from marginal analysis.

That industry does not adapt its plants and processes to varying wage rates in the manner assumed by marginalists seems to be indicated by data recently collected by the author.[31] Executives of 112 firms with plants in both the north and the south were asked in January 1945 the following question: 'Have lower wages in the south *themselves* caused your company to use production techniques or methods in its southern plant(s) that require more labor and less machinery than the proportions of labor to machinery used in its northern plant(s)?' Of 44 replies, one was vaguely affirmative, one was indefinite, and 42 answered 'no'. Of the 42, a total of 35 stated that, for all comparable jobs, average wages in their southern plants were below the average for their northern plants. On that basis the wages in the southern plants averaged per firm from 5 to 30% below the northern plants, with the average north–south differential for all 35 firms at 15%. Those 35 replying firms represent a wide variety of industries[32] and had a total of over half a million employees in 150 plants in the south and 491 plants in the north. Some of them stated that the existence of lower wages in the south did not influence the type of machinery installed nor the processes used there, that 'the most efficient equipment available' is used in every plant regardless of location or relative wage levels.

The sample probably contains offsetting biases: in favor of concerns in a good position to make close comparative cost

30. See his unpublished Ph.D. thesis, 'Wages and unemployment, a preliminary analysis' (Princeton University Library, 1944), p. 122.

31. These data are more fully discussed and explained in an article in the *Journal of Political Economy* entitled 'Effectiveness of factory labor, south–north comparisons'.

32. Including 7 cotton and rayon textile firms, 5 building materials producers, 4 food companies, 3 rubber companies, and 2 firms in each of the following industries: clothing, hosiery, oil, chemicals, paper and pulp, metals, furniture and plywood, and aircraft and construction equipment.

calculations and in favour of large firms with relatively low labor-to-total-cost ratios. Nevertheless, it should be pointed out that included in the 35 concerns are 15 in industries that, on the average, have labor costs amounting to 25–40% of total production costs[33] and 11 that were paying wage rates in the south from 20 to 30% below their comparable northern rates. Surely, if wage rates were as important in determining the proportion of factors of a firm's employment as the textbooks imply, the completely negative results from this test would not have been possible.

A T.N.E.C. study of wage rates, labor costs, and technological change in two shoe companies, two paper companies, two mills of a textile company, and plants of the International Harvester Company in the 1930s indicated that increases in wage rates were not the most important or decisive factor – in fact may have no significant influence – in the determination and timing of technological changes. For the most part there appeared to be little casual connection between increased labor costs and the introduction of capital improvements.[34]

There is no need to discuss at length in this paper the technical difficulties involved in any attempt to discover the marginal product of an added unit of labor in large-scale industry and to impute to that unit of labor its value contribution to a joint, multi-processed product. Such difficulties have been discussed elsewhere in detail by the author.[35] More recently W. J. Eiteman has succinctly explained the 'hopeless complexity' that would attend any attempt to apply marginal analysis to modern manufacturing establishments.[36] His demonstration leaves no doubt that it would be utterly impractical under present conditions for the manager of a multi-process plant[37] to attempt, by means of repeated variation in the number of men employed, to work out and equate marginal costs and marginal returns for each productive factor.

33. Cotton textiles, full-fashioned hosiery, furniture, cotton clothing, and rubber.

34. See *Industrial Wage Rates, Labor Costs and Price Policies*, T.N.E.C. monog. no. 5, pp. xxv, 25, 42, 53, and 136.

35. *Economics of Labor* (1941), pp. 175–84.

36. 'The equilibrium of the firm in multi-process industries', *Quart. Journ. Econ.*, vol. 59 (February 1945), pp. 280–6.

37. A plant in which more than one type of operation or process is performed and which has, therefore, more than one 'cost center'.

IV

The foregoing discussion and data throw light on experience under the Fair Labor Standards act that has been difficult to explain by conventional marginal theory, and they also help to illuminate the answers of southern business executives to a group of questions on probable adjustments to an increase in their wage rates relative to those paid by competitors in other regions.

For example, the south–north wage differential in the men's cotton-garment industry (shirts, collars, nightwear, work clothes, and pants) was reduced, on the average, by one-third between March 1939 and March 1941 primarily as a result of the establishment of a statutory minimum of 30 cents in October 1939 under the Fair Labor Standards act and an industry wage order setting minimum wages in the industry at 32½–40 cents (depending on the product), effective in July 1940; yet between March 1939 and March 1941 employment in 180 identical plants increased more than one and a half times as fast in the south as in the north.[38]

The same pressure of minimum wages had similar results in the wood furniture industry. Between October 1937 and February 1941 the south–north wage differential was reduced about 7% for 72 identical wood furniture plants, with the establishment of a statutory minimum of 25 cents in October 1938 and 30 cents in October 1939 and the setting of minima from 32½ to 40 cents in the principal industries competing with southern furniture manufacturers for labor.[39] Not only did employment for the industry as a whole increase the most in firms with the lowest average hourly earnings in 1937, where the statutory minima obviously had the greatest direct and immediate effect; but employment in the southern plants increased 26%, whereas it decreased slightly in competing northern firms during the period (October 1937 to

38. Separate figures for branches of the industry show somewhat varying results. Employment did decrease slightly in southern plants producing shirts, collars, and nightwear, where the north–south wage differential was being practically eliminated, but in the work clothing and cotton pants branch, employment increased more than twice as fast in the south as in the north despite a reduction of more than 50% in the north–south wage differential. See 'Earnings in the men's cotton-garment industries, 1939 and 1941', *Mo. Lab. Rev.*, vol. 55 (August 1942), p. 349.

39. Seamless and full-fashioned hosiery, men's cotton clothing, and cotton textiles.

February 1941); and, within the south, employment expanded more than twice as fast in the lower-wage firms[40] whose wages were increased 10% as it did in the higher-wage firms where the increase in wages was less than 2%.[41]

Various factors were, of course, responsible for employment results so contrary to the presuppositions of conventional marginalism in such industries as men's cotton clothing and wood furniture. For the purposes of this paper there is no need to analyse individual cases where the results are so opposite to the expectations of marginal analysis and to assess the responsibility of each factor for those results.[42] Such data have been mentioned here merely to indicate that the replies of the southern business executives discussed in this section do have some basis in fact and experience. Furthermore, furniture and men's cotton-clothing concerns constitute half of the 43 southern firms that gave full answers to a group of questions concerning the adjustments they would make to a sharp narrowing of the north–south

40. Averaging under 35 cents an hour in 1937.

41. The actual changes in hourly earnings and employment in 72 wood furniture plants from October 1937 to February 1941 were as follows:

Plants with average hourly earnings in 1937	Percentage increase in average hourly earnings, 1937–41		Percentage increase in employment, 1937–41	
	U.S.	South	U.S.	South
Under 32·5 cents	11·2%	10·2%	26·3%	29·1%
32·5 and under 35·0 cents	7·6	9·9	38·1	38·1
35·0 and under 37·5 cents	8·3	1·7	30·7	18·5
37·5 cents and over	2·4	1·7	0·4	16·8

Sources of data: *Earnings and Hours in the Furniture Industry, February 1941*, U.S. Bur. of Lab. Stat., Serial No. R. 1330, 1941, Table 3, p. 11, and *Minimum Wages in the Wood Furniture Manufacturing Industry*, Wage and Hour Division of U.S. Dept. of Labor, June 1941, pp. 24–8. The employment increase for the south of 16·8% was calculated from data in the latter publication on p. 28.

42. The notion that variations in geographic wage differentials and changes therein fairly accurately reflect geographic differences in labor effectiveness so that 'efficiency wages' are approximately the same for all regions or areas seems to be disproved by a north–south comparison that the author made between wages and labor efficiency in 41 firms with plants in both regions (see 'Effectiveness of factory labor, south–north comparisons', in the *Journal of Political Economy*).

wage differential in their industry.[43] The basic question was as follows:

Suppose that during the first three years after the defeat of Japan the average north–south wage differential in your industry should be cut in half, causing southern wage rates in your line to rise relative to those of your competitors in the north. Assuming no other change in your costs and no decline in the nation's demand for the type of products you manufacture, how would your firm be likely to adjust to such a permanent 50% reduction in the north–south wage differential?

The executives were requested to rate each factor in terms of the relative importance or share in the total adjustment for which it would be responsible, the rating being in percentage terms on the basis of a composite of 100%. The following list of factors was provided:

a. Install additional labor-saving machinery.

b. Improve efficiency through better production methods, organization, supervision, incentives, workloads, etc.

c. Change the price, quality, or kind of products manufactured.

d. Increase sales efforts so as to expand sales and production.

e. Reduce production by deliberately curtailing output.

f. Other adjustments (please specify).

The replying firms estimated their wage rates to be from 5 to 40% under the average for comparable jobs in the north. The average for all replying was 18·2%, so that the question involves, on the average, an increase of 11% in the wage scale of replying firms in the south, assuming no change in the wage level of their northern competitors.

As the replying firms are mostly in industries that experienced some narrowing of the north–south wage differential under the National Recovery Act and Fair Labor Standards Act, their answers are founded on recent experience. Indeed, the replies are extremely helpful in interpreting that experience. They are

43. Ten firms declined to answer this set of questions on the ground that there was at present no differential, or only a negligible one, between their wage rates and average rates for comparable jobs in the north. Four of the 10 were in men's cotton clothing, in which previous figures have shown the north–south differential was rapidly reduced between 1939 and 1941.

summarized and classified by industry and labor-cost ratios in table 3. Also, table 3 contains a summary for the 11 firms that estimate their wage rates to be from 25 to 40% under the average rates of their northern competitors for comparable jobs, and it is

Table 3

Adjustments of 43 Southern Firms to Sharp Narrowing of North–South Wage Differentials, Factors Weighted According to Percentage of Importance

Classification of firms	a (labor-saving machinery)	b (improved methods and efficiency	c (price-product changes)	d (increased sales efforts	e (curtail output)	f (other)
Number of firms giving factor weight	35	36	19	31	4	4
Average weight per stressing firm	33%	36%	41%	29%	43%	20%
43-firm average of weights	26·1%	29·6%	17·5%	20·7%	4·1%	20%
Average for 14 furniture firms	19·6	23·2	34·3	17·9	0·7	4·3
Average for 7 men's cotton-clothing firms	24·3	40·0	17·1	18·6	—	
Average for 10 metal-working firms	35·0	28·5	5·5	20·0	11·0	—
Average for 12 other firms	27·5	32·4	8·8	24·3	5·0	2·0
Average for 11 firms with north–south wage differential of 25–40%	25·0	30·5	10·9	20·0	10·0	3·6
Average for firms with labor-to-total-cost ratios from						
40–60% (8 firms)	41·9	23·1	19·4	13·1	1·2	1·3
30–39% (8 firms)	33·1	28·7	14·4	15·0	6·3	2·5
21–29% (10 firms)	17·8	32·8	31·1	18·3	—	
12–20% (9 firms)	22·8	36·2	7·8	26·7	1·0	5·5

significant that the averages for those 11 firms (for which the question posits a selected wage increase of 17–33%) are very similar to the averages for all 43 firms.[44]

The adjustment most frequently mentioned by the 43 firms was

44. The principal exception is that the factor of curtailing output has an average of 10% for the 11 firms compared with an average of 4·1% for all 43 firms. Responsibility for that result rests on one metal-working firm with a north–south wage differential estimated at 25%, which rated this factor 100%. Elimination of that firm would reduce the average for the factor of curtailing output to 1% for the remaining 10 firms with large north–south wage differentials. The firm, subsequently discussed, failed to report its ratio of labor costs to total costs so it is not included in the last group of figures in table 3.

factor *b*, improvements in efficiency through better management, incentives, etc. Introduction of labor-saving machinery is the second most significant adjustment according to the results in table 3, and increased sales efforts ranks third. Price–product changes are considered the most important adjustment by some furniture concerns (3 of them placing sole stress on that factor),[45] but for the other firms such changes are considered of minor significance.[46]

It is especially noteworthy that deliberate curtailment of output, an adjustment stressed by conventional marginal theory, is mentioned by only 4 of the 43 firms.[47] Two of them, rating it at 10%, had reported decreasing unit variable costs up to 100% of plant capacity; however, their percentage decreases in moving from 70 to 100% of plant capacity totaled only 8% in each instance. The third firm, rating this factor 50%, is the chemical concern in table 2 that reported sharply increasing unit variable costs between 95 and 100% of capacity and maximum profits in peacetime at 75% of capacity. The fourth firm, a fabricator of steel structures and tanks with 125 employees, although reporting maximum profits at 100% of capacity and decreasing unit variable costs between 70 and 100% of capacity, places sole stress on this factor, making the following statement: 'Volume of production would be reduced to small sales for a local market. The only

45. One furniture executive said he would enter a new field of manufacture of advanced products in furniture and veneers. However, another furniture manufacturer reported: 'Such a change would affect us but very little as 90% of our market is in the south.'

46. 'Other' adjustments were: 'Use only higher skilled employees', 'Replace inefficient labor with efficient labor', and 'Several'.

47. Yet reasoning on the basis of conventional theory, D. K. McKamy and John V. Van Sickle argue that elimination of the north–south wage differential by government action would result in 'an enormous and legislated growth of unemployment', because 'those enterprises in the areas of labor surplus which are unable to earn enough money to pay the imposed wage would have to go out of business or reduce employment to the point where the last workers employed were worth as much as the imposed minimum' (see *Statement of D. K. McKamy and Dr John V. Van Sickle with regard to the demand of the union for elimination of geographical wage differentials*, Company's Exhibit No. 28, in the matter of Carnegie–Illinois Steel Corporation *et al.*, and United Steelworkers of America, before the Steel Panel of the National War Labor Board, case no. 111–6230–D [14–1 *et al.*], 7 June, 1944, p. 51).

reason we can now compete with the large northern firms is due to the difference in wage scale. They have enormous advantages in freight rates and more skilled type of workman.'

That business concerns stress item *b*, improved management and efficiency, may seem surprising to economists, who have generally reasoned as one replying executive, who stated: 'Doing all these things is a continuous process with us. I don't see what the wage level has to do with it.' Nevertheless, experience under the N.R.A. and the Fair Labor Standards Act indicates that the spur of increased wages does lead to improved plant organization. An executive of one of the largest cotton-textile concerns in the south has testified that, under the N.R.A. requirement that the same wages be paid for 40 hours of work as formerly were paid for 55 hours, the firm's actual increase in labor costs was less than one-third of the expected or calculated increase, the difference being explained by 'the utilization of improved machinery, better arrangement of processes and application of skilled labor, and the more adequate scheduling of the flow of production and better selection of raw materials'.[48]

Greatest stress on factor *b*, better management and work procedures, is understandable in men's cotton clothing, where the possibilities of making savings through labor-reducing equipment are generally less than in metal-working plants, which gave the factor of additional labor-saving machinery the primary weight.[49] Also, as might be expected the firms with the highest

48. *Textile Industry, Findings and Opinion of the Administrator*, Wage and Hour Division, U.S. Dept of Labor, 29 September 1939, p. 35.

49. The possibilities of better management practices have frequently been emphasized in discussions of minimum-wage experience (see, for example, John F. Moloney, 'Some effects of the Federal Fair Labor Standards Act upon southern industry', *Southern Econ. Journ.*, vol. 9 [July 1942], p. 22, and H. M. Douty, 'Minimum wage regulation in the seamless hosiery industry', *Southern Econ. Journ.*, vol. 8 [October 1941], p. 186).

In the seamless hosiery industry, with the introduction of 25-cent and 32½-cent minima in 1938 and 1940, respectively, employment declined more in the firms with average hourly earnings in the lowest wage classifications, largely due to increased use of labor-saving equipment in those firms (see Douty, *Southern Econ. Journ.*, vol. 8, pp. 183-9). However, there is no evidence that total output or sales of those low-wage firms, most affected by the wage minima, experienced any decline relative to the average for the industry.

rates of labor to total cost are the ones that place the most emphasis on new labor-saving machinery. Indeed, there is a notable inverse correlation between stress on that factor and the relative importance of labor in total costs. Exactly the reverse is true of the factor of increased sales efforts. Less stress is placed on sales efforts the larger is the percentage of labor in total costs. The implication is that large non-labor costs and increasing returns up to full capacity production bring to the fore the importance of keeping sales up when profits begin to be squeezed.

Economists brought up on the conventional theory may discount the stress placed by the business executives on increased sales efforts, considering it to be an irrational and uneconomic reaction to a wage increase. Previous data on the relationship between rates of output and unit variable costs indicate, however, that such stress on increased sales efforts may have some rationality. It may help to raise and retain output near capacity operations. Data at the beginning of this section indicate that expanding sales, output, and employment may, at times, be one of the results in firms most affected by wage increases. Business men are acutely aware of the fact that unit costs vary with output, that wage rates which seem extremely burdensome at half-capacity operations may not seem unduly high as full-capacity production is approached. Unlike economists, business executives tend to think of costs and profits as dependent upon the rate of output, rather than the reverse (the rate of output as dependent upon the level of cost).

V

This paper raises grave doubts as to the validity of conventional marginal theory and the assumptions on which it rests. Admittedly the data used are imperfect and are based, for the most part, on opinions of business executives. Many of the replying executives are, however, heads of 'small' businesses in highly competitive industries, so that they are good test cases for the theory. There may, of course, be questions concerning the representativeness of the samples, the completeness of the data, the content and character of the questions asked. etc. It may be argued, if somewhat unconvincingly, that business executives as a group do not learn from past experience and do not know their own businesses.

Nevertheless, the answers of the replying executives are sufficiently consistent, firm by firm, and so overwhelmingly support certain reasonable conclusions that there can be little doubt about the correctness of the general results.

While awaiting the fruits of further investigation and analysis, the following tentative conclusions can be drawn from the data contained in this paper:

1. Market demand is far more important than wage rates in determining a firm's volume of employment.[50] Indeed, for employment determination, market demand is considered by business executives to be almost five times as important as all other factors combined,[51] and the wage level or changes in wages are considered to be no more important in determining a firm's employment than the level of non-labor costs and changes in such non-labor costs.

2. Most manufacturing concerns apparently are considered by their executives to be operating at decreasing unit variable costs all along the scale between 70 and 100% of plant capacity. Consequently, it is seldom practical for a firm to curtail output (and, therefore, employment) simply in response to an increase in wage rates.

3. In modern manufacturing, a firm's level of costs per unit of product is influenced considerably by its scale of output; the reverse, as assumed by conventional marginalism, is not generally true.

4. Interregional firms, except in rare cases, do not adjust their use of labor and capital equipment to compensate for sectional differences in wage rates. For many manufacturing concerns it is not feasible, or would prove too costly, to shift the proportion of productive factors in response to current changes in wages, in the manner suggested by marginal analysis.

50. The 56 replying firms gave market demand an average rating of 87·5 compared with an average of 3·8 for the level of wages or changes therein, which, taken literally, would mean that market demand is more than 26 times as important as wage rates in determining the volume of employment of a firm.

51. The relative importance of market demand was assessed by the executives of 56 firms at 82·5 compared with 17·5 for all other factors influencing a firm's employment. The ratio is 65 to 35 for the 28 firms rating two or more factors (see table 1).

5. The practical problems involved in applying marginal analysis to the multi-process operations of a modern plant seem insuperable, and business executives rightly consider marginalism impractical as an operating principle in such manufacturing establishments.

6. Of the three adjustments stressed by business executives to meet a rise in wages relative to those paid by competitors, two – better management practices and increased sales efforts – are neglected by conventional marginalism; whereas the adjustment stressed by marginalism – curtailment of output – is considered so unimportant and exceptional as to be mentioned in only 1 out of every 11 replies. Indeed, experience seems to indicate that, on an individual-firm basis, the adjustments considered important by the business executives may, at times, even result in larger firm employment at a higher wage level.

These tentative conclusions indicate a new direction for investigations of employment relationships and equilibrating adjustments in individual firms.

2 F. Machlup

Marginal Analysis and Empirical Research

Excerpt from Machlup, F. (1946) Marginal analysis and empirical research. *Amer. Econ. Rev.*, **36**, 547–54.

[. . .]

Marginal Productivity and Wage

Empirical research designed to verify or disprove marginal-productivity theory in the analysis of input of the individual firm is beset with difficulties. Few systematic endeavors have been made and none has led to any suggestion, however vague or tentative, of an alternative theory. Whereas in certain price-research projects those who felt compelled to reject the marginal theory have advanced the average-cost theory of pricing as a substitute, no substitute theory has been forthcoming from those who decried marginal-productivity theory.

Statistical research

Empirical research on cost, price, and output of the individual firm has resulted in several interesting attempts to derive marginal cost functions from statistical data; and also in one or two attempts to derive price elasticities of demand for a firm's products. But nobody, to my knowledge, has ever undertaken to construct from actual data a marginal net revenue productivity curve for a given type of labor employed by a firm. The difficulties are formidable and, since the raw material for the calculations could not come from any records or documents, but merely from respondent's guesses of a purely hypothetical nature, the results might not be much more 'authentic' than the schedules made up by textbook writers for arithmetical illustrations.

Statistical studies of the relationship between wage rates and employment in large samples of individual firms or industries would be nearly useless because we have no way of eliminating the simultaneous effects of several other significant variables, especially those of a psychological nature. An increase in wage rates may have very different effects depending on whether the employer (1) (*a*) has foreseen it, (*b*) is surprised by it; (2) (*a*) reacts quickly to it, (*b*) reacts slowly to it; (3) (*a*) expects it to be reversed soon, (*b*) expects it to be maintained, (*c*) expects it to be followed by further increases; (4) (*a*) assumes it to be confined to his firm, (*b*) assumes it to affect also his competitors, (*c*) believes it to be part of a nation-wide trend; (5) connects it with an inflationary development; or is influenced by any other sort and number of anticipations. Most of these moods and anticipations can be translated by the economist into certain shapes or shifts of the marginal productivity functions of the firms; but since the researchers cannot ascertain or evaluate these conjectural 'data' for the large number of firms contained in a representative sample, statistical investigations of the wage–employment relation of individual firms are not likely to yield useful results.

Questionnaire on employment

It has been pointed out [. . .] why the method of mailed questionnaires without supporting interviews is hopelessly inadequate for empirical studies of business conduct. Even the most intelligently devised set of questions would not assure reliable and significant answers. Questions designed to achieve the necessary separation of variables would be so complicated and call for so high a degree of 'abstract thinking' on the part of the questioned business men that questionnaires of this sort would be too much of an imposition, and cooperation would be too small. Although the questions in Professor Lester's research project on employment did not even approach these standards, he received only 56 usable replies from 430 manufacturers whom he had asked to fill out his questionnaires.[1]

Professor Lester's questionnaires suffered not merely from the inherent weaknesses of the method but also from defects in formulation. These defects were so serious that even the most complete, reliable, and intelligent answers could not have yielded significant findings. The business men were asked to rate the

1. Reading no. 1, pp. 16.

'importance' of several factors determining the volume of employment in their firms. No explanation was given whether this importance of a variable – that is, I presume, its responsibility for changes in the employment volume – should refer to (*a*) the frequency of its variations, (*b*) the extent of its variations, or (*c*) the effects of its variations. Surely, the variable rated as least important – perhaps because it varied less frequently than the others – may be just as strategic as any of those with higher importance ratings. What we really need to know, however, is not the *comparative* importance of several factors but rather the effects of variations of each factor separately while the others remain unchanged.

If I want to know by how much an increase in the price of spinach may affect its consumption in an individual household, I shall not get very far by asking the householders to give a percentage rating to each of several listed factors that are believed to be 'important' influences on spinach consumption. If it were tried, we should not be surprised to find changes in family income, the number of children and guests at dinner, and the notoriety of Popeye the Sailor's gusto for spinach, receiving much higher percentage ratings than changes in the price of spinach. (In a number of households price may not be a factor at all.) Nobody, I hope, would conclude from such a poll that price is an unimportant factor in the consumption of spinach.

Yet Professor Lester followed just this procedure when he wanted to find out how important wage rates were in determining the volume of employment in the individual firm. He asked the executives of the companies to 'rate' the following factors 'in terms of the percentage of importance of each':

a. Present and prospective market demand (sales) for your products, including seasonal fluctuations in demand.

b. The level of wage rates or changes in the level of wages.

c. The level of material costs and other non-wage costs and changes in the level of such non-labor costs.

d. Variations in profits or losses of the firm.

e. New techniques, equipment, and production methods.

f. Other factors (please specify).

Of these items the first unquestionably excels all others in frequency and extent of variations. That it won first prize in Professor Lester's importance contest is therefore not surprising. If several respondents gave ratings to item *d* (variations in profits or losses) and at the same time also to other items, they obviously did not realize that this variable comprised all the others. Professor Lester does not explain why he listed it when he knew that it was not 'completely independent' and that 'for example, wages affect profits'.[2] Nor does he state whether the 43 firms which failed to mention changes in wage rates as an important factor meant that they would continue in business and continue to employ the same number of workers regardless of any degree of wage increase. If this is what they meant, they can hardly be taken seriously. If they meant something else, then it is not clear just what the replies should indicate about the probable effects of wage increases upon employment.

The strangest thing about Professor Lester's list of possibly important variables is that all – except *f*, the unspecified, and *d*, the all-inclusive profit-and-loss item – are essential variables of the very analysis which he means to disprove. The prize-winning item, *a*, the demand for the product, is certainly a most crucial determinant of marginal productivity. Items *c*, non-labor cost, and *e*, production techniques, are two other determinants of marginal productivity. How Professor Lester came to think that the results of this poll would in any sense disprove or shake marginal productivity analysis remains a mystery.

Questionnaire on variable cost

Professor Lester asked his business men also some questions on unit variable costs and profits at various rates of output. The information obtained in answer to these questions might have been useful had it not been based on an undefined concept of 'plant capacity'. Unfortunately, it must be suspected that not all firms meant the same thing when they referred to '100% of capacity'.

Economic theorists use different definitions of capacity. One widely used definition marks as 100% of capacity that volume of output at which short-run total cost per unit is a minimum;

2. Reading no. 1, p. 17.

another definition fixes the 100% mark at the output at which variable cost per unit is a minimum. The former definition implies decreasing average total cost, the latter decreasing average variable cost, up to '100% capacity'. Professor Lester after painstaking empirical research arrives at the following finding:

> The significant conclusion from the data in this section is that most of the manufacturing firms in the industries covered by this survey apparently have decreasing unit variable costs within the range of 70–100% of capacity production. . . .[3]

Has Professor Lester asked himself whether this is not merely a self-evident conclusion implied in the definition of capacity used by his respondents?

The steepness of the reported decline in unit variable cost, however, would be an interesting observation – if the data were reliable. (Few of Professor Lester's firms had 'constant unit variable costs', or anything approaching this situation, over a considerable range of output.[4]) It is rather peculiar that unit variable costs should decrease steeply (at an increasing rate!) down to a certain point and then abruptly start rising – as one must infer from the term '100% capacity'. Where equipment is not utilized for 24 hours a day, the steep decline and abrupt rise of the unit cost is somewhat questionable.

Professor Lester, nevertheless, has sufficient confidence in his findings to draw conclusions – conclusions, moreover, which could not even be supported if the findings were of unquestionable validity. He states:

> If company output and employment policies are based on the assumption of decreasing marginal variable cost up to full capacity operations, much of the economic reasoning on company employment adjustments to increases and decreases in wage rates is invalid, and a new theory of wage–employment relationships for the individual firm must be developed.[5]

This deduction simply does not follow from the premises. There is no reason why decreasing marginal costs should invalidate the conventional propositions on factor cost and input. Professor

3. Reading no. 1, p. 22.
4. Reading no. 1, p. 21.
5. Reading no. 1, p. 23.

Lester could have found dozens of textbook examples demonstrating the firm's reactions under conditions of decreasing marginal cost.

Professor Lester may have been deluded by a rather common confusion between related concepts: from decreasing marginal cost he may have jumped to the assumption of increasing labor returns,[6] and from increasing physical returns he may have jumped to the assumption of increasing marginal productivity of labor. Both these jumps are serious mistakes. For instance, the very conditions which may cause a firm to restrict the employment of labor to a volume still within the phase of increasing physical productivity per unit of labor are likely to result in decreasing marginal net revenue productivity of labor. These conditions are:

(a) an indivisibility of the firm's physical plant facilities,[7] combined with either (or both);

(b) a low elasticity of the demand for the firm's products,[8] or (and)

(c) a low elasticity of the supply of labor to the firm.[9]

The first condition, (a), makes a phase of increasing physical productivity of labor in the firm a practical possibility; the other conditions, (b) or (c), make that phase relevant for actual operations by providing the pecuniary incentive to operate the plant inefficiently. Condition (b), the low elasticity of demand for the product, will cause marginal net revenue productivity of labor to be diminishing in a range of employment in which average or even marginal physical productivity of labor are still increasing.

It is not possible from Professor Lester's exposition to find out whether his failure to see these relationships was at the bottom

6. Reading no. 1, p. 19.

7. i.e., the firm cannot adjust the number of machines or production units to smaller production volumes but must instead produce small outputs with an inefficiently large productive apparatus.

8. i.e., the firm realizes that it can charge much higher prices for smaller outputs or cannot dispose of larger outputs except with substantial price reductions.

9. i.e., the firm realizes that it can enjoy much lower wage rates at lower employment levels or cannot obtain more labor except with substantial wage increases.

of his faulty theorizing on this point. In any event, his findings on variable costs contain nothing that would even vaguely bear on the validity of marginal analysis.

Questionnaire on adjustments

Professor Lester's fact-finding and theorizing on substitution between labor and capital and on other adjustments of the firm to changes in wage rates are also marred by inconsistencies and misunderstandings.

After trying to make the most of increasing returns to labor and only a few lines after referring to 'unused plant capacity', Professor Lester asserts that 'most industrial plants are designed and equipped for a certain output, requiring a certain work force. Often effective operation of the plant involves a work force of a given size.'[10] To operate within the phase of increasing returns is to operate inefficiently, that is, with an employment of less labor with a given plant than would be compatible with efficient operations. (Because an increase in employment would raise output more than proportionately.) 'Effective operation', on the other hand, logically implies employment at or beyond the point where diminishing returns set in. Professor Lester does not seem to be clear which way he wants to argue.[11]

Professor Lester seems to think that substitution between capital and labor can occur only in the form of installation of new or scrapping of existing machinery[12] and that it is supposed to occur 'readily' and would, therefore, be 'timed' with the wage changes.[13] These are rather common but nevertheless mistaken views.

Professor Lester does not discuss a glaring contradiction in his findings: On the basis of replies to one questionnaire he states that his data indicate 'that industry does not adapt its plant and processes to varying wage rates in the manner assumed by marginalists'.[14] But on the basis of another questionnaire

10. Reading no. 1, p. 24.
11. Absolutely fixed proportions between factors of production would imply that short-run marginal productivity of labor drops precipitously to zero at the full capacity level of employment.
12. Reading no. 1, p. 25.
13. Reading no. 1, p. 25.
14. Reading no. 1, p. 26.

about adjustments to increases in relative wages, he reports that the introduction of 'labor-saving machinery' was given the highest rating in relative importance by the questioned firms whose labor costs were more than 29% of total cost.[15]

The last-mentioned questionnaire apparently was designed to show that wage increases had no important effects upon employment. Six alternative adjustments to increases in relative wages were listed and manufacturers had to give percentage ratings for relative importance. In this popularity contest an item called 'deliberate curtailment of output' got the booby prize. Quite apart from the fact that the words were loaded against this item, the result is not in the least surprising. For it is a well-known fact that where competition is not pure (as it rarely is in industrial products), output adjustments to higher production costs take place by way of changes in selling price. Price and product adjustments were another of the alternative items and scored rather well in the poll. If all employment-reducing adjustments – labor-saving machinery, price increases, and deliberate output curtailment – are taken together, they clearly dominate in the importance ratings by the firms.[16] This, or anything else, may not mean much in such an 'opinion poll', but it certainly does not prove what Professor Lester wanted to prove. Nevertheless, he contends that 'it is especially noteworthy that deliberate curtailment of output, an adjustment stressed by conventional marginal theory, is mentioned by only four of the 43 firms'.[17] And he concludes that marginal analysis is all but done for, that 'there can be little doubt about the correctness of the general results' of his tests,[18] and that 'a new direction for investigations of employment relationships and equilibrating adjustments in individual firms' is indicated.[19]

Conclusions

I conclude that the marginal theory of business conduct of the firm has not been shaken, discredited, or disproved by the empirical tests discussed in this paper. I conclude, furthermore, that

15. Reading no. 1, p. 31.
16. Reading no. 1, p. 31.
17. Reading no. 1, p. 32.
18. Reading no. 1, p. 35.
19. Reading no. 1, p. 36.

empirical research on business policies cannot assure useful results if it employs the method of mailed questionnaires, if it is confined to direct questions without carefully devised checks, and if it aims at testing too broad and formal principles rather than more narrowly defined hypotheses.

The critical tone of my comments on the research projects discussed in this paper may give the impression of a hostile attitude towards empirical research as such. I wish to guard against such an impression. There should be no doubt that empirical research on the economics of the single firm is badly needed, no less than in many other fields. The correctness, applicability, and relevance of economic theory constantly need testing through empirical research; such research may yield results of great significance.

Sharp criticism of bad research can be constructive in two respects: it may save some of the waste of time which the published research findings are apt to cause if they remain undisputed and are allowed to confuse hosts of students of economics; and it may contribute to the improvement of research. The chief condition for improved research is a thorough understanding of the theories to be tested. Supplementary conditions are a certain degree of familiarity with the technological and institutional peculiarities of the fields or cases on which the research is undertaken and a grasp of the research techniques employed.

Part Two The Supply of Labour

Wage theory has tended to collapse because of a lack of understanding of supply forces. Rottenberg outlines the economist's theory of job choice in a manner which suggests that jobs like goods yield utility and this theory is then used for examining various attempts to criticize economic theory. Becker's article is representative of the revived interest in job choice and places labour supply in the wider context of household behaviour. The problem of skills and skill acquisition is dealt with in the Penguin Modern Economics Readings volume entitled *Education*, edited by Mark Blaug.

3 S. Rottenberg

On Choice in Labor Markets

Rottenberg, S. (1956) On choice in labor markets. *Indus. Labor. Relat. Rev.*, **9**, 183–99.

A voluminous literature reporting on empirical research on labor markets has been published in recent years. Some of this literature has contributed much to understanding of the limitations on fruitful use in *real* markets of the *theory* of worker behavior in labor markets. Some of it, however, has charged the theory with errors it does not contain. This paper proposes to examine conventional theory and the nature of the criticism which has been made of it.[1]

The Classical Theory

Criteria for choice among alternatives in labor markets and the consequences of choice were discussed by Adam Smith in some detail in a classic chapter, 'Of wages and profit in the different employments of labour and stock'.[2] A number of economists who wrote in the early and middle parts of the nineteenth century – among them Senior, McCulloch, and Mill – developed the

1. The large volume of research on labor markets in the last decade and a half has been motivated by the belief that economic theory is an unsatisfactory instrument for understanding resource allocation and compensation in labor markets.

'Since 1940 there has been considerable interest in the movement of labor within a local labor market. This interest grew out of a dissatisfaction with the traditional assumption of economic theory about the movement of workers from one job to another in response to differences in wage rates' (Charles A. Myers, 'Labor mobility in two communities', in E. W. Bakke *et al.*, *Labor Mobility and Economic Opportunity*, The Technology Press, and John Wiley and Sons, [Cambridge, Mass. and New York, 1954], p. 68).

2. Adam Smith, *An Inquiry into the Nature and Causes of the Wealth of Nations*, Modern Library edition (Random House, New York, 1937), book 1, ch. 10.

subject, interpreting Smith here, revising him there, and describing more up-to-date versions of labor market behavior.

Smith summarized the theory of the labor market in this way:

The whole of the advantages and disadvantages of the different employments of labour and stock must, in the same neighbourhood, be either perfectly equal or continually tending to equality. If, in the same neighbourhood, there was any employment evidently either more or less advantageous than the rest, so many people would crowd into it in the one case, and so many would desert it in the other, that its advantages would soon return to the level of the other employments. This at least would be the case in a society where things were left to follow their natural course, where there was perfect liberty, and where every man was perfectly free both to chuse what occupation he thought proper, and to change it as often as he thought proper. Every man's interest would prompt him to seek the advantageous and to shun the disadvantageous employment.[3]

The theory has two parts. One relates to the nature of occupational choice: 'every man' will pursue his interest and this will 'prompt him to seek the advantageous, and to shun the disadvantageous employment'. The other relates to the consequences of this behavioral choice system: 'the whole of the advantages and disadvantages' of all employments will be equal or will tend toward equality. Any disparity in net advantage will cause persons to redistribute themselves. Greater numbers in the relatively more advantaged employments, and fewer in the relatively disadvantaged, will tend to restore equality of net advantage in all.

Inequalities may occur in the short run, while the process of adjustment works itself out; in this period, net advantage will be only 'tending to equality'. Inequalities may also occur when things are not left at perfect liberty and men are not free to choose among alternative employments. Otherwise, in Smith's system, net advantage will be equal in all employments.

It is of primordial importance to understand that the early economists said that it was '*the whole of the advantages and disadvantages*' in all employments that would be equal. This is so apparent from their writings that there should be no confusion about it. They did *not* say *wages* are equal in all employments.

3. A. Smith, p. 99.

Smith, who knew the economy of his time in remarkable detail, despite the rudimentary state of the statistical arts, knew that wages were different in various employments and explicitly enumerated the causes of difference. Wages would vary, he said, with the ease or hardship, the cleanliness or dirtiness, the honorableness or dishonorableness of the employment; with the easiness and cheapness or the difficulty and expense of its learning; with its constancy or inconstancy; with the small or great trust which is reposed in the worker; and with the probability or improbability of success in the employment.

Those who followed Smith added other causes of difference; when we search for what is common to all, we find that it is the influence which the circumstances of different employments have upon the numbers who will make themselves available in them. Thus, if men prefer an agreeable employment to a disagreeable one, they will tend to move into the former and away from the latter; increasing numbers in the one and diminishing numbers in the other will have opposite effects upon wages in the two employments; when the differential in wages is just large enough to overcome the difference in the agreeableness-property of the two, movement between them ceases, because men are now indifferent in choice and this just-sufficient differential persists.

Occupations equal in other respects would tend to be equal in price, but occupations *unequal* in other respects would be *unequal* in price. Just as price differentials compensate for differentials in other qualities, so differentials in other qualities compensate for differentials in price. Thus occupational choice was understood by the economists to be made with reference to the total complex of attributes which attach to jobs.

This is, of course, a description of the process which operates in free labor markets. The classical economists knew, however, that real world markets are not always free. In the second part[4] of his chapter 'Of wages and profit in the different employments of labour and stock', Smith discussed the restrictions on 'perfect liberty' in real markets. Here, he dealt with three types of circumstances in the labor markets of his time in which men were distributed among occupations by other criteria than relative net advantage. First, some persons who were disposed to enter a trade

4. A. Smith, p. 118 ff.

were prevented from entering it. Second, some were encouraged to enter a trade that they would otherwise not be disposed to enter. Third, some were obstructed from moving from one employment to another.

Differences in wages among employments thus can be of two classes. They can be 'compensating', in which case they are a function of differences in the nonwage qualities of different jobs. Or they can be 'real', in which case they are a function of restrictions on freedom of occupational choice.

The classical thesis respecting the distribution of workers among employments was only a specific application of the general principle which the classical economists understood to govern the distribution of all resources among uses. This is what Kenneth Boulding calls the principle of 'equal advantage' – which operates to move resources 'from the low-advantage locations where there are "too many" to the high-advantage locations where they are "too few".'[5]

In the ensuing discussion, criticisms of the classical theory of the labor market, as made in recent labor-market studies, are presented in paraphrased form and subjected to analysis.[6]

Relative Prices and Occupational Choice

Economists in the classical tradition say that men make occupational choices in terms of relative prices in different occupations. If we ask people why they have chosen to enter their crafts or why they have (or have not) made job changes, we find that most workers make choice decisions with reference to the 'human relations' factors which attach to jobs or for 'personal reasons', for example, and that the structure of wages plays a very small role in the choice process.[7]

5. K. E. Boulding, 'Toward a general theory of growth', *The Canadian Journal of Economic and Political Science* (August 1953), p. 338.

6. In addition to paraphrasing the criticism, I have drawn specific references from the recent literature of the labor market. That part of the literature which is consistent with conventional doctrine is not discussed at all. For a review of the critical literature, the reader is referred to Herbert S. Parnes, *Research on Labor Mobility* (Social Science Research Council, New York, 1954).

7. An example of this criticism can be found in Richard A. Lester, *Hiring Practices and Labor Competition* (Industrial Relations Section, Princeton University, Princeton, 1954), p. 96 ff. 'Accepted theory is

We must distinguish here between the early classical economists and their neoclassical successors. The classical economists did not say that choice was made with reference to price alone. They did not formulate hypothetical models; the world of their theory was the real world as they perceived it. Abstraction from complex reality was a later innovation in the methodology of economics. The simple case, which could be dealt with precisely and mathematically and in which functional relationships could be drawn between pairs of variables, was a contribution of more recent times. Even Marshall, who used the analytical and expository technique of *ceteris paribus* much and with great care, is the despair of young students who hunger for neat solutions, for Marshall is full of 'ifs' and 'buts' and qualifying clauses.[8]

---

based primarily on interfirm mobility of labor and on job applications and acceptances differentiated according to relative levels of compensation ... paid by companies. ... The wage-mobility focus of traditional theory is too narrow. Some of the important relationships are more varied, indirect, and subtle than the theory assumes. ... In view of the character of the employment process in most of the interviewed firms, traditional theory appears to give a misleading impression of precision and unique solutions. ... In resource allocation, economic theory assumes price to be the indicator and governor. Relative wage changes are presumed to be the mechanism for bringing about the proper redistribution of labor.'

Professors Myers and Maclaurin found, in their study of the Fitchburg labor market, that 'In terms of total inter-factory moves, differences in wage rates were not an important cause of movement' (Charles A. Myers & Rupert Maclaurin, *The Movement of Factory Workers* [John Wiley and Sons, Inc., New York, 1943], p. 19).

Generalizing from a number of labor-market studies, Clark Kerr has written, 'Two processes, among others, are going on all the time in our economy: wage rates are changing and individuals are moving among jobs. The two processes may or may not be closely connected' (Clark Kerr, 'Labor markets: their character and consequences', *American Economic Review* [May 1950], p. 278 ff.).

8. Marshall wrote of his own work: 'Though urged by the late Professor Walras about 1873 to publish [his, Marshall's, diagrammatic illustrations of economic problems], he had declined to do so because he feared that if separated from all concrete study of actual conditions, they might seem to claim a more direct bearing on real problems than they in fact had. He began, therefore, to supply some of the requisite limitations and conditions'. Contributed by Marshall to a German compilation, *Portraits and Short Lives of Leading Economists*, and quoted by J. M. Keynes, 'Alfred Marshall, 1842–1924', in A. C. Pigou, ed., *Memorials of Alfred Marshall* (Macmillan Co., Ltd., London, 1925), p. 21.

Labor market of classical economics

In the labor markets of Adam Smith and the economists who followed him, workers made occupational choices in terms of comparative total net advantages, not in terms of comparative wages. McCulloch saw, for example, that some workers might prefer low-wage, healthful employment to high-wage, unhealthful employment. 'The agreeableness and healthiness of their employments,' he said, 'seem to be the principal cause of the redundant numbers, and consequent low wages, of workmen in ordinary field labor.'[9] Adam Smith said that the price of labor in constant employments must compensate for the 'anxious and desponding moments' which the casual worker suffers when he thinks of the instability of his situation. This is the same as saying that workers consider instability as well as price in making choice. Nassau Senior, on the other hand, maintained that steady, regular labor is disliked by workers and that 'the opportunities for idleness afforded by an occupation of irregular employment' will cause the long-period earnings of irregular employment to be less than the common average of regular employments. Though Smith and Senior pursued the principle to opposite judgments, what is relevant for us is that neither saw workers choosing solely in terms of relative price. For one, choice was made in terms of relative price and relative instability; for the other, it was made in terms of relative opportunity for idleness. For neither was choice made in terms of relative price, standing alone.

Examples from Senior and Mill

Examples can be multiplied almost without end, but reference will be made only to a few more. Employment in the slave trade, Senior wrote, implies 'fatigue, hardship, and danger, public execration, and, if a slave trader can be supposed to reflect on the nature of his occupation, self reproach'.[10] Earnings in this employment must be great, therefore, to compensate for the

9. J. R. McCulloch. *A Treatise on the Circumstances Which Determine the Rate of Wages and the Conditions of the Labouring Classes*, 2nd edn (G. Routledge and Co., London, 1854), p. 55.

10. Nassau W. Senior, *An Outline of the Science of Political Economy*, Library of Economics edition (George Allen and Unwin Ltd., London, 1938), p. 202.

odium which attaches to it. This clearly means that the decision whether to accept employment in the slave trade depends upon price *and* the odious character of the trade.

A father, Senior said again, does not 'have his child nursed in the country at 2s. a week till he is eight years old, and then [have him] removed to a farm-yard or a cotton-mill' and he does not reflect that 'in giving him a more expensive education he is engaging in a speculation which is likely to be unprofitable', because, 'with all men, except a few outcasts, one of the greatest sources of immediate gratification' is to witness a son's daily improvement.[11] Just as relative price is not the exclusive criterion of occupational choice for adults in the classical system, it is not the exclusive criterion of the occupational choices which parents make for their offspring.

Mill writes of the handloom weavers who cling to their craft 'in spite of the scanty remuneration which it now yields' because they have 'freedom of action' in this employment, and he quotes Mr Muggeridge's report to the Handloom Weavers Inquiry Commission:

He can play or idle as feeling or inclination lead him; rise early or late, apply himself assiduously or carelessly, as he pleases, and work up at any time, by increased exertion, hours previously sacrificed to indulgence or recreation. There is scarcely another condition of any portion of our working population thus free from external control. . . . The weaver will stand by his loom while it will enable him to exist, however miserably.[12]

Thus Mill indicated that the handloom weaver did not choose his employment in terms of wages, but preferred lower to higher wage employment, because it was otherwise attractive to him and the wage difference was not sufficiently large to overcome this attraction.

Senior spoke of the choice between employment as a Manchester weaver or spinner or work as an agricultural laborer, carpenter, or coal heaver as depending not only upon the weekly wage in each occupation but also upon the opportunities for

11. N. W. Senior, pp. 205–6.
12. John Stuart Mill, *Principles of Political Economy* (George Routledge and Sons, Ltd., London, 1895), p. 266.

employment of wives and children. Even here, he pointed out, choices must be seen in net terms. From the gain in earnings of secondary income earners in the family must be subtracted certain costs: 'the wife is taken from her household labours', 'the moral inconveniences' are great, 'the infant children suffer from the want of material attention and those who are older from the deficiency of religious, moral, and intellectual education, and childish relaxation and amusement'.[13]

Thus, it is clear that total net advantage and not price alone is the touchstone of occupational choice and change in the theory of the economists, and it is total net advantage and not price alone that is said to be equal in all employments.

Price–quantity curves

Latter-day economists, who have developed more elegant systems of analysis than the classicists, *do* use price as the instrument for allocating labor among alternative uses, and their supply curves are drawn to relate quantity to price. Price–quantity curves are drawn, however, upon other-things-equal assumptions, but since economists are not repetitively explicit about this, it is sometimes forgotten.

Quantity is related to price in formal economic analysis for several reasons. First, price is continuously quantifiable; other qualities which attach to occupations may not be quantifiable at all or may be discontinuous. Second, preference patterns related to price are consistent; preference patterns related to other qualities are not. Other things being equal, all persons prefer a higher price for their services to a lower one; but all individuals do not, for example, prefer security to risk. Some are timid and others are gamblers by nature. Third, the analytical model which assumes that behavioral choices are related to price, *ceteris paribus*, gives tolerably good predictive results. Everywhere there is massive aggregative evidence that people move from low-income areas to high, and from areas of thin opportunity, where long-run earnings are likely to be low, to thick opportunity areas, where long-run earnings are likely to be high. Irishmen move to Scotland, Mexicans to the United States, southerners to the

13. Nassau W. Senior, *Three Lectures on the Rate of Wages* (John Murray, London, 1830), pp. 8–9.

north, rural people to the towns, and Europeans to the New World; net flows are not in the opposite directions.

Despite this, it is not inconsistent with the classical model for another attribute than price to operate as an allocating instrument. If, for example, an employer finds that he is losing his workers to other employers because, given the structure of other differentials, the difference between the wage he pays and the wage paid by the others draws the workers away, he has a variety of tactics open to him to induce them to stay. He may offer more wages, or better housing, or superior schooling for the workers' children, or less obnoxious foremen, or more security, or a more acceptable system of advancement to better jobs. But, though tactical choices are open in great variety, there is only a single strategy and this is to reduce the differential of total net advantage between employment with others and employment with him. This is all the classical economists said; they did not say the price differential itself must be changed. Any choice of method made by an employer is consistent with their understanding of the system by which workers are distributed among occupations.

While the employer may contrive any tactic to make employment in his enterprise relatively more attractive, he will usually find that the supply of labor is more elastic to a money price than to a nonmoney price and that it will be usually cheaper, therefore, to increase the wage he pays than to improve the quality of the employment in some other way. This is so because preferences are diverse among men, and money is a more efficient instrument of exchange than any other commodity. Consider, for example, the employer who wants to attract workers to an occupation. Assume two choices are open to him: he may pay more wages or he may 'pay' free gifts of spirituous beverages. Those who have a strong preference for spirits over other commodities may be indifferent to the 'currency' in which they are paid; if they received money payments, they would, in any case, exchange it for spirits. Others, who prefer liquor less, will seek to exchange it for other things which they prefer more. The latter persons will suffer some inconvenience in seeking out others willing to make an exchange, and it will be necessary to compensate for this inconvenience by paying more in spirits than would have been necessary to pay in money. The inconvenience effect applies especially to the class of cases where nonmoney payments are made in commodities which workers can acquire easily through normal purchase. It applies somewhat less to cases where payments are made in non-marketed 'commodities' like plant ventilation, for which only imperfect substitutes (such as respiratory masks which filter out dust fragments) are purchasable. It is inapplicable only for non-marketed 'commodities' which are not at all substitutable by marketed goods, such as decent and compassionate supervisors.

Complexity of motivation

Real life is complex, and the behavior of men has diverse motivations. If many variables affect a result, however, it does not mean that a particular one is without influence. As Lionel Robbins has remarked, the thermometer reading in his room in winter is affected by the opening of his window, as well as by the intensity of the fire in the grate. It may be uncomfortably cold in the room with the window open, but Robbins is surely right to say that the room will be warmer if there is a fire. For some purposes it is useful to hold other things constant and examine the consequences of differentiation in a single variable. This is what Robbins does when he remarks that his room will be warmer if the fire is high. It is what the economist does when he says workers will choose a high wage in preference to a low one. Robbins does not say that the temperature of the room is a unique function of the efficiency of the fire; the economists do not say that occupational choice is a unique function of relative price.

Complex motivation in real life does not destroy the truism of simple motivational behavior in the abstract neoclassical model of the labor market. Other things equal, it can be a correct description of real life behavior to say that workers make job choices with reference to relative prices.

The test of meaningfulness

If the model is to be meaningful, it must be correct and also useful. It is *correct*, other things equal, if workers prefer higher prices to lower; it is incorrect if workers prefer lower prices to higher, or if workers are indifferent toward price and make random choices as between higher and lower prices. It is *useful* if from among the multiple motivations which influence worker occupational choice a significant one has been selected against which to examine choice.

How can we know if the model is meaningful? Following Friedman,[14] we may attempt to ascertain this by seeing whether workers do distribute themselves among employments consistently with the distribution which a theory constructed upon the model tells us to expect. If behavior conforms to these expectations more frequently than to those generated by some alternative theory, then the model is meaningful.[15]

14. Milton Friedman, *Essays in Positive Economics* (University of Chicago Press, Chicago, 1953), part 1, 'The methodology of positive economics'.

15. There is some confusion in the literature of the labor market on the nature of theory. The ordinary form which theory takes is that of a postulated functional relationship between variables, one dependent and at least one independent, which has the power to give predictions at some level of generalization and which is testable. If the machine lacks generalized predictive power, it is not a theory but only an apparatus for describing unique phenomena or, at best, a taxonomic tool for distinguishing likes and unlikes. If it has the power to predict, but results are functions of 'too many' variables, it *is* theory but lacks the capacity to be manipulated; it is therefore useless and there is nothing to do with it but keep it in storage in a kind of intellectual warehouse. With 'too many' independent variables, a theory has no capacity to be verified; its goodness cannot be tested.

The model (the postulated functional relationship between variables) need not be realistic to give good results. 'Bohr's theory of the atom, with its circulating electrons, was at first taken to be a faithful picture of the objective reality. It was only later that it came to be realized that *any other picture* [italics supplied] will do equally well, provided it leads to the same mathematical equations. And the modern Schroedinger atom, with its waves in multidimensional space, presents us with a picture which is frankly incredible' (J. W. N. Sullivan, *The Limitations of Science*, [Viking Press, New York, 1949], p. 157).

To draw another example from the physical sciences, John Dalton, the Manchester schoolmaster, found regularity in the chemical composition of various substances. '[He] now cast about for an *explanation* of the composition of matter. . . . He made the assumption . . . [of] the famous *atomic hypothesis. If the truth of this hypothesis be granted*, the laws of chemical combination may be deduced directly, and are made intelligible. . . . It is . . . important to note that the hypothesis is nothing more than a *mentally constructed and quite imaginary* mechanism, accounting for the facts. *We must be under no illusion that our pictorial conception is representative of the actual machinery of nature* [italics supplied]. Whether there are such things as atoms, and whether the atomic hypothesis is actually in accordance with nature, we have no real knowledge whatever. . . . It must be carefully borne in mind that *all we know* is that certain chemical processes take

Elements in job attractiveness

Some of the recent literature takes the position that wage differentials have little to do with job choice. Workers are asked why they take jobs, why they change jobs. They reply that a constellation of considerations influences their decisions, that alternative wages are only one component of this constellation, and that other factors than alternative wages weigh more heavily on choice. Such choice criteria are consistent, however, with conventional doctrine, which permits choice to be made in terms, let us say, of the cleanliness or dirtiness of jobs. In the classical system, a worker may choose a job because it is clean and reject another because it is dirty. The classicists only argue that other things equal, the clean job will carry a lower wage than the dirty job and that the difference in the wage will be only enough to compensate for the cleanliness properties of the two jobs, if workers are permitted to move freely between jobs.

Occupational choice in terms of relative wages is made only in a framework in which other job properties are given. If a dirty occupation is expanding and must attract workers from a clean

place *as if* the hypothesis were true' (F. W. Westaway, *Scientific Methods* [Hillman-Curl, Inc., New York, 1937], pp. 250–1).

Or consider the process of 'continuous creation'. 'Where does the created material come from? It does not come from anywhere. Material simply appears – it is created. At one time the various atoms composing the material do not exist, and at a later time they do. This may seem a very strange idea, and I agree that it is, *but in science it does not matter how strange an idea may seem so long as it works – that is to say, so long as the idea can be expressed in precise form and so long as its consequences are found to be in agreement with observation*' [italics supplied] (Fred Hoyle, *The Nature of the Universe* [Harper and Brothers, New York, 1950], pp. 123–4).

'Sometimes palpably fictitious theories have been more fruitful in producing new discoveries than perfectly correct but quite abstract formulae' (A. D. Ritchie, *Scientific Method* [Kegan Paul, Trench, Trubner & Co., Ltd., London, 1923], p. 159).

In economics, as in the physical sciences, the consistency of the model with observed experience is not the measure of the goodness of a theory; it is the predictive results that count. I think that Professor Reynolds, for example, is on the wrong road when he writes, 'A proper test of competitive labor market theory would require factual evidence sufficient to test the key assumptions of this theory' (Lloyd G. Reynolds, *The Structure of Labor Markets* [Harper and Brothers, New York, 1951], p. 207).

occupation, then the wage differential between the two must be, for a time, larger than when the distribution of workers between the two is in equilibrium. It can be seen that given other job properties, choice will be made in terms of relative wages, if one asks whether workers can be attracted to otherwise unattractive employments by offering very, very high wages. There surely is some wage high enough to move workers. The principle that relative wages are meaningful in job choice can be proved by arguing the case of the extremely high wage. The economists' position is simply this: that workers will be indifferent between clean and dirty occupations, if the wage differential is just sufficient to compensate for differential cleanliness; that they will prefer the clean job, if the wage differential is less than this; that they will prefer the dirty job, if the wage differential is more than this. It does not matter whether we say that they choose jobs in terms of cleanliness properties, *wages being given*, or that they choose jobs in terms of relative wages, *cleanliness properties being given*. In either case, we say the same thing.

The money wage becomes the determinant of choice only when other attributes are compared. This does not say that choice is made only in terms of relative prices.

Responses to questions on job choice

The trade of common informer cannot be made more agreeable short of revising the values of our culture, but given the odium which attaches to the trade, a price can be attached to it, such that some are willing to engage in it. They are paid 'at a rate quite disproportioned to the quantity of work they do. They are paid not so much for encountering toil as for being pelted and hissed.'[16] Ask a man why he does not become an informer and he will answer that it will make him unpopular with his fellows, but we cannot be led by this to the judgment that price is irrelevant to his choice. At some price differential between the informer's trade and others, he will accept work of this kind. Men do act as informers. The relevance of price to choice is not nullified by the response that the trade is eschewed because of the odium in which it is held. If the informer's wage becomes very high, and

16. Nassau W. Senior, *Industrial Efficiency and Social Economy* (Henry Holt, New York, 1928), vol. 2, p. 248.

this same man does enter the trade, he will answer, when asked why he accepted the job, 'Because the price is high.' The values of this worker may not have changed at all, but one response has reference to the odious character of the work and the other to its high price. No appropriate inference on the weights attached by workers to different qualities in jobs can be drawn from the replies to questions about motivations for job-taking and job-changing.

Another example may be helpful. Consider a worker with a given criteria system. If he rejects an offer of work in Greenland, he will explain his choice by saying, 'It's too cold up there.' If he accepts the offer, he will explain by saying, 'They're paying good money.' When he said, 'It's too cold,' what he really intended was, 'It's too cold, for the money they're paying'; and when he said, 'They're paying good money,' what he really intended was, 'They're paying good *enough* money, even for the cold I will experience in Greenland.'

Two things can be inferred from this example. First, job choices are not made in single-motivational terms; and, second, responses couched in single-motivational terms have other motivations implicitly embedded within them. The same man, with the same criteria system, is here seen to respond differently. The relative importance he attaches to wages and warmth has not changed, but his replies have. His response is determined by the *whole* complex of circumstances that confront him, all taken together.[17]

17. Much of the recent research in labor markets has precisely involved the methodology of putting questions to samples of workers and inferring their criteria systems from their responses (see Parnes, op. cit., pp. 147 ff.). This methodology was (mistakenly, I think) thought to be appropriate by a group of economists who met at Harvard in 1948, under the auspices of the Committee on Labor Market Research of the Social Science Research Council. '[Do] wage rates have a marked influence on workers' job choices [?] The direct approach to this problem is to interview workers who have recently changed jobs concerning their reasons for leaving the previous job and for taking the the present job' (Lloyd G. Reynolds, *Research on Wages:* Report of a conference held on 21–2 February 1948 at the Littauer Center, Harvard University Social Science Research Council, [New York, 1948, mimeo.], p. 20).

Professor Myers seems to support the view expressed in this paper. He says, 'The answer [to the question of "what workers want in jobs"] will depend on what they already enjoy in their work' ('Labor mobility in two communities', p. 75).

S. Rottenberg

Knowledge and Ignorance in Job Choice

If workers are to make job choices with reference to the comparative net advantages in different employments, they must have knowledge of the qualities which attach to jobs. Frequently, however, they make choices in conditions of ignorance, and the most extreme case is the one in which the worker moves from unemployment to a job or from a job to unemployment. In these cases, comparison is not possible.[18]

Comparisons by unemployed workers

It seems to be a plausible proposition that even unemployed workers assess alternatives and choose among them. Consider a worker who is unemployed and who is offered a job with properties x, y, and z. Is comparison possible here? It is, and it is comparison with a dual facet.

The worker makes, first, a comparison between a continued status of unemployment and the job offered. He would not, under all circumstances, accept the job. If it were offered, for example, at a wage of one penny per year, he would prefer unemployment.

18. Professor Reynolds says, '[Workers'] knowledge of wage and non-wage terms of employment in other companies is very meager' (*The Structure of Labor Markets*, p. 213).

Professor Parnes says, 'There are at least three different circumstances in which workers voluntarily terminate employment. A worker may quit a job because he has found another which is more attractive to him; because of dissatisfaction with his present job and the hope that he will find a more satisfying one; or with no intention of seeking other work. Only separations of the first type are clearly relevant in research intended to test empirically the premises of traditional economic theory relating to labor mobility' (Parnes, op. cit., p. 149). Paraphrasing the findings of the Myers and Schultz study of the Nashua labor market, Professor Parnes reports that 'fully a third [of the sampled workers] had not "chosen" the job in any real sense, but had either drifted into it or had taken it because they could find no other' (op. cit., p. 156). Parnes believes that the evidence that workers possess incomplete knowledge of alternatives weakens the analytical power of economic theory. 'Unless workers have reasonably accurate and complete knowledge of the extent and nature of employment opportunities, there is no basis for assuming a purposeful movement of workers among jobs, and the foundation for the entire theoretical analysis is weakened. The evidence on this point is not reassuring. The average manual worker seems to have very limited knowledge of job opportunities in the labor market and even less information regarding the specific characteristics of jobs in establishments other than his own' (op. cit., p. 187).

A 'job' with full leisure at zero income would be preferred to a job with less leisure at a one-penny-per-annum wage. The wage differential would not be sufficient to compensate for the relatively less advantageous nonwage properties of the penny-per-annum job.

The worker makes, secondly, a comparison between the net advantages of the job offered and the net advantages of other jobs not offered and not known in any specific sense, but which are known in some expectational sense. This only says that the choice is made in conditions of uncertainty. Most economic choices are made in conditions of uncertainty; we have only to look at business mortality rates to verify this fact. But this does not mean that choice cannot be made in any other way than randomly. The worker knows the properties of the job offered to him; he estimates the properties of other jobs which he expects may become available; and he compares the two and chooses whether to accept the first or wait for another.[19] Assume that the worker quits his job (about whose properties he has knowledge) but has no other job immediately available to him. He may move to unemployment, but still be available for other employment. In the same way as has already been discussed, there is a comparison made and choice is possible. The choice here is between a known job and an unknown, expected job whose properties are estimated. If the worker moves from a known job to 'out-of-the-labor-force status' and is not available for work, again he compares and chooses. Here, the properties of the known job were not sufficiently advantageous to compensate for the attractions of leisure.

The notion that when unemployed workers take jobs 'because they are unemployed', choice is made by them outside a framework of comparison is, thus, not correct. An unemployed worker can be expected to reject work at a very low wage or, what is the same thing, work at a very high wage which is so hazardous that he has perfect certainty that it will cause his death. Unemployed

19. By omitting the possibility of estimation in uncertainty, I think that Professor Reynolds underestimates the number of alternatives by which workers consider, in some implicit sense, that they are confronted. He says of New Haven workers, 'The decision to take or to keep a job usually depends on a comparison between the characteristics of the job and the worker's minimum standards, rather than on a comparison of the job with other known alternatives' (*The Structure of Labor Markets*, p. 212).

workers, thus, do not take 'any' job or 'the first job offered'. Persistent unemployment will be preferred to some jobs. If the 'first job offered' is taken, it is because the worker, having made an estimate, decides that all things considered, he is better off with it than he would be if he continued to be unemployed and waited for a next offer.

'Pushes' and 'pulls'

Some writers have attempted to distinguish between 'pushes' and 'pulls' to explain worker behavior in the labor market.[20] If a worker is discharged or demoted, or if something else distasteful to him transpires in his present place, he is said to be 'pushed' to make a change. If he is offered or becomes aware of a higher wage or otherwise superior position elsewhere, he is said to be 'pulled' to make a change.

Because 'pushed' workers move to other jobs more frequently and because a disproportionately large number of new job-takers are of this class, they may appear to be more actively engaged in calculating net advantage among alternatives than those who are 'pulled'. But appearance may be deceptive. It may be only that differential rates of movement for 'pushed' and 'pulled' workers reflect different magnitudes for the two classes in the net advantages of present and new situations. The average difference between the net advantage of their present position and that of a new situation may be very much larger for 'pushed' workers than the average difference between the two for workers who are merely 'pulled'. If this is so, we should expect a higher rate of movement between jobs by 'pushed' workers, even if the propensity to calculate and compare were equal for the two classes.

If choices are rational, they are made in terms of the worker's assessment of difference between two situations. It is not the fact that he is badly off, by any absolute measure, in his present place that causes him to move; it is rather that he is badly off relative to what he estimates his position will be after moving. If he

20. See, for example, Clark Kerr. 'There is some real question how effective a wage structure can be in distributing labor in any event. Wages are only one of several important considerations which repel workers from some jobs and attract them to others. The push of unemployment, for example, is often more effective than the pull of higher wages' (*Labor Markets: their Character and Consequences*, p. 288).

believes that he can improve his lot by going elsewhere, he will go; if he does not, he will stay. What is important to his decision is difference; to understand the nature of choice in labor markets, we must look at response to difference.

The comparison of estimated alternatives is made in a context of more or less correct understanding of the 'going rate' in different employments, of the 'worth' of the worker's services, or of the availability of alternative opportunities. There is verification of this behavioral pattern in the empirical studies themselves, which show that quits are more frequent in times and places of expanding employment than in those of constant or diminishing employment.

The unemployed worker who sets a minimum standard for jobs which he will find acceptable is making a choice with respect to the comparative attractiveness of alternatives. In substance, the worker is saying, 'For work of this kind, I shall not accept a wage of less than X cents per hour; because I believe that if I wait, I shall find this price.' Seen in this way, the case of the minimum standard turns out to be a specific variation of the general case of calculation and choice on the basis of comparative net attractiveness. Even if, as the empirical studies have found, 'workers' knowledge of job alternatives is fragmentary and imperfect',[21] movement of workers can equalize earnings in equal employments. Some will overestimate the relative value of a new job and will move more rapidly and frequently than they would if they had full knowledge. Some will underestimate and will move less rapidly and frequently than they would if they had full knowledge. If over and underestimation is randomly distributed among workers, the differences will cancel, and movement will tend to be just that required to equalize net advantage. This may be a sensible expectation of what happens in the labor market.

Uncertainty and job selection

Estimates made in uncertainty may lead, of course, to some wrong directional movement. Even if the cancelling-out process which is here suggested does operate in labor markets, therefore, and

21. George P. Schultz, 'Recent research on labor mobility', in *Proceedings, Industrial Relations Research Association* (Boston, 1951), p. 116.

appropriate allocation of labor among uses is finally achieved, economists will still be interested in enlarging knowledge and diminishing uncertainty, because the more certain are the conditions within which choice is made, the smaller will be the number of moves necessary to reach the optimum.

Empirical research has found that workers who leave a present employment with another specific employment already arranged move to higher gross weekly earnings positions more often than do workers who leave without a specific alternative arranged. From this the conclusion has been drawn that the classical understanding of the nature of worker behavioral choice is more consistent with reality in the former case than in the latter. In both cases, however, workers may well be searching for greater advantage. The conclusion we can appropriately draw from the evidence is that choice in a context of less uncertainty is more successful than choice in a context of more uncertainty. This is only like saying that the incidence of mortality of firms with certain futures is less than the incidence of mortality of firms with uncertain futures. We cannot infer from differential mortality rates differential motivations or differential behavioral patterns.

We can say that uncertainty retards optimum resource distribution in the cases of both firms and workers and hinders equation of net advantages in different uses, but this is all. We cannot say that uncertainty prevents these tendencies or that it leads to nonoptimum distribution and nonequivalence.

The retarding process operates in two ways. First, movement between occupations is more frequent in conditions of uncertainty than in conditions of certainty; second, each movement is less complete than it otherwise would be. But long-distance movement can occur by a chain of short-distance moves. Equivalence of new advantage in positions A and Z can be achieved without specific movement between them, if only there is movement from A to B, from B to C, etc. An examination of the pattern of internal migration in the United States will show precisely this kind of movement. Just as not every worker need move for equivalence to occur, not every moving worker need make a full move. It is only necessary that movement tend to be from less to more advantageous employments.

Desire of Workers for Security

Workers value security highly. They prefer present employment at lower prices to other employment at higher, because moving will diminish their security. Therefore, workers are unresponsive to differentials in prices in alternative employments.[22] Workers are especially insecure in periods of less than full employment, and especially in these periods, price differentials will not move them to change jobs. Therefore, the classical doctrine is especially deficient for an understanding of behavior at time of cyclical troughs.

Surely, workers give attention to security, along with price, in making job decisions. The security attribute is one of the comparative components, along with price, upon which workers make choices. Workers who have acquired security of tenure or who are employed by firms which are expected to be successful in the future may prefer to stay at a lower wage, rather than moving to other employments at a higher wage. But this is no proof that actual behavior of workers is at variance with the classicists' perception. The economists realized that workers *do* give weight to the expected duration of employment in making behavioral choices.

Adam Smith listed as one of the cases of variableness in wages the constancy or inconstancy of employment. Paraphrasing him, Nassau Senior spoke of the London porter, who works inconstantly and thus must be paid more to induce him to pursue that calling than the hodman, whose work is more severe but can 'always find a market for his services'. Their discussion was of prices in different employments in relationship to the qualities of casualness or regularity that attach to different jobs. But, in principle, the classic proposition was that other things equal, a lower wage attaches (will attract workers) to regular employment than to irregular employment; it requires no revision to read it as saying that a worker will accept a lower wage in a secure employment in preference to one somewhat larger wage in an insecure (or less secure) employment. The important role played by seniority rules, in recent years, for rationing dismissals and promotive vacancies among workers merely puts a new face on

22. ' "Oldtimers" were . . . frequently unwilling to risk the security of their present positions by moving' (Myers and Maclaurin, op. cit., pp. 50–1).

Adam Smith's point that a constant employment will be preferred to an inconstant one. In his day, workers were willing to pay a price for the short-run security of constant employment; in ours, they are willing to pay a price for the long-run security of seniority status. Just as inconstancy could be paid for by a higher wage then, the loss of seniority status can be paid for now. There is some earnings difference that will induce even very long-service workers to take up new employment.

Choice is not made by workers in terms of instantaneous earnings differences, and it was not understood by the economists that it would be. It was 'obvious' to Senior that 'the labourer's situation does not depend on the amount which he receives at any one time, but on his average receipts during a given period – during a week, a month, or a year; and that the longer the period taken, the more accurate will be the estimate'.[23] He saw, too, that the number of competitors in the medical and legal professions was diminished, not only by the high cost of learning these arts but also because, for a period of some years of apprenticeship or study, the earnings of practitioners are very low.[24]

Thus it is consistent with the theory that in periods of less than full employment, the relative hourly wage should be less important in motivating job changes than in periods of full employment. A sensible worker accepts a 'low' wage in present employment,

23. *Three Lectures on the Rate of Wages*, p. 7. Professors Reynolds and Shister wrote, 'Economists have tended to assume that even when a worker has a job he will keep his eyes continuously open for something better and will be willing to switch to a superior job at the drop of a hat' (Lloyd G. Reynolds and Joseph Shister, *Job Horizons* [John Wiley and Sons, Inc., New York, 1949], p. 45).

If a 'superior job' means merely a job paying a higher wage, then two things need to be said: (1) the classical economists did not assume such behavior; and (2) the neoclassical economists may have assumed such behavior, but this assumption was not intended to be descriptive of real life. The usefulness of the abstraction from the real world in which th e as sumption appears depends not upon its 'realism' but upon the degree of conformity of predictions derived from the abstraction with observable experience. If, on the other hand, 'superior job' means one which is, on balance, superior, *all things considered*, then it seems indeed to be sensible to assume that a worker '*will* be willing to switch'. Any other assumption has the worker making choices according to the rule that he shall be disadvantaged. It is doubtful that many workers are guided by such a rule.

24. *An Outline of the Science of Political Economy*, p. 207.

at the trough of the cycle, because he has a low estimation of his future earnings prospects if he should leave to search for an alternative. A comparison of long-run earnings in different employments (one known and others estimated) diminishes the influence of hourly wages upon choice in trough periods. In periods of cyclical peak, on the other hand, when opportunities for work elsewhere are many, the expectation of long-run earnings in other employment is high, and hourly wage rates weigh more heavily upon choice.

It is even consistent with the theory that in conditions of lay-offs in particular labor markets, workers move from 'better' previous employment to a 'worse' present one. The worker who makes a job choice must be thought to calculate net advantage in long-run rather than instantaneous terms. He may, therefore, choose a secure employment at a lower wage over an insecure employment at a higher wage, even in periods of full employment. Just so, in times of unemployment he accepts a job with reference to his calculation of long-run prospects, and this may lead him to conclude that a lower wage job than he has held is still for him the more advantageous one.

Rationality of Worker Behavior

Workers do not act rationally in labor markets. They do not make comparisons of net advantage in alternative employments. They do not even examine the evidence which is available to them. Their decisions stem more from habit than from rational calculation.[25]

The idea that choice is made in terms of relative net advantage does not imply that comparison and calculation by workers be explicit. Professor Machlup's driver decided whether to pass a truck on the highway without explicitly solving some formidable equations.[26] In some implicit sense, of course, he did solve them.

25. Myers and Maclaurin found in Fitchburg, for example, 'There were large groups of employees . . . who had become sufficiently habituated to their working environment so that they were not interested in moving to another concern that promised immediate payment of better wages for comparable types of work' (op. cit., pp. 49–50).

26. Fritz Machlup, 'Marginal analysis and empirical research', *American Economic Review* (September 1946), pp. 534–5.

That his solution might not have been correct we know from the incidence of highway accidents, but in event of a mishap most observers would say that the driver had 'miscalculated'. Few, if any, would assume he had made no calculation of the situation.

Calculation in labor markets occurs in the same way; wrong choices (miscalculations) are not infrequent.[27]

Meaning of rational choice

When we assume that workers choose rationally among employment alternatives, we mean that they make choice decisions which are consistent with their goals. If the goal is A, choice which leads to the achievement of A is rational; choice which leads to achievement of B, when the chooser believes it leads to A, is also rational. Choice is irrational, if the goal is A, and the choice leads to B, when the chooser believes it leads to B. Choice is random, when there is no goal (when there is indifference among ends) and selection is made as though it depended upon the turn of a coin.

If, therefore, workers' goals are to maximize net advantage and if they make choices which they believe will maximize net advantage, they are making rational choices. They may miscalculate and come to wrong decisions, but wrong decisions

27. The notion that *explicit* calculation must occur, if there is to be comparison, seems to be held by Professor Parnes, who has written, 'In many voluntary job changes the worker simply is not in a position to make a conscious comparison of the advantages of alternative jobs', (Parnes, op. cit., p. 158, n. 11), 'A good deal of voluntary movement – perhaps most of it – is not the product of deliberate and careful comparison of alternative job opportunities, but rather the result of workers' leaving jobs that are distasteful in order to cast around for others which they hope will be more satisfactory' (op. cit., pp. 161–2).

Reynolds and Shister suggest that theory assumes explicit calculation. '[In the economic theory of job choices], the worker is regarded as behaving like a scientist, carefully gathering all of the relevant facts, and then choosing the job which promises the greatest net advantage' (*Job Horizons*, p. 80).

Professor Shister elsewhere describes the actual process of job choice in this way: 'Most workers who are changing jobs take the first one they find if it meets certain *absolute* standards that they have developed. The evaluation of the new job is not based on drawing comparisons with other jobs' (*Economics of the Labor Market*, J. B. Lippincott Company, New York, 1949, p. 395). Of first-job taking, he says, 'Workers gaining full-time employment for the first time do not indulge in rational comparisons involving net economic advantage' (op. cit., p. 398).

are not irrational decisions and do not destroy the classical thesis.

It may be said that the qualities which attach to jobs are so large in number and so diverse that calculated comparison of jobs is not possible. To this there are two answers. First, though comparison is difficult, comparison occurs; we know this because we know that choices are made and that the pattern of choice does not distribute people randomly in the economy but puts them more or less where they are wanted. Second, comparison is diverse among individuals. The qualities of an employment do not attach to it in any intrinsic, objective sense. An occupation has qualities only as workers perceive them, and their perceptions are diverse. Some will think dirtiness very disagreeable; others will think it only somewhat disagreeable. Some will have a preference for security; others for risk. If John Doe believes that wages aside, job *A* is only slightly preferable to *B*, Richard Roe may believe it is preferable by far. Doe, who, let us say, was on the margin of moving to *B*, can be induced to move by a small differential in wages; a large differential will be necessary to move Roe.

It is because there is variation among workers in the evaluation of jobs that we have an upward sloping supply curve of labor of a craft and the possibility of equalization of net advantage by adjusting relative wages, with only fractional response by workers to a changing wage structure.

It is not correct, of course, to conclude that workers do not behave as the economists assume they do, because we find cases in which workers sometimes move from employments that pay well to those that pay badly. It cannot be said that in these cases workers made no comparison or that they chose irrationally. The choice may be simply incorrect, but still rational, and as has been suggested, wrong choices only slow down the process of advantage equalization. Or it may not be incorrect at all, for a high wage is preferable to a low wage only in other-things-equal circumstances and other things may not have been equal. Depending upon circumstances, workers may maximize net advantage by moving to a new occupation which pays more, less, or the same rate, and any one of the three can be consistent with the classical doctrine.

Habit and calculated comparison

The apparent persistence of wage differentials in similar employments in a labor market does not necessarily mean that calculated comparison does not occur. What seem to be similar employments may not be similar at all in the worker's perception of them, and there also may be errors in observation. What appears to be 'the same kind of work' may really be different when account is taken of all the qualities considered by workers in making occupational choices. Some of these are surely so subtle that they escape detection.

The distinction between choice from habit and choice based upon calculation is not clear-cut, and what seems to be habitual behavior may be consistent with calculated behavior. Senior remarked, for example, that 'ten [English mechanics] go to America for one who will venture to France', although their wage gain would be greater if they went to France.[28] This can be interpreted as pursuit of the habitual idiom, but it can also be seen as calculated avoidance of the real cost of assimilating an unhabitual one.

If there are persistent price differentials in truly similar employments, it may only be because adjustment is not quickly brought about. McCulloch said on this point:

It often happens that, owing to an attachment to the trade, or the locality in which they have been bred, or the difficulty of learning other trades, individuals will continue, for a lengthened period, to practice their peculiar trades, or will remain in the same district, when other trades in that district and the same trades in other districts, yield better wages to those engaged in them. But how slowly soever, wages, taking everything into account, are sure to be equalized in the end.[29]

Conclusions

If we accept the argument that workers make employment choices without respect to wages, or in ignorance or randomly, we are then confronted with some questions. How shall we ex-

28. *An Outline of the Science of Political Economy*, p. 222.
29. *A Treatise on the Circumstances Which Determine the Rate of Wages and the Condition of the Labouring Classes*, pp. 67–8.

plain, for example, the massive evidence that the geographical movement of workers is from low, long-run earnings opportunities to high? Or how shall we explain why occupations requiring rare talent or long and arduous training for their successful performance carry a higher price than those requiring talents possessed by many and skills that are come by easily?

Can we sensibly believe that gross behavior which is consistent with the conventional theory is the result of accidental circumstance and random choice? It seems unlikely that this should be so. The economic theory of the labor market is logically defensible and gives good gross predictive results, if allowance is made for the time necessary for the allocational process to work itself out. Where it has been said to contain errors, it seems to be for these reasons:

1. Empirical research has sought to test the theory by measuring the *assumptions* of the abstract and simple neoclassical model of worker behavior against the complicated motivational system of real workers, rather than by measuring the predictive *results* derived from the use of the analytical apparatus against observed experience.

2. Wrong inferences about the valuation of job qualities by workers have been drawn from responses to interview questions.

3. Exposition intended to characterize whole and general universes have been interpreted to apply to the unique individuals of which they are composed.

4. Disbelief exists that predictions from simple models can give good results in complicated real worlds.

5. The part of the theory which was relevant to free markets was applied to markets in which there are constraints on choice.

6. It was believed that conditions of certainty (of perfect knowledge) are necessary to rational choice.

7. The theory was incorrectly thought to assume uniformity and instantaneity, or at least rapidity, in responsive behavior among workers.

8. It was thought that rational choice required conscious and explicit calculation.

4 G. S. Becker

A Theory of the Allocation of Time

Excerpts from Becker, G. S. (1965) A theory of the allocation of time. *Econ. J.*, **75**, 493–517.

Introduction

Throughout history the amount of time spent at work has never consistently been much greater than that spent at other activities. Even a work week of fourteen hours a day for six days still leaves half the total time for sleeping, eating, and other activities. Economic development has led to a large secular decline in the work week, so that whatever may have been true of the past, today it is below fifty hours in most countries, less than a third of the total time available. Consequently the allocation and efficiency of non-working time may now be more important to economic welfare than that of working time; yet the attention paid by economists to the latter dwarfs any paid to the former.

Fortunately, there is a movement under way to redress the balance. The time spent at work declined secularly, partly because young persons increasingly delayed entering the labour market by lengthening their period of schooling. In recent years many economists have stressed that the time of students is one of the inputs into the educational process, that this time could be used to participate more fully in the labour market, and therefore that one of the costs of education is the forgone earnings of students. Indeed, various estimates clearly indicate that forgone earnings is the dominant private and an important social cost of both high-school and college education in the United States.[1] The

1. See T. W. Schultz, 'The formation of human capital by education', *Journal of Political Economy* (December 1960), and my *Human capital* (Columbia University Press for the N.B.E.R., 1964), ch. 4. I argue there that the importance of forgone earnings can be directly seen, e.g., from the failure of free tuition to eliminate impediments to college attendance or the increased enrolments that sometimes occur in depressed areas or time periods.

increased awareness of the importance of forgone earnings has resulted in several attempts to economize on students' time, as manifested, say, by the spread of the quarterly and tri-mester systems.[2]

Most economists have now fully grasped the ·importance of forgone earnings in the educational process and, more generally, in all investments in human capital, and criticize educationalists and others for neglecting them. In the light of this it is perhaps surprising that economists have not been equally sophisticated about other non-working uses of time. For example, the cost of a service like the theatre or a good like meat is generally simply said to equal their market prices, yet everyone would agree that the theatre and even dining take time, just as schooling does, time that often could have been used productively. If so, the full costs of these activities would equal the sum of market prices and the forgone value of the time used up. In other words, indirect costs should be treated on the same footing when discussing all non-work uses of time, as they are now in discussions of schooling.

In the last few years a group of us at Columbia University have been occupied, perhaps initially independently but then increasingly less so, with introducing the cost of time systematically into decisions about non-work activities. J. Mincer has shown with several empirical examples how estimates of the income elasticity of demand for different commodities are biased when the cost of time is ignored;[3] J. Owen has analysed how the demand for leisure can be affected;[4] E. Dean has considered the allocation of time between subsistence work and market participation in some African economies;[5] while, as already mentioned, I have

2. On the cause of the secular trend towards an increased school year see my comments, op. cit., p. 103.

3. See his 'Market prices, opportunity costs, and income effects', in *Measurement in economics: Studies in mathematical economics and econometrics in memory of Yehuda Grunfeld* (Stanford University Press, 1963). In his well-known earlier study Mincer considered the allocation of married women between 'housework' and labour force participation (see his 'Labor force participation of married women', in *Aspects of Labour Economics* [Princeton University Press, 1962]).

4. See his *The supply of labor and the demand for recreation* (unpublished Ph.D. dissertation, Columbia University, 1964).

5. See his *Economic analysis and African response to price* (unpublished Ph.D. dissertation, Columbia University, 1963).

been concerned with the use of time in education, training, and other kinds of human capital. Here I attempt to develop a general treatment of the allocation of time in all other non-work activities. Although under my name alone, much of any credit it merits belongs to the stimulus received from Mincer, Owen, Dean, and other past and present participants in the Labor Workshop at Columbia.[6]

The plan of the discussion is as follows. The first section sets out a basic theoretical analysis of choice that includes the cost of time on the same footing as the cost of market goods, while the remaining sections treat various empirical implications of the theory. These include a new approach to changes in hours of work and 'leisure', the full integration of so-called 'productive' consumption into economic analysis, a new analysis of the effect of income on the quantity and 'quality' of commodities consumed, some suggestions on the measurement of productivity, an economic analysis of queues, and a few others as well. Although I refer to relevant empirical work that has come to my attention, little systematic testing of the theory has been attempted.

A revised theory of choice

According to traditional theory, households maximize utility functions of the form

$$U = U(y_1, y_2, \ldots, y_n) \tag{1}$$

subject to the resource constraint

$$\sum p'_i y_i = I = W + V \tag{2}$$

where y_i are goods purchased on the market, p'_i are their prices, I is money income, W is earnings, and V is other income. As the introduction suggests, the point of departure here is the systematic incorporation of non-working time. Households will be assumed to combine time and market goods to produce more basic commodities that directly enter their utility functions. One such commodity is the seeing of a play, which depends on the input of actors, script, theatre, and the playgoer's time; another is sleeping

6. Let me emphasize, however, that I alone am responsible for any errors.

which depends on the input of a bed, house (pills?), and time. The commodities will be called Z_i and written as

$$Z_i = f_i(x_i, T_i) \tag{3}$$

where x_i is a vector of market goods and T_i a vector of time inputs used in producing the ith commodity.[7] Note that, when capital goods such as refrigerators or automobiles are used, x refers to the services yielded by the goods. Also note that T_i is a vector because, e.g., the hours used during the day or on weekdays may be distinguished from those used at night or on week-ends. Each dimension of T_i refers to a different aspect of time. Generally, the partial derivatives of Z_i with respect to both x_i and T_i are non-negative.[8]

In this formulation households are both producing units and utility maximizers. They combine time and market goods via the 'production functions' f_i to produce the basic commodities Z_i, and they choose the best combination of these commodities in the conventional way by maximizing a utility function

$$U = U(Z_i, \ldots Z_m) \equiv U(f_1, \ldots f_m) \equiv \\ U(x_1, \ldots x_m; T_1, \ldots T_m) \tag{4}$$

subject to a budget constraint

$$g(Z_i, \ldots Z_m) = Z \tag{5}$$

where g is an expenditure function of Z_i and Z is the bound on resources. The integration of production and consumption is at odds with the tendency for economists to separate them sharply, production occurring in firms and consumption in households. It should be pointed out, however, that in recent years economists

7. There are several empirical as well as conceptual advantages in assuming that households combine goods and time to produce commodities instead of simply assuming that the amount of time used at an activity is a direct function of the amount of goods consumed. For example, a change in the cost of goods relative to time could cause a significant substitution away from the one rising in relative cost. This, as well as other applications, treated in the following sections.

8. If a good or time period was used in producing several commodities I assume that these 'joint costs' could be fully and uniquely allocated among the commodities. The problems here are no different from those usually arising in the analysis of multi-product firms.

increasingly recognize that a household is truly a 'small factory':[9] it combines capital goods, raw materials, and labour to clean, feed, procreate, and otherwise produce useful commodities. Undoubtedly the fundamental reason for the traditional separation is that firms are usually given control over working time in exchange for market goods, while 'discretionary' control over market goods and consumption time is retained by households as they create their own utility. If (presumably different) firms were also given control over market goods and consumption time in exchange for providing utility the separation would quickly fade away in analysis as well as in fact.

The basic goal of the analysis is to find measures of g and Z which facilitate the development of empirical implications. The most direct approach is to assume that the utility function in equation (4) is maximized subject to separate constraints on the expenditure of market goods and time, and to the production functions in equation (3). The goods constraint can be written as

$$\sum_1^m p_i x_i = I = V + T_w \bar{w} \tag{6}$$

where p_i is a vector giving the unit prices of x_i, T_w is a vector giving the hours spent at work, and $\bar{w}$ is a vector giving the earnings per unit of T_w. The time constraints can be written as

$$\sum_1^m T_i = T_c = T - T_w \tag{7}$$

where T_c is a vector giving the total time spent at consumption and T is a vector giving the total time available. The production functions (3) can be written in the equivalent form

$$\left. \begin{array}{l} T_i \equiv t_i Z_i \\ x_i \equiv b_i Z_i \end{array} \right\} \tag{8}$$

where t_i is a vector giving the input of time per unit of Z_i and b_i is a similar vector for market goods.

The problem would appear to be to maximize the utility function (4) subject to the multiple constraints (6) and (7) and to the production relations (8). There is, however, really only one basic constraint: (6) is not independent of (7) because time can be

9. See, e.g., A. K. Cairncross, 'Economic schizophrenia', *Scottish Journal of Political Economy* (February 1958).

converted into goods by using less time at consumption and more at work. Thus, substituting for T_w in (6) its equivalent in (7) gives the single constraint[10]

$$\sum p_i x_i + \sum T_i \bar{w} = V + T\bar{w} \tag{9}$$

By using (8), (9) can be written as

$$\sum (p_i b_i + t_i \bar{w}) Z_i = V + T\bar{w} \tag{10}$$

with
$$\left. \begin{array}{l} \pi_i \equiv p_i b_i + t_i \bar{w} \\ S' \equiv V + T\bar{w} \end{array} \right\} \tag{11}$$

The full price of a unit of Z_i (π_i) is the sum of the prices of the goods and of the time used per unit of Z_i. That is, the full price of consumption is the sum of direct and indirect prices in the same way that the full cost of investing in human capital is the sum of direct and indirect costs.[11] These direct and indirect prices are symmetrical determinants of total price, and there is no analytical reason to stress one rather than the other.

The source constraint on the right side of equation (10), S', is easy to interpret if $\bar{w}$ were a constant, independent of the Z_i. For then S' gives the money income achieved if all the time available were devoted to work. This achievable income is 'spent' on the commodities Z_i either directly through expenditures on goods, $\sum p_i b_i Z_i$, or indirectly through the forgoing of income, $\sum t_i \bar{w} Z_i$, i.e. by using time at consumption rather than at work. As long as w were constant, and if there were constant returns in producing Z_i so that b and t_i were fixed for given p_i and $\bar{w}$ the equilibrium condition resulting from maximizing (4) subject to (10) takes a very simple form:

$$U_i = \frac{\partial U}{\partial Z_i} = \lambda \pi_i \qquad i = 1, \dots m \tag{12}$$

where λ is the marginal utility of money income. If $\bar{w}$ were not constant the resource constraint in equation (10) would not have

10. The dependency among constraints distinguishes this problem from many other multiple-constraint situations in economic analysis, such as those arising in the usual theory of rationing (see J. Tobin, 'A survey of the theory of rationing', *Econometrica* [October 1952]). Rationing would reduce to a formally identical single-constraint situation if rations were saleable and fully convertible into money income.

11. See my *Human capital*.

any particularly useful interpretation: $S' = V + T\bar{w}$ would overstate the money income achievable as long as marginal wage-rates were below average ones. Moreover, the equilibrium conditions would become more complicated than (12) because marginal would have to replace average prices.

The total resource constraint could be given the sensible interpretation of the maximum money income achievable only in the special and unlikely case when average earnings were constant. This suggests dropping the approach based on explicitly considering separate goods and time constraints and substituting one in which the total resource constraint necessarily equalled the maximum money income achievable, which will be simply called 'full income'.[12] This income could in general be obtained by devoting all the time and other resources of a household to earning income, with no regard for consumption. Of course, all the time would not usually be spent 'at' a job: sleep, food, even leisure are required for efficiency, and some time (and other resources) would have to be spent on these activities in order to maximize money income. The amount spent would, however, be determined solely by the effect on income and not by any effect on utility. Slaves, for example, might be permitted time 'off' from work only in so far as that maximized their output, or free persons in poor environments might have to maximize money income simply to survive.[13]

Households in richer countries do, however, forfeit money income in order to obtain additional utility, i.e. they exchange money income for a greater amount of psychic income. For example, they might increase their leisure time, take a pleasant job in preference to a better-paying unpleasant one, employ unproductive nephews, or eat more than is warranted by considerations of productivity. In these and other situations the amount of money income forfeited measures the cost of obtaining additional utility.

Thus the full income approach provides a meaningful resource

12. This term emerged from a conversation with Milton Friedman.

13. Any utility received would only be an incidental by-product of the pursuit of money income. Perhaps this explains why utility analysis was not clearly formulated and accepted until economic development had raised incomes well above the subsistence level.

constraint and one firmly based on the fact that goods and time can be combined into a single overall constraint because time can be converted into goods through money income. It also incorporates a unified treatment of all substitutions of nonpecuniary for pecuniary income, regardless of their nature or whether they occur on the job or in the household. The advantages of this will become clear as the analysis proceeds.

If full income is denoted by S, and if the total earnings forgone or 'lost' by the interest in utility is denoted by L, the identity relating L to S and I is simply

$$L(Z_1, \ldots, Z_m) \equiv S - I(Z_1, \ldots, Z_m) \qquad (13)$$

I and L are functions of the Z_i because how much is earned or forgone depends on the consumption set chosen; for example, up to a point, the less leisure chosen, the larger the money income and the smaller the amount forgone.[14] Using equations (6) and (8), equation (13) can be written as

$$\sum p_i b_i Z_i + L(Z_1, \ldots, Z_m) \equiv S \qquad (14)$$

This basic resource constraint states that full income is spent either directly on market goods or indirectly through the foregoing of money income. Unfortunately, there is no simple expression for the average price of Z_i as there is in equation (10). However, marginal, not average, prices are relevant for behaviour,

14. Full income is achieved by maximizing the earnings function

$$W = W(Z_1, \ldots Z_m) \qquad (1')$$

subject to the expenditure constraint in equation (6), to the inequality

$$\sum_1^m T_1 \leqslant T \qquad (2')$$

and to the restrictions in (8). I assume for simplicity that the amount of each dimension of time used in producing commodities is less than the total available, so that (2') can be ignored; it is not difficult to incorporate this constraint. Maximizing (1') subject to (6) and (8) yields the following conditions

$$\frac{\partial W}{\partial Z_i} = \frac{p_i b_i \sigma}{1 + \sigma} \qquad (3')$$

where σ is the marginal productivity of money income. Since the loss function $L = (S - V) - W$, the equilibrium conditions to minimize the loss is the same as (3') except for a change in sign.

and these would be identical for the constraint in (10) only when average earnings, $\bar{w}$, was constant. But, if so, the expression for the loss function simplifies to

$$L = \bar{w}T_c = \bar{w}\sum t_i Z_i \qquad (15)$$

and (14) reduces to (10). Moreover, even in the general case the total marginal prices resulting from (14) can always be divided into direct and indirect components: the equilibrium conditions resulting from maximizing the utility function subject to (14)[15] are

$$U_i = T(p_i b_i + L_i) \qquad i = 1, \ldots, m \qquad (16)$$

where $p_i b_i$ is the direct and L_i the indirect component of the total marginal price $p_i b_i + L_i$.[16]

Behind the division into direct and indirect costs is the allocation of time and goods between work-orientated and consumption-orientated activities. This suggests an alternative division of costs; namely, into those resulting from the allocation of goods and those resulting from the allocation of time. Write $L_i = \frac{\partial L}{\partial Z_i}$ as

$$L_i = \frac{\partial L}{\partial T_i}\frac{\partial T_i}{\partial Z_i} + \frac{\partial L}{\partial x_i}\frac{\partial x_i}{\partial Z_i} \qquad (17)$$

$$= l_i t_i + c_i b_i \qquad (18)$$

where $l_i = \frac{\partial L}{\partial T_i}$ and $c_i = \frac{\partial L}{\partial x_i}$ are the marginal forgone earnings of using more time and goods respectively on Z_i. Equation (16) can then be written as

$$U_i = T[b_i(p_i + c_i) + t_i l_i] \qquad (19)$$

15. Households maximize their utility subject only to the single total resource constraint given by (14), for once the full income constraint is satisfied, there is no other restriction on the set of Z, that can be chosen. By introducing the concept of full income the problem of maximizing utility subject to the time and goods constraint is solved in two stages: first, full income is determined from the goods and time constraints, and then utility is maximized subject only to the constraint imposed by full income.

16. It can easily be shown that the equilibrium conditions of (16) are in fact precisely the same as those following in general from equation (10).

The total marginal cost of Z_i is the sum of $b_i(p_i + c_i)$, the marginal cost of using goods in producing Z_i, and $t_i l_i$, the marginal cost of using time. This division would be equivalent to that between direct and indirect costs only if $c_i = 0$ or if there were no indirect costs of using goods.

The accompanying figure shows the equilibrium given by equation (16) for a two-commodity world. In equilibrium the slope of the full income opportunity curve, which equals the ratio of

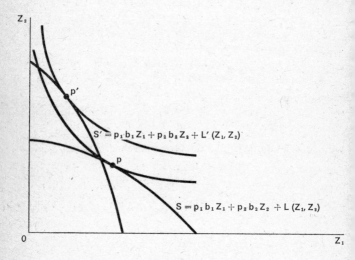

marginal prices, would equal the slope of an indifference curve, which equals the ratio of marginal utilities. Equilibrium occurs at p and p' for the opportunity curves S and S' respectively.

The rest of the paper is concerned with developing numerous empirical implications of this theory, starting with determinants of hours worked and concluding with an economic interpretation of various queueing systems. To simplify the presentation, it is assumed that the distinction between direct and indirect costs is equivalent to that between goods and time costs; in other words, the marginal forgone cost of the use of goods, c_i, is set equal to zero. The discussion would not be much changed, but would be more cumbersome were this not assumed.[17] Finally, until [the penultimate section] goods and time are assumed to be used in fixed proportions in producing commodities; that is, the coefficients b_i and t_i in equation (8) are treated as constants.

Applications

Hours of work

If the effects of various changes on the time used on consumption, T_c, could be determined, their effects on hours worked, T_w, could be found residually from equation (7). This section considers, among other things, the effects of changes in income, earnings, and market prices on T_c, and thus on T_w, using as the major tool of analysis differences among commodities in the importance of forgone earnings.

The relative marginal importance of forgone earnings is defined as

$$\alpha_i = \frac{l_i t_i}{p_i b_i + l_i t_i} \tag{20}$$

The importance of forgone earnings would be greater the larger l_i and t_i, the forgone earnings per hour of time, and the number of hours used per unit of Z_i respectively, while it would be smaller the larger p_i and b_i, the market price of goods, and the number of goods used per unit of Z_i respectively. Similarly, the relative marginal importance of time is defined as

$$\gamma_i = \frac{t_i}{p_i b_i + l_i t_i} \tag{21}$$

If full income increased solely because of an increase in V (other money income) there would simply be a parallel shift of the opportunity curve to the right with no change in relative commodity prices. The consumption of most commodities would have to increase; if all did, hours worked would decrease, for the total time spent on consumption must increase if the output of all

17. Elsewhere I have discussed some effects of the allocation of goods on productivity (see my 'Investment in human capital: A theoretical analysis', *Journal of Political Economy*, special supplement [October 1962], Sect. 2); essentially the same discussion can be found in *Human capital*, ch. 2.

commodities did, and by equation (7) the time spent at work is inversely related to that spent on consumption. Hours worked could increase only if relatively time intensive commodities, those with large γ, were sufficiently inferior.[18]

A uniform percentage increase in earnings for all allocations of time would increase the cost per hour used in consumption by the same percentage for all commodities.[19] The relative prices of different commodities would, however, change as long as forgone earnings were not equally important for all; in particular, the prices of commodities having relatively important forgone earnings would rise more. Now the fundamental theorem of demand theory states that a compensated change in relative prices would induce households to consume less of commodities rising in price. The figure shows the effect of a rise in earnings fully compensated by a decline in other income: the opportunity curve would be rotated clockwise through the initial position p if Z_1 were the more earnings-intensive commodity. In the figure the new equilibrium p' must be to the left and above p, or less Z_1 and more Z_2 would be consumed.

Therefore a compensated uniform rise in earnings would lead to a shift away from earnings-intensive commodities and towards goods-intensive ones. Since earnings and time intensiveness tend

18. The problem is: under what conditions would

$$\frac{-\partial T_w}{\partial V} = \frac{\partial T_c}{\partial V} = \sum t_i \frac{\partial Z_i}{\partial V} < 0 \qquad (1')$$

when $\qquad \sum(p_i b_i + l_i t_i)\frac{\partial Z_i}{\partial V} = 1 \qquad (2')$

If the analysis were limited to a two-commodity world where Z_1 was more time intensive, then it can easily be shown that $(1')$ would hold if and only if

$$\frac{\partial Z_1}{\partial V} < \frac{-\gamma_2}{(\gamma_1 - \gamma_2)(p_1 b_1 + l_1 t_1)} < 0 \qquad (3')$$

19. By a uniform change of β is meant

$$W_1 = (1 + \beta)W_0(Z_1, \ldots Z_n)$$

where W_0 represents the earnings function before the change and W_1 represents it afterwards. Since the loss function is defined as

$$L = S - W - V$$
$$= W(\hat{Z}) - W(Z),$$

then $\qquad L_1 = W_1(\hat{Z}) - W_1(Z)$
$$= (1 + \beta)[W_0(\hat{Z}) - W_0(Z)] = (1 + \beta)L_0$$

Consequently, all opportunities costs also change by β.

to be positively correlated,[20] consumption would be shifted from time-intensive commodities. A shift away from such commodities would, however, result in a reduction in the total time spent in consumption, and thus an increase in the time spent at work.[21]

The effect of an uncompensated increase in earnings on hours worked would depend on the relative strength of the substitution and income effects. The former would increase hours, the latter reduce them; which dominates cannot be determined *a priori*.

The conclusion that a pure rise in earnings increases and a pure rise in income reduces hours of work must sound very familiar, for they are traditional results of the well-known labour–leisure analysis. What, then, is the relation between our analysis, which treats all commodities symmetrically and stresses only their differences in relative time and earnings intensities, and the usual analysis, which distinguishes a commodity having special properties called 'leisure' from other more commonplace commodities? It is easily shown that the usual labour–leisure analysis can be looked upon as a special case of ours in which the cost of the commodity called leisure consists entirely of forgone earnings and the cost of other commodities entirely of goods.[22]

20. According to the definitions of earning and time intensity in equations (20) and (21), they would be positively correlated unless l_i and t_i were sufficiently negatively correlated. See the further discussion later on.

21. Let it be stressed that this conclusion usually holds, even when households are irrational; sophisticated calculations about the value of time at work or in consumption, or substantial knowledge about the amount of time used by different commodities, is not required. Changes in the hours of work, even of non-maximizing, impulsive, habitual, etc., households would tend to be positively related to compensated changes in earnings because demand curves tend to be negatively inclined even for such households (see G. S. Becker, 'Irrational behavior and economic theory', *Journal of Political Economy* [February 1962]).

22. Suppose there were two commodities Z_1 and Z_2, where the cost of Z_1 depended only on the cost of market goods, while the cost of Z_2 depended only on the cost of time. The goods-budget constraint would then simply be

$$p_1 b_1 Z_1 = I = V + T_w \bar{w}$$

and the constraint on time would be

$$t_2 Z_2 = T - T_w$$

This is essentially the algebra of the analysis presented by Henderson and Quandt, and their treatment is representative. They call Z_2 'leisure', and Z_1 an average of different commodities. Their equilibrium condition that

As a description of reality such an approach, of course, is not tenable, since virtually all activities use both time and goods. Perhaps it would be defended either as an analytically necessary or extremely insightful approximation to reality. Yet the usual substitution and income effects of a change in resources on hours worked have easily been derived from a more general analysis which stresses only that the relative importance of time varies among commodities. The rest of the paper tries to go further and demonstrate that the traditional approach, with its stress on the demand for 'leisure', apparently has seriously impeded the development of insights about the economy, since the more direct and general approach presented here naturally leads to a variety of implications never yet obtained.

The two determinants of the importance of forgone earnings are the amount of time used per dollar of goods and the cost per unit of time. Reading a book, taking a haircut, or commuting use more time per dollar of goods than eating dinner, frequenting a night-club, or sending children to private summer camps. Other things the same, forgone earnings would be more important for the former set of commodities than the latter.

The importance of forgone earnings would be determined solely by time intensity only if the cost of time was the same for all commodities. Presumably, however, it varies considerably among commodities and at different periods. For example, the cost of time is often less on week-ends and in the evenings because many firms are closed then,[23] which explains why a famous liner intentionally includes a week-end in each voyage between the United States and Europe.[24] The cost of time would also tend to be less for commodities that contribute to productive effort, traditionally called 'productive consumption'. A considerable

---

the rate of substitution between goods and leisure equals the real wage-rate is just a special case of our equation (19) (see *Microeconomic theory* [McGraw-Hill, 1958], p. 23).

23. For workers receiving premium pay on the week-ends and in the evenings, however, the cost of time may be considerably greater then.

24. See the advertisement by United States Lines in various issues of the *New Yorker* magazine: 'The S.S. *United States* regularly includes a week-end in its 5 days to Europe, saving [economic] time for businessmen' (my insertion).

amount of sleep, food, and even 'play' fall under this heading. The opportunity cost of the time is less because these commodities indirectly contribute to earnings. Productive consumption has had a long but bandit-like existence in economic thought; our analysis does systematically incorporate it into household decision-making.

Although the formal specification of leisure in economic models has ignored expenditures on goods, cannot one argue that a more correct specification would simply associate leisure with relatively important forgone earnings? Most conceptions of leisure do imply that it is time intensive and does not indirectly contribute to earnings,[25] two of the important characteristics of earnings-intensive commodities. On the other hand, not all of what are usually considered leisure activities do have relatively important forgone earnings: night-clubbing is generally considered leisure and yet, at least in its more expensive forms, has a large expenditure component. Conversely, some activities have relatively large forgone earnings and are not considered leisure: haircuts or child care are examples. Consequently, the distinction between earnings-intensive and other commodities corresponds only partly to the usual distinction between leisure and other commodities. Since it has been shown that the relative importance of forgone earnings rather than any concept of leisure is more relevant for economic analysis, less attention should be paid to the latter. Indeed, although the social philosopher might have to define precisely the concept of leisure,[26] the economist can reach all his traditional results as well as many more without introducing it at all!

Not only is it difficult to distinguish leisure from other

25. For example, *Webster's collegiate dictionary* defines leisurely as 'characterized by leisure, taking *abundant time*' (my italics); or S. de Grazia, in his recent *Of time, work and leisure*, says, 'Leisure is a state of being in which activity is performed for its own sake or as its own end' (The Twentieth Century Fund, New York, 1962, p. 15).

26. S. de Grazia has recently entertainingly shown the many difficulties in even reaching a reliable definition, and *a fortiori*, in quantitatively estimating the amount of leisure (see ibid., ch. 3 and 4; also see W. Moore, *Man, time and society* [Wiley, New York, 1963], ch. 2; J. N. Morgan, M. H. David, W. J. Cohen, and H. E. Brazer, *Income and welfare in the United States* [McGraw-Hill, New York, 1962], p. 322, and Owen, op. cit., ch. 2).

non-work[27] but also even work from non-work. Is commuting work, non-work, or both? How about a business lunch, a good diet, or relaxation? Indeed, the notion of productive consumption was introduced precisely to cover those commodities that contribute to work as well as to consumption. Cannot pure work then be considered simply as a limiting commodity of such joint commodities in which the contribution to consumption was nil? Similarly, pure consumption would be a limiting commodity in the opposite direction in which the contribution to work was nil, and intermediate commodities would contribute to both consumption and work. The more important the contribution to work relative to consumption, the smaller would tend to be the relative importance of forgone earnings. Consequently, the effects of changes in earnings, other income, etc., on hours worked then become assimiliated to and essentially a special case of their effects on the consumption of less earnings-intensive commodities. For example, a pure rise in earnings would reduce the relative price, and thus increase the time spent on these commodities, *including the time spent at work*; similarly, for changes in income and other variables. The generalization wrought by our approach is even greater than may have appeared at first.

Before concluding this section a few other relevant implications of our theory might be briefly mentioned. Just as a (compensated) rise in earnings would increase the prices of commodities with relatively large forgone earnings, induce a substitution away from them, and increase the hours worked, so a (compensated) fall in market prices would also induce a substitution away from them and increase the hours worked: the effects of changes in direct and indirect costs are symmetrical. Indeed, Owen presents some evidence indicating that hours of work in the United States fell

27. Sometimes true leisure is defined as the amount of discretionary time available (see Moore, op. cit., p. 18). It is always difficult to attach a rigorous meaning to the word 'discretionary' when referring to economic resources. One might say that in the short run consumption time is and working time is not discretionary, because the latter is partially subject to the authoritarian control of employers. (Even this distinction would vanish if households gave certain firms authoritarian control over their consumption time; see the discussion in [the second section].) In the long run this definition of discretionary time is suspect too because the availability of alternative sources of employment would make working time also discretionary.

somewhat more in the first thirty years of this century than in the second thirty years, not because wages rose more during the first period, but because the market prices of recreation commodities fell more then.[28]

A well-known result of the traditional labour–leisure approach is that a rise in the income tax induces at least a substitution effect away from work and towards 'leisure'. Our approach reaches the same result only via a substitution towards time-intensive consumption rather than leisure. A simple additional implication of our approach, however, is that if a rise in the income tax were combined with an appropriate excise on the goods used in time-intensive commodities or subsidy to the goods used in other commodities there need be no change in full relative prices, and thus no substitution away from work. The traditional approach has recently reached the same conclusion, although in a much more involved way.[29]

There is no exception in the traditional approach to the rule that a pure rise in earnings would not induce a decrease in hours worked. An exception does occur in ours, for if the time and earnings intensities (i.e. $l_i t_i$ and t_i) were negatively correlated a pure rise in earnings would induce a substitution towards time-intensive commodities, and thus away from work.[30] Although this exception does illustrate the greater power of our approach, there is no reason to believe that it is any more important empirically than the exception to the rule on income effects.

28. See op. cit., ch. 8. Recreation commodities presumably have relatively large forgone earnings.

29. See W. J. Corbett and D. C. Hague, 'Complementarity and the excess burden of taxation', *Review of Economic Studies*, vol. 21 (1953–54); also A. C. Harberger, 'Taxation, resource allocation and welfare', in the *Role of direct and indirect taxes in the federal revenue system* (Princeton University Press, 1964).

30. The effect on earnings is more difficult to determine because, by assumption, time-intensive commodities have smaller costs per unit time than other commodities. A shift towards the former would, therefore, raise hourly earnings, which would partially and perhaps more than entirely offset the reduction in hours worked. Incidentally, this illustrates how the productivity of hours worked is influenced by the consumption set chosen.

The productivity of time

Most of the large secular increase in earnings, which stimulated the development of the labour–leisure analysis, resulted from an increase in the productivity of working time due to the growth in human and physical capital, technological progress, and other factors. Since a rise in earnings resulting from an increase in productivity has both income and substitution effects, the secular decline in hours worked appeared to be evidence that the income effect was sufficiently strong to swamp the substitution effect.

The secular growth in capital and technology also improved the productivity of consumption time: supermarkets, automobiles, sleeping pills, safety and electric razors, and telephones are a few familiar and important examples of such developments. An improvement in the productivity of consumption time would change relative commodity prices and increase full income, which in turn would produce substitution and income effects. The interesting point is that a very different interpretation of the observed decline in hours of work is suggested because these effects are precisely the opposite of those produced by improvements in the productivity of working time.

Assume a uniform increase only in the productivity of consumption time, which is taken to mean a decline in all t_i, time required to produce a unit of Z_i, by a common percentage. The relative prices of commodities with large forgone earnings would fall, and substitution would be induced towards these and away from other commodities, causing hours of work also to fall. Since the increase in productivity would also produce an income effect,[31] the demand for commodities would increase, which, in turn, would induce an increased demand for goods. But since the productivity of working time is assumed not to change, more goods could be obtained only by an increase in work. That is, the higher real income resulting from an advance in the productivity of consumption time would cause hours of work to *increase*.

Consequently, an emphasis on the secular increase in the

31. Full money income would be unaffected if it were achieved by using all time at pure work activities. If other uses of time were also required it would tend to increase. Even if full money income were unaffected, however, full real income would increase because prices of the Z_i would fall.

productivity of consumption time would lead to a very different interpretation of the secular decline in hours worked. Instead of claiming that a powerful income effect swamped a weaker substitution effect, the claim would have to be that a powerful substitution effect swamped a weaker income effect.

Of course, the productivity of both working and consumption time increased secularly, and the true interpretation is somewhere between these extremes. If both increased at the same rate there would be no change in relative prices, and thus no substitution effect, because the rise in l_i induced by one would exactly offset the decline in t_i induced by the other, marginal forgone earnings ($l_i t_i$) remaining unchanged. Although the income effects would tend to offset each other too, they would do so completely only if the income elasticity of demand for time-intensive commodities was equal to unity. Hours worked would decline if it was above and increase if it was below unity.[32] Since these commodities have probably on the whole been luxuries, such an increase in income would tend to reduce hours worked.

The productivity of working time has probably advanced more than that of consumption time, if only because of familiar reasons associated with the division of labour and economies of scale.[33] Consequently, there probably has been the traditional substitution effect towards and income effect away from work, as well as an income effect away from work because time-intensive commodities were luxuries. The secular decline in hours worked would only imply therefore that the combined income effects swamped the substitution effect, not that the income effect of an advance in the productivity of working time alone swamped its substitution effect.

Cross-sectionally, the hours worked of males have generally declined less as incomes increased than they have over time. Some

32. So the 'Knight' view that an increase in income would increase 'leisure' is not necessarily true, even if leisure were a superior good and even aside from Robbins' emphasis on the substitution effect (see L. Robbins, 'On the Elasticity of Demand for Income in Terms of Effort', *Economica* [June 1930]).

33. Wesley Mitchell's justly famous essay 'The backward art of spending money' spells out some of these reasons (see the first essay in the collection *The backward art of spending money and other essays* [McGraw-Hill, New York, 1932]).

of the difference between these relations is explained by the distinction between relevant and reported incomes, or by inter-dependencies among the hours worked by different employees;[34] some is probably also explained by the distinction between working and consumption productivity. There is a presumption that persons distinguished cross-sectionally by money incomes or earnings differ more in working than consumption productivity because they are essentially distinguished by the former. This argument does not apply to time series because persons are distinguished there by calendar time, which in principle is neutral between these productivities. Consequently, the traditional substitution effect towards work is apt to be greater cross-sectionally, which would help to explain why the relation between the income and hours worked of men is less negatively sloped there, and be additional evidence that the substitution effect for men is not weak.[35]

Productivity in the service sector in the United States appears to have advanced more slowly, at least since 1929, than productivity in the goods sector.[36] Service industries, like retailing, transportation, education, and health, use a good deal of the time of households that never enter into input, output, and price series, or therefore into measures of productivity. Incorporation of such time into the series and consideration of changes in its productivity would contribute, I believe, to an understanding of the apparent differences in productivity advance between these sectors.

An excellent example can be found in a recent study of productivity trends in the barbering industry in the United States.[37] Conventional productivity measures show relatively little

34. A. Finnegan does find steeper cross-sectional relations when the average incomes and hours of different occupations are used (see his 'A cross-sectional analysis of hours of work', *Journal of Political Economy* [October 1962]).

35. Note that Mincer has found a very strong substitution effect for women (see his 'Labor force participation of married women', op. cit.).

36. See the essay by Victor Fuchs, 'Productivity trends in the goods and service sectors, 1929–61: A preliminary survey', N.B.E.R. Occasional Paper, October 1964.

37. See J. Wilburn, 'Productivity Trends in Barber and Beauty Shops', mimeographed report, N.B.E.R., September 1964.

advance in barbers' shops since 1929, yet a revolution has occurred in the activities performed by these shops. In the 1920s shaves still accounted for an important part of their sales, but declined to a negligible part by the 1950s because of the spread of home safety and electric razors. Instead of travelling to a shop, waiting in line, receiving a shave, and continuing to another destination, men now shave themselves at home, saving travelling, waiting, and even some shaving time. This considerable advance in the productivity of shaving nowhere enters measures for barbers' shops. If, however, a productivity measure for general barbering activities, including shaving, was constructed, I suspect that it would show an advance since 1929 comparable to most goods.[38] [. . .]

The division of labour within families

Space is too limited to do more than summarize the main implications of the theory concerning the division of labour among members of the same household. Instead of simply allocating time efficiently among commodities, multi-person households also allocate the time of different members. Members who are relatively more efficient at market activities would use less of their time at consumption activities than would other members. Moreover, an increase in the relative market efficiency of any member would effect a reallocation of the time of all other members towards consumption activities in order to permit the former to spend more time at market activities. In short, the allocation of the time of any member is greatly influenced by the opportunities open to other members.

Substitution between Time and Goods

Although time and goods have been assumed to be used in fixed proportions in producing commodities, substitution could take place because different commodities used them in different proportions. The assumption of fixed proportions is now dropped in order to include many additional implications of the theory.

38. The movement of shaving from barbers' shops to households illustrates how and why even in urban areas households have become 'small factories'. Under the impetus of a general growth in the value of time they have been encouraged to find ways of saving on travelling and waiting time by performing more activities themselves.

It is well known from the theory of variable proportions that households would minimize costs by setting the ratio of the marginal product of goods to that of time equal to the ratio of their marginal costs.[39] A rise in the cost of time relative to goods would induce a reduction in the amount of time and an increase in the amount of goods used per unit of each commodity. Thus, not only would a rise in earnings induce a substitution away from earnings-intensive commodities but also a substitution away from time and towards goods in the production of each commodity. Only the first is (implicitly) recognized in the labour–leisure analysis, although the second may well be of considerable importance. It increases one's confidence that the substitution effect of a rise in earnings is more important than is commonly believed.

The change in the input coefficients of time and goods resulting from a change in their relative costs is defined by the elasticity of substitution between them, which presumably varies from commodity to commodity. The only empirical study of this elasticity assumes that recreation goods and 'leisure' time are used to produce a recreation commodity.[40] Definite evidence of substitution is found, since the ratio of leisure time to recreation goods is negatively related to the ratio of their prices. The elasticity of substitution appears to be less than unity, however, since the share of leisure in total factor costs is apparently positively related to its relative price.

39. The cost of producing a given amount of commodity Z_i would be minimized if

$$\frac{\partial f_i / \partial x_i}{\partial f_i / \partial T_i} = \frac{P_i}{\partial L / \partial T_i}$$

If utility were considered an indirect function of goods and time rather than simply a direct function of commodities the following conditions, among others, would be required to maximize utility:

$$\frac{\partial U / \partial x_i}{\partial U / \partial T_i} \equiv \frac{\partial Z_i / \partial x_i}{\partial Z_i / \partial T_i} = \frac{p_i}{\partial L / \partial T}$$

which are exactly the same conditions as above. The ratio of the marginal utility of x_i to that of T_i depends only on f_i, x_i, and T_i, and is thus independent of other production functions, goods, and time. In other words, the indirect utility function is what has been called 'weakly separable' (see R. Muth, 'Household production and consumer demand functions', unpublished manuscript).

40. See Owen op. cit., ch. 10.

The incentive to economize on time as its relative cost increases goes a long way towards explaining certain broad aspects of behaviour that have puzzled and often disturbed observers of contemporary life. Since hours worked have declined secularly in most advanced countries, and so-called 'leisure' has presumably increased, a natural expectation has been that 'free' time would become more abundant, and be used more 'leisurely' and 'luxuriously'. Yet, if anything, time is used more carefully today than a century ago.[41] If there was a secular increase in the productivity of working time relative to consumption time [... there would be an increasing incentive to economize on the latter because of its greater expense (our theory emphatically cautions against calling such time 'free'). Not surprisingly, therefore, it is now kept track of and used more carefully than in the past.

Americans are supposed to be much more wasteful of food and other goods than persons in poorer countries, and much more conscious of time: they keep track of it continuously, make (and keep) appointments for specific minutes, rush about more, cook steaks and chops rather than time-consuming stews and so forth.[42] They are simultaneously supposed to be wasteful – of material goods – and overly economical – of immaterial time. Yet both allegations may be correct and not simply indicative of a strange American temperament because the market value of time is higher relative to the price of goods there than elsewhere. That is, the tendency to be economical about time and lavish about goods may be no paradox, but in part simply a reaction to a difference in relative costs.

The substitution towards goods induced by an increase in the relative cost of time would often include a substitution towards more expensive goods. For example, an increase in the value of a mother's time may induce her to enter the labour force and spend less time cooking by using pre-cooked foods and less time on child-care by using nurseries, camps, or baby-sitters. Or barbers' shops in wealthier sections of town charge more and provide quicker service than those in poorer sections, because waiting by barbers is substituted for waiting by customers. These examples

41. See, for example, de Grazia, op. cit., ch. 4.
42. For a comparison of the American concept of time with others see Edward T. Hall, *The silent language* (Doubleday, New York, 1959), ch. 9.

illustrate that a change in the quality of goods[43] resulting from a change in the relative cost of goods may simply reflect a change in the methods used to produce given commodities, and not any corresponding change in *their* quality.

Consequently, a rise in income due to a rise in earnings would increase the quality of goods purchased not only because of the effect of income on quality but also because of a substitution of goods for time; a rise in income due to a rise in property income would not cause any substitution, and should have less effect on the quality of goods. Put more dramatically, with total income held constant, a rise in earnings should increase while a rise in property income should decrease the quality chosen. Once again, the composition of income is important and provides testable implications of the theory.

One analytically interesting application of these conclusions is to the recent study by Margaret Reid of the substitution between store-bought and home-delivered milk.[44] According to our approach, the cost of inputs into the commodity 'milk consumption at home' is either the sum of the price of milk in the store and the forgone value of the time used to carry it home or simply the price of delivered milk. A reduction in the price of store relative to delivered milk, the value of time remaining constant, would reduce the cost of the first method relatively to the second, and shift production towards the first. For the same reason a reduction in the value of time, market prices of milk remaining constant, would also shift production towards the first method.

Reid's finding of a very large negative relation between the ratio of store to delivered milk and the ratio of their prices, income, and some other variables held constant, would be evidence both that milk costs are a large part of total production costs and that there is easy substitution between these alternative methods of production. The large, but not quite as large, negative relation with income simply confirms the easy substitution between methods, and indicates that the cost of time is less important

43. Quality is usually defined empirically by the amount spent per physical unit, such as pound of food, car, or child (see especially S. J. Prais and H. Houthakker, *The analysis of family budgets* [Cambridge, 1955]; also my 'An economic analysis of fertility', op. cit.).

44. See her 'Consumer response to the relative price of store versus delivered milk', *Journal of Political Economy* (April 1963).

than the cost of milk. In other words, instead of conveying separate information, her price and income elasticities both measure substitution between the two methods of producing the same commodity, and are consistent and plausible.

The importance of forgone earnings and the substitution between time and goods may be quite relevant in interpreting observed price elasticities. A given percentage increase in the price of goods would be less of an increase in commodity prices the more important forgone earnings are. Consequently, even if all commodities had the same true price elasticity, those having relatively important forgone earnings would show lower apparent elasticities in the typical analysis that relates quantities and prices of goods alone.

The importance of forgone earnings differs not only among commodities but also among households for a given commodity because of differences in income. Its importance would change in the same or opposite direction as income, depending on whether the elasticity of substitution between time and goods was less or greater than unity. Thus, even when the true price elasticity of a commodity did not vary with income, the observed price elasticity of goods would be negatively or positively related to income as the elasticity of substitution was less or greater than unity.

The importance of substitution between time and goods can be illustrated in a still different way. Suppose, for simplicity, that only good x and no time was initially required to produce commodity Z. A price ceiling is placed on x, it nominally becomes a free good, and the production of x is subsidized sufficiently to maintain the same output. The increased quantity of x and Z demanded due to the decline in the price of x has to be rationed because the output of x has not increased. Suppose that the system of rationing made the quantity obtained a positive function of the time and effort expended. For example, the quantity of price-controlled bread or medical attention obtained might depend on the time spent in a queue outside a bakery or in a physician's office. Or if an appointment system were used a literal queue would be replaced by a figurative one, in which the waiting was done at 'home', as in the Broadway theatre, admissions to hospitals, or air travel during peak seasons. Again, even in depressed times the likelihood of obtaining a job is positively related to the time put into job hunting.

Although x became nominally a free good, Z would not be free, because the time now required as an input into Z is not free. The demand for Z would be greater than the supply (fixed by assumption) if the cost of this time was less than the equilibrium price of Z before the price control. The scrambling by households for the limited supply would increase the time required to get a unit of Z, and thus its cost. Both would continue to increase until the average cost of time tended to the equilibrium price before price control. At that point equilibrium would be achieved because the supply and demand for Z would be equal.

Equilibrium would take different forms depending on the method of rationing. With a literal 'first come first served' system the size of the queue (say outside the bakery or in the doctor's office) would grow until the expected cost of standing in line discouraged any excess demand;[45] with the figurative queues of appointment systems, the 'waiting' time (say to see a play) would grow until demand was sufficiently curtailed. If the system of rationing was less formal, as in the labour market during recessions, the expected time required to ferret out a scarce job would grow until the demand for jobs was curtailed to the limited supply.

Therefore, price control of x combined with a subsidy that kept its amount constant would not change the average private equilibrium price of Z,[46] but would substitute indirect time costs for direct goods costs.[47] Since, however, indirect costs are positively related to income, the price of Z would be raised to higher-income persons and reduced to lower-income ones, thereby redistributing consumption from the former to the latter. That is,

45. In queueing language the cost of waiting in line is a 'discouragement' factor that stabilizes the queueing scheme (see, for example, D. R. Cox and W. L. Smith, *Queues* [Wiley, New York, 1961]

46. The social price, on the other hand, would double, for it is the sum of private indirect costs and subsidized direct costs.

47. Time costs can be criticized from a Pareto optimality point of view because they often result in external diseconomies: e.g. a person joining a queue would impose costs on subsequent joiners. The diseconomies are real, not simply pecuniary, because time is a cost to demanders, but is not revenue to suppliers.

women, the poor, children, the unemployed, etc., would be more willing to spend their time in a queue or otherwise ferreting out rationed goods than would high-earning males.

Summary and Conclusions

This paper has presented a theory of the allocation of time between different activities. At the heart of the theory is an assumption that households are producers as well as consumers; they produce commodities by combining inputs of goods and time according to the cost-minimization rules of the traditional theory of the firm. Commodities are produced in quantities determined by maximizing a utility function of the commodity set subject to prices and a constraint on resources. Resources are measured by what is called full income, which is the sum of money income and that forgone or 'lost' by the use of time and goods to obtain utility, while commodity prices are measured by the sum of the costs of their goods and time inputs.

The effect of changes in earnings, other income, goods prices, and the productivity of working and consumption time on the allocation of time and the commodity set produced has been analysed. For example, a rise in earnings, compensated by a decline in other income so that full income would be unchanged, would induce a decline in the amount of time used at consumption activities, because time would become more expensive. Partly goods would be substituted for the more expensive time in the production of each commodity, and partly goods-intensive commodities would be substituted for the more expensive time-intensive ones. Both substitutions require less time to be used at consumption, and permit more to be used at work. Since the reallocation of time involves simultaneously a reallocation of goods and commodities, all three decisions become intimately related.

The theory has many interesting and even novel interpretations of, and implications about, empirical phenomena. A few will be summarized here.

A traditional 'economic' interpretation of the secular decline in hours worked has stressed the growth in productivity of working time and the resulting income and substitution effects, with the former supposedly dominating. Ours stresses that the substitution effects of the growth in productivity of working and consumption time tended to offset each other, and that hours worked declined secularly primarily because time-intensive commodities have been luxuries. A contributing influence has been the secular decline in the relative prices of goods used in time-intensive commodities.

Since an increase in income partly due to an increase in earnings would raise the relative cost of time and of time-intensive commodities, traditional cross-sectional estimates of income elasticities do not hold either factor or commodity prices constant. Consequently, they would, among other things, be biased downward for time-intensive commodities, and give a misleading impression of the effect of income on the quality of commodities consumed. The composition of income also affects demand, for an increase in earnings, total income held constant, would shift demand away from time-intensive commodities and input combinations.

Rough estimates suggest that forgone earnings are quantitatively important and therefore that full income is substantially above money income. Since forgone earnings are primarily determined by the use of time, considerably more attention should be paid to its efficiency and allocation. In particular, agencies that collect information on the expenditure of money income might simultaneously collect information on the 'expenditure' of time. The resulting time budgets, which have not been seriously investigated in most countries, including the United States and Great Britain, should be integrated with the money budgets in order to give a more accurate picture of the size and allocation of full income.

Part Three **Trade Unions**

The problems of trade-union growth, structure, and government have implications for union wage policy. Union growth and structure have usually been examined in terms of a classification of unions into craft, general, and industrial unions, but Turner finds this typology unhelpful as a guide to current trends and it is instructive to examine the changes he observes in the language of Marshall's determinants of the elasticity of derived demand.[1] Reder builds on the earlier controversies surrounding the determinants of union wage policy, his theory has strong similarities with the growth theories of the firm presented by Baumol[2] and Marris[3] and the discretionary theory of Williamson,[4] while his predictions seem to be in conformity with Gregg Lewis' statistical findings.[5] Reder's stress of the sociological and political role of unions in a second-best world finds an echo in Weinstein's article: featherbedding (or restrictive practices) frequently arises from the nature of the innovational process with the result that the best practices do not spread rapidly, workers are immobile, and unions provide some solution to the problems that occur when the economy is operating inside the production-possibility frontier.

References

1. MARSHALL, A. (1920) *Principles of economics* (Macmillan, London, 8th edn).
2. BAUMOL, W. J. (1959) *Business behaviour, value and growth* (Macmillan, New York).
3. MARRIS, R. L. (1964) *The economic theory of 'managerial' capitalism* (Macmillan, London).

4. WILLIAMSON, O. E. (1964) *The economics of discretionary behaviour, managerial objectives in a theory of the firm* (Prentice Hall, Englewood Cliffs).
5. LEWIS, H. G. (1963) *Unionism and relative wages in the United States* (University of Chicago Press).

5 H. A. Turner

Trade Union Organization [1]

Turner, H. A. (1955) Trade union organization. *Political Quarterly*, **25**, 57–70.

I

Of all industrial disputes, few are more likely to induce a baffled incomprehension among those not concerned, in none is irritation at public inconvenience less mollified by sympathy with the workers' cause than those that spring from dissension between the unions themselves. Indeed, that the wave of disputes in early 1955 should have invoked a crop of parliamentary and press proposals for further legal control of strikes was not least attributable to the fact that its three major stoppages – those occurring in the railways, the national newspapers, and the docks – each involved an inter-union conflict.

Trade unionists have themselves been uneasily and continually conscious of the effect of discordant sectionalisms upon their movement. 'Closer unity' has been a permanent motive of its organizational trends, a motive that found a first effective expression in the great craft amalgamations of the 1850s and continued in this century through the linking-up of unskilled workers' associations in so-called general and industrial unions. From 1874 on, the Trades Union Congress adopted successive resolutions called for 'a federated union'. Its 1918 resolution *envisaged* a quite elaborate scheme of structural reform, and at that time, certainly, trades unionists at large would have endorsed the Webbs' remark that '. . . to competition between overlapping unions is to be attributed nine-tenths of the ineffectiveness of the trade union world'. It was a prime instruction to the newly formed T.U.C. General Council of 1920 that it should 'endeavour

1. A more extensive discussion of trade union organization is to be found in this author's *Trade union growth, structure and policy* (Allen & Unwin, 1961).

to adjust disputes and differences between affiliated Unions' – an instruction of which its standing Disputes Committee is a partial fulfilment. On that committee's motion, the 1924 Congress adopted certain 'main principles for the avoidance of disputes' (the Hull rules) and over the three following years pursued an extensive and active review of union structure and inter-relationships – a review repeated between 1943 and 1946.

Such reformist movements have certainly had a considerable effect – though perhaps less in their specific recommendations than in creating an ideological climate that reinforced economic and institutional pressures towards merger and centralization, in confirming certain canons of good behaviour between unions, and in obviating (by providing a less public ventilation and adjustment of inter-union differences) the fratricidal and almost annual rows that once undignified the meetings of Congress. Too much weight, however, may perhaps be given to such things as the contrast between the increased union membership and the reduced number of unions, or the decline in the number of disputes submitted to the T.U.C. The growth of individual unions has – witness the docks disputes – to some extent only transferred the structural problem, from one *between* to one *within* unions.

The events of early 1955 may be dismissed as unrepresentative and unfortunately coincidental; but their causes persist. Instances in which common policy is only enforced upon related unions by the refusal of employers to distinguish between them are still to be found: while continued allegations of 'restrictive practice' against trade unionism find such substance as they possess partly in the recurrence, especially in such trades as construction and shipbuilding, of demarcation disputes arising from rival union claims to particular jobs. Individual leaders, students, and sympathizers of labour have criticized the slow pace of the unions' structural evolution and its seeming directional illogicality: and they have contrasted these things both with union demands for planning in *other* spheres and with the apparent tidiness of union structure in certain other countries.

II

It is, of course, one thing to project (as West German trade unionists were able to do in 1945) a fabric from its first foundation and in an uncluttered field, and quite another to make a harmonious whole from existing constructions of differing antiquity and fashion. And a general view that things should be better by no means implies agreement on how to improve them. The unions' problem of 'closer unity' is sometimes represented as one of conflicting organizational theories – of 'craft' versus 'industrial', and 'industrial' versus 'general' unionism. Such terms have a certain historical validity: existing unions represent the deposit of successive waves of trade union expansion, each of which has generally been crested with doctrinal assertion. And contemporary disputes can sometimes be interpreted in their light: so that when the National Union of Railwaymen contests the London Society of Compositors' claim to printers of railway time-tables, or the National Union of Funeral and Cemetery Workers challenges the Amalgamated Union of Building Trades Workers' right to organize monumental masons, they can be described as illustrating the clash of industrial with craft theories.

But in practice, and apart from certain smaller associations of apprenticed craftsmen (like that of the Lancashire shuttlemakers), pure forms are hard to find. With those exceptions, no union has completely realized its preferred organizational ideal in face of competing bodies: even the National Union of Mineworkers, despite the definiteness that nationalization gave to its announced field of industrial recruitment and the preponderance in that field of its ancestral organizations, did not succeed in assimilating the National Coal Board's clerical employees and has experienced digestive difficulties with several grades of specialist workers. Still more to the point, few unions, when it comes to a test, have been willing to renounce a likely membership for the sake of a theory. The larger craft unions – like the Amalgamated Society of Woodworkers and the Electrical Trades Union – have accepted workers of successively less obvious degrees of skill. 'Industrial', 'occupational', and 'employment' unions have discovered the boundaries that first defined their ambitions to be conveniently elastic, so that the N.U.R. finds reason to recruit road transport workers and the Union of Shop, Distributive and Allied Workers to organize factory operatives and laboratory assistants, while the National Association of Local Government Officers sees the step into state services as logically necessary. Even the A.U.B.T.W. – which appeared above in the role of craftsman's friend – was within a year or two embarrassingly adjudged guilty (again, by the T.U.C. Disputes Committee) of 'poaching' builders' labourers from the National Union of General and Municipal Workers.

Organizational theories have, in fact, often served for little more than to justify the immediately hopeful ambitions of particular unions. The Amalgamated Engineering Union for long refused to join the federal association of engineering operatives on the ground that only a complete amalgamation of the unions concerned (in which its own membership would have been dominant) would meet the case. The N.U.R., in a similar situation, has similarly refused a merely co-operative arrangement with the minority railway unions. Such theories have generally proved proportionately adjustable – as when, the war-time growth of rival unions having robbed its announced principle both of realism and one element of attraction, the A.E.U. joined the Confederation of Shipbuilding and Engineering Unions. To interpret inter-union relationships, then, one needs a more realistic instrument than the customary organizational classifications – which, in any case, fail to accommodate so many existent unions as to be of little use.

III

One clue to the realistic analysis of trade union structure is the marked growth of certain unions. Half the T.U.C.'s affiliated membership is to be found in six unions, and over two-thirds in a score of major associations. The other clue lies in the comfortable survival, despite the general trend to merger and specific competition from very large organizations, of a number of relatively small unions – like the United Patternmakers' Association and the Associated Society of Locomotive Engineers and Firemen; and with this may be associated the occasional embarrassment of the larger unions by such secessionist movements as that of junior officers from the Fire Brigades Union.

Our contemporary union structure may be described as the product of contrasting (but nevertheless, related) membership policies: 'expansionist' and 'restrictionist'. The motives that drive a union to increase not merely the *number* of its members but the *variety* of their occupations are not far to seek. It is nice to be big, of course. But a more specific pressure is that to achieve an organization which is viable from the point of view of the union's purposes. Industrially, this may involve the recruitment of workers in trades or occupations which might otherwise compete with and undermine the standards of its existing membership. Financially, the necessity of a large reserve fund (to support strikes, essential services or other action) may contrast with the inability or unwillingness of its members to pay a large subscription per head. For a union which seeks improvement through political action (whether to secure statutory wage minima and other labour legislation, or such broader industrial reforms as nationalization) the number of its constituents will itself be important. And so on.

The form that growth imposes on a union is very largely shaped by its starting point, which itself indicates certain lines of recruitment. Thus, it may expand by adding new classes of members whose employment is associated in particular firms with that of its foundation group, as labourers are employed with craftsmen, or warehousemen with shop assistants. Alternately, it will certainly tend to expand where its existing membership's tenure of employment is *integrally* related to that of some as yet unorganized section – for instance, where skilled grades of worker are customarily drawn from less-skilled employees in the same industry, or where nominally distinct crafts are substitutable in a significant range of jobs. The direction of a union's growth is thus heavily influenced by the employment structure of the occupations among which it commences to organize. The two general unions have leapt from industry to industry because their initial membership, being unskilled, was also both mobile between, and dependent for the maintenance of its wages on conditions in, a wide range of trades. Such so-called industrial unions as the N.U.R. and the British Iron, Steel and Kindred Trades' Association, on the other hand, will be found to operate mainly in industries where workers are promoted from one grade to another, so that union organization has either followed its members in their progress within the trade or anticipated future promotions.

It is thus useful to distinguish between *horizontal* and *vertical* forms of union organization, according to the main direction of particular growths. But these directions are not mutually exclusive: while many unions exhibit a clear predominance of one trend rather than the other, alternative opportunities have usually appeared. Thus both the N.U.R. and the old Railway Clerks' Association (now the T.S.S.A.) recruited road passenger workers because the railway companies had interests in bus firms, and B.I.S.A.K.T.A. has organized workers in heavy engineering because they were employed in neighbouring establishments and had not yet been recruited to an engineers' union (although their minimum rates were fixed by the C.S.E.U.). The principle animating the apparently haphazard growth of British union structure has been simply that nature abhors a vacuum. Organizational vacuums have usually been filled by the nearest union to hand that desired to grow.

The second determinant of individual union growth has thus been the stimulant or restriction of rival organizations. The major craftsmen's associations, for instance, did not consider it worth while to recruit the unskilled until the appearance of independent labourers' unions threatened to deprive their own membership of the advantage of exclusive organization. Nearly every union extending into an as yet uncultivated field has sooner or later encountered another busily ploughing in a different direction; and it is this that has given amalgamation so much importance as an alternative method of expansion to recruitment. Two unions which cannot achieve viability because of their separate existence must face the necessity of merging, and this represents, historically, the first phase of the amalgamation movement. The second and more recent stage came with the realization, among many smaller unions, that they must surrender their hope of enlarging their inadequate base, and look for protection to whichever of the more viable unions would offer the most favourable terms of incorporation. This has given larger unions additional avenues of extension. That most omnipresent of all labour organizations, the Transport and General Workers' Union, owes its universality not least to an internal structure ingeniously designed to encourage smaller unions to accept adoption.

So much for 'expansionist' unionism: the 'restrictionist'

variety can be more shortly dealt with. The motive that leads a union deliberately to confine its membership to certain defined and related occupations, to a specific occupation or even (as in the notable case of the L.S.C.) to a particular district within those categories is in essence similar to that which drives other unions to expand. But in the restrictionist case, viability in relation to the union's purposes is already largely achieved, and that on a basis of such strength – in relation to its particular labour market, the possibilities of controlling the intake of new workers, and so on – that the subordination of its existing membership's interest to a broader one would only disadvantage the former. Examples of such restrictionist unions are, however, to be found not only in such old-style associations of apprenticed craftsmen as still exhibit a comfortable survival but in unions of more recent type. The A.S.L.E.F., for instance, does not restrict itself to skilled foot-platemen alone, but covers all grades concerned in the actual running of locomotives from the most lowly-paid cleaners upwards.

These alternative tactics of trades unionism may be regarded, by a military analogy, as that of the 'wide front' versus the 'strong point'. But, again, they are not absolutely exclusive. A restrictionist union may be driven to change its character by, for instance, technical change – as the National Union of Vehicle Builders was forced to adopt an expansionist policy by the decline of its old coach-building crafts before mass-production. Or the acceptance of a tempting amalgamation offer from a smaller body may involve such a union, unforeseen, in a recruiting campaign to defend its new commitment.

But more important is the effect upon expansionist unions of their own success. To build a restrictionist union from new requires a certain natural position of strength. But the extension and reinforcement of a 'wide front' inevitably leads to the creation of 'strong points' within it. Particular groups within a wider organization derive such strength and sectional identity from their first association with it that continued membership of the parent body (with its implied adjustment to the pace of weaker brethren) comes to seem a constraint rather than a support.

Most larger unions have been afflicted at some time by 'breakaway' organizations: the railway signalmen from the N.U.R., the winding-enginemen from the N.U.M., the aeronautical engineers from the A.E.U. The northern dockers' secession from the T. & G.W.U. – of which their former membership had produced so remarkable an elevation in their status – threatens to become a classic case. The tendency, however, is less involved in the size of trade unions than their heterogeneity: however indefinite the boundaries a union's external circumstances set to its expansion, an *internal* limit is set by its capacity to placate a growing diversity of interests.

IV

This is an interpretation of trade union structure. But it also provides a guide to inter-union disputes, four types of which may be distinguished. First, those arising from differences in the industrial policy – especially in regard to wages – of the different unions that deal with particular employers or associations of employers. For obvious reasons, the latter do not like to discriminate between their workpeople merely according to the organizations to which they belong. Yet a restrictionist union may hold out for a bigger wage increase than (or a differential over) the expansionist bodies with which it is usually compelled to associate, but the expectations of which are keyed to their less strongly placed members: this, in essence, is the history of recurrent disunity between the printers' unions in matters of wage policy. Or expansionist unions may seek to demonstrate their superiority to prospective recruits by a competing militancy in wage demands: both engineering and the railways provide ample illustration.

Second, therefore, comes the direct dispute arising from rival union claims to the membership of a particular group of workers (or even an individual worker). Such 'jurisdictional' contests constitute the majority of those reported to the T.U.C., and are associated with disputes as to the recognition of additional unions by employers. They are commonly caused by the intrusion of an expansionist union into a new field. The third type of dispute is usually associated with restrictionist unions, the strength of which customarily derives from the assertion of a monopoly in particular jobs: this is the 'demarcation' conflict – as to which union's members should do what work. And finally comes the contest with a 'breakaway' union, an immanent phase of which may be an 'unofficial' movement – which is not, of course, to say that an incompatibility of a union's various sectional interests is the sole, or even the major, cause of 'unofficial' action.

All these disputes are contests of sectional interest. In this, there is nothing improper. It is only when considered ideally and altogether that trade unions represent some more general purpose such as that of the working class. The first and legitimate intent of individual unions is the particular interest of the people who form and subscribe to them, and within that reference subordination to a broader claim (such as that of the industry, the labour movement, or – still vaguer – the community) is strictly arguable only to the extent that it offers the best method of forwarding particular needs. It cannot be expected that the wider interest will always be found, even in justice, overwhelming. It is, indeed, rather to the credit of British trades unionism that its fraternal disputes have been almost entirely confined to such issues, and have very little involved either such incidents concerning the personal aggrandizement of leaders and labour racketeering as have marred the American unions' history, or the politico-religious dissensions of continental trade unionism.

It also follows, however, that such disputes cannot be resolved by merely organizational devices. Their incidence is affected by economic circumstances: if these were to straiten, the preservation of particular group standards would weigh forcibly against tolerance of the interest of others. The problem is also one of general policy: a common interest will more evidently exist if it is expressed in concrete objectives – such as a programme of economic and industrial reform: it is perhaps not quite accidental that major inter-union disputes have followed the demise of the Labour Government. And education is also involved: if a common interest exists, those affected must become conscious of it. It is for this reason that one of the most important of the T.U.C. General Council's contributions to labour unity has been the dissemination of an elementary code of good behaviour between unions – involving such things as the recognition of established 'organizational rights' and the acceptance of a duty to inform other unions where one's action (whether in recruiting or negotiating) may affect their interest.

V

With that general comment, we may consider resolution of the four types of inter-union dispute in detail. For conflicts of industrial policy, the main remedy of both the trade union movement and officialdom has been conciliation and compromise – an extension, indeed, of the techniques developed in collective bargaining with employers. Recognition of the right of other unions to exist and practice in one's own field, and of the desirability of concerting one's policy with theirs, is expressed by affiliation to such federations of unions as operate in the engineering, building, and cotton trades. These bodies have usually acquired other functions than those of bargaining. By such formal or informal devices most negotiations are in fact handled. It is the exceptional case, where a union persists in an independent line, that causes trouble.

It is at this point that a development in the powers of the T.U.C. General Council may prove important. Until 1955, that body's rules, provided that it should be informed (and if it thought necessary, inform unions) of the course of industrial disputes ... 'in particular where such ... may involve large bodies of workers', but it could only itself intervene if negotiations actually broke down. It was as a consequence of its experience with the three stoppages already referred to that it sought and secured an amendment empowering it to require the union concerned to consult and receive advice if a deadlock in its negotiations *seemed likely*. The amended rule is broadly worded, and opponents of the amendment suggested (in the Congress debate) that it might lead to a considerable and discriminatory intervention by the General Council in sectional bargaining. In theory, it would certainly permit the elaboration of something like a central wage policy. But in practice, the voluntary character of the Congress affiliation and the ability of many individual unions to stand alone limit the initiative of the General Council. It is itself composed of leaders of individual unions, and the latter have been traditionally insistent upon their ultimate independence in industrial policy. It is likely to be long before T.U.C. intervention goes far beyond a mediatory initiative.

This refers, of course, mainly to national negotiations. At the work-place itself, co-operation between separate unions has mainly developed through joint action by their shop stewards. The shop-steward system is integral to some unions' practice, and has by now received at least a conditional recognition in most rule books. Its *de facto* authority, however, often exceeds its constitutional status: it has not merely provided a platform for alternative leaderships within trade unions, but – through 'joint shop-stewards' movements' – the framework of what have been, in potential, alternative union structures, extending across and conflicting with established union boundaries. But the discussion of this borders on another topic – the relations between union officials and the rank and file.

It is in the second type of dispute – the 'jurisdictional' – that attempts to establish co-operation between unions have probably been most successful. An important instrument of this has been the 'sphere of influence' agreement: in the rayon and leather industries and in catering, separate unions have allocated establishments or districts between themselves, and in other trades local agreements have even shared out the different departments or workshops of a factory. The Joint Relations Committee of the two great general unions provides a standing mechanism for such arrangements. It is in this field, too, that the T.U.C. has operated most fruitfully. Its 'Bridlington rules' provide both a standard recruiting procedure by which unions may avoid committing unawares the sin of 'poaching', and a principle for the adjudication of rival membership claims that has been effectively operated by the T.U.C. Disputes Committee. This recognizes no exclusive jurisdictional claims, but asserts that where, in particular establishments, a union has established a majority membership of particular grades no other union should commence to organize them without its consent. The rule has been applied with a reasonable flexibility and has generally provided – except in one or two trades, like docks and railways, where a minor guerrilla of fringe 'poaching' has been endemic – an acceptable formulation of organizing rights. The 'Bridlington' procedure has even been accepted by one of the two major non-affiliated unions, N.A.L.G.O.[2]

Demarcation issues, by contrast, have proven singularly

2. This union has since joined the T.U.C.

intractable. These disputes involve the very existential basis of restrictionist unions, and where they have been resolved without a fight it has usually been by direct bargaining between the groups concerned. Such bargaining is, indeed, a considerable duty of shipyard union officials: the Boilermakers' Union is even obliged to limit its members' transfer between its own crafts. One or two demarcation disputes have been referred (from railway workshops) to the Industrial Court, but arbitrators generally (whether of the independent or union variety) have found them hot to touch. They were excluded from the provenance of the Industrial Disputes Tribunal. And although the T.U.C.'s rules permit unions to apply to its Disputes Committee in these disagreements as in others, they have been ruled by Congress as inappropriate to the 'Bridlington' procedure; in those few instances where the Committee has made an award, it has usually done so with reluctance, and has hedged its decision with such reservations as that it shall be temporary only or shall not be treated as a precedent. The A.E.U. has announced that it will not, on principle, accept arbitration in demarcation issues; the printing unions (in odd contrast to their disunities in wage policy) have developed a procedure for adjusting these issues within their Federation but their occupational distinctions are sharp and simple. Demarcation disputes seem most stubborn where there is a difference between the wage rates of the rival claimants to particular jobs: it is curious that the Webbs' apparently practical suggestion that unions should concentrate on fixing the rate *for the job* and leave individual employers to choose its occupant (and individual workers to accept or reject it) should have been so little explored.

As regards the 'breakaway' union, established organizations have only one specific: anathema. It is upon such bodies, rather than upon bona fide unions whose quarrels disturb the movement's amity, that the emotional force attaching to the ideal of closer unity is discharged. Indeed, considering the bitterness the generality of trades unionists display towards such secessions, the T.U.C.'s procedure for identifying and publicizing them as 'proscribed organizations', the reluctance of employers and arbitrators (knowing the indignation it would arouse in the established unions with which they must deal) to recognize them, and the exclusion from employment which has in at least one case fallen upon their members, the remarkable thing is that such bodies exist and survive.

VI

It is not evident (even if it were seriously proposed) that such stoppages of work as result from inter-union disputes would be reduced if the latter were submitted to legal controls. There is, of course, in all such controls the difficulty of enforcement; but in this particular instance no formal control seems to offer an advantage over the unions' existing procedure. The United States' arrangement, providing for supervised elections at the work-place to determine the 'exclusive bargaining agent', in some respects facilitates 'raiding' between unions and in any case assumes a different system of collective bargaining to that in Britain. The provision of certain European countries for periodic work-place elections, to select from the nominees of different union groups a representative council, merely symbolizes and perpetuates the party character of their labour conflicts. And, as the Terrington Committee discovered in its review of the G.P.O.'s 'Listowel formula' of 1946, legalism multiplies litigants: the formula (which applied certain automatic tests to the claims of minority associations for acceptance) was held to have encouraged a situation in which thirty-one internal unions were recognized by the Post Office.

Beyond such detailed arrangements for the mutual regulation of inter-union dealings as have already been discussed, the main prospect of closer unity lies in structural reform. While some trades unionists continue to assert the virtue of industrial union-ism, the main body of union opinion has abandoned a theoretical approach as impractical in face of the factual irregularity of union forms. But it would, I think, be true to say that no rival organiza-tional doctrine commands the same appeal as the industrial. Its past associations with the evolution of socialist thought through syndicalism and (particularly in the U.S.A.) with the organization of the lower-paid, provide a historical explanation, but its con-tinuing attraction is harder to understand. Its superficial neatness disappears before such realities as the imprecision of industrial boundaries and the existence of inter-industry identities: in no country where unions are independent of the state, for instance, have salaried and professional employees been wholly convinced that their interest lies with manual workers who appear on the same pay-rolls as themselves rather than with each other. Of course, where trades unionism is an instrument of economic planning, convenience suggests vertical demarcations as coinciding with the state's industrial administrations: even from such a viewpoint, however, a horizontal form of union organization, with its emphasis upon mobility of labour and upon those universal skills and techniques which are becoming increasingly central to the growth of productivity, has much to recommend it. But any voluntary trades unionism must accommodate *alternative* alliances of particular interests: its need is less for a structure that appears aesthetically satisfying than for one which is flexible to changing circumstance.

The T.U.C.'s efforts have been concentrated upon a reduction in the number of unions by amalgamation. Hence the emphasis, in its General Council's policy, upon the federation of unions as an immediate step: it is hoped that the development, in such federations, of common services (for negotiating, policy formation, and so on) will both reduce the merely institutional obstacles to amalgamation and influence the latter in a broadly 'industrial' direction. But as this programme progresses, it encounters an increasing constraint. There are the successfully restrictionist unions to which merger offers no apparent gain. Beyond that, however, the intricacy of the overlaps between the expansionist unions' coverages, the criss-cross of horizontal and vertical growths, means that in very few fields could amalgamation now realize a single unit to negotiate, not merely with the appropriate employers' association but with the larger employers, without its involving the amalgamation of all unions. Maintenance mechanics are employed in all industries: hence the universality of the A.E.U. and E.T.U. The two general unions already recognize, I think, that despite the outstanding kinship of their interests they are too big to merge.

Continued amalgamations would, of course, reduce the workers' choice of union. That, however, is already diminished by the multiplicity of jurisdictional agreements. And in the world of labour, freedom is less involved in individual choices (which are few by circumstance) than in group standards and status – with the preservation of which random transfers of allegiance are incompatible. But by implication, the ability to express such sectional interests is fundamental. To submit too heterogenous a membership to the restraints of a centralized amalgamation invites later insurrection.

Ideally, again, all this suggests that amalgamation of existing unions should be accompanied by their regrouping: this involving the transfer of fragmentary memberships at present dispersed over several associations, and in some cases the formation of new bodies. There are probably instances, indeed (like that of nurses), where the growth of trades unionism would have been much encouraged if the various unions which had secured a scant foothold in the field had surrendered their claims to a specially formed organization. But the T.U.C. has sponsored only one such union, and that in an employment – private domestic – both dwindling and singularly unrewarding to its other affiliates. One item of the 1918 Congress resolution – proposing exchange and transfer of members between unions – was lapsed in 1925 owing to the negative response of individual unions to the suggestion of a Trade Union clearing house.

The alternative appears to be that as the amalgamations grow they should become less centralized. In this, as in other respects, the forgotten 1918 resolution displayed an advanced conception – in essence that a union combining various interests should give them a certain autonomy, with powers to form federal associations with similar sections of other unions. Centralized amalgamation has been a dominant theme of trade union constitutional history since the days of the 'New Models'. It may well be that the unions will be driven, as their number declines, to revive the virtues of such older and more federal forms as are still partly preserved in the cotton unions and (for all its apparently monolithic façade) the N.U.M. The problem of closer unity between unions becomes one of freedom within them.

6 M. W. Reder

Job Scarcity and the Nature of Union Power

Reder, M. W. (1959) Job scarcity and the nature of union power. *Indus. Lab. Relat. Rev.*, **13**, 349–62.

In the last few years there has been considerable discussion of what labor unions can and do accomplish for their members, and also what effect these accomplishments have on the general functioning of the economy. Much of this discussion has been focused on the question of how much economic power unions possess. This is undeniably an important matter. It is my belief, however, that it is secondary to the question of how unions use whatever power they do have.

A convenient point of departure for our discussion is the question of what it is, if anything, that unions are attempting to maximize or 'optimize' in their demands for wages and fringes. As we conceive it, in their wage-setting activities, unions 'satisfice' rather than 'optimize'.[1] That is, union leaders seek to satisfy the wage expectations of their members, so as to avoid dissatisfaction, but do not go looking for trouble with employers simply because it might be possible to obtain still more. Hence the determinants of member expectations, Ross's 'orbits of coercive comparison', play an active role in determining union wage demands.

This is hardly a new story, but certain of its implications are not generally appreciated. As we show, first, the proximate objectives of union wage–employment policy differ substantively when there is unemployment (among the membership) and when there is not. Only in the presence of unemployment do unions tend to become 'job rationers' à la Perlman; however, as the next part of this paper contends this is not a peculiarity of unions, but

1. See J. G. March and H. A. Simon, *Organizations* (John Wiley, New York, 1958), p. 140 ff. The view that unions attempt to maximize something or other is put forward in J. T. Dunlop *Wage determination under trade unions*, 2nd edn (Augustus Kelley, New York, 1950), ch. 2.

reflects a behavior pattern common to many institutions. One consequence of this argument is that the 'economic power' *exerted* by unions over wages – though not necessarily the power *possessed* – varies with the unemployment of the membership. The implications of this for the definition and measurement of union economic power, and its effect upon wages, are then discussed. The general tenor of the argument up to this point is that unions have but a limited and intermittent influence over wage rates and related variables. But if this is so, why fuss about the legal status of unionism? The last two sections offer a partial answer to this question.

Job Scarcity and Union Wage Policy

Let us begin by supposing that labor unions behaved as if they were organizations concerned primarily with defining and protecting the job rights of their *present* members;[2] these job rights are assumed to be 'scarce' in the economic sense. Specifically, let us assume that at a wage rate somehow established, not all 'qualified'[3] job applicants can find employment.[4] Then the union will attempt to reserve these scarce jobs for its present members, excluding outsiders unless and until all the present members are employed. Moreover, if jobs are so scarce that not all of its members can find employment, then a union will attempt to determine the allocation of these jobs among its members in accordance with some set of rules. Obviously, this view of union objectives is very similar to that of Selig Perlman;[5] as will be

2. i.e. their members on some given initial day on which our analysis begins.

3. 'Qualified' as defined by employers; i.e. there will be said to be unemployment of qualified workers at the union wage scale if there are idle workers whom employers would consider as perfect substitutes for workers currently employed, were they choosing among them *prior to initial hiring*. The reason for the qualifying phrase is to abstract from the effects of 'learning on the job', which tend to make any current employee more valuable to a firm than a new one, other things equal.

4. For simplicity, we assume that the work week is not variable; this changes nothing of importance, however.

5. Selig Perlman, *The theory of the labor movement*, 1928 reissued, Augustus M. Kelley, New York, 1949), ch. 6.

seen, however, we avoid the particular psychological assumptions upon which Perlman based his argument.[6]

A view of union behavior that stresses the primacy of job allocation over other possible economic objectives immediately poses a question of where wage determination enters the picture. If there is a chronic scarcity of jobs, it would seem to follow that the relevant wage rates must be chronically above their equilibrium levels. From this it would follow, in turn, that a union's concern with job control is simply the obverse side of its attempt to set wage rates in excess of competitive equilibrium levels, and that to assign priority to either job control or wage setting as a union objective is arbitrary and misleading.[7] This argument overlooks, however, an important aspect of the matter.

Consider: in periods of substantially full employment, most unions have all their 'old' members employed and admit new members without attempting to handicap them in their attempts to obtain *current* employment. Thus, some unions issue work permits to persons who are not full-fledged members in periods when the demand for labor at the current union scale is greater than can be satisfied by the regular membership. More frequently, unions freely admit new members, subject to the condition that, in the event of future decreases in employment, layoffs will be in reverse order of seniority. On the other hand, if there are unemployed members looking for work, unions usually refuse admission to new applicants.[8]

The typical union thus behaves as follows: when demand for labor is sufficient to employ all current union members, it interposes no obstacle (beyond work-permit fees) to an increase in employment, provided the job rights of current members are

6. To wit: that 'manualists', as distinguished from businessmen, believe that their economic opportunities are limited and strive to allocate them in some equitable manner rather than scramble for all they can get.

7. This is essentially the contention of a very interesting paper by Simon Rottenberg, 'Wage effects in the theory of the labour movement', *Journal of Political Economy* (August 1953), pp. 346–52.

8. In some unions the refusal is outright; in others, rigid enforcement of seniority in job allocation accomplishes the same objective without formal closing of the union's books. I conjecture that those unions which close their books formally tend to be those that share work opportunities more or less equally among the members; i.e. where seniority preference in allocating jobs is either nonexistent or of little consequence.

protected in the event of a subsequent decline in labor demand. Furthermore, the typical union does not regard demand for more labor than the current membership can supply as evidence that it has set the wage rate too low, as would an income-maximizing union monopoly. However, excess labor supply (i.e. unemployed union members) will lead it to curb severely new admissions to the union; to insist upon seniority in layoffs or some plan of work sharing, etc.

For the purpose of this paper, union wage policy may be left unexplained, save for two stipulations which follow from the previous argument: (1) in the presence of full employment of its present membership and a rising demand for its labor, unions do not usually attempt to raise wage rates so high as entirely to choke off the increase in demand; and (2) in the presence of unemployment among its members, a union resists wage cuts big enough to eliminate the unemployment. To separate union policies on wages and entry restriction in this fashion is valid only for the purposes of short-run analysis; over a period of years, unions setting high wages relative to a competitive market equilibrium will be more likely to engage in restriction on entry than those setting low ones.

Union failure to prevent employment expansion when all members are employed, or even seriously to attempt to do so, implies that unions do not attempt to get the highest (union) scale attainable without creating unemployment among the current membership. The widespread phenomenon of wage-drift,[9] which tends to raise straight-time earnings above union scales under conditions of full employment, is evidence for this contention. This does not deny, however, that unions may, in situations of increasing employment, make wages higher and the *increase* in employment smaller than otherwise.

Nonunion Rationing of Scarce Opportunities

Whenever there is member unemployment, jobs tend to be rationed (on a non-price basis) and, as Perlman so cogently argued, unions seek to control this allocation. There are several

9. See B. C. Roberts, *National wages policy in war and peace* (George Allen and Unwin, London, 1958), pp. 88 ff., 160 ff.

reasons why Perlman should have stressed job allocation as the essential function of unions; not the least of these is that he desired to emphasize – in opposition to the Marxists – the forces that work to disrupt working-class solidarity. But whatever his motives, his argument required that jobs should be scarce most of the time; with full employment of its members, unions lose – in Perlman's view – their raison d'être. Moreover, Perlman felt that concern with rationing scarce economic opportunities was peculiar to, or at least more characteristic of, 'manualists' than others. The examples discussed below, at least by implication, contradict this view and show that restrictionism is more widespread than Perlman believed. Rather, job allocation is not a new factor introduced into labor markets by unions but antedates unionism and is rooted in other social institutions.

As an example of nonunion entry restriction, consider government policy toward immigration. Under full employment, when jobs are plentiful, immigration curbs tend to be relaxed. Conversely, when there is substantial unemployment, these curbs are tightened in order to exclude new job seekers and even expel foreign workers already in the country. During the depressed years of the 1930s, for example, many European countries drastically restricted immigration in an effort to save jobs for citizens. France, Britain, and Switzerland were outstanding examples of this practice, but they were far from alone.[10] Indeed, during this period France actually reduced its labor force by expelling foreign workers.[11]

In some cases, immigration restriction was overt; in others, it was accomplished by requiring immigrants to prove that they would not become public charges. Obviously, such requirements have a more restrictive effect under conditions of substantial unemployment than otherwise.[12] Not only have sovereign states

10. J. Isaac, *Economics of migration* (Kegan Paul, London, 1947), pp. 36, 54–9, and 218. As Isaac points out, the intent of these regulations is indicated by the fact that persons of working age were subject to more severe entry restrictions than others.

11. J. J. Spengler, *France faces depopulation* (Duke University Press, Durham, N.C., 1938), pp. 200–2.

12. Isaac, op. cit., pp. 56–8. American practice is discussed in R. A. Divine, *American immigration policy, 1924–1952* (Yale University Press, New Haven, 1957), ch. 4.

done this, but many American state governments also have sought to minimize their relief burdens by establishing residence requirements for public assistance. In the full employment years since 1945, governmental behavior has been very different. There has been appreciable relaxation of barriers against immigration in Europe, in Australia, and in Canada; the policy of the United States is a notorious exception.[13]

The economic reason for restricting immigration, it is important to notice, cannot be rationalized on the hypothesis that some group is attempting to maximize the earnings of native workers. The objective is more nearly to reserve jobs at 'minimum living standards' for natives *when such jobs* are scarce; when jobs are not scarce, economic restrictions (on immigration) tend to fall into abeyance.

Thus, the behavior of governments in restricting immigration is strikingly parallel to that of unions in rationing jobs. It would not be a very great exaggeration to say that governments behave as though they were a union of all resident job holders, striving to reserve job opportunities (when they are scarce) for 'resident members'. Indeed, France actually pursued a policy of issuing work permits to foreigners during the prosperous 1920s, and then, by withdrawing the permits, compelled foreign workers to leave when labor demand became slack in the 1930s.[14] Of course, this type of government policy is strongly supported by unions, but it can hardly be termed simply a union policy. It reflects the attitude of the vast majority of the population.

Immigration   restriction   benefits   (native)   wage   earners

13. Unfortunately, one cannot readily infer the extent of governmental entry restriction from fluctuations in the volume of migration, because the number of persons desiring to migrate tends to increase with the demand for labor in the country of immigration, and vice versa; i.e. the temporal pattern of governmental restriction parallels that of 'desired emigration'.

Moreover, the volume of desired migration itself reflects the effect of informal restrictionism. This can be seen from the following consideration: when the labor-market situation in the recipient country makes it difficult for new immigrants to find employment, the costs of 'acclimating' an immigrant, which falls upon friends and relatives, become heavier. This leads these friends and relatives to encourage new arrivals to return home, and others not to come (see H. Bernardelli, 'New Zealand and Asiatic migration', *Population studies*, vol. 6 [July 1952]).

14. Spengler, op. cit.

primarily; but there are other government policies, similar in operation to immigration restriction, that benefit other groups. For example, in many Western European countries – especially France – government licensing and other regulations which promote restrictive price and output policies of business firms stem from a determination to prevent economic competition from destroying the less efficient firms.[15] While these regulations are aimed at preserving the existence of (inefficient) firms, they do little or nothing to help them grow. Another example to the same point is the American method of supporting farm prices. When a surplus threatens to become 'too big' at a given support price, the Department of Agriculture attempts to restrict output, but when demand lifts prices above support levels, market forces are given full sway. Yet another example is the administration of American tariffs: an industry in difficulties because of foreign competition can plead for (and often obtain) additional protection, but an argument that profits (though 'adequate') could be made greater by raising the tariff would certainly be rejected. Finally, we might mention the widespread tendency of business firms, in times of 'shortage' of their products, to refrain from charging all the market will currently bear and to ration output so as to favor long-term customers and/or those who 'ordered first'. Such practices, in effect, protect places in a buyer's queue.

The Ethics of the Queue

The principle underlying these various practices would seem to be that the right to an acquired position ought to be protected by treating it as a species of property right. Governments, business enterprises, and unions, as well as informal social groups, all display respect for this right in the presence of shortages. This respect is rooted in what we may term the 'ethics of the queue'. Briefly, the ethics of the queue state that newcomers shall not usurp the 'places' of those already having them or, more generally, that scarce and desired things shall be rationed 'first come, first served'. The ethics of the queue are manifested in the

15. See Herbert Luethy, *France against herself* (Meridian Books, New York, 1957); T. Scitovsky, 'Economies of scale, competition and European integration', *American Economic Review* (March 1956), pp. 71–91.

rationing of telephones, apartments, etc., when they are in short supply; in registration lines of all kinds; and, above all, in the rationing of jobs.

There is an obvious conflict between the ethics of the queue and the price system, and most Western communities believe in both principles.[16] The ethics of the queue apply when there are sharp changes in the relative positions of supply and demand schedules, and price adjusts slowly, so that for a time there is felt to be a shortage either of buyers or sellers. Wherever price rationing is abandoned for a substantial period of time, however, it tends to assert itself in violation of other rationing principles,[17] though not without bitter protest.

Thus, union entry restrictions and job allocations are not practices peculiar to 'manualists', as Perlman thought, but are manifestations of the ethics of the queue which are accepted throughout most of the community.[18] Unions accept and attempt to enforce these ethical practices, but do not create them. And where unions are unable to act as effective instruments of job allocation at given wage rates, other 'institutional' forces[19] perform the task. For example, the employer's social conscience often acts in more or less the same way as union rules, subject to vagaries of personality and the necessity for avoiding losses.[20] That is, employers tend, unions or no, to protect the jobs of employees of long-standing without slashing wages to the full extent *currently* permitted by the labor market. The occasional failure of

16. And a few others, to boot. For example, in the event of sudden severe shortages of 'necessities', the idea of 'fair shares' for all acquires enormous popular support.

17. e.g. via 'black' or 'gray' markets.

18. Indeed, what distinguishes thorough-going advocates of *laissez faire* from the rest of the community is their refusal to accept the ethics of the queue and to demand price rationing – in situations where the former is normally unchallenged.

19. Examples of nonunion institutional job protection include governmental restrictions on layoffs; customary restrictions on layoff, as in Japan; the social obligation to give employment to family retainers in certain backward areas, as stressed by W. A. Lewis, 'Economic development with unlimited supplies of labour', *Manchester School of Economics and Social Studies* (May 1954).

20. This is not to allege that such behavior is irrational; in establishing long-term relations with employees or customers, conspicuous manifestation of a sense of decency may be very profitable.

employers to behave in this way has prompted expressions of strong disapproval and, in some circumstances, to legislation.

The best evidence that employers engage in non-market job rationing is the behavior of wages and job turnover in areas or in periods of 'substantial' unemployment when unions are absent. Wages do decline, but in a notoriously sluggish way,[21] and most job holders (successfully) cling to their jobs as to dear life. Though there is little systematic evidence, it would seem plausible to suppose that, even in the absence of unions, the order of layoff is roughly inverse to seniority within the firm. However, in the absence of unions, the layoff process does not conform rigidly to any particular principle; managerial judgments of merit and personal favoritism flavor the whole process.[22] The effects of unionism are mainly to formalize the process and to assert the claims of seniority when they conflict with managerial preference. Where layoffs are regulated by legislation, yet another set of non-market criteria affect job allocation. However, these criteria usually do not differ greatly from those applied by unions, as both spring from the ethics of the queue.

To stress the ethics of the queue and related phenomena in the job allocation process opens wide the door to promulgating an 'institutional' wage theory, as Barbara Wootton has done.[23] This is not the intention, however. Rather, it is asserted merely that the ethics of the queue affect the adjustment process of labor markets, but only rarely their equilibrium values (*when the employer is a business enterprise*). Since our argument emphasizes the similarity of union and nonunion labor markets *as they are found*, and their common difference from textbook competitive markets, it would seem that we believe union and nonunion markets to be very similar in operation and results. Such a conclusion would be compatible with our argument, but it is not implied by it. Our argument is compatible with unions having a

21. As Dunlop indicates (op. cit., ch. 7), there was a considerable association during the 1929–33 and 1937–38 depressions between the size and timing of wage reductions and product price cuts. Where product prices are sticky, so are wages.

22. Job selling, kickbacks, etc., also occur. They would seem the exception rather than the rule, however.

23. Barbara Wootton, *The social foundations of wage policy* (W.W. Norton, New York, 1955).

substantial upward effect on wage rates, in the long run, as compared with actual nonunion markets. Specifically, it is possible that union wage pressure shifts labor markets from equilibria where jobs are not scarce to those where they are.

The Concept and Measurement of Union Power

If the term 'union power' be interpreted – as it often is – to mean power to raise wages, then the above argument raises certain conceptual problems. It implies that union 'power' will not always be used to raise wages, and therefore that overt wage *behavior* will not be a reliable indicator of union power to influence such behavior.[24] Nor will actual behavior of unions in rationing jobs be an effective indicator of union power to ration, as the extent of job rationing will depend on the state of the labor market; indeed, the maximum power to ration jobs may never be displayed.

In other words, there is an important distinction between a union's power to accomplish a given result and the extent to which it uses that power. Failure to keep this distinction in mind consistently has produced considerable confusion. For example, it is sometimes contended that a union's power to raise wages is inversely related to the ratio, R, of its (members') wage bill to the total cost of a typical employer.[25]

24. For example, see G. S. Becker, 'Union restrictions on entry', in *The public stake in union power* (University of Virginia Press, Charlottesville, Va., 1959), pp. 209–24. Becker defines the ratio of union wages to the competitive equilibrium wage as a measure of union power over wages. He also defines a measure of union power over quantity – power to restrict entry – as one plus the ratio of the number who wish to enter the union (in order to secure work) to the number actually admitted (op. cit., pp. 212–13).

These measures are conceptually different from those used in bargaining discussions which define A's power over B as the (monetary value of the) difference in B's level of satisfaction if A behaved as a competitor rather than choosing the course of action least favorable to B. Any of a number of variants of this measure may be used. The important difference between any definition of this type and Becker's is that this type allows for the effect of 'all or none' offers but Becker's does not; i.e. Becker assumes implicitly that unions do not force employers off their demand curves.

Except where otherwise specified, we shall 'measure' union power as Becker's power to affect wage rates.

25. The *locus classicus* of this argument is Alfred Marshall's *Principles*

This contention depends upon the following assumptions: (1) an inverse association between R and the elasticity of derived demand for the union members' services; (2) that power to obtain a given wage increase (over the competitive level) varies among unions inversely with the cost of obtaining it, where cost includes only foregone employment.

Let us explain: we assume that a union can place itself anywhere it chooses on the employer's demand curve (nonunion competition is barred). The only cost it incurs by raising its wage rate is reduced employment. Hence, given the derived demand curve for its members' services, a specific union's 'power' to raise its wage rates is the inverse of its willingness to sacrifice employment. As we assume all unions to be alike in the willingness to trade employment for wage increases, power to raise wages varies inversely with the elasticity of derived demand.[26] From this it follows that unions will set wages so that the elasticities of derived demand for the services of each union's members are the same.

Granting (2) for the sake of argument, it follows from (1) that unions with low Rs would tend to force up the wage rates of their members relative to those with higher Rs. But something is wrong with this. Consider: if we had two unions with identical 'tastes' for substituting higher wages for employment, and neither feared nonunion competition, then the relative wages of the two

of economics 8th edn (London, 1920), pp. 384–6. It is also found, in modified and improved form, in J. R. Hicks, *The theory of wages* (London, 1932), pp. 241–6, and in Joan Robinson, *The economics of imperfect competition* (London, 1933), ch. 22; also, Milton Friedman, 'Some comments on the significance of labor unions for economic policy', in *The impact of the union*, D. McWright, ed. (New York, 1951), pp. 207–8. Recently, G. W. Nutter, 'The limits of union power', in *The public stake in union power*, pp. 297–8, has (properly) criticized the Marshall–Friedman analysis, though continuing to accept its main conclusions for somewhat different reasons.

Lloyd Ulman in 'Marshall and Friedman on union strength', *Review of Economics and Statistics* (November 1955), pp. 384–401, has denied that in practice it is 'important to be unimportant'. Though Ulman is correct in this contention, it is aside from the present argument.

26. This assumption is far from trivial and might well be disputed. It implies that union morale, worker preferences for leisure, and the like are either unimportant or vary little from one union to another.

unions would be in equilibrium only when the elasticities of derived demand for their members' services were equal. But then an *observed* difference in the *R*s of the two unions, if any, would not indicate a difference in their 'power' to raise wages further; it could indicate only the existence of differences in the other determinants of the elasticity of derived demand. To put the same point vividly, though rather inexactly, if one union's *R* was below that of another, *ceteris paribus*, the union with the lower *R* would raise its relative wage until the elasticity of derived demand for its members' services fell to the same level as that of the other union.

In other words, the Marshall–Friedman hypothesis concerning the relation of *R* to wage-raising power cannot refer both to the potential – but as yet unused – power to raise wages, and to an observed association between low *R*s and relatively high excesses of actual over competitive wages.[27]

So far as I am aware, none of the authors who have discussed the relation of *R* to wage-raising power has distinguished between these two different concepts of power. The context of their remarks, however, makes it likely that they were referring to the relation existing at a particular time; it is quite possible that the relation between *R* and wage-raising power is as they allege.[28]

27. This statement will not apply in all cases, but only *cet. par.*, because of the varying influence of the other determinants of the elasticity of derived demand for the factor. That is, either the difference in *R*'s will have been eliminated, or the inverse association of them with the elasticity of derived demand will have been eliminated.

Professor Albert Rees has persuasively contended, in discussion, that the *R* for a given group of workers is likely to vary much less as a result of a shift from nonunion to union wage-setting than the intergroup variations among the *R*s. From this it would follow that, granting the inverse association between *R* (at the nonunion wage) and union wage-raising power, a low observed *R* would tend to be associated with a high ratio of union to nonunion equilibrium wages. This certainly is one possible interpretation of the Marshall–Friedman hypothesis. However, if this interpretation is correct either (1) the alleged inverse association between *R* and the elasticity of derived demand does not exist (at the union wage rate) or (2) unions do not systematically exploit their wage-raising power.

28. Ulman, op. cit., might disagree. I am not sure whether he would contend that 'it ain't necessarily so' or that 'it just ain't so'. In any event, there is no systematic empirical study of this matter to which we can refer for guidance.

But, if so, then either low values of R are not empirically associated with large degrees of union power (i.e. (1) is false), or unions do not use the power they have. We cannot exclude the former possibility, but in line with the argument of the first section, let us stress the second.

Unions may not raise wages as much as they are 'able' for at least two reasons: (1) Employer resistance, however irrational, to 'out-of-line' wage scales and/or public resentment of such scales act as a curb upon union demands; indeed, the existence of such attitudes may well limit the 'power' of unions to raise wages.[29] (2) Unions may be very willing not to squeeze the maximum possible from employers, provided they obtain enough to satisfy the demands of the membership. By holding potential wage and other increases 'in reserve', they put themselves in a position to obtain without difficulty such increases as may be required to match rises in living costs, wage gains of other unions, and so on.

A tactic of holding wage increases presently obtainable (though under duress) in reserve would tend to create the kind of situation in which one party – the one not taking full advantage of his power – is said to have the other 'in his power'. For example, when A can, within wide limits, compel B to do his bidding, A is said to have B 'in his power'. But this implies that A has not already extracted the maximum possible concession from B. That is, A has not already taken so much that, rather than yield more, B will let him do his worst. For example, when a heavy campaign contributor has a particular politician in his power, he is able to compel the politician to do his bidding in a large number of ways; but obviously he does not usually squeeze him to the point where there is no 'consumer's surplus' in office

29. This is a matter on which there might well be discussion. However, I propose to adopt the arbitrary verbal correction of saying a union has the power to do anything (about employment terms) it could legally 'press' an employer to accept, even though fear of public reaction prevents it from using a great part of this 'power'.

Ulman, op. cit., correctly argues that, where an employer deals with several unions, the wage demands of the individual unions are closely interrelated. This is an important reason for an employer to resist demands from one union (for a wage increase) that are greater than he could afford to extend to all.

holding. The utility of power often lies in the capacity to protect one's interests when they are threatened.

The Uses of Reserve Power

Viewed in this way, the power of a union *organization* over wages lies not in what it has achieved but in what it can achieve in order to protect its interests. Obviously, a ranking of unions in order of their power over wages in this sense might be very different from their ranking in terms of the ratio of actual to competitive wage rates. Though it would not be easy to measure unused power to raise wages in any precise manner, empirical evidence of 'reserve power' over wages could be inferred from the extent of over-scale payments or other benefits to union members over and above what is required by the union contract.

The idea that unions hold power in reserve may be conveniently rationalized by the hypothesis that, in the wage field at least, they are 'satisficing' rather than 'optimizing'. When union wage achievements are sufficient currently to satisfy the members, the leaders let well enough alone, rather than push further, and devote their time and resources to other objectives (including a quiet life). By not seeking all they can get without causing unemployment among the present members, union leaders reduce the risks of strikes; they also avoid creating antagonism among employers which may lead to vindictive countermoves if circumstances change, and finally they create a 'reservoir' of potential wage hikes they can obtain when and if the members press for them.

Hence, given full employment of a union's membership, its wage demands are likely to be determined by the various requirements of its members: for example, to keep up with similarly situated workers, to keep up with rising living costs, to get a 'fair share' of the gains of increasing productivity, and so on. In short, when a union's members are fully employed, its wage claims are likely to be determined by the sociopolitical forces suggested by the term 'orbit of coercive comparison'.

When there are demands for a wage cut by employers, the members may demand that the union resist or, at least, minimize the extent of the cut. Under such circumstances, the leaders must, in order to satisfice, exert the union's full economic power to make wages higher than they would have been in a competitive market, by resisting a wage cut. As demands for wage cuts occur mainly when there is unemployment of members,[30] this means that, when union members appear to be doing badly, the unions may well be *exercising* more economic power over wage rates than when the members are prospering.

So much for the power that unions exert over wages. There are, however, dimensions of union power, other than the capacity to raise member wage rates, which are of concern to students of labor problems. The *amount* of financial injury, including foregone profits, that a union can impose upon an employer is often an excellent indicator of what it can compel him to do. For example, a union (call it X) with a large R might be able to raise wages only slightly above competitive levels without driving an employer out of business, while a union (call it Y) with a smaller R could bring its members greater gains per hour of employment. However, the former could, by a strike threat, force management to adopt a variety of personnel practices or status-enhancing concessions to the union, which it found unpalatable though not cost-increasing (in large amounts), whereas similar demands by the latter union would be met with great resistance. The reader might well ask, 'If this is true, then why would the employer agree to raise the wages of Y's members proportionately more than those of X's?'

The answer lies in the properties of the employer's utility function. If the employer by nature or the rigors of competition is a pure profit maximizer, our argument is wrong. But employers with true entrepreneurial rents (from the viewpoint of the industry), or with prospects of long-lived quasi-rents in an expanding industry, or with downright monopoly power might indulge their preference for good employee relations by 'buying off' a union with a small R, even though they felt unable to afford the same policy with regard to a union with a large R, because the reduction in money profits would be so much greater in the latter case.[31]

30. This does not mean that wage cuts become an issue whenever there is member unemployment, but merely that substantial member unemployment is virtually a necessary (but not a sufficient) condition for wage cuts.

31. Nutter, op. cit., contends that it is erroneous to suppose that 'A firm will be moved to economize only in proportion to the saving gained through

Another aspect of union power emerges in dealings with governmental agencies. A union big enough to create a national emergency or contribute a million dollars to a political campaign clearly has more power to get White House attention to its complaints than one with, say, 500 members, whatever their respective wage gains per hour.

In short, union power has a number of different aspects, and, in order to measure, or even discuss, it meaningfully, it is necessary to specify whether or not the power is fully used. Moreover, to measure union power it is necessary to specify the manner in which the power is to be exerted, over whom it is to be exercised, and the purpose for which it is to be used.

The Social Function of Union Power

One major implication of our argument is that when unions appear to be economically strong in the sense of being able to force up wage rates, that is, when members are fully employed, they tend to stay their hand. It is when they appear to be weak, plagued by unemployment and confronted with demands for wage cuts that unions use to the fullest whatever power they have. In short, when unions are relatively strong (in the wage-raising sense), they do not use all their power, and when they exert their power, they cannot raise wages much – if at all.[32]

This raises the question: 'What good are unions, anyway?' To say that they prevent wage cuts in the presence of unemployment is a weak argument in view of the earlier contention (pp. 123–7) that in this connexion unions are more or less substitutes for other institutions. At most, unions merely intensify resistance to wage cuts, and this may not always be desirable. Consequently, if unionism in anything like its present form in Western countries

---

each economizing action taken by itself'. This is true, however, only when competition and demand growth are such as to keep quasi-rents at or below the tolerable current minimum, and/or management is interested only in money income.

32. This is, of course, an oversimplification. There are many individual unions to whom it would not apply; but it is a correct statement concerning both a majority of unions and a majority of union members.

is to be defended as socially desirable, it is necessary to find other grounds.[33]

Two such grounds are offered: (1) the effect of unions on employer–employee relations, and (2) the political role of unions.

The concept of economic power is especially pertinent to discussions of employer–employee relationships. It is usually argued that in a competitive market both individual workers and employers would be indifferent as to whether a particular employment relation is terminated, since a perfect substitute would be always available to both. It is very doubtful that this is true even in situations which are competitive in all other respects; it seems reasonable to suppose that the employer's interests are best served by paying wage earners more than the bare minimum necessary to keep them from quitting. For the essence of the employment relation is, in many cases, that the employee shall perform work under the direction of the employer or his representative;[34] obviously, efficiency implies that an employee shall not be so close to indifference as to whether he is fired that defiance of directions is frequent. Hence, the net advantages of continuing employment with the present employer must normally be appreciably above the long-run transfer price to the employer. However, given the costs of transfer both to workers and employers,[35] neither party can be completely indifferent to a threatened rupture of even an individual employment relation. But, as an employer usually employs many wage earners, each of whom works only for him, the percentage loss of income from ending an employment relation is much less to him than to the worker. Consequently, in the absence of collective bargaining,

33. This is not to reject completely the possibility that unions may have an appreciable – and desirable – influence on wages and income distribution. However, this influence is at best uncertain and much disputed; consequently, it cannot, at least for the present, serve as a basis for recommendations concerning public policy.

34. On this point see H. A. Simon, 'A formal theory of the employment relation', *Econometrica* (July 1951), pp. 293–305.

35. For example, workers who change employers may lose accumulated seniority rights and, sometimes, pension benefits, in addition to the psychic costs of changing work environment and the loss of special skills valuable only to one particular firm. Employers lose an investment in training (either formal or on the job); and must also bear the cost of a new hiring and, sometimes, the cost of reduced efficiency because of lowered worker morale.

the employer has more 'power'[36] over any of his employees than they have over him.[37] This power can be used in a variety of ways to alter working conditions, change job assignments, or cut money wages, to the dissatisfaction of the worker without actually inducing him to quit. But, it might be argued, it would be irrational for an employer to use his power in this way for, in the long run, he would become known for such behavior and would consequently have to pay more than other employers to secure a given quality of worker – if workers really objected to the exercise of employer power.[38]

To argue in this way, however, is to ignore the possibility that employers may hold their power in reserve for special occasions. To be sure, some employers enjoy exercising power under any circumstances, and presumably will have to pay for the privilege. But many will exercise their power only when pressed to do so by inadequate current profits – perhaps only after a managerial reshuffling. In such cases, superior employer bargaining power is used to force a particular distribution between labor costs and quasi-rents from 'inadequate'[39] sales receipts.

The effect of collective bargaining, in such cases, is to reduce the class of attainable distributions of sales proceeds. The long-run effect of this is to increase the employer's risk of loss and

36. 'Power' as used here and in the following paragraphs refers to power to cause income loss by severing the employment relation – 'all or nothing' power – rather than power to affect wage rates (see fn. 24).

37. There are notable exceptions to this statement, especially among executives and in situations where one 'worker' has many 'employers', e.g. a doctor. Nevertheless, the statement in the text applies to the overwhelming majority of wage earners. It does not, of course, deny that bargaining strength may vary with the absolute losses the parties can inflict on each other, as well as the relative losses.

38. In the terminology of Becker (G. S. Becker, *Economics of discrimination* [University of Chicago Press, Chicago, 1958]) and Lewis (H. G. Lewis, 'Competitive and monopoly unionism', in *The public stake in union power*, pp. 181–208), if employers have a taste for the exercise of power – and workers a distaste – the former will, save for peculiar cases, have to pay extra for indulging it. Albert Rees, 'Some non-wage aspects of collective bargaining', in *The public stake in union power*, pp. 124–42, reaches substantially the same conclusion but by a different argument.

39. i.e. quasi-rents which are inadequate to satisfy stockholder expectations.

perhaps reduce the inducement to invest.[40] Of course, when a firm is hard pressed, its employees will usually accept a reduction in wages and/or heavier work loads, union or no. The fact that this is so often the case provides evidence for our interpretation of the way employers use economic power; but the distribution of the 'burden' and the form in which it is borne may be very different, depending on the presence or absence of collective bargaining.[41] Collective bargaining gives the worker the power to compel the employer to consider his interests in distributing the burden of economic adversity. However, under more prosperous circumstances, employers pursuing a policy of long-run rationality may not attempt to exploit their economic power.

The foregoing has a direct relation to public policy questions concerning the limits of union control over job opportunies. For unions to bargain effectively often requires that they be given some quasi-governmental status; that is, in the words of the late Lloyd Fisher, that they be legitimized as 'private governments'. An individual worker may gain by the restraint upon employer behavior imposed by a union, but that need not lead him to contribute to its finances; when permitted, he may take a 'free ride'. The argument for compulsory[42] dues payments in bargaining units where a union has been chosen by majority vote as bargaining representative is precisely analogous to that for permitting governments to levy taxes: a collective benefit is conferred by institutional action which cannot be withheld from individuals for failure to contribute. To facilitate this collective activity by a union (or make it at all practicable), it is necessary to extend some limited tax power to the union. Whether the benefits conferred by unions upon their members are such as to justify this

40. That is, the reduced inability of employers to compel workers to share short-run losses in the event of adversity will increase the risk of long-run losses on any given project and will, *cet. par.*, act as a deterrent to investment. This argument implies that unions have an impact upon unit labor costs in situations where employers are moved to attempt wage cuts.

41. In the absence of a union, an employer may be quite arbitrary about the distribution of wage cuts, additional work loads, etc. A union makes all such decisions subject to negotiation and compels observance of some sort of equity.

42. 'Compulsion' here is short of legal compulsion, but may involve loss of an employment opportunity which is very valuable to an individual recalcitrant.

delegation of tax power is a difficult question involving both issues of fact and value upon which there is disagreement. While I strongly favor permitting unions this power, I do not propose to argue the point here.

Because the tax power may, by legislation, be given or withheld from an institution, it follows that conditions may be attached to such an award. For example, to be permitted to require financial contributions from individuals as a condition of employment, unions might well be compelled by law to desist from certain activities or to engage in others.

It should be recognized explicitly that to give unions taxing power is to give them a special and privileged status under the law. Each grant of quasi-governmental power to an institution must be defended in terms of the social function that the institution is to perform, and the relation of the grant of power to that function. That such grants of power may and have been abused, and that the grantees may require constant surveillance, must be conceded. But from this it does not follow that there should be no such grants.[43]

Let it be conceded that this particular function of unions could be performed by other institutions. For example, a system of labor courts could be established, which would have power to hear and adjust grievances of individual workers. These could be completely independent of unions, but we do not have such a set of courts and are not likely to get them. Hence, *faute de mieux*, worker grievances on the job must be negotiated by unions.

Unions as Political Instruments

In any modern society, inter-election political decisions, both legislative and administrative, are made under duress of political pressure from a variety of sources. When a measure is proposed that affects the interests of wealthy persons or corporations, they are able, either individually or as small coalitions, to make their

43. P. D. Bradley, 'Involuntary participation in unionism', in *Labor unions and public power* (Washington, 1958), pp. 47–91, argues the reverse of this on the ground that the alleged benefits of unionism to members are illusory. All I can do here is register dissent.

wishes known and threaten reprisal if they are not heeded. In principle, individual wage earners can do the same. However, the problem of financing the production of collective benefits once again arises; any one of a small group of (wealthy) men involved in a political undertaking can appreciably affect the strength of the coalition by contributing his 'share' or withholding it. The individual worker, one among millions, has no such ability; a free ride is always possible. Moreover, the large contributor can communicate directly with any of the other parties involved in any decision-making process and has a reasonable chance of affecting the final outcome; the personal satisfaction and possible economic advantage of this is not available to a negligible contributor.

Since there are greater difficulties in mobilizing economic resources for political combat by voluntary contributions from large numbers of small contributors than from small numbers of large ones, those interested in enhancing the political influence of many small (potential) contributors will feel sympathy for some form of nonvoluntary contributions to institutions, such as labor unions, which support their interests. Whether one shares this sympathetic attitude depends upon whether he wants organized labor to exercise substantial political influence. To want this does not imply complete, or even substantial, agreement with the policies that organized labor advances. It implies only being in favor of having such views powerfully advocated – along with other views that are strongly supported by wealthy individual contributors. After all, relatively low income families have interests concerning tax policy, social legislation, and, to a limited degree, even international policy that differ from those of wealthier ones. In Western democracies, labor representatives push measures that are intended to advance the economic interests of the former group, and conservative spokesmen the interests of the latter. To desire that both sets of interests should be powerfully supported does not imply a desire that either should completely dominate. Nor does it imply belief that the consequences of adopting particular union-supported policies will bear out the expectations of their advocates.

It might well be asked why unions should be singled out for special treatment in this connexion. Although their members are, in the relevant sense, a 'low income' group,[44] there are other groups that could be singled out whose average income would be even lower and whose economic interests are not always identical with those of organized labor. Two examples of such groups might be the aged and small farmers.

But I make no special plea for unions in this connexion. It is simply that they happen to have evolved into an instrument (though a very imperfect one) for lobbying on behalf of all low income groups.[45] To cripple or abolish this union function by impairing union sources of revenue, or forbidding their use for political purposes, would in my judgment greatly weaken the political strength of the loose alliance of pressure groups striving to help lower income recipients generally.

Summary and Conclusions

This article has attempted to analyse the nature of union power and how it is used. The conclusions of those sections which deal with this power as it affects wage setting are: (1) that union power to raise wages is not used to its maximum when current members are fully employed; (2) that union power over wages is more fully exerted when there is some member unemployment; (3) that, although unions ration jobs, à la Perlman, when there is member

44. The 'low income' group includes, for this purpose, roughly the lower nine deciles of the family income distribution. The 'upper income' group includes all of those (individually) rich enough to be able to affect political action by offers – and threats – of financial support. The politically potent rich are, of course, but a small part of the upper income group, but they protect the interests of the remainder. The lower groups have no such 'protectors' save for a few rich sympathizers and organizations such as unions.

45. Specifically, I refer to union demands for such things as a more highly progressive tax system, more liberal social security benefits, higher minimum wage legislation, greater public works expenditures during depressions, more federal aid to home buyers, etc. This is not to deny that unions also sometimes lobby for higher tariffs, or featherbedding laws, which harm other low income groups. Nor is it to accept the views of union spokesmen – and, more often than not, of their opponents – as to the ultimate consequences of their legislative demands. All that is implied here is that the collection of measures governing general tax and expenditure policy that is considered 'liberal' – in the twentieth century sense – is strongly and effectively backed by labor union lobbyists.

unemployment, rationing also exists in nonunion labor markets; and (4) that because union power over wages is not always fully utilized, it is misleading to measure union power over wages solely as an increasing function of the difference between union wage rates and what would have obtained in a competitive labor market.

Because the effect of this argument is to minimize the significance of union power over wages, two positive and, in the author's opinion, beneficial functions that unions do perform are presented and discussed. They are: (1) unions can protect the worker against arbitrary employer action better than the market can; and (2) unions provide an effective means of mobilizing the political power of low income groups.

7 P. A. Weinstein

The Featherbedding Problem

Weinstein, P. A. (1964) The featherbedding problem. *Amer. Econ. Rev.*, **54**, 145–2.

A growing number of disputes appear to involve the problem of featherbedding. At the heart of these conflicts is the question of who should bear the cost of technological change. While there are a number of theoretical alternatives to technological displacement, featherbedding is the most satisfactory from the position of both the union and the potentially displaced workers. There has been increasing pressure on unions not to resort to featherbedding demands, but external pressure, even when directed by the President, has not proved effective. Some collective bargaining agreements have offered alternatives to featherbedding when there is a structural change, but the advice to follow the lead of constructive agreements that propose to end constraints on firms and effect a better utilization of our manpower resources has gone unheeded. The failure to settle featherbedding issues has cast doubt upon collective bargaining and the market as an appropriate institution.

This paper will treat the following topics: first, the necessary and sufficient conditions for the emergence and continuance of featherbedding; second, the impact of the featherbedding rules on decision making in both the short and long run; third, alternatives to featherbedding for meeting structural unemployment.

Conditions for Featherbedding

Employment insecurity gives rise to featherbedding under special circumstances. The following generalizations are significant in understanding the acceptance or rejection of this particular response to the problem of insecurity.

Featherbedding occurs in industries that are characterized by noncompetitive operation prior to formalization of the rules. The economic environment for featherbedding is very similar to that required for racketeering. In both cases the firms must have some expropriatable surplus, or else the working rule or extortion leads to downward instability. In the main, the distinction between these two phenomena is in the utility functions of the maximizing institution and the division of the rewards. Therefore, it is inappropriate to examine the impact[1] of the rules on the assumption that they disturb an optimal competitive position.

For example: the industries protesting most about these rules – and where in fact they are found in abundance – are the transportation industries and the building trades. Both are noncompetitive in character. The railroads, for example, are under extreme control in nearly every activity, from quality of product to price, while the building trades continue to be a hotbed of localized monopoly in which the government has a role through licensure and demand. Given this state of affairs, some might suggest we dismiss the problem merely as one of internal allocation of quasi-rents. Featherbedding ties up manpower in unproductive activities, and to dismiss the problem as one internal to the firm leaves the larger manpower problem unresolved. It is better to have a higher utilization of human resources even if there is monopoly, though quite obviously it is best to free both labor and product markets.

The spread of these practices, which increase costs, to competing industries reduces one of the constraints on the union imposing them. The rationale is identical to the explanation of the failure of featherbedding in pure competition. The market restraints on unions are diluted when competitive industries work under similar circumstances. For example, it is clearly advantageous to the railroads to have airlines face the problem of manning requirements on jet services, as well as the problem of restrictions on abandonment by public authorities. A great comfort to the Brotherhood of Locomotive Firemen and Helpers should be the increase in the crew consist on some commercial airlines resulting from the joint demands of flight engineers and the Airline Pilots Association.

1. Norman J. Simler, 'The economics of featherbedding', *Indus. Labor Relat. Rev.*, (October 1962), p. 100.

The unions involved in featherbedding are narrowly organized along craft lines. There is almost a total absence of these rules in industrial or multicraft unions. The economics of this is important in understanding the role of the market in eliminating restrictive practices and restricting their introduction. The advantages of featherbedding accrue to a specific group, and this serves as a restraint upon gains to other workers in the firm. In an industrial union small groups rarely elicit the support of the entire organization for their own narrow ends, because the larger group has nothing to gain.

Union rivalry also leads to featherbedding as a defensive strategy. Featherbedding is found when there is a cluster of craft unions in an industry. These unions abide with each other under unstable conditions for a number of reasons. The organizations are competitive, pursuing individual goals with little regard for the impact of their policies on nonmember employees.

A current [1964] dispute in the airline industry concerns the manning of the third seat in the cockpit. Should it be a member of the Flight Engineers with some pilot training or a pilot with an engineer's license? One result of course has been the three pilot/one engineer crew on some lines. The emergency boards examining this dispute have pointed to the need for union merger as a necessary condition for the settlement of the problem.

While employment goals of unions are not frequently dominating, much of the literature on trade-union utility functions implies that this is an aberration. These older models of trade unions, like those of Fellner, Ross, and Dunlop, were influenced by the flush labor markets of the 1940s. Such a position can hardly be accepted in the light of recent labor experience. While an interest in employment has long been noted in craft unions, one notes the growing interest of industrial unions in employment security. More and more we observe union leaders placing increased emphasis on employment factors rather than on wages. The type of activity pursued by unions with employment interests varies markedly from featherbedding at one extreme to the program recently effected by Kaiser, the I.L.A.-P.M.A., and Armour. It would appear that there is a series of alternative trade-union utility functions and that there is a need for a systematic analysis of why a trade union chooses one alternative rather than another.

The technological requirements for featherbedding are at least as important as the industry and union structure. An almost universal characteristic is the gradual substitution of one form of technology for another. The displacement is evolutionary, wiping out the wage–rent differential of skilled groups. This type of change establishes the conditions for the imposition of the rules, as well as pointing the way toward their elimination. Thus, the type of rule we are concerned with arises shortly after the commercial introduction of a technology that is likely to adversely affect a relatively small and usually skilled group in the work force. Quite frequently featherbedding emerges from the carrying forward of a set of practices appropriate for one technology to another where it is alien.

The specific labor groups engaged in featherbedding do not allow employers to modify the job assignments of the workers. This fact along with analysis of broader categories of inputs implies that the elasticity of substitution for specific groups in a firm is zero or close to it.[2] To analyse the effects of featherbedding with the aid of a Cobb–Douglas function[3] having a positive and constant elasticity of substitution for other factors appears most inappropriate. The results using that model imply that the marginal productivity of capital increases as a result of featherbedding – a conclusion that evaporates when a more realistic production function is employed. However, this is an empirical problem, and one that needs examination before a definitive answer to the impact of featherbedding can be provided.

The Impact of Restrictive Rules

There are two avenues of analysis open: static analysis, which is fairly well developed, and dynamics, which is largely in an embryonic state. Some conclusions about featherbedding under static conditions are summarized, while some interesting dynamic questions are posed.

2. K. J. Arrow, H. B. Chenery, B. S. Minhas, and R. M. Solow, 'Capital labor substitution and economic efficiency', *Rev. Econ. & Statis.* (August 1961), pp. 225–50; also, Jora R. Minasian, 'Elasticity of Substitution and constant output demand curves for labor', *Journ. Polit. Econ.* (June 1961), pp. 261–70.

3. Norman J. Simler, op. cit., pp. 96, 97.

Theoretically a featherbedding rule could require a fixed amount of labor to be hired for a specified economic period. Under this procedure labor would be a semivariable cost and thus be analogous to any other lumpy factor.

However, the rules considered under the rubric of featherbedding do not specify that a fixed amount of labor be hired. On the contrary, they usually call for the retention of an existing labor–output ratio. Examples are the 'bogus' role, double heading, and standby. In each case the amount of redundant work to be performed by the firm is a function of output, thus affecting the height and slope of variable costs, and, given the structure of the industry, reduced output. Consequently, we can say that the rules do reduce output and raise costs and prices in a short run.

The first dynamic question concerns the impact of featherbedding on supply. Does the existence of featherbedding affect the labor supply function? Unfortunately this is not easily answered, but let me point out the implications under either of two sets of conditions. First, if we assume that there is some onus connected with a job that is reputed to involve featherbedding, then the supply to the industry would shift to the left and in the extreme would possibly disappear; i.e. would be perfectly inelastic at zero offerings over the relevant wage range. In the long run, the problem might then be self-correcting from the supply side. An alternative would be for the wage rate to be adjusted upward to compensate for the disutility of being in an undesirable occupation. Thus, a consequence of featherbedding would be an upward pressure on wages that cannot be stopped in a short run. If the rule does not adversely affect supply, then the problem can never be self-adjusting from the supply side. This obviously opens the question to some other type of policy.

A second dynamic problem concerns the impact of the rules on the rate of technological change and investment. It is commonly assumed that these restrictive rules retard progress. Clearly the intent of the rules is to lower the marginal efficiency of investment on laborsaving changes. The employer is not free to reap the full cost-reducing advantages of the change and unless the demand for the final product is perfectly inelastic some of the increase in cost must be shifted to ownership or other factors. The meager work on this problem is inconclusive, but indicates that the rules have some, though marginal, negative effect. I would argue that it is theoretically possible for the rules to stimulate change under certain conditions.

Let us assume that there is a new technology that allows the production of a product without the use of a factor used in the old technology. Assume further that there is a rule requiring a fixed labor–output ratio for one of the factors. Then the level of the featherbedding cost as measured by the slack variable depends on the mix of the two techniques. In the early stages of the substitution of the technologies there is little of the new and much of the old. Therefore the cost of the rule is minor. However, the more the new technology is substituted for the old, the higher is the relevant featherbedding cost. The maximum cost is obtained prior to the complete substitution of the new technology. When the last unit of capital using the old inputs is scrapped, the workers are entirely superfluous. The absolute cost of featherbedding through time depends on the length of time it takes to complete the change in technology. If this is perceived, then the featherbed rule should foster the more rapid introduction of a new technology and one that is radically different.[4] While research on this is not complete, it is suggested that this model is fruitful in explaining the history of the dispute concerning crew consist rules in the railroads. The critical factors are thus the character of the new production function and the time period between introduction and total substitution.

A less optimistic result comes about if it is assumed that some skills are still required even under the new technology. In this instance one sees that the problem is not corrected from the demand side and in fact may grow at a rate consistent with the increase in some parameter, such as the amount of matrix work in the printing trades.

In the former case, that involving the complete change in technology, the market can resolve the problem of the firm in the long run, but not in the latter case. Given that there are supply and demand conditions which may forestall a resolution of the problem, is there any way out of the featherbedding dilemma? One might also point out the fact that even though the problem, say, from the supply side is soluble in the long run, it may be

4. This assumes absence of co-operation by other unions, *supra*.

deemed that the period is too long, both from the firm's position as well as in tying up manpower resources.

Private Programs

The threat of technological unemployment can give rise to programs to ease the adjustments. Recent experiments, such as the Armour, West Coast, and Kaiser agreements, have been proposed as models to be followed in other agreements. The advantages of these plans are that they are arrived at privately and do not countenance redundant labor. It would appear that the market is effective in ending the problem of featherbedding by providing a more attractive alternative to the parties. Are these programs desirable alternatives? If they are desirable, what conditions are necessary for their adoption?

Longshoring has a fragile existence as a separate industry or trade. The rationale for a separate union stems from the historic irregularity of shipping, yielding a fluctuating labor demand and with low integration in the industry, separate and corrupt unions.[5] Whenever the trade is regularized, as in coastwise shipping, or the market decasualized, through restricted entry in the hiring hall, the unions cease to have a separate identity and become submerged into teamster or ocean shipping unions. The restrictive rules have arisen out of the corrupt, casual labor market and have tended to disappear with organization. Faced with technological change, as well as hostility from the Teamsters, the I.L.W.U. leadership stressed demands on their membership for a program that allowed management to institute work rules changes. The *quid pro quo* was a management financed fund of some $29 million to be used for early and regular retirement benefits, death benefits, and the stabilization of workers' income against declines due to changes in technology. The primary burden of disemployment resulting from technological change was to be borne by the workers last to arrive in the industry, many of whom are not members of the union. The union agreed not to object to alterations in rules and new technology, except in the case of speed-up. However, the I.L.W.U. have opposed changes quite regularly, as shown by the heavy use of arbitration.

5. The corruption arises from the ease of discriminating pricing.

The agreement has been advantageous to the parties. Management has added flexibility. The union has ended the hostile period with management and can concentrate on protecting itself against the Teamsters and resolving international problems.

In the meat industry, the Armour program has devoted considerable energies in studying displacement problems caused by plant shut-downs or elimination of divisions, as well as alternative ways of dealing with the workers' problems. The Armour Automation Committee has sponsored useful research that has resulted in some steps that have aided the displaced. For example, an early warning system for plant shut-down and the T.A.P. program. The activities that have received most attention are in the labor market sphere of retaining and placement.

Featherbedding was never an alternative open to the meat industry unions. The structure of the industry precluded such strong union policy. The emergence of new plants and firms in geographic areas that are difficult and costly to organize, as well as lower entry barriers, has made the industry more competitive.

The unions in the meat industry show increasing dissatisfaction with this endeavor. This plan has been in jeopardy because of union frustration that reflects their inability to enforce an employment guarantee solution. It is also important to note that this is the only plan that has actually lived with the problem of structural unemployment.

The Kaiser sharing plan has as one of its activities a program for employment security in addition to productivity sharing. The plan allows the employer to introduce new techniques and alter work rules, but alleviates the insecurity usually associated with this. Workers displaced by technological changes are bumped into the plant-wide pool, maintaining their former wages.

There has been no real test of the plan, and the high attrition rate at the Fontana plant makes it unlikely that the pool will be too costly. The high attrition rate, estimated at 8%, and the twenty-six week eligibility requirement were originally viewed as being in excess of manpower reductions due to altered operations. The company has bought the freedom to adjust procedures with an employment guarantee of dubious value. The union has acceded to changes in technology elsewhere and in fact is not known either for featherbedding or particular concern about permanently unemployed steelworkers.

The reason for this lack of interest, in addition to the character of the union utility function, is basic to understanding the limited role of private agreements in handling the displaced. These programs are adequate for avoiding the conflicts but are not in fact perfect substitutes for featherbedding, as the institution of featherbedding or its continuance in the case of longshoring was not a real alternative.

The cause of featherbedding is employment insecurity. The restrictive rules maintain jobs for the displaced. The alternative for featherbedding is the placement of displaced workers in other jobs and this normally means outside the firm or industry. While the Armour program attempts this, it is at once hampered by the inadequacies of public services and is an alternative to public services. Labor market functions performed by either the former employer or union are likely to be on a crisis basis. To adequately move workers from their old jobs implies careful planning based upon labor market surveys, employment projections, and training techniques in diverse industries. To invest in this activity would require a considerable incentive, and it is on this point that the future of these plans in handling employment insecurity breaks down.

The return to both labor and management of shifting workers smoothly out of their own province is either zero or close to it. What incentive is there for a particular union to invest in preparing workers for membership in another union and, *a fortiori*, management investing for the benefit of other firms. Today the Armour Automation Committee is resorting to public services more and more – for these are best suited for handling the real problems. The main contribution that the programs can make is in mobilizing the public service. However, a really efficient service would hardly need this catalyst.

Conclusion

While the market through substitution can end the problem of redundant labor under specified conditions, it can only offer a superficial answer to the real problem of union insecurity. Both the limited interest of labor and management and the technical requirements of appropriate labor market policy require that a more vigorous program of public labor market activity be adopted. Further, it is to the interest of the economy to broaden the industrial basis of union organizations. The market does not seem to aid, and in fact may retard, broader trade-union organization. Without the broadening of their scope, even plans for labor market activity as positive alternatives to featherbedding may collapse against the weight of organizational self-preservation.

Part Four **Bargaining Theory**

The economist's main theory of wages is essentially a theory
of wage determination in the long run when competitive forces
are envisaged to be strong. However, these forces are slow-
moving and difficult to discern in the short run, so that there
occur points of time when labour markets are in disequilibrium
and there exists a constellation of wages which are compatible
with momentary conditions: the agreed wage is then dependent
upon the abilities of the negotiators. Stevens discusses how
the bargain may be reached, his article being of particular
interest on account of the use made of work carried out by
psychologists.

8 C. M. Stevens

On The Theory of Negotiation

Stevens, C. M. (1958) On the theory of negotiation. *Quart. Journ. Econ.*, **73**, 77–97.

I

In recent literature, increasing attention has been paid to the theory of bargaining and negotiation.[1] This is a most desirable development since, in the light of the number and importance of the economic and other transactions (and interactions) thus mediated, there can be little doubt of the real need for a good theory of the negotiation process.

Interesting as have been some of the contributions to particular aspects of negotiation theory, no general statement of such a theory has yet emerged.[2] As a contribution to the development of such a general theory, I herein suggest the adaptation of a psychological choice theory model to the analysis of negotiation.

Throughout this paper, collective bargaining over terms and conditions of employment is used as an example of the negotiation process. However, the format of the analysis is intended to be applicable to negotiations of many sorts.[3]

1. Perhaps the most comprehensive recent effort is Neil W. Chamberlain's *A general theory of economic process* (New York, 1955). For an earlier quite comprehensive formulation see G. L. S. Shackle, *Expectation in economics* (Cambridge, England, 1949), ch. 6, 'A theory of the bargaining process'. See Harvey M. Wagner ('A unified treatment of bargaining theory', *Southern Economic Journal*, vol. 23 [April 1957], pp. 380–97) for a recent discussion of three approaches (bilateral monopoly, risk evaluation, and the theory of games) to bargaining theory. See also J. Pen, 'A general theory of bargaining', *American Economic Review*, vol. 42 (March 1952), pp. 24–42.

2. See, for example, T. C. Schelling, 'An essay on bargaining', *American Economic Review*, vol. 46 (June 1956), pp. 281–306.

3. Including, for example, not only negotiation, which is part of 'economic' relations in the usual sense of this term, but also negotiation which may be part of intranational and international political relations, etc.

Emphasis is upon developing the analytical framework rather than upon application of this framework to particular problems. The major points are:

(1) A reasonably self-contained description of the choice theory model to be employed in the analysis.

(2) An explanation, in terms of the model, of why the parties negotiate at all, i.e. rather than selecting some alternative method for mediating the transaction in question.

(3) An analysis, in terms of the model, of the negotiation process itself, i.e. the significance of the information exchanged in the course of negotiation.

(4) An illustrative application of the model to the disputed problem of the 'real' function of the so-called basic criteria used in wage negotiations (e.g. comparative wage rates, ability to pay, etc.).

(5) An explanation of the five analytically separable ways in which negotiation may terminate. (It develops that, from this point of view, there is an important asymmetry in the effects of different negotiation tactics.)

The choice theory model employed is of the stable equilibrium 'conflict' choice type, basically different from models usually employed in the analysis of economic choice behavior. Although herein applied only to negotiation theory, this model may well be of much more general interest to students of economic choice behavior. It may also be noted that since this is an equilibrium model, it permits, analogously to comparative statics analysis generally, prediction of the direction of shift in the variable of interest (e.g. wage rate), consequent, *ceteris paribus*, upon shifts in certain environmental parameters of interest. In this sense, then, it makes the outcome of negotiations theoretically determinate.

II

In much of the literature the terms 'bargaining' and 'negotiation' are used more or less interchangeably, as if they had reference to the same phenomena. However, it is helpful to maintain a distinction between the two. In any exchange transaction, for example, an ordinary retail purchase, a bargain (regarding the terms of exchange) is struck, and hence, a kind of bargaining may be said to have taken place. But, as in this instance, there need be no negotiation involved. Only certain exchange transactions are featured by negotiation, although all may be viewed as instances of bargaining.[4] Thus negotiation is just one of several ways in which a bargain may be concluded. In order to mediate any transaction, A and B must exchange some minimum amount of information, namely the initial terms upon which either (or both) is willing to conclude the transaction (on a take-it-or-leave-it basis), and subsequent acceptance or rejection of the offered terms.[5] However, A and B may be said to negotiate if they exchange information relevant to some prospective transaction in addition to this minimum amount. I subsequently discuss the kinds and functions of such additional information.

III

Let us now consider the choice theory model used in the subsequent analysis. It has been observed that a subject, when confronted with a choice between goal objects, may behave in either of two distinctly different ways:

(1) The subject may immediately elect one or the other. Call this a nonconflict choice.

(2) The subject may immediately elect neither goal. Rather he will remain uncertain for a period of time in a sort of behavioral equilibrium between the two. Call this a conflict choice.

How is this difference between nonconflict and conflict choice behavior to be explained?[6]

4. On this point see Chamberlain, op. cit., especially chs. 6, 7, and 8. As Chamberlain illustrates, the concept 'bargaining power' may be elaborated with respect to numerous transactions in which no negotiation takes place.

5. This exchange of information need not be of the *vis-à-vis* variety nor need it involve verbalization.

6. Economic choice theory might suggest this explanation: in the conflict choice situation the objects are equally preferred or indifferent, whereas in the nonconflict choice situation the relative preference for one is much greater than that for the other. This explanation is not, however, on any simple interpretation of it, adequate. Psychological choice theory suggests that all nonconflict choices will be made quickly, the matter of relative preference being manifest operationally in the probability that one rather than the other will be elected. Thus, in the case of a nonconflict choice involving two goals of equal preference, we should expect, on a series of

The model here described bases the explanation of behavioral equilibrium in the conflict choice situation upon the concepts of the 'approach gradient' and the 'avoidance gradient'.[7] Just as an individual may learn approach tendencies to rewarding (positive) goals, so also he may learn avoidance tendencies to goals such that to elect them involves an expectation of punishment or non-reward (negative goals). The approach gradient is a name given the hypothesis that the strength of an individual's tendency to approach a positive goal is a decreasing function of his distance from the goal. Analogously, the avoidance gradient is a name given the hypothesis that the strength of an individual's tendency to avoid a negative goal is a decreasing function of his distance from the goal.[8] A number of stable and unstable equilibrium choice models can be constructed in terms of these gradients. This analysis will make use only of the avoidance gradients. That is, the choice theory model employed is the avoidance–avoidance type. This model is represented in [the] figure.[9] (At present, the reader should ignore the graph labels in brackets.) In [the] figure, view the goals A and B as negative goals. The function AA is an avoidance gradient for goal A, representing the increasing strength of the tendency to avoid goal A as the subject gets closer to it. And, analogously, BB is the avoidance gradient for goal B. At a position such as D1, the strength of the tendency to avoid goal A is equal to the strength of the tendency to avoid goal B. At such a position, the individual is in a stable equilibrium position. If, in this avoidance–avoidance situation, the individual be momentarily displaced from a position such as D1, say to D2, he will

---

trials, that each would be selected immediately about half of the time. (This is, indeed, the operational definition usually given the concept of indifference in experimentation associated with economic choice theory.) The conflict choice situation is of a generically different sort.

7. John Dollard and Neal E. Miller develop the model I shall here describe (see their *Personality and psychotherapy* [New York, 1950], especially ch. 22). Dollard and Miller do not apply their model to the negotiation problem.

8. See Dollard and Miller, op. cit., for a discussion of the inductive and deductive bases for these hypotheses.

9. The linear assumptions incorporated in the figure are not significant. For this analysis there is no need for restrictions on the shape of these functions other than their general slopes.

tend to return to *D1*. The reason for this is that in a position such as *D2*, the strength of the tendency to avoid goal *A* is stronger than the strength of the tendency to avoid goal *B*. Hence there is a net avoidance tendency operating to drive the individual toward goal *B*, i.e. back towards position *D1*. An analogous argument applies to displacements on the other side of *D1*, closer to goal *B*.[10]

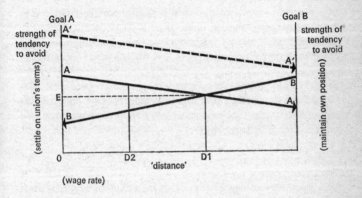

Suppose the individual to be in equilibrium at position *D1*. Further suppose that, due to a change in environmental circumstances, the individual's avoidance gradient *AA* shifts upward to occupy the position *A'A'* (the dotted line function). In this instance, the avoidance gradient to goal *A* lies everywhere above that to goal *B*, hence everywhere there is a net tendency to avoid *A*. In this circumstance, the individual will elect goal *B*. It is only in such a circumstance that, in spite of the avoidance–avoidance nature of the choice, one goal will be immediately elected.

It will be observed that the model determines two variables: (1) the distance of the subject from each goal, in equilibrium; (2) the strength of the tendency to avoid both goals, which is the same for both goals in equilibrium. In [the] figure and for position *D1* this is measured by *OE*. Regarding this latter variable,

10. It may be noted with respect to the figure that if *A* and *B* are viewed as positive goals, and *AA* and *BB* as approach gradients, then the model is of the unstable equilibrium type.

conflict choice situations involving this kind of behavioral equilibrium are apt to be an uncomfortable experience for the individual. Such situations give rise to a drive stimulus commonly termed 'tension' (or anxiety, etc.). The level of tension experienced in such an equilibrium choice situation is an increasing function of the strength of tendency to avoid which the individual feels in equilibrium, and of the length of time the subject is in the equilibrium situation. High or long-experienced levels of tension are apt to be associated with a variety of aberrant behaviors, e.g. reduced learning capacity, reduced ability to pay attention, etc. The theory of conflict choice involving this kind of behavioral equilibrium suggests that if there is available some compromise behavior, other than electing either of the two negative goals, the individual should be expected to choose it. (For example, escape from the choice situation altogether, or some compromise response 'between' the two goals.) We shall have use for these considerations subsequently.

IV

Given this general background, let us turn to what is the first task of a theory of negotiation. This is to explain why it is that, in a type of situation such as collective bargaining, the parties negotiate at all.[11] Negotiation is not after all the only way in which the transaction might be mediated. Why should not the parties elect some alternative method, e.g. 'take-it-or-leave-it', for mediating the transaction in question? In seeking an answer to this question it will be helpful to investigate a simple alternative model.

Assume a well organized union whose members comprise the major portion of the company's work force. Further assume that the company would have extreme difficulty in replacing the union members should they strike, and that, in such an event, the union members would experience extreme difficulty in finding alternative employment. Now assume a market procedure as follows: The union unilaterally states its terms (demand for a wage increase) on a take-it-or-leave-it basis, no compromise possible, and with the understanding that should the company

11. Such considerations as the existence of a statutory requirement to bargain are not at this point relevant.

elect to leave-it, a strike would be a certainty.[12] In this situation, two choices are available to the company:

(1) insisting upon its own position, the existing terms;
(2) settling on the union's terms.

Economic choice theory might suggest that the company's choice in this situation should turn simply upon the maximization of expected utility, taking into account such factors as the relative probability and cost of a strike, on the one hand, and the probable cost of paying the rate increase, on the other. That is, the company would immediately elect one goal or the other, depending upon the outcome of such a 'calculation'.

However, this is a conflict choice situation conforming to the avoidance–avoidance model. The company confronts two negative goals, i.e. there is an expectation of cost consequent upon the election of either. Company choice 1 exposes the company to a strike and the costs associated therewith. Company choice 2 means, *ceteris paribus*, loss of profit due to paying the higher rate.[13] In consequence, one should expect the company to elect neither of its available choices immediately. Rather, the company will remain uncertain, unable to 'make up its mind', i.e. in a sort of behavioral equilibrium between the two. It will also be recalled

12. This was, indeed, very much the way in which 'collective bargaining' was carried on in this country in the early nineteenth century. In so far as the point made in this section is concerned, we might alternatively suppose the company to quote the terms, unilaterally. The following analysis applies to both cases.

In a negotiation situation, the union's initial statement of terms would not be its final offer, but rather a 'gambit' price enough above its final offer to leave room for bargaining. This, however, is a take-it-or-leave-it situation and the initial statement of terms is the final one.

For a discussion of the various prices with which a bargainer may be subjectively concerned see Shackle, op. cit.

13. This way of looking at the matter is in line with Hicks's depiction of the employer's position in the bargaining situation, viz.: '. . . either he must pay higher wages than he would have paid on his own initiative (and this generally means a prolonged reduction in profits) or on the other hand must endure the direct loss which will probably follow from a stoppage of work' (see J. R. Hicks, *The theory of wages*, pp. 141 *et seq.*; see also Chamberlain's elaboration of the concept of 'bargaining power', in Neil W. Chamberlain, *Collective bargaining* [New York, 1951], ch. 10). Chamberlain adopts a modification of Hicks's view.

that in such a choice situation the company should be expected to perform some compromise response *were such available*. Thus the company might prefer that the rules of the market game permitted an additional choice, viz.:

(3) seeking a compromise, via negotiation.[14]

The market 'game' as I have here presented it (the take-it-or-leave-it model) is what I shall term an unnatural, purposive game.[15] I define a purposive game as one in which the relation between the game and its associated economic transaction is such as to make the game a means to an end, namely, to mediate the economic transaction.[16]

14. Or perhaps the company might attempt escape from the choice situation entirely, e.g. obtain a court indictment of the union as a criminal conspiracy, or seek injunctive relief against the strike, etc. From this point of view, the existence of a statutory requirement to bargain is significant, i.e. as blocking off certain potential escape routes.

15. One might, of course, construct alternative models. One feature of the model presented was a certain asymmetry in the amount of information available to the parties. The union made its demand with no knowledge of the company's position whereas the company made its choice with perfect knowledge of the union position which would lead to a strike if rejected. We might remedy this feature by providing that the union and the company are to state their terms simultaneously (e.g. the wage rate) on a take-it-or-leave-it basis. This would now be a two person, two strategy game in which the union had available strategies analogous to those available to the company in the example cited. Provision might also be made that the parties must reveal information with respect to their choices simultaneously. Investigation of such additional models does not, however, seem to lead to conclusions substantially different from those involved in the simple model above discussed.

16. This is in contrast to certain parlor games in which the relationship between the game and its associated economic transaction (wager) is the reverse of this. In these games, the game itself is the end, and the economic transaction a means to the end, i.e. to lend interest to the playing of the game.

The distinction between purposive and nonpurposive games is an important one for the reason that the two classes may differ with respect to properties crucial to analysis. Thus, for example, one would hazard the guess that purposive games are more apt to give rise to conflict choice situations involving the experience of uncomfortable tensions than are parlor games. Consequently, it would seem more important to consider this possibility in an analysis of purposive games. On the other hand, a game theory elaborated chiefly with respect to nonpurposive games might neglect this possibility.

The take-it-or-leave-it game is considered unnatural in the avoidance–avoidance choice situation because, in this situation, the player is highly motivated (by tensions generated in the choice situation) to seek strategies in addition to those made available by the rules. Of course, in any game, increasing the number of opportunities available may, *ceteris paribus*, increase the value of the payoff. However, I do *not* here argue that, in the case of an unnatural game, the player seeks an additional strategy (negotiation) because he may thus probably be assured a more favorable outcome of the game.[17] Rather, I argue that the avoidance–avoidance conflict choice situation is inherently and generically of such a nature that the game take-it-or-leave-it must give rise to strong motivations to discover alternative responses. In this situation the individual cannot immediately make up his mind which goal to elect. He is in a kind of behavioral equilibrium such that strategies other than those available in take-it-or-leave-it are psychologically necessary if the game is to be an appropriate (natural) one for mediating the transaction in question.

I conclude, then, that in the kind of bilateral monopoly situation represented by collective bargaining, the parties would probably prefer to play the game negotiation rather than the game take-it-or-leave-it. This conclusion would seem to be somewhat at odds with Schelling's approach to the theory of bargaining. Schelling's major point is that an important class of tactics in bargaining is that class which enables a player to convert the choice confronted by his adversary into one of the take-it-or-leave-it variety.[18] However, in the light of the above analysis of why the parties negotiate, this tactic should not be of prime importance (at least at the outset) in many negotiations. I have argued that (for rational or other reasons) the parties choose to

17. Such a rationality principle argument can be made. Suppose that a solution 'no deal' has an extremely low value. Suppose further that, as contrasted with negotiation, take-it-or-leave-it greatly increases the chance of such an outcome. Then one might choose to mediate the transaction via negotiation precisely for the reason that this increases the probable payoff.

18. That is, player A contrives to so bind himself that B is convinced that A will not concede, i.e. B is confronted with a take-it-or-leave-it offer. This tactic may well be of great importance in some kinds of bargaining situation (see Schelling, op. cit.).

play the game negotiation rather than the game take-it-or-leave-it in certain kinds of choice situation (i.e. conflict choice of the avoidance–avoidance type). It would not seem plausible, then, that a primary negotiation tactic should be an attempt immediately to convert the game negotiation into one of the take-it-or-leave it variety.

V

The next task is an analysis of the negotiation process itself. For this purpose let us again utilize the avoidance–avoidance paradigm. Assume that the sole bargaining issue is the wage rate. We shall explicitly consider just one side of the situation, i.e. the choice problem as confronted by the employer and the negotiation task as seen by the union. The principles involved will likewise apply to the situation seen from the other side. [The] figure [p. 159] now represents the employer's position, the goal A being 'settle on union's terms', and the goal B being 'maintain own position'. Since this is a negotiation situation, the union's demand and the company's position must be viewed as 'gambit' prices, i.e. announced prices, leaving room for negotiation, rather than necessarily final prices. We need an appropriate conceptualization of the concept 'distance' (from goal) – the horizontal axis in [the] figure. In this content, distance will have to be interpreted in some subjective sense rather than in a literal spatial sense. Generally speaking, postulation of this kind of behavioral equilibrium results in dividing choice behavior into two stages: (1) the initial stage of deliberation or 'making up the mind'; (2) a subsequent stage of actual overt choice behavior which will take place once stage (1) is resolved.[19] The concept of 'distance' from goal A shall be interpreted as 'nearness to having made up one's mind' to choose goal A. This concept of distance is, perhaps, susceptible to operational definition only in terms of an individual's responses upon interrogation. It seems probable that in many instances a subject would be able to testify on this matter only in an ordinal sense. In the collective bargaining situation,

19. As Macfie has noted, such a division of the choice problem into two stages, which is not characteristic of choice theory in economics, is characteristic of much psychological choice theory (see A. L. Macfie, 'Choice in psychology and as economic assumption', *Economic Journal*, vol. 63 [June 1953], pp. 352–67).

the two goals represent certain wages rates (the announced positions of the parties), and hence the distance between the two may be thought of as scaled in terms of such rates. Suppose the company's announced position to be $1.50 and the union's announced position to be $2.00. An equilibrium position halfway between would be represented by a rate of $1.75. The individual in such an equilibrium position will be supposed ready to accept a rate of $1.75, *if there were any way to do so*. The 'distance' between the equilibrium position and the goal $2.00 is $.25 – and the individual may be thought of as this near to having made up his mind to elect the goal $2.00.

Again with reference to [the] figure, the goals confronting the company are negative goals. To elect the goal *B* may result in a strike. The expected cost calculation on this score must presumably be compounded of two parts:

(1) an estimate of the probable cost to the company of a strike, should it occur;

(2) an estimate of the probability that the company's insisting upon its own position will indeed eventuate in a strike.

Goal *A* is also a negative goal, the cost being lower profits in consequence of higher wage rates, *ceteris paribus*. The company may be viewed as initially in equilibrium at position *D1* – unable to make up its mind either to insist upon own position or settle on the union's terms.

The union will accomplish its negotiation task by means of information exchanged during the course of negotiations. One important aspect of this task is to move the company's equilibrium position in a direction favourable to the union, that is, toward the company's goal *A*, i.e. settling on the union's terms (see figure, [p. 159]).[20] Two classes of negotiation tactics which will have this effect must be distinguished:

Class I: Tactics which will raise the company's avoidance gradient to the company's goal *B*, i.e. insisting upon its own position.

20. The other important part of the task is for the union to communicate information regarding its own equilibrium position without at the same time destroying whatever negotiation power it may have. This matter is discussed subsequently.

Class II: Tactics which will lower the company's avoidance gradient to the company's goal *A*, i.e. settling on the union's terms.

Subsequently, tactics of class I will be referred to simply as raising the avoidance gradient, and tactics of class II will be referred to as lowering the avoidance gradient, the goals of reference being understood.[21]

It might be objected that these classes of tactics are not really independent. That is, that a tactic which will increase the company's tendency to avoid its own position (class I) will, at the same time, decrease the company's tendency to avoid the union's position (class II). The implications of this way of putting the matter are misleading. It is true, of course, that a union tactic which will move the company's equilibrium position farther from the company's goal *B* (maintaining its own position) will, at the same time, move that equilibrium position closer to the company's goal *A* (settling on the union's terms). However, tactics of classes I and II are not distinguished in terms of movements of the equilibrium position, but rather in terms of movements of the avoidance gradients, i.e. tendencies to avoid viewed in the *schedule* sense. In these latter terms, the independence of the two classes seems plausible. The company's avoidance tendencies are based

21. Adaptation of the avoidance–avoidance model to analysis of collective bargaining results in a conceptualization of that process similar in many ways to approaches suggested in the literature (see, for example, Hicks, op. cit.). Compare also Chamberlain's definition of 'bargaining power'. (see n. 4, p. 78; see also his *Collective bargaining*, ch. 10). Using Hicks's analysis as a point of departure, Chamberlain defines *A*'s bargaining power *vis-à-vis* *B* as the ratio of the cost to *B* of disagreeing with *A* on *A*'s terms to the cost to *B* of agreeing with *A* on *A*'s terms. The significant thing about Chamberlain's concept of bargaining power is not that it results in a coefficient of that power in any particular situation. Rather, the significant thing is the theory of the negotiation process implied by it. His scheme, unlike much discussion of bargaining, recognizes both what we have termed class I and class II tactics. Beyond such similarities to the avoidance–avoidance model, there are also important differences. For example, Chamberlain does not develop any explicit equilibrium theory of conflict choice situations. Thus his scheme does not explain *why* it is that if, in his terms, *A*'s coefficient of bargaining power *vis-à-vis* *B* is greater than one, *B* doesn't simply settle on *A*'s terms – rather than go on bargaining (as, he indicates, may indeed be the case).

upon calculation of expected cost associated with paying a higher wage rate, on the one hand, and a strike, on the other hand. Let us suppose, for example, that the information exchanged during negotiation will revise downward the company's estimate of the cost associated with paying a higher rate (a successful union class II tactic). There is no *prima facie* reason to suppose that this tactic must necessarily have a class I effect, e.g. cause a revision of the company's estimate of the probable cost associated with a strike.

VI

An analysis of the negotiation process in terms of this schema is in large part an analysis of the shift parameters relevant to the avoidance functions. Thus, e.g. party one's various negotiation tactics will be seen as attempts to shift party two's avoidance functions so as to move two's equilibrium position closer to (and if possible coincident with) one's demand.

It has been my intention to present a framework in terms of which negotiation processes may be analysed. It is not my intention to undertake an extensive analysis of these processes. However, an example to illustrate at least the application of this framework would seem desirable in order to make the nature of such application more concrete.

Consider the problem of the function of the so-called 'basic criteria' used in wage negotiations, e.g. ability to pay, productivity, comparative rates, etc. This is an interesting example because of the widespread use of such principles in the course of negotiations, and because of the nature of the discussion which has surrounded the practice.

In many wage negotiations, the participants spend considerable time and energy in gathering data relevant to, and in debating the applicability of, various of these basic criteria. This circumstance would seem to constitute at least *prima facie* evidence that these principles must play some functionally important role in the wage negotiation process. However, much discussion of the use of these principles takes a position, in one way or another, that would lead to the conclusion that these principles play no substantively important role in the negotiations.[22] (For example, a

22. For example, Lindblom, viewing this matter from the point of view of union wage aims, deems these principles mere 'window dressing'

substantively important role in the sense of serving to define the 'real' wage objectives of the parties, etc.)

Looked at from the point of view of the negotiation theory herein developed, it becomes apparent that use of such principles may well serve important tactical purposes. Let us consider the comparative rates criterion. Suppose the union to contend that its own demands are justified and, indeed, minimal in the light of rates prevailing in a somehow defined comparable labor market area. What function might this communication serve?

It might actually serve to change the company's mind with respect to this aspect of its environment, i.e. serve to convince the company that its rates were indeed low on a comparative basis. If this were the effect, and if the labor market area selected for the comparison contained the company's important competitors, then the comparative rates argument might serve as a class II negotiation tactic (decreasing the company's tendency to avoid accepting the union position). This would be so to the extent that the company had previously avoided accepting the union position for fear of being thereby put at a comparative disadvantage.

However, there is the additional and perhaps more likely possibility that this comparative-rates argument has its major effect as a class I negotiation tactic. From this tactical point of view, the important functional role of the union's comparative-rates argument is less to communicate information to the company about the company's wage-rate environment than to communicate

---

utilized by the union for 'expediency's sake', (cf. Charles E. Lindblom, *Unions and capitalism* [New Haven, 1949], ch. 3). Bloom and Northrup explain their lack of attention to these wage criteria on the ground that '. . . these criteria are basically rationalizations pressed into service to support demands which need justification', and point out that these '. . . slogans should not, however, be confused with the practical realities of union–management wage determination . . .' (cf. Gordon F. Bloom & Herbert R. Northrup, *Economics of labor and industrial relations* [Philadelphia, 1950], p. 204). Reynolds likewise views these criteria as 'rationalizations', and points to the 'lack of substance' and 'frailty' of arguments involving these criteria (cf. Lloyd G. Reynolds, *Labor economics and labor relations* [New York, 1954], p. 575, *et seq.*). This list of citations could be extended, but the sample is representative of the point of view here in question, and sufficient to make the point.

information to the company about the *union's beliefs* on this matter.[23] That is, the argument may serve to convince the company *that the union believes itself (the union) to be correct in asserting its demands to be minimal in accordance with the comparative rates criterion.* If this were the effect of the argument, then it would constitute a class I argument. The reasons why this is so are as follows:

(1) It will be recalled that the expected cost calculation tending to make the company avoid insisting upon its own terms was comprised of two elements: (*a*) the estimated cost of a strike, should it occur; (*b*) the probability that a strike would indeed eventuate.

(2) The company may believe that, to the union officials, because of their status as elected officials who must satisfy the membership, comparative rates parity is an extremely important matter.

(3) If the comparative rates argument had the effect hypothesized (see italicized passage), it would be apt, in the light of (2), to revise upward the company's estimate of the probability that a strike would eventuate should the company insist upon its own position. And this upward revision would shift the avoidance gradient upward, moving the company towards the union's demand.[24]

Other wage 'principles' and, indeed, any other negotiation tactic (e.g. striking, taking a strike vote, appealing to the public, etc.) are susceptible to analysis in terms of the conceptual scheme here presented. I shall not here attempt a demonstration of this assertion.[25]

23. This does not carry the implication that the union is aware of or intends this effect.

24. Note that the factor of the probability that a strike would occur, not the factor of the cost of a strike should it occur, has been the expected cost element influenced by this particular tactic. In general, one should expect that negotiation tactics might operate upon either or both elements.

25. The above analysis suggests that negotiation arguments, e.g. those concerning the basic criteria, may take on a new significance if viewed from what might be termed a 'tactical' rather than a 'substantive' point of view. (Regarding this distinction, see my 'Regarding the determinants of union wage policy', *Review of Economics and Statistics*, vol. 35 [August 1953]). This suggestion is in line with that made by Schelling, op. cit. Indeed, the

VII

To complete this conceptual framework for the analysis of negotiation, it is necessary to explain why and in what ways the negotiations may come to an end. There appear to be at least five analytically distinguishable ways in which the negotiations may end, viz.:

(1) Compromise
    (*a*) unilateral
    (*b*) bilateral
(2) Noncompromise
    (*a*) type I
    (*b*) type II
(3) Breakdown

Although we have thus far been looking at the negotiation process largely from one side of the table, i.e. possible effects of

---

interpretation of the comparative rates argument as a class I negotiation tactic makes it similar in effect to that particular class of tactics to which Schelling intended to draw attention. There are these important differences in emphasis, however: (1) The union does not, in my example, bind itself in an all-or-none fashion by converting the game of negotiation into one of take-it-or-leave-it. In my example, the effect is a much more subtle one, tending to increase (in the company's eyes) the degree of adherence of the union to its position. (2) The effect of the tactic is not to result either in a unilateral compromise (by the company to the union position) or no deal. Rather, it serves just to move the company's equilibrium position somewhat closer to the union's terms. Thus it may help to set up the conditions necessary for a compromise. A good bit of argument remains before we can explain how compromise is possible in a purposive game such as collective bargaining over terms and conditions of employment.

Martin Fishbein has suggested another interpretation of the role of the basic criteria in wage negotiations (see his *A social–psychological approach to collective bargaining*, unpublished B.A. thesis, Reed College, 1957). Fishbein draws attention to Nicholas Pastore's suggested modification of the Dollard (*et al.*) frustration–aggression hypothesis. According to Pastore, an aggressive response to frustration is less likely if the subject perceives the obstacle to his goal achievement as 'reasonable' (i.e. nonarbitrary). Fishbein suggests that through widespread use in the process of collective bargaining, the basic criteria may be becoming institutionalized as 'reasonable' obstacles to union–management goal achievement (e.g. lower wage rates, in the case of the company goal), thereby decreasing the probability of aggressive responses in the bargaining context.

the union's negotiation tactics on the company's equilibrium position, it will be recalled that the analysis is intended to apply symmetrically to both sides of the table. From now on it will often be helpful to think in terms of two figures, such as [the] figure [on p. 159], one representing the union's conflict choice situation and equilibrium position and the other representing the company's conflict choice situation and equilibrium position. In these terms, the status of any particular collective bargaining negotiations at any particular time may be represented by values, e.g. as assembled (for subsequent use) in [the] exhibit below:

EXHIBIT*

	Status 1	Status 2	Status 3	Status 4
Union's announced demand	$1·25	$1·25	$1·25	$1·25
Union's equilibrium position	1·15	1·12	1·20	1·12
Company's equilibrium position	7·10	1·12	1·13	1·05
Company's announced offer	1·00	1·00	1·00	1·00

* All figures represent hourly rates.

By the outcome 'compromise' I mean simply termination of the negotiations with an agreed price, i.e. with a position to which both parties assent. In outcome (1) (a), unilateral compromise, the agreed price is the same as the announced position of either party.[26] Unilateral compromise will be the outcome if the negotiation tactics of one party, say the union, succeed in shifting the equilibrium position of the other party to its (the union's) announced position.

Compromise, unilateral or bilateral (to be discussed subsequently), may well follow the occurrence of a strike, as well as numerous other negotiation tactics. It is important in the analysis of negotiation to realize that what I term the 'legitimate' strike is not an instance of the 'breakdown' of negotiations (category 3 in the above classification of terminations). The legitimate strike, as a deliberate attempt on the part of the union in this way to increase the company's tendency to avoid adherence to its own position, is perhaps best viewed as an effective way of communicating information. Previously the company has experienced the threat of a strike. The actual occurrence of the strike raises to a value of one the company's estimate of the probability that

26. This position need not be the initial gambit price.

a strike will occur if the company insists upon its own position. Hence, as an integral part of the negotiation process (not as a result of the breakdown of that process), a legitimate strike may be instituted by the union if the union thinks that the company:

(*a*) underestimates either the cost to it, or the probability of a strike; and

(*b*) would probably assent to the union's demand were a correct estimate made.[27]

If, in such a case, the union were correct on points (*a*) and (*b*), the legitimate strike may be followed by a compromise, the company modifying its position.

By definition, in outcome (1) (*b*), bilateral compromise, the agreed price will lie somewhere between the announced positions of the parties.

The development of a good theory of bilateral compromise is at once one of the most important and most difficult problems in the development of a general theory of negotiation. It will not do simply to assume that bilateral compromise is in some sense a 'natural' outcome of the negotiation process. A negotiation theory must explain how it is possible for the parties to achieve bilateral compromise.[28]

The conflict choice analysis indicates that it is a necessary condition for the occurrence of bilateral compromise that the equilibrium positions of the parties be brought, via negotiation, to the same position. For example, with reference to [the] exhibit, status 1 represents a situation in which bilateral compromise is not possible, and status 2 one in which it is possible. One definite task to be accomplished by the exchange of information in negotiation is to bring this equality (necessary but not sufficient for bilateral compromise) about. Further, the parties must somehow

27. This would suggest that (*A*) might protect himself against a legitimate strike by *B* by convincing *B* that he, *A*, held the highest possible estimate of both the probability of a *B* strike and the cost of a *B* strike when it occurred. From this point of view, perhaps the present tendency in international relations to lay great stress upon the likelihood of atomic war and the tremendous destruction sure to follow serves a useful purpose.

28. There is also the question of *why* the parties seek bilateral compromise. The discussion in section IV of this paper may be taken as directly relevant to this question.

be informed of the similarity of their equilibrium positions if the fact of this similarity is to create a compromise route. But how is this information to be conveyed? Suppose with respect to a particular negotiation that, with reference to [the] exhibit, status 2 obtains. That is, at the time in question, the conditions necessary for bilateral compromise obtain. Suppose now the union simply announce its equilibrium position, i.e. $1.12 (which is the same as the company's position, but the union does not know this). This announcement, rather than resulting in immediate bilateral compromise, may serve to stiffen the company's position by causing the company to revise downward its estimate of the probability that adhering to its own announced position will result in a strike.[29] In terms of [the] exhibit, for example, the union's announcement of its position may cause the negotiations to shift from status 2 (status at time of announcement) to status 4 (where the necessary conditions for bilateral compromise are no longer met).

In the light of these considerations, what is the second major function of the exchange of information during negotiations becomes clear. This second function is to enable A, for example, to inform B of his (A's) equilibrium position in such a way as not to destroy A's bargaining power by the very process of the communication.

The question of precisely how such a communication may be accomplished is an important one, and one to which I cannot deliver a definite answer. However, it should be noted that M. W. Reder has made some suggestions of interest from this point of view.[30] On Reder's view, the problem in the bargaining duel is to

29. This point has been made elsewhere in the literature, for example, by Chamberlain (see his *Collective bargaining*, op. cit., ch. 10). In his terms, A's attempt to 'increase bargaining power' by reducing the magnitude of a demand (which will reduce B's cost of agreement) may fail to increase bargaining power because it may also decrease B's notion of the cost of disagreeing with A. In general, Chamberlain views alterations in the magnitude of demands, as well as all other bargaining and negotiation tactics which, in our terms, would be viewed as shift parameters in the avoidance functions, as ways in which to change the magnitude of bargaining power. It would seem better to view these tactics as the utilization of bargaining or negotiation power, whatever its magnitude, to achieve an objective.

30. See his 'The theory of union wage policy', *Review of Economics and Statistics*, vol. 34 (December 1952), pp. 34–45.

define 'fair treatment'. This is so because, although within limits
any settlement is better than no settlement, the parties '. . . do not
wish to appear over-eager for agreement (lest they tempt the
other party to take advantage of them), and they wish to be
treated "fairly".'[31] Reder then points out that among the principal ingredients of equitable treatment will be Ross's notion of
orbits of coercive comparison (the comparative rates criterion).
The other basic criteria may likewise be viewed as relevant from
this point of view. This suggestion may be interpreted somewhat
as follows. Suppose the union's announced price to be $1.25 and
its equilibrium price $1.12. As previously indicated, the union's
simple and direct communication of information regarding its
equilibrium price may be destructive of its bargaining power.
However, the union may be able to argue in terms of the comparative rate (and other basic wage) criteria in such a way as to
convey information that some price less than its announced demand would still be considered acceptable as 'fair'. What is here
implied, then, is that an 'orderly' retreat (based on 'principle')
from an asking price to a 'fair' price, may not be destructive of
bargaining power (i.e. on Reder's terms, will not cause the other
party to 'take advantage' of the party so involved).

Turning now to the outcome noncompromise, let us mean by
this the termination of negotiations without an agreed price. Such
a termination of negotiations implies some sort of strike or lock-
out (before or after such termination), but not a permanent sever-
ance of the relationship between the parties.[32] Suppose that, after
negotiations have terminated and the union is out on strike, the
strike is broken. That is, there is a nonunion-ordered return of
union (and nonunion) members to work on company terms to
which the union has not assented. In such a situation the union
may ultimately sign a contract on company terms, if only to sal-
vage its status as bargaining agent. In terming such an outcome
noncompromise, i.e. one in which there is no agreed price, I mean,
in effect, that it is an outcome which is the result of a breakdown

31. *Review of Economics and Statistics*, vol. 34 (December 1952), p. 39.
32. The outcome noncompromise may follow a legitimate strike, as well
as other negotiation tactics. This will be the case if, in the light of the information conveyed by the legitimate strike, the company still does not
agree to the union position.

of an 'alliance' on one side – in this case, the union and its members. Such an outcome (although it involves in some sense an 'agreed' price), does not represent a compromise in our sense, i.e. a compromise between two parties which retain their organizational integrity. Rather, it represents the destruction of the organizational integrity of one of the parties.

Within the general outcome category noncompromise, it is helpful to distinguish:

(2) (*a*) type I;

(2) (*b*) type II.

This distinction is based upon the two general functions which the exchange of information in negotiations is supposed to serve. The first of these, it will be recalled, was to alter the equilibrium positions of the parties by shifting the avoidance gradients up and down. It is clear that negotiation may fail to result in compromise because this function has not been served in such a way as to set up the conditions necessary for compromise – i.e. to bring the equilibrium positions of the parties into consonance. This is a type I noncompromise outcome.

Even if the necessary conditions for compromise have been achieved, however, a noncompromise outcome may still be the result if the parties are unable mutually to inform each other of this fact so as to turn the fact of this equivalence into an actual compromise route. A failure on these grounds constitutes a type II noncompromise outcome.

It would appear that the institution of mediation is primarily useful in preventing negotiation failures of the type II noncompromise variety. The parties while not free, for reasons explained, to communicate information directly regarding their true equilibrium positions to each other, are free to do so to a neutral third party, the mediator. The latter is in a position with this knowledge to inform the parties if and when they have indeed achieved the condition necessary for bilateral compromise. Thus the mediator, in a sense, performs the second of the two major functions of the exchange of information in the negotiation process.[33]

33. This would suggest that perhaps mediation (of a sort) should be a part of many negotiation proceedings *from their inception*. Thus it might be required that the parties continuously submit, during the course of negotiations, information regarding their true equilibrium positions to a neutral

Let us turn finally to the possibility of breakdown as an outcome of the negotiation process. It will be recalled that the avoidance–avoidance model determined not only the individual's equilibrium distance from the negative goals but also the strength of the individual's tendency to avoid these goals, which, in equilibrium, is the same for both goals. (Referring again to [the] figure, for distance $D1$ the strength of tendency to avoid is measured by OE.)

The possibility of the outcome breakdown is suggested by the second of these two variables. For, as pointed out in section III, the conflict choice situation is apt to give rise to tension or anxiety. Further, the amount of tension experienced in this choice situation is apt to be an increasing function of the strength of tendency-to-avoid experienced in equilibrium. High levels of tension may lead to various forms of aberrant behavior, e.g. reduced learning capacity, reduced ability to pay attention, etc. Such behavior might, *per se*, reduce the chances of finding a compromise solution via negotiation. Beyond this, a part of such behavior might be simply to 'bolt' the bargaining situation in a precipitate and nondeliberate fashion.[34] Such a termination of the negotiations is what we here term a breakdown of the negotiations – to be distinguished from the outcome noncompromise.

It should be emphasized that the argument here is not that, typically, collective bargaining negotiations will involve the kind of emotional content probably leading to breakdown.[35] Rather, the

---

third party. It would be understood and agreed that the sole function of this neutral third party would be to receive the information in question and announce the fact of conditions necessary for bilateral compromise – if and when such conditions should eventuate. The value of employing mediation of this sort from the outset is that it might prevent the parties from destroying a condition necessary for bilateral compromise in their unaided attempts to discover the fact of its existence.

34. Unlike, for example, a calculated legitimate strike.

35. Although this factor is probably important in some negotiations. Edward Peters (*Conciliation in action* [New London, 1952], pp. 28–9), after warning against an overemphasis upon the emotional factor and pointing out that disputes are based first and foremost upon the relative strengths of the parties, goes on to point out: 'This does not mean that deadlocks are not marked by a tense emotional atmosphere. It does mean taking into account that the contestants usually exhibit strong emotions because of the issues

position is this: If, indeed, the avoidance–avoidance paradigm is conceptually appropriate for analysis of the negotiation choice problem, then the possibility of breakdown must be taken into account in the analysis.

The above considerations suggest the possibility of an important asymmetry in the effects of the two classes of negotiation tactics. It will be recalled that class II tactics, as used by, say, party one, serve to decrease party two's tendency to avoid agreement with one. Such an effect will drive two closer to one's position. It will also serve to *decrease* the amount of tension experienced by two in equilibrium. Class I tactics, on the other hand, serve to increase two's tendency to avoid his own position. Such an effect will likewise serve to drive two closer to one's position, and in this sense may be equally efficacious with the class II tactic. Unlike the class II tactic, however, the class I tactic will increase the degree of tension experienced by two in equilibrium. On the basis of the earlier argument, then, negotiations featuring heavy emphasis upon class I tactics should, *ceteris paribus*, be more apt to terminate in breakdown than negotiations featuring relatively heavier emphasis upon class II tactics.

VIII

One final point warrants brief attention. In thinking about general conceptual schema adequate to the analysis of negotiation, should not some place be given to game theory? Attempts have been made to analyse aspects of bargaining in these terms.[36] However, in this writer's opinion, the game theory format is essentially inappropriate to the analysis of negotiation. This is for reasons beyond the often mentioned nonzero sum nature of most negotiated games. Game theory emphasizes a rationality-type solution with the calculation of optimal strategy elaborated with respect to a supposedly known or somewhat arbitrarily assumed payoff matrix. But in most negotiated, purposive games, precisely

---

between them and not, as is often supposed, that there are issues between them because of angry passions and deep emotions. The emotions are not the cause of the deadlock. They are one of its effects.' Agreeing with this general position, one may then go on to argue that these emotions themselves may have additional effects.

36. See, for example, Wagner, op. cit.

the major task of the exchange of information during negotiation is to change the negotiators' perception of the values comprising the payoff matrix. Herein lies the essence of the analysis. Elaboration of techniques for the calculation of optimal strategies on the basis of known payoffs would not seem to add much to the analysis of this type of situation.

Part Five The Allocation of Labour

In Part Two the economist's theory of job choice was presented and certain tests based on interviews and questionnaires were made. This section takes up the problem of movements in relative wages and employment in more detail. Wages are found to alter and workers change jobs, but there appears to be little or no association between the two: custom, frozen in institutions, is found to regulate wage movements and workers move according to the availability of jobs. The implications for incomes policies are, of course, important, since opponents of incomes policies have pointed out that wages are not only incomes but serve to allocate labour between jobs. The Reddaway article suggests that the allocative role of wages can be ignored by proponents of incomes policies.

9 W. B. Reddaway

Wage Flexibility and the Distribution of Labour

Reddaway, W. B. (1959) Wage flexibility and the distribution of labour. *Lloyd's Bank Rev.*, **54**, 32–48.

The Nature of the Problem

Most discussions about the usefulness or otherwise of a 'wages policy' have been primarily concerned with the question of the *general* level of wages, rather than with the question of the relative wages of particular industries and occupations. The latter point has, however, commonly been raised as a related issue, partly because it is considered important for securing desirable changes in the distribution of the country's labour force. It is this second question – of *relative* wages and the distribution of labour between industries and occupations – with which this article is concerned.

It may help to focus the issue by starting with a quotation from the first report of the Cohen Council, which in fact inspired the research on which the article is based. In paragraph 146 the report says:

> We think it most important that the flexibility of relative wages in response to changes in the demand for labour should be preserved, since in a free enterprise economy without direction of labour this is the main means on which we must rely for ensuring the most efficient distribution of the country's labour force.

This view may perhaps be contrasted with a different one, which starts from the idea that, whether we like it or not, wages are not fixed in this way in response to the forces of supply and demand; for example, Lady Wootton has stressed the importance of social considerations in the fixing of relative wages. If one takes this view of the way in which wages are fixed, then the fact that the distribution of labour between industries and occupations does in fact change substantially, necessarily implies that there is some other force which is responsible. This alternative view of the labour market may perhaps be set out as follows:

Changes in the demand for labour in the various industries and occupations operate to secure a redistribution of the labour force mainly through direct changes in the 'job opportunities' made available by employers, and the vigour (or lack thereof) with which the employers seek to recruit workers.

This hypothesis does not, of course, deny that employers will find it easier to fill posts if they offer higher wages. It asserts rather that in the main employers adjust their labour force, whether upwards or downwards, by varying the number of men whom they are willing to take on or whom they dismiss. An industry which is experiencing an increased demand for its products, or in which firms wish to increase their labour force for other reasons, will typically be an easy one in which to get a job because nearly all employers are willing to take on men nearly all the time – and perhaps not too fussy about qualifications: the effective demand in that industry is widespread in space, time, and perhaps 'character'. In an industry which is contracting, on the other hand, 'no vacancies' is the rule at all firms, and some men may be dismissed. The wage in the former industry may be no higher[1] than in the latter, but the desired changes will be effected without the rates being changed.

It is not, of course, necessary to believe that adjustments work *exclusively* in this way, without any assistance from changes in the wages offered. The essential characteristic of this 'alternative hypothesis' is that the *main* way in which employment will be either increased or reduced is through 'direct action' by the employers, and that only exceptionally will they have to include a change in the relative wage offered in order to secure the desired number of workers – or at least that the change in relative wage

1. An important additional point is that potential entrants need to take account of all sorts of factors besides the cash wage, and comparison of these may be difficult, quite apart from the fact that different people will attach different degrees of importance to particular factors. There is no reason to be surprised if *either* of two industries in a town would secure a reasonable flow of new recruits if it announced vacancies – even at a time of 'full employment'.

will usually be so small that it is hard to detect in a world where other wages are also changing.

If we are to compare the validity or plausibility of this hypothesis and the one put forward by the Cohen Council, it is first necessary to clarify somewhat the meaning of the latter. The word 'preserved' seems to imply that we have had such flexibility of relative wages in the past; but the passage quoted comes immediately after a statement that the forces of supply and demand are apt to be impaired by the 'persistence of customary differentials, based on abstract notions about the comparable merits of different types of job and no longer corresponding to contemporary requirements'. Perhaps we should assume that in the Council's view, there had been *some* of the desired flexibility, but not as much as they would have liked.

Nor is it altogether clear what the consequences would be if relative wages do not show the desired flexibility. Perhaps the most natural meaning is that too few workers would be attracted to occupations or industries which ought to expand, whilst too many would remain attached to industries which are contracting. It is easy enough to picture the consequences of the first of these. For example, in the immediate post-war years there was a shortage of typists, which particularly affected government departments, where the typists' wage was fixed by a scale in which the typist had traditionally occupied a relatively low place. So long as no more than this wage was offered for a typist, government departments found that they suffered from a chronic shortage and could not in fairness prevent some of their typists from applying to be promoted to vacancies in other ranks in the service where they were much less needed but where the pay was higher. The result was a 'bottle-neck', revealed to the public in the form of duplicated letters sent to inquirers saying that their letter had been received, and that a reply had been drafted and sent to Scotland for typing.

So far as the contracting industries are concerned, however, the position is not so clear. There is usually nothing which compels an employer to retain workers whom he does not need – at the very least, he can refrain from replacing normal wastage. Consequently, even if the relative wage is not lowered in the way regarded by the Cohen Report as desirable, there seems no reason to suppose that the numbers *in employment* in the industry will fail to contract. And it seems unrealistic to think that an undesirably large number of workers will remain 'attached' to the industry on the strength of a maintained wage-rate, if a sizeable proportion of them are unable to find a job at that wage; unemployment is at least as powerful an incentive to move elsewhere as a wage-cut *for the people affected*.

The Cohen Council would, I think, hardly deny that contractions in an industry's labour force, or in the number of some particular type of workers, can be secured without a fall in relative wages, through dismissals and non-replacement of wastage. The argument in favour of wage flexibility here would have to run in more subtle terms. Thus, they might argue that a wage-cut would reduce the number of transfers needed, and so the risk of unemployment – e.g. by enabling the industry to quote lower prices, or by making it possible to continue a little longer the use of traditional craftsmen rather than to switch entirely to machines. Or they might argue that dismissals are liable to be concentrated on workers who cannot easily transfer to other jobs, whilst a lowering of the wage would stimulate mobile people to leave, and let the immobile stay at work. Or they might advocate wage-cuts in contracting industries and occupations on quite other grounds, such as the need to keep down the general level of prices.

There may be some force in these arguments, but for the question in hand – the distribution of labour between industries and occupations – they are probably secondary: an industry's labour force clearly *can* be contracted without a cut in relative wages, by a reduction in the jobs offered. Moreover, the labour market is inevitably not left to the unfettered working of atomistic competition, and the co-operation of the unions is likely to be needed both over a sound system of redundancies and over measures to raise productivity (and so the wage which can be paid to a reduced labour force). There are real advantages in not *also* asking them to agree to a major cut in their customary differential in the interests of 'wage flexibility'.

The real question comes with industries or occupations in which the demand for labour is expanding. In a sense, perhaps the difference between the two view-points is only a matter of degree. Clearly, the industries cannot expand without an increased number of jobs being offered – the advocates of wage flexibility doubtless 'take that as read', and would hardly deny that some expansion can be secured by that means alone.[2] On the other side, it is not denied that an increase in relative wages would help, and might indeed on occasions be essential – especially if it is a matter of increasing greatly the number of people in an occupation which traditionally carried a low wage. In particular, the difference of views would be small if the advocates of wage flexibility believe that workers will respond freely to a *very small* change in relative wages – assuming of course that it is backed up by an increased number of jobs being offered in expanding industries, and by dismissals in contracting ones. The proponents of the alternative hypothesis might then say that they find it hard to believe that an industry can recruit workers easily by offering an improvement of (say) 2% in the relative wage, but that this 'flexibility' is vital: they might well add, however, that the issue is of no real importance on that basis, because such a small change, if vital, will be easily secured – if only through better chances of earning over-time or securing promotion in an industry which is short of labour.

The Cohen Council did not, however, say that very small changes in relative wages would suffice; indeed, by implication they seemed to deny this, since they regarded it as 'most important' to have flexibility of relative wages in response to changes in the demand for labour, and in effect contrasted this with the views about 'fair wages' and the like which are stressed in a process of collective bargaining. There is therefore an issue of practical importance: is it really necessary to try to persuade negotiators to change their ways or not? What would this process of education mean, and could it be achieved if considered desirable?

The changes would not be all on the unions' side, though one tends to think first of persuading them to agree that wages in

2. In text-books on supply and demand the quantity offered in a market is commonly represented as depending on the price offered by buyers: this may explain why economists are liable to underestimate the extent to which the quantity offered responds to increases in the quantity demanded without any change in price, especially if the increased supplies are actively sought. Such a response can be particularly important if the demand progressively grows at a modest pace – as often happens in the labour market.

contracting industries should be reduced, 'even though highly skilled workers would then be earning no more than routine workers elsewhere'. Wage flexibility would also require that employers should not be inhibited in *raising* the pay of a type of labour which is scarce at the moment by views about 'customary differentials' or the inherent skills involved (or not involved). Moreover, the policy would not work unless both sides assumed that wages in future would similarly be settled in the light of circumstances *then* prevailing. It must be at least tacitly agreed that acceptance of a low wage now, because there is too much labour in the industry, would not in any way imply continuance of that wage when it (and dismissals) had duly diverted the surplus to other industries. Similarly it must be assumed that payment of scarcity rates of wages now would not imply their continuance after more workers had been attracted.

So far as the distribution of labour is concerned, the most important part of the change would be the acceptance of the view that wages should be freely raised above their normal rating for types of workers in short supply (and then freely lowered again if and when the shortage is overcome). Failure to get cuts in relative wages in declining industries would not, as we saw above, prevent their labour force from declining: dismissals are a substitute for low wages as a means of diverting workers, whereas there is no corresponding 'forcible' means of securing an increased labour force if the wage is too low to attract workers (even when supported by vigorous advertising of vacancies, etc.).

This asymmetry may perhaps provide an additional reason – over and above the simple influence of 'job opportunities' – why the distribution of labour has been reasonably responsive to changes in the demand for labour, even though the negotiators of collective agreements have not made that an overriding principle in fixing their bargains. For employers with an expanding demand who find that they cannot attract recruits for the jobs which they offer are not usually prohibited from offering higher pay, and this latitude may well have been used to overcome real bottle-necks.

The Role of Research

What, then, can research into the facts do to throw light on the need, or lack of need, for a campaign to influence the principles followed in wage-fixing? The answer seems to be that it can establish nothing conclusively, but that it is nevertheless helpful to examine such things as the extent to which industries which have changed their relative share of the labour force have in fact raised (or lowered) the wages which they pay relative to the average, or have ended up by paying more or less than the average. The *amount* of the movement in relative wages is important, as well as the frequency with which expanding industries have had to improve their relative pay.

The limited objective of such procedure must be stressed:

(*a*) It is concerned solely with finding out what did happen – not with whether some other method of reaching the new labour force would have been possible or preferable. (As already stressed, the 'job opportunity' theory does not in any way deny that it is *easier* to fill vacancies if you raise the pay: we do not need research in order to establish that most people prefer a job with higher pay to one with lower pay if they consider that other things are equal and the choice is effectively open to them at the critical moment.)

(*b*) For the moment at least we are not concerned with causation, merely with what things are associated. Thus, higher numbers might be associated with higher relative wages because the unions seized the opportunity to demand these, although the additional workers would in fact have come if the job opportunities had been made available without the rise in wages. Lower numbers might fail to be associated with lower relative wages because the unions in contracting industries were strong enough to resist a cut, even though the individual workers might have preferred a lower relative wage and a smaller risk of dismissal.

(*c*) In particular, it is always *possible* that an increase in numbers originated from a change on the supply side, which was independent either of the wage offered or of job opportunities. Thus, the great increase in the number of clerks and other white-collar workers which has been observed over the last half-century or more, despite a fall in their relative wages, is clearly to be explained mainly by the system of universal education. It would not, of course, have happened if the number of job opportunities in this line had not grown greatly with the greater complexity of life in a wealthier community; but without the improved educational system it *might* have been necessary for employers, in order to attract the necessary numbers, to raise the relative wage offered, instead of lowering it.[3]

When the facts have been assembled, it will be possible to review alternative interpretations of them. But further discussion of that is best left to [p. 194].

The Data

Manufacturing industries taken singly

The first set of data presented relates to the 111 separate manufacturing industries covered by the Ministry of Labour's earnings inquiries.[4] For each of these we have the average hourly earnings

3. The obverse of the above case is more complex, but really lies outside the scope of this article. The number of people doing various labouring jobs, of a simple but often disagreeable kind, has fallen, whilst their wage has risen relatively to the average (though usually remaining below it). This is partly because improved education has reduced the number of people incapable of holding a better post, but largely because full employment has greatly increased the number of better posts which are in fact available. The case for wage flexibility as against customary differentials is probably at its strongest when stressing the need for paying enough for such 'dirty' jobs to attract the numbers whom we need; in a sense it is a testimony to the power of job opportunities (plus mechanization and selective immigration) that we are not suffering from acute shortages of some goods and services which used this type of labour.

4. For *employment*, the figures used are the Ministry of Labour statistics for May of each year, and for hourly *earnings* the Ministry's returns for April of each year.

The years used were selected essentially on the basis of convenient availability of figures at the time the research was done. *Average earnings* were used rather than agreed wage-rates for two reasons: (*a*) wage-rates were not available for all the various industries; (*b*) it was considered desirable to work with statistics of actual payments, rather than agreed rates, since otherwise the force of 'wage attraction' would be underestimated by omitting the influence of changes in the extent to which employers pay more than

of men in April 1951 and April 1956, so that we know the percentage increase over the period. We also know the percentage movement from 1951 to 1956 in the number of males employed. Each industry therefore provides one point or observation in the diagram (p. 190), which gives a convenient way of seeing two things:

(a) What sort of movements took place, both in wages and employment; and, in particular, how varied the movements were in each case from industry to industry.

(b) How far industries with a high increase in employment also had a high increase in wages.

So far as the actual movements are concerned, the results can be summarized as follows:

Employment. The average change in numbers employed was an increase over the five years of 5·3%, but the individual industries showed very great variations – far greater, perhaps, than one might expect from some discussions of the rigidity produced by the welfare state and its full employment pledge. Without taking the individual extreme cases, we can note that 10 industries showed increases of over 30%, and 10 showed *decreases* of more than 15%. If we want a more conservative indicator of the variations, we can say that one-third (37) of the industries showed rises

---

the agreed rates. *Hourly* earnings were used in preference to *weekly*, so as to minimize the influence of short-time and overtime work in the week in question, which might be purely ephemeral factors. (To the extent that overtime is paid at more than the ordinary time rate, some influence of overtime does remain in the hourly figures.) Figures for *men* were used rather than those for 'all workers', so as to avoid any distortion of the earnings comparison which might be produced by changing proportions of women and juveniles as between the two years. A separate calculation might have been made for *women*, but the statistics would have been of no real use in a fair proportion of industries, where the number of women employed is very small; it was not found necessary to reject any industry on grounds of an inadequate number of men. The fact that the employment statistics relate to *all males*, rather than to *men*, is thought unlikely to make any significant difference to the comparison; figures for men only were not available. Similarly, the fact that the earnings figures relate to the United Kingdom, whilst the employment figures relate to Great Britain only, is considered unlikely to make any significant difference to a comparison of *movements*.

of 9·6% or more, and one-third showed falls of 2·5% or more. Whatever the mechanism, big changes in the distribution of labour were in fact effected.

Hourly earnings. The average increase in hourly earnings over the five years was 42·3% – measured, of course, in money. By comparison with the movements in employment, however, the

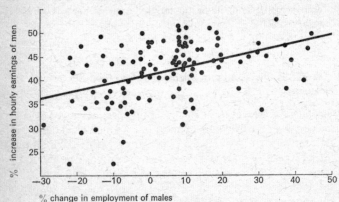

Notes: 1. Each dot represents one industry
2. The line down (regression of y on x) has equation $y = 41.5 + 0.165x$
3. The aircraft industry had too large an increase in employment (62.3%) to include in the figure; its earnings increase was 52.3%

Percentage changes 1951–56 in employment and hourly earnings in 111 manufacturing industries

variations from industry to industry were much smaller. If, as before, we exclude the top and bottom ten, the range is from 33% to 50%; if we exclude one-third at each end, we find that the middle third is in the narrow range from 40·8% to 45·2%.

How far, then, do the biggest increases in employment tend to go with the biggest increases in earnings? The diagram gives a general picture: there clearly is some tendency for this to happen – the points show some tendency to cluster round a line running from the south-west to the north-east. But the association is not very close.

This general impression may perhaps be clearer from table 1, which summarizes the diagram by dividing the industries into 'high', 'medium', and 'low' groups in respect of both employment change and earnings change. There is clearly a tendency for an industry which is rated high on employment increase to be rated high on wage increase also: 56 out of the 111 industries (i.e. one half) get the same rating on each test. But these ratings are very broad, and even so there are some interesting exceptions: 8 industries which come in the top category for employment increase come in the bottom one for wage increase.[5]

Table 1

Cross-Classification of 111 Manufacturing Industries by Percentage Changes between 1951 and 1956 in:

(a) number of males employed

(b) average hourly earnings of men

% Increase in earnings	% Change in employment Decrease of 2·5 or more	−2·5 to +9·3	+9·6 and over	Total
45·2 and above	5	15	17	37
40·8–45·2	9	16	12	37
up to 40·5	23	6	8	37
Total	37	37	37	111

One final statistical device is also useful. A straight line has been fitted to the diagram so as to tell us what value of the wage-change one will *tend* to find in an industry whose employment change is of any size we may select. The equation is given under the diagram: expressed in words it tells us, for example, that an industry with an employment change 10% greater than the average (i.e. 15·3% instead of 5·3%) will *tend* to have a wage

5. It is also useful to express the result in a statistical measure, the correlation coefficient, which is about 0·43. The square of this coefficient (0·185) tells us that between one-sixth and one-fifth of the variations in one of the variables (e.g. wage movements) from its mean can be 'explained' by reference to the variation in the other; it cannot of course tell us anything about the *causal* process. This degree of statistical explanation is *interesting* – the figure is far too high for one to say that it has arisen as a matter of statistical chance – but the explanation is clearly far from complete.

increase 1·7% greater than the average (i.e. 44% instead of 42·3%). The emphasis here must, however, be strongly on the word 'tend': the diagram shows that in some industries the actual wage increase was very different from the one indicated by the line.

Manufacturing industries by groups

Before attempting to interpret these results, it is useful to see the picture as it emerges when the various industries are grouped into the 14 industrial orders used in the Standard Industrial Classification (i.e. when we have, for example, a single employment figure for 'textiles', instead of 15 separate ones for cotton spinning, cotton weaving, wool, and so on).

The result is shown in table 2, in which the orders have been arranged according to the size of their change in employment. On this basis there is, as was to be expected, a smaller spread of movements in employment, though it is still considerable. The greatest increase shown by a single order is 18·7% (for vehicles), and the biggest fall is 17·2% (for leather, etc.). Without these two extreme cases, the range is from +13·3 to −8·9%. For *earnings* movements the spread is also somewhat reduced, but not very much: without the highest and lowest orders the increases range from 48·6 to 34·1%, which is not much less than we obtained for the individual industries, after cutting out ten at each extremity.

The most striking feature of the results is, however, the much more marked association between the two movements. All the highest increases in earnings come near the top of the table and all the lowest near the bottom. The orders were in fact arranged according to the size of their employment movement, but they are also roughly in the order of their rise in earnings. In statistical terms, the correlation coefficient has indeed gone up from 0·43 to 0·92; more significantly, its square has gone up from 0·185 to 0·85 – and even with perfect correlation (i.e. all points exactly on the regression line)[6] the coefficient is only 1·0.

6. The equation of the regression line is now $y = 40·5 + 0·508x$. In words, this says that an order with an employment increase 10% greater than the average will tend to have an earnings increase 5% greater than the average. If one used this formula to 'predict' the change in wages for an order with a given change in employment, one would now be fairly near the mark in most cases – the worst exception being paper and printing, with an actual wage increase of 49·5% instead of a calculated one of 45·9%.

Table 2

Industrial order	Changes 1951–6 in number of males employed	Rise 1951–6 in average hourly earnings of men	
	%	% Deviation from average rise	Actual % rise
Vehicles	+18·7	+12·0	47·0
Engineering, shipbuilding, electrical goods	+13·3	+15·9	48·6
Paper and printing	+10·8	+18·0	49·5
Chemicals, etc.	+9·4	+4·4	43·8
Miscellaneous manufacturing	+7·8	+3·9	43·6
Metal manufacture	+5·5	+9·4	45·9
Food, drink, and tobacco	+5·1	+3·9	43·6
Precision instruments, jewellery etc.	+4·8	+2·0	42·8
Bricks, china, glass, etc.	+3·6	−3·0	40·7
Miscellaneous metals	+2·8	+5·1	44·1
Wood and cork	−7·1	−19·4	33·8
Clothing	−8·2	−15·6	35·4
Textiles	−8·9	−18·0	34·4
Leather, etc.	−17·2	−18·7	34·1
Average	+2·87		41·9

Industries within the groups

In view of the pictures revealed in the above two sections, it is of importance also to examine the movements in employment and earnings for the industries *within* each of the various orders. Unfortunately, this information is not so easy to present in detail, but the general conclusion is clear enough.

The engineering order (more strictly, 'engineering, shipbuilding, and electrical goods') will serve as a good illustration. The 17 industries comprised within this order show a very wide range of employment movements between 1951 and 1956, ranging from three decreases (including one of 17% for textile machinery) to two increases of over 40% (for wireless apparatus, etc., and valves, etc.). On the other hand, the *earnings* movements are all grouped within a rather narrow range, from 40·2 to 52·9%; indeed twelve of them fall within the range 45 to 50%. Moreover, statistical analysis shows no real association between the movements. In effect, the industries all have much the same wage-movement but widely different movements in employment; and there is no significant tendency for such variations in wage-movement as there are to be associated with variations in the same direction for employment.

The other orders do not all show quite such clear-cut results, and many of them have too few industries within them to permit much of a conclusion.[7] Nevertheless, it is a fair general summary to say that within an order the wage-movements are usually fairly similar, and that the association between wage-movements and employment movements is negligible.[8]

Interpretation of the Results

Before attempting to give interpretation of all these results, one must start by re-emphasizing the point that they cannot possibly *prove* anything: the most that one can hope to do is to see what they *suggest*, and in particular to see whether the results are of the kind one would expect on various assumptions. Apart from anything else, there are too many different ways in which the things react, or may react, upon one another: a higher wage might be necessary to attract workers to an expanding industry, or it might simply reflect the fact that the union concerned has

7. The results for orders with more than twelve industries are:

Food drink, and tobacco $r^2 = 0·004$
$r^2 = 0·24$ Textiles

It is also interesting to note that if we expand the 'engineering' group to include vehicles, r^2 is still negligible (0·058); and if we also include metal manufacture and metal goods to give one big 'metal' group, 32 out of 38 industries show wage-increases between 40% and 50%, and r^2 is again negligible (0·073).

8. The correlation in several orders, including engineering, is weakly *negative*: this is the sort of result which chance factors would be likely to produce if there were no significant underlying tendency for the two variables to be associated within an order.

taken advantage of the increasing level of demand to negotiate a higher wage, even though enough workers would in fact have been forthcoming at the old wage in response to offers of employment. We cannot hope to establish that the wage increase was *necessary* to attract workers, we can only see what in fact *happened*. Similarly, we cannot be sure that the expanding industries attracted as many workers as they would have liked, but can only measure how many they did in fact attract.

With this general warning, it is perhaps helpful to consider two ways in which people might attempt to summarize the probable conclusions to be learnt. They are deliberately put in a slightly extreme form, in order to clarify the issue, but of course there is no reason why one should not believe that some element of what each says is really embodied in the true explanation.

The first way of presenting the conclusions, which might appeal to somebody starting from the ideas embodied in the Cohen Report, could be set out as follows:

Within the individual industrial orders, workers move freely from one industry to another, without needing any significant incentive in the way of differential wages. It is perhaps a little paradoxical to find that the expanding industries within the order are as likely to show a wage increase below the average as they are to show one above the average, but the differences are usually not great, and this result might perhaps be due to imperfections in the statistics or purely 'chance' causes. In particular, expanding industries often have to take a bigger proportion of learners or people in junior grades; this tends to lower the average earnings, even though the industry may be paying well to each grade.

When one comes, however, to a question of increasing the size of one industrial order relatively to the size of others, the problem of movement is a much more substantial one, and the statistics suggest that it requires a significant change in relative wages to induce workers to move. On the whole, it is reassuring to find that these wage differentials do not have to be *very* large: an order which expanded its employment by 10% more than the average (a substantial change) only raised its relative wage by some $3\frac{1}{2}\%$.[9] But our original view that wage flexibility of this kind was important is supported by the statistics for the 14 orders.

9. As a percentage of 1951, earnings in 1956 would be: 'average' order 144%, 'expanding' order 149% – a change in relative wages of about $3\frac{1}{2}\%$.

A second view, which would perhaps appeal more naturally to somebody starting from the ideas embodied in the 'alternative hypothesis' might be set out as follows:

The figures for the industries within the various orders show that it is possible for industries to expand very substantially without any change in relative wages. This seems to be a clear illustration of the power of 'job opportunities' to secure changes in the distribution of labour, without having to invoke the aid of changes in relative wages. The fact that in some orders the expanding industries had the smaller wage increase is particularly suggestive on this point.

The high correlation between wage increases and employment increases for the 14 orders might at first sight suggest that this was necessary to enable the expanding industries to secure additional workers. An alternative possibility, however, is simply that the more employers in an order wanted to expand, the more the union(s) concerned insisted on higher wages, even though the workers might have been attracted without the increase in wages. This also explains the position at the bottom end, since a contracting industry is commonly one in which the ordinary processes of collective bargaining would lead to smaller wage increases than elsewhere. One cannot say that cuts in relative wages in the contracting orders were *necessary* to get rid of the workers, since the employers could always reduce their labour force by non-replacement or dismissals. This is not to deny that the movement of relative wages may have *helped* somewhat to secure the change in the distribution of labour, with less need for expanding industries to have continuous active recruiting campaigns; but the experience within the individual orders suggests that probably the only thing really *needed* was a good supply of job opportunities at a wage regarded as 'acceptable' according to conventions which are more social than economic.

In part the difference between the two positions is one of words rather than of substance, but there are some points of real importance to be made.

First, the imaginary 'Cohen' view is trying to gloss over much too easily the striking difference between the results *within* an order and *between* orders. In many cases, perhaps most, it is just not true that movement from one industry to another within an order is easy; in many cases there is only a very broad similarity in the type of work and the industries are in quite different locations. Indeed, there is no real presumption that the expanding industries within the food, drink, and tobacco order, for example, recruited many workers from the contracting ones: each expanding firm simply drew on the general pool of labour in its district, whilst the contracting ones largely allowed wastage to operate. Thus, the two industries with the biggest expansion of employment are chocolate and sugar confectionery ($+39\%$) and biscuits ($+36\%$); the two biggest contractions are bread, etc., baking, (-11%) and tobacco (-9%). Doubtless the biscuit industry recruited some displaced bread-bakers but there does not seem to be much other scope for simple movement, and the biscuit industry is much more highly localized.[10] The earnings-increases were all much the same, except that tobacco showed a significantly *higher* one than any other industry in the order. There is clearly some force which produced the big changes in the distribution of labour, and there seems no reason to look beyond the 'obvious' one, which we have christened job opportunities. Nobody need *regret* the fact that substantial changes in the distribution of labour can be secured in response to changing demands without the need for 'corresponding' changes in the wage-pattern, which would be hard to secure.

What, then, of the very high correlation at the 'order' level between movements in employment and in earnings? Is the 'alternative explanation' entitled to dismiss this as something which was likely to emerge from the process of wage bargaining, but which had little or no effect in helping to secure the redistribution of the labour force? And if so, ought not the imaginary proponent also to explain why the process of wage bargaining did not produce the same sort of result within the orders?

It is easiest to take the second question first. If one follows the idea that wage bargains are largely determined by 'social' and 'conventional' considerations, then it is not difficult to understand why the various industries within an order tend to have much the same wage increase, despite the differences in both their character and their fortune. In some cases there is really only a single bargain covering the whole of an order, or virtually the whole (e.g. engineering). In orders, it is regarded as almost

10. Similarly, in the engineering order there is no 'easy' transfer from the declining textile machinery industry to the expanding radio and television; in vehicles, the expanding aircraft industry would not draw on the contracting locomotive manufacture; and so on.

axiomatic that the wage increases should be made closely similar to those in some broadly related industry (which will commonly be in the same order, e.g. some other branch of the food industries), even though the labour forces overlap only to a modest extent if at all, and the fortunes of that industry are moving differently. 'Customary differentials' (or perhaps we should say 'customary relativities, including equalities') are likely to be particularly strong within an order – though there is of course still *some* scope for variations in the wage-movement, particularly for the wages actually paid.

As between orders, the force of these customary relativities is weaker – though it clearly still exists, and the boundary of the statistical order is not necessarily the crucial point at which the pattern can most easily be distorted. The people who stress the social and conventional factors in wage bargaining would not perhaps *expect* a high correlation between movements in employment and in wages at the 'order' level;[11] but this result would not be particularly *surprising* to them, so long as one adds that the differences in the wage-movement are not very *big*. In a period of full employment, it is quite understandable that the economic forces of changing demand should have a modest, systematic effect on the wage-bargain – and perhaps rather more effect on the wages actually paid – even though the social and conventional factors prevent any real 'flexibility' in relative wages from being established.

This leaves the crucial question of the contribution of the wage-changes to securing the redistribution of labour between orders. The answer seems to me to be essentially a matter of personal judgment. There can be no doubt that the changes in the wage-pattern between orders, though not very substantial, would be operating in the right direction to help secure a redistribution of the labour force. How important they were, and how easily (if at all) the redistribution could have been secured without them, is a matter which cannot be answered by statistics. For my own part, I am inclined to think that their role was probably a fairly

11. Indeed, various previous researches have shown that groups of industries which are expanding their labour force did *not* have particularly big wage increases, but sometimes tended to have one which was below the average.

small one, essentially because the basic units which expand their employment are *not* 'orders', but rather 'industries' or more strictly 'firms'. It seems fairly clear that, where the wage-change was much the same (e.g. within orders), the pattern of the labour force could nevertheless be greatly changed; hence it also seems plausible that substantial changes could have occurred as between industries in different orders, if the wage-change had in fact been much the same there also. In a sense, the 'order' is little more than a convenient statistical abstraction, so far as this problem of redistribution is concerned.

The above view can be only tentative, in the sense that it cannot be proved, and it must not be taken as implying any *objection* to the sort of wage-changes which have occurred as between orders. If one wants to secure a redistribution of the labour force, then obviously it is all to the good if the force of 'wage attraction' is on the whole pulling in the right directions. The most one can conclude is that it is probably not worth while to undertake a difficult campaign to induce wage-negotiators to change their practices, when redistribution seems to be obtainable without such a campaign, largely via the (socially more acceptable) route of varying job opportunities.

Perhaps one may conclude by reverting to the point made towards the end of [the first section]. A campaign to secure wage flexibility on the Cohen lines means attacking inhibitions against 'absurd' wage-increases where labour is short, just as much as inhibitions against 'unfair' wage-cuts where labour is in oversupply. If the campaign is to find its logical justification in the need to secure desirable changes in the distribution of labour, it is the *first* of these which provides the really strong case, and it is at least possible that that half of the campaign would be considerably more successful than the other. Does the prospective gain from a better system for redistributing labour justify the risk of aggravating the rise in prices? Since the one thing which is certain is that very substantial changes in the distribution of labour have been secured (with relatively small changes in relative wages) with the existing system of wage-fixing, that is the crucial question to ask before embarking on a campaign to alter the system.

Part Six **Wage Differentials**

If wage differentials play no part in allocating labour, then
wage differentials may be the product of non-economic forces.
The articles by Turner and Reder present the main competing
explanations of the movement of occupational wage differentials.
According to Turner the narrowing of wage differentials
coincides with the emergence of mass unionism, while in
Reder's view the narrowing of wage differentials is due to
variations in the hiring standards set by employers.

10 M. W. Reder

The Theory of Occupational Wage Differentials

Reder, M. W. (1955) The theory of occupational wage differentials. *Amer. Econ. Rev.*, **44**, 833–52.

Although data on occupational wage patterns are far from plentiful – and, at best, none too firm – there is a body of such material about which some theoretical speculation (and controversy) has arisen.[1] This paper is an attempt to construct a theoretical model which can be used to interpret the existing data, and to clarify some of the points in dispute. Its first section deals with the structure of the model; the second section uses the model to explain temporal changes in American occupational wage differentials; the third deals with interregional and international differentials, while the fourth considers alternative arguments. [The last section] attempts to extend the analysis (previously

1. In addition to other references cited hereafter, readers interested in this literature should consult the following: T. P. Kanninen, 'Occupational wage relationships in manufacturing, 1952–53', *Mo. Lab. Rev.*, vol. 76, (November 1953), pp. 1171–8; K. G. J. C. Knowles and D. J. Robertson, 'Differences between the wages of skilled and unskilled workers, 1880–1950', *Bull. Oxford Inst. Stat.*, vol. 13 (April 1951), pp. 109–27; D. W. Oxnam, 'The relation of unskilled to skilled wage rates in Australia', *Econ. Record*, vol. 26 (June 1950), pp. 112–18; R. A. Lester, 'A range theory of wage differentials', *Indus. Lab. Rel. Rev.*, vol. 5 (July 1952), pp. 483–500; S. Lebergott, 'Wage structures', *Rev. Econ. Stat.*, vol. 29 (November 1947), pp. 274–85; R. L. Raimon, 'The indeterminateness of wages of semi-skilled workers', *Indus. Lab. Rel. Rev.*, vol. 6 (January 1953), pp. 180–94; K. G. J. C. Knowles and T. P. Hill, 'On the difficulties of measuring wage differentials', *Bull. Oxford Inst. Stat.* vol. 16 (November and December 1954), pp. 393–409; L. G. Reynolds, *The structure of labor markets* (New York, 1951), pp. 195–8, 236–40; H. A. Turner, 'Trade unions, differentials and levelling of wages', *Man. School Econ. Soc. Stud.* vol. 20 (September 1952), pp. 227–82; E. H. Phelps-Brown and S. V. Hopkins, 'Seven centuries of building wages', *Economica*, vol. n.s. 22 (August 1955), pp. 195–206; E. E. Muntz, 'The decline in wage differentials based on skill in the United States', *Internat. Lab. Rev.* vol. 71 (June 1955), pp. 575–92.

confined to hourly wage differentials) to the differences in annual incomes that are associated with differences in skill.

Theoretical Considerations

Economic theory has a ready-to-hand technique for analysing the wage differentials associated with skill (hereafter called 'skill differentials' or 'skill margins'); i.e. treat workers of different grades of skill as representing different factors of production, and analyze the behaviour of their relative wage rates by means of the theory of related (factor) markets. However, if not carefully used, this mode of analysis can be highly misleading because the wage rates paid for particular jobs are not analogous to factor prices. The skill and other characteristics of workers who apply for given jobs vary with the state of the labor market, and the wage rates paid on given jobs are therefore affected by 'quality' variations in the job applicants. As the 'quality' variable has not been accorded much attention in wage theory, it will pay us to examine it with some care.

Quality variations in labor markets arise through upgrading and downgrading of members of the labor force relative to the jobs they are to fill. When applicants became scarce, employers tend to lower the minimum standards upon which they insist as a condition for hiring a worker to fill a particular job – and vice versa when applicants become plentiful.[2] These minimal hiring standards may be stated explicitly as age, sex, educational, racial, and other prerequisites that must be satisfied as a precondition of hiring. Or they may be the consequence of the unarticulated habits and prejudices of persons responsible for hiring decisions. But whatever the degree of explicitness, minimum hiring (and firing) standards do exist for most jobs in modern industrial communities.

The prevalence of these hiring standards is so widespread as to make it difficult to find situations from which they are absent. Such situations can be found, but they are rare. Their scarcity can be appreciated if it is remembered that jobs without hiring

2. One set of hiring standards, A, is said to be lower than another, B, if the job applicants meeting A include all who also meet B, as well as some who do not.

requirements are, by definition, jobs for which selection is non-existent (i.e. all applicants are taken) or is made by a process unrelated to any social or economic characteristic of the applicants (e.g. by lot). Jobs where selection among applicants is minimal tend to occur where there is no guarantee of minimum earnings and no capital to injure or destroy; e.g. selling on a 'straight commission' basis; piecework with no guarantee of minimal earnings and no equipment to damage.[3]

The ability to discriminate among job applicants on the basis of putative differences in quality implies that variations in relative scarcity of job applicants can be met by varying either (or both) of two determinants of hiring policy; i.e. employers may adjust: (1) wage rates; (2) hiring standards; or some combination of the two. There are a number of factors that affect the relative emphasis that a given employer will place upon these two factors. A brief survey of these will clear the ground for the succeeding argument:

1. The employer will be particularly concerned with maintaining hiring standards when there is danger of property loss from incompetent workmen, and the prospective amount of such loss is considerable, relative to the difference in wage cost (per unit of product) between superior and inferior workmen. For example, a processor of gem diamonds is not likely to risk using an inexperienced diamond cutter to save the additional expense of hiring one who is fully qualified. Or if very delicate machinery is to be used, an employer is likely to be insistent upon the workers being fully qualified, even if production must be delayed in order to recruit them. Conversely, among assembly-line workers, employers frequently relax hiring standards to speed recruitment.

2. Where agreements among employers against 'labor piracy' are operative, expansion of the firm's labor force will tend to be accomplished more by 'quality deterioration' and less by wage

3. L. H. Fisher, *The harvest labor market in California* (Cambridge, Mass., 1953) gives an example of this type of situation. In California harvesting almost anybody is accepted for employment. However, they are paid a flat piece-rate per box with no guaranteed hourly minimum; as they use practically no equipment, there is no risk in having them work, and therefore the employer can profitably accept any and all comers, once the decision to begin harvesting has been taken.

increases than otherwise. Oligopsonistic agreements in restraint of labor market competition are rarely of a formal nature, but their operation is frequently reported and there is good reason why employers should adhere to them. For if an employer attempts to secure more workers in a 'tight' labor market by raising wages, competing employers are likely to match his increases. And, as knowledge of the wage increase is likely to reach rival employers before it reaches many prospective job applicants, it is unlikely to give the aggressive firm even a temporary advantage.

3. A third factor relates to wage discrimination.[4] If a firm should need additional workers of a particular grade (and cannot obtain them at the going wage rate), it may promote some of its own employees of a lower grade. Promoting workers – new or old – has one advantage over bidding up the wage rate; the increased compensation need be paid only to the promoted workers. But if a wage increase is granted to one worker, others doing similar work – and accustomed to similar rates – must, in practice, get similar increases.

A related advantage of adjusting 'quality rather than price' is the greater ease of downgrading workers as compared with lowering wage rates. Shifting workers, reclassifying jobs, etc., are more or less continuous processes, and therefore not subject to the time-lags attendant upon changing contractual prices, i.e. union wage rates. Furthermore, although unions may and do protest against unfavorable job shifts, they are less prone to resist demotions which affect only a few workers at a time than wage cuts which give many workers a common grievance.

4. Frequently the quality of workers can be improved by training. The costs and yields of such training, relative to existing wage differentials between different grades of labor, are the important factors in determining an employer's choice as between raising wage rates and altering hiring standards.[5] Where needed

4. I am indebted to my colleague, Tibor Scitovsky, for a discussion of this point.
5. It should be noted that we speak of an employer's hiring standards with reference only to a particular job or job-type. This implies that promoting workers within the firm is regarded as *hiring* workers for the job to which they are being promoted.

skill can be acquired in a short period and the margin for skill is large, the tendency (*ceteris paribus*) will be to recruit by changing hiring standards; where the reverse is true, the tendency will be toward raising wage rates.

As workers, once trained, are under no obligation to remain with the employer who bore the cost of their training, employers will not usually invest in such training unless the prospective net gain (if any) from hiring an untrained instead of a trained worker can be realized very quickly. This means, in practice, that employers are reluctant to train workers if it involves a substantial out-of-pocket loss during the training period. Therefore, such training occurs mainly when labor is in such short supply and the demand for output so strong that even the slim marginal contribution of trainees to current output is worth almost as much as their current wage; i.e. such training tends to be concentrated in extreme booms.

In short, there are several important reasons why employers should sometimes prefer to adjust to changes in labor market conditions by altering worker quality[6] together with, or instead of, wage rates. However, both quality and price respond to labor market pressure; the rather notorious stickiness of wage rates is one indication of the importance of quality variation in the labor market.

Now let us examine the implications of this fact for the behavior of skill margins. To do this let us study the behavior of the wage rates[7] paid to the holders of specific jobs. We assume employers aim at minimizing the total cost of producing their chosen rate

6. It is important that our use of the term 'worker quality' should not be misunderstood. It is not implied, necessarily, that workers currently hired (but not hirable under previous standards) are inferior to those previously hired in any sense except that the employer would previously have rejected them. The *wisdom* of hiring policies – from the employer's own viewpoint – is, in many cases, questionable; hiring policies that involve arbitrary age, race, or sex criteria may not be conducive to profit maximization. Furthermore, one wonders whether investing in on-the-job training – and reducing skill differentials – might not be profitable even when labor is plentiful.

7. By wage rates, we mean straight-time hourly earnings. We abstract from the effect of incentive systems, perquisites, and nonpecuniary satisfactions.

of output by adjusting, among other things, the quality of the workers hired for, and the wage rates paid to workers on particular jobs. The wage rates paid (to the holders of particular jobs) will be the higher of (1) the market rate for workers with the characteristics necessary for getting hired and (2) the rate the firm negotiates with the relevant union.[8] Where (2) exceeds (1), the firm is said to have 'labor slack' for the given job;[9] labor slack is manifested by the presence of more applicants who meet its hiring standards (for the given job) than it wishes to hire. As a result, a firm with labor slack is compelled to ration the relevant jobs on the basis of 'first come, first hired', or in some other way that is of no concern to the *employer*.[10] For simplicity, we shall assume that all firms pay the same wage rate and have similar hiring requirements for similar jobs.[11]

Suppose there should be a general increase in demand for all grades of manual labor of such size that (with given wage rates and hiring standards) labor slack is eliminated from the market for every kind of job. Competition for workers able to meet current hiring standards on the most skilled jobs would then tend to raise their wage rates. However, there would be a brake upon this rise because some workers, previously unable to secure employment in the most highly skilled job categories, would be

8. It sometimes happens that employers pursue a 'generous' wage policy; i.e. they pay a wage rate higher than (1) despite the absence of union pressure. We may treat such behavior as though it resulted from collective bargaining; the employer's conscience serves as the worker's bargaining agent.

9. The most frequent occurrence of labor slack is where firms reserve jobs for their current holders without attempting to reduce wages, refusing new applicants as well qualified as those presently employed. Similar situations arise where workers, holding lower-paid jobs in a firm, wait for vacancies in better jobs for which they are as fully qualified as the present incumbents. Nevertheless, the reader should not suppose that the presence of labor slack is evidence of employer irrationality; labor slack is often an unavoidable incident in a long-run policy aimed at making a firm an attractive place to work.

10. It is, of course, possible that the union may be vitally concerned with the method of job rationing adopted.

11. This assumption is for convenience only. Another assumption, implicitly made, is the absence of monopsony power; this, too, is solely for convenience and could easily be dropped if and when necessary.

available at lower rates. Therefore, if the spread between the wage rates of the most skilled and those closest to them in skill should become too large, substitution would tend to occur.[12] This substitution would involve either (1) training the 'inferior' workers or (2) altering the production process (and/or product) somewhat so as to facilitate the use of less skilled workers or some combination of the two.[13]

But whatever the process, the substitution of less for more skilled workers reduces (*ceteris paribus*) the supply of persons possessing specified minimum qualifications[14] who are available for jobs requiring less than the highest degree of skill. This would tend to raise the equilibrium rates paid on these jobs; however, it is possible to substitute less for more skilled workers on these jobs also. This, in turn, reduces the supply of workers holding still less skilled jobs, etc. Now if we assume what is often contrary to fact – full employment and a fixed size of labor force – it follows that the supply of labor for the least skilled jobs could not be increased by attracting those employed on still less attractive jobs (or unemployed). Hence employers wishing to use the cheapest grade of labor would have to scramble for a reduced supply, tending to drive up the wage rate.

It cannot be *deduced* from this consideration that, under the specified conditions, wage rates paid on the lowest grade of jobs would rise proportionately more than the rates on others. But if for other reasons we knew that this did occur, then the relatively greater reduction in the supply of workers available for

12. This does not require that there be a great deal of worker mobility among firms. Much of this substitution may occur via intrafirm promotions and the remainder by hiring some new job applicants at higher job grades than they had previously held.

13. Where there is labor slack, this process of substitution is costless (requiring no adjustment whatever) and inhibits any rise in skilled wage rates.

14. Including, where relevant, being in an appropriate place on a promotion list. For the sake of brevity, we assume that workers substituted 'up the job hierarchy' have hitherto held less skilled jobs than those to which they have been promoted. In some cases this is contrary to fact; jobs sometimes command a premium because of tradition. However, the interrelation among skill and other attributes (education, sex, race, etc.) that are related to labor market premiums is so great as to make it reasonable to assume that a relaxation of hiring standards implies a sacrifice of skill.

these jobs would afford an important clue to the explanation of its occurrence. And, as we shall see under 'Evidence Bearing on the Theory', page 213, skill margins have varied with labor demand in the manner indicated in those cases where the 'labor reserve' had been absorbed. Accordingly, we offer the hypothesis that the association of short-period variations in skill margins with the level of aggregate employment is due to the fact that a rise in the level of employment for all grades of labor reduces the supply of labor available for unskilled jobs (at initial wage rates) proportionately more than it reduces the supply available for others. This hypothesis is presumed to hold only when labor demand increases sufficiently to absorb the labor reserve; the operational significance of this proviso will be indicated below.

It is not alleged that there is any particular pattern of variation among the wage rates for skilled and semiskilled jobs. It is alleged only that, under the conditions specified, rates on unskilled jobs are driven up relatively to those on semiskilled (which compete most keenly for labor with the unskilled jobs) and that this, in turn, results in a diminution in the spread between the rates on skilled and unskilled jobs.

But before accepting this hypothesis, it is necessary to consider the effects of unemployment and of a variable size of labor force. It is well known that the business sector of most economies usually possesses a labor reserve in the form of unemployed work-seekers, low-income farm youths, oldsters, juveniles, housewives, etc., who will accept jobs in the business or government sectors of the economy at going wage rates whenever such jobs are available. As the bulk of these persons are available for unskilled jobs, they serve as a replacement for the unskilled workers attracted to better jobs. Therefore, an increase in aggregate labor demand would not be expected to affect skill margins (as far as our hypothesis is concerned), unless the increase were more than sufficient to absorb the entire labor reserve at going wage rates. However, when such large increases do occur, within a short-period (e.g. during both world wars), skill margins would be expected to contract – and they have.[15]

15. The reader should not suppose that the existence of a labor reserve is a special case of labor slack. The workers in the labor reserve may (although they need not) be inferior to those regularly employed.

Now let us consider the implications of the labor reserve concept for wage theory. Allegation of the existence of a labor reserve immediately provokes the question, 'Why doesn't the unskilled wage rate fall until the labor reserve's members either find employment or cease to desire it?' The answer lies in what we shall, for brevity, call *SM* (for social minimum). *SM* is the minimum (straight-time) hourly wage rate at which a business firm or government – as distinguished from a household or family farm – can hire an hour of labor. *SM* may be set by statute (e.g. a minimum wage law), by social custom and/or by trade union policy. *SM* is also related, indirectly, to the assistance from social security, friends, family, etc., that a wage earner can obtain. However, when *SM* is not effectively set by statute or union policy, it becomes a very slippery concept. Therefore we shall treat *SM* as established by statute or effective union policy, although its bases are far more complicated than this assumption would suggest.

SM is often set higher for men than for women, for workers in the prime of life than for juveniles or aged workers; also, it tends to vary in the same direction as living costs. It is not an absolute minimum rate below which workers are never hired; it is a rate below which workers, especially adult males in the prime of life, are not hired by a business firm or government. However, households often hire servants, men, and boys for odd jobs, etc., on whatever terms they can obtain them. Also travelers 'hire' porters, etc., for tips; and on family farms, the members share in what the 'enterprise' earns. Indeed, when there is substantial unemployment, the unemployed have frequently set themselves up as small entrepreneurs (e.g. in garment-making and retail trade). They are able to pay their employees only on some sort of receipts-sharing basis; this implies little more than that wages will not be negative.

In the midst of large-scale unemployment, such attempts at self-help are not likely to be obstructed; but whether substantial businesses can exploit the existence of unemployment to reduce the wage rates they pay their workers below some minimum level depends upon social attitudes. For example, in early nineteenth-century England (under the famous Speenhamland system), workers would frequently eke out a 'surviving' by combining

parish aid and wages.[16] And, apparently, it was not then considered improper to hire labor that required public assistance in
order to survive. But nowadays it would certainly be considered
improper, when not illegal, to employ labor and at a wage so
low that it had to be supplemented by public assistance; and it
would be illegal for workers to accept most forms of public
assistance while employed. In short, we now have laws and mores
that place a floor under the minimum wage rate that a worker
need or will accept on a 'steady job' with a business firm or
government.

Outside the business and government sectors, there is really no
effective minimum to wage rates, except reluctance to accept
employment at still lower rates. Whether an unemployed worker
accepts on offer of a 'day's' casual employment depends upon
(1) the relative importance of the earnings as compared with his
leisure (and shame at working for too little) and (2) his expectation of finding a more attractive employment opportunity during
the 'day', if he keeps looking. Wage rates paid on odd jobs are
rarely recorded; but, we suspect, they are subject to marked short-
period fluctuations and considerable dispersion on any given day.
In other words, unskilled wage rates have downward rigidity
only in the business and government sectors; elsewhere, they are
determined in a 'classical' manner. Unemployment is, therefore,
either voluntary or frictional. However, the frictions (e.g. imperfect communication, intermittent demand, geographic immobility,
etc.) that impede the operation of labor markets outside the business and government sectors are far greater than 'classical' wage
theory would suggest.

Evidence Bearing on the Theory

Let us first consider the evidence against which it may be possible
to test the hypothesis concerning the behavior of skill margins
during large short-period increases in employment. If the hypothesis were true, it would follow that, in periods of general labor
shortage, the skill margin would tend to decline. Table 1 indicates

16. J. H. Clapham, *An economic history of modern Britain, 1820–1850*,
2nd edn (Cambridge, England, 1950), p. 124 *et seq.* and p. 357 *et seq.*;
also P. Mantoux, *The industrial revolution in the eighteenth century*, 2nd edn
(London, 1928), pp. 447–50.

Table 1
Margins for Skill in the United States, 1907–47

A. Manufacturing industries

Year	Median skill Margin *
1907	205
1918–19	175
1931–2	180
1937–40	165
1945–7	155

B. Building industries

Year	Skill margin	Year	Skill margin
1907	185	1931	179
1908	188	1932	179
1909	191	1933	182
1910	192	1934	178
1911	195	1935	179
1912	197	1936	175
1913	197	1937	172
1914	199	1938	170
1915	199	1939	170
1916	199	1940	169
1917	191	1941	167
1918	183	1942	160
1919	180	1943	159
1920	166	1944	158
1921	168	1945	154
1922	174	1946	147
1923	180	1947	143
1924	180	1948	140
1925	181	1949	141
1926	177	1950	139
1927	180	1951	138
1928	179	1952	138
1929	179		
1930	177		

Sources: for 1907–47, Harry Ober, 'Occupational wage differentials, 1907–47', *Mo. Lab. Rev.*, vol. 67 (August 1948), p. 130; for 1948–52, H. M. Douty, 'Union impact on wage structures', *Proc. Indus. Rel. Res. Assoc.*, (1953), pp. 61–76.

* The median skill margin is the median of the ratios of the straight time average hourly earnings of the skilled workers (in various manufacturing industries) to those of the unskilled.

that this is what occurred during both world wars; indeed, that this happened is a matter of common knowledge.[17] There is no definite evidence that the skill margin has any very definite cyclical pattern apart from the tendency to shrink during wartime (major) booms. But our hypothesis does not imply that it should vary with *small* changes in business conditions; the 'ordinary' period of prosperity does not usually absorb a large enough fraction of the labor reserve to induce a sharp rise in unskilled rates. It is only in the really big outbursts of economic expansion that this occurs – at least in present-day Western countries.

But there is more evidence for our hypothesis than the behavior of wage rates; the hypothesis implies that when aggregate labor demand increases sufficiently there will be a tendency for the manual labor force, especially the unskilled, to move toward better jobs and for their places to be filled, if at all, by erstwhile members of the labor reserve. This implies a shift of workers from agriculture to industry, from unskilled to semiskilled jobs, etc. And, it is common knowledge that this has happened in the United States during both world wars and in the full employment period since 1945;[18] it has also occurred, during the same periods, in other countries.

Unfortunately, our hypothesis does not seem to be 'reversible'. That is, the skill margin does not seem consistently to widen during major depressions – conversely to what happens during major booms. In the two major depressions, 1920–1 and 1929–33

17. Behavior similar to that presented in table 1 is to be found also in book and job printing. The annual data for 1907–46 are presented in Appendix, table 117, pp. 761–2 of W. S. Woytinsky and associates, *Employment and wages in the United States* (New York, 1953). In the building industries there was a substantial widening of the skill margin between 1907 and 1914. However, this tendency did not appear in the printing trades, and it is therefore difficult to determine which industry was more 'representative'. In the absence of additional information, speculation is pointless.

18. See H. S. Parnes, *Research on labor mobility*, Social Science Research Council Bull., no. 65 (1954), pp. 91–3, and the literature cited therein. Further evidence will be found in the report of the National Manpower Council, *A policy for skilled manpower* (New York, 1954), Chs. 2, 8, and 9, esp. pp. 76–80, 236–8. Also Harold Goldstein, 'The changing occupational structure', *Mo. Lab. Rev.*, vol. 65 (December 1947), pp. 654–9.

(the only ones for which we have data), the skill margin widened during the former, but did not change much – if at all – during the latter. The different behavior of the skill margin during the two depressions can be 'rationalized' as follows: the 1920–1 depression followed hard upon the First World War labor shortage during which skill margins declined and hiring standards loosened substantially. The depression of 1920–1 largely represented a return to prewar 'equilibrium' skill margins and hiring standard.[19] The fact that unions in the skilled trades survived the depression of 1920–1 far better than those in the unskilled trades contributed, no doubt, to the greater decline in unskilled rates. However, it is submitted that the greater strength of the skilled unions was largely the result of employer policy governing hiring standards.[20]

The situation in the 1929–33 depression was different – especially in the market for unskilled labor. Unlike the situation a decade earlier, wage cutting – particularly for low-wage earners – was widely condemned, and many employers, especially larger ones, were very reluctant to cut the wages of unskilled workers as much as market forces alone might have dictated.[21] In terms of the analysis [in the first section], the unskilled wage rate in 1920–21 was well above SM, and subject to downward pressure. But the ideology of 'welfare capitalism' and the general social climate of the 1920s so raised SM that, by 1929, it had more or less caught up with the prevailing wages rates for unskilled labor. In many situations, this hampered the operation of market forces upon unskilled wage rates; this was especially true for large and

19. In the period since the Second World War, there has been no major depression, and increasing demand for workers in skilled and semiskilled jobs has maintained an upward pressure on unskilled rates in the United States, causing a further diminution in skill margins. T. P. Kanninen, op. cit., p. 1171, reports that the skill margin of 55% reported in 1947 had been reduced to 37% by 1952–3.

20. i.e. employers could not get 'adequate' substitutes for skilled workers to operate during a strike, but could do so in the case of unskilled strikers. The interested reader may consult S. Perlman and P. Taft, *History of labor in the United States, 1896–1932* (New York, 1935), chs. 37, 38; Leo Wolman, *Ebb and flow in trade unionism* (New York, 1936), ch. 3.

21. On this point see P. W. Bell, 'Cyclical variations and trends in occupational wage differentials in American industry since 1914', *Rev. Econ. Stat.*, vol. 33 (November 1951), pp. 329–37.

wealthy firms that continued to pay dividends and high salaries throughout the depression.[22]

An upward shift in SM may also be credited with the narrowing of the skill margin from 1933–40. (Considering the level of unemployment, it is hardly likely that this could be explained as the result of a shortage of skilled labor compelling a relative relaxation of hiring requirements.) It would seem reasonable to suppose that New Deal legislation and the associated social climate did boost SM relative to the level of skilled rates. New Deal measures that might have been expected to have this effect were National Recovery Administration code requirements, Works Progress Administration wage policies, and after 1939, the Fair Labor Standards Act. But more important than any one governmental measure or policy was the attitude that underlay all of them, an attitude of impatience with low wages and the employers who paid them.

Another but related factor was the direction of union wage policy coupled with the growing strength of unions. The unions newly organized in the 1930s had a larger proportion of unskilled workers than the older ones. This fact, together with the known tendency for new unions to obtain greater percentage hourly wage increases than old ones, would lead to a reduced (average) margin for skill.

To summarize: in the only two periods of economic expansion in which it could be tested (the two world wars) our theory was compatible with the data for the United States. Similar tendencies

22. This argument is a rationalization of the facts presented in table 1. However, I consider it quite possible that these 'facts' are misleading. That is, the data in table 1 refer only to firms whose existence was sufficiently permanent to permit them to be included in wage surveys. But these firms would tend to be relatively more sensitive than others to the social pressures that shore up SM. That is, wage surveys tend to miss the fly-by-night enterprises that are most willing to cut prices and wages, and which, during depressions, tend to grow in relative importance as sources of employment. Furthermore, where social pressures to maintain wages are severe, actual wages may tend to fall below those that are reported, because of unpaid overtime (in small firms, especially in textiles and clothing manufacture), kickbacks, and/or downright falsification of records. It is also very likely that unskilled wage rates in agriculture, domestic service, and other non-business sources of employment fell proportionately more than the unskilled rates reported by business firms.

have also been observed in several European countries.[23] Unfortunately, however, the behavior of skill margins during major depressions has not shown a consistent pattern. This is due, at least in part, to independent variations in *SM*. It is also necessary to invoke *SM* as an explanatory factor to account for the events of the 1930s in the United States. The need to lean on *SM* indicates weakness in the theory; *SM* is an exogenous variable – a *deus ex machina* – which is blamed for some failures of the theory. However, this cannot be helped; variations in *SM* are a powerful economic force which must be taken into account.

As an explanation of secular trends in skill margins our theory does somewhat better than in accounting for short-run behavior. As is well known, there has been a marked reduction in skill margins, in most Western countries, over the past half century or so. This is what our theory would predict, if it be granted that laborers are more able to acquire new skills the higher the level of their education; for then the secular improvement in the education of working class children would tend to increase the ease of substituting less- for more-skilled workers.[24] Furthermore, mechanization and specialization of equipment tends greatly to reduce the need for broadly skilled workers, thereby facilitating the utilization of partially skilled operatives, whose highly specialized training can be acquired quickly. This tends further to increase interskill substitutability.[25]

In other words, the long-run trend toward improved working class education has increased the percentage of workers able to satisfy the hiring standards for skilled jobs, and this tends to act as a brake upon increases in their wage rates. The obverse side

23. See, for example, Walter Galenson, *The Danish system of labor relations* (Cambridge, Mass., 1952), table 26, p. 179, and Knowles and Robertson, op. cit., p. 111.

24. This point is well argued by A. G. B. Fisher, 'Education and relative wage rates', *Internat. Lab. Rev.*, vol. 25 (June 1932), pp. 742–64.

25. If it is accepted that improved education has increased the ease of substituting less- for more-skilled workers, then it may be that the tendency for skill margins to contract in association with large short-period increases in aggregate employment has not always operated. That is, it may be that in the nineteenth century the substitution of less- for more-skilled workers was so difficult that short-period booms led to as great (or greater) increases in skilled rates as in unskilled.

of this trend is a reduction in the share of the work force that is seeking unskilled jobs; this trend has been reinforced by the gradual extinction of child labor (which was almost entirely unskilled) and by the sharp relative rise in demand for semiskilled machine tenders. The result has been to put upward pressure upon unskilled rates. (The possible role of union pressure in this secular process is considered [under 'Alternative Hypotheses', p. 222].)

Interregional and International Applications of the Model

The model outlined in [the] first section can also be applied to explain differences in the skill margins that exist among different regions of the United States and among different countries. These differences result from two forces, both affecting the ease of substituting less- for more-skilled workers: (1) different minimum educational levels[26] of the labor force in different areas make it easier to substitute less- for more-skilled workers in those places where educational levels are relatively high; (2) competition of skilled labor has much less effect upon the wages of the unskilled than competition of semiskilled; i.e. it is not nearly so easy to substitute an unskilled worker for a fully skilled one as for a semiskilled machine tender.[27] However, some of the relatively more-skilled machine tenders can perform many of the tasks of a skilled job, and some of the 'intermediately skilled' operatives can handle jobs now held by slightly more-skilled, etc., down to the unskilled. Hence labor market competition between the skilled and the unskilled will tend to be more effective where it is

26. As unskilled workers are the least educated part of the labor force, it is their educational level that is important. The higher this is, up to some point, the better able they are to adjust to more complicated jobs. Education, as used here, refers not only to formal schooling but also to the whole complex of informal instruction from parents, relatives, etc. However, years of schooling completed is probably a fair index of educational attainment in this broader sense.

27. In this connexion, the relation of substitution is more asymmetrical than in, say, the theory of consumer choice. That is, relative increases in the wage rates of less-skilled workers will not lead to a substitution of more- for less-skilled workers (assuming the wage rates of the latter continue higher than those of the former). But the reverse of this may very well happen if the wages of the more-skilled rise relative to those of the less-skilled.

indirect; i.e. where it operates via several links of semiskilled workers.[28] Therefore, where manufacturing industries, which provide most of the semiskilled jobs, are relatively unimportant sources of employment, labor market competition between skilled and unskilled workers tends to be relatively weak.

In general, the greater the ease of substitution between skilled and unskilled workers, the smaller will be the skill margin. However, when the elasticity of substitution is low, circumstances arising in either of the separate markets for skilled and unskilled workers may have an important effect upon skill margins. All sorts of such circumstances may arise (and have arisen), but one particular type – relevant to interarea differences in unskilled wage rates – is of such significance as to warrant special mention. This circumstance is a change in the capital–labour ratio (i.e. the ratio of capital stock to labor force plus labor reserve) in a given area.

Abstracting from the effects of short-period fluctuations in effective demand, the primary determinant of the level of the unskilled wage rate in a given area is the capital–labor ratio. The higher this ratio, the higher will be the employment of unskilled – or low-skilled – workers at a given wage rate.[29] Consequently, the higher the capital–labor ratio, the less the unemployment at any given SM and the lower the cost to the community of maintaining that level of SM. This, in turn, suggests (but does not prove)[30] that the higher the capital–labor ratio, the higher the wage rate of unskilled workers.[31]

Because of the positive association of both a high proportion

28. The presence of a large number of semiskilled workers in a community tends, after a period, to diffuse more widely the requisite knowledge and the habits of mind helpful to performance of such jobs. Of course, the presence of a large number of fully skilled workers will accomplish the same, or better, results.

29. This is a conventional and familiar proposition in economic theory; i.e. the larger the quantity of one factor, the greater the marginal product of the cooperant factor (in a two-factor situation).

30. It does not, and could not, constitute proof because different communities have different SMs. By and large, one community's SM will be higher or lower than another's if its per capita output (highly correlated with the capital–labor ratio) is higher; but there are exceptions to this statement.

31. Interarea differences in the level of unskilled wage rates are associated with differences in industrial structure. Where unskilled rates are relatively low, all sorts of low-wage industries tend to flourish, absorbing a large part

of manufacturing employment and a high (minimal) level of education[32] with the level of per capita income, there is a tendency for wide skill margins to be associated with low levels of economic development, and vice versa. This tendency is reinforced by the tendency of more developed countries to remove inferior workers, especially children, the aged, and the infirm, from the labor market. As these workers are largely unskilled, removing them from the market tends to increase the ease of substitution between skilled and unskilled workers.

If this theory is correct, then one would expect that, within the United States, the south – where semiskilled manufacturing jobs are relatively infrequent, minimum educational standards are low, and racial prejudice acts as a barrier to substitution of unskilled Negroes for skilled whites[33] – would be an area where the skill margin would be relatively high. In the far west where minimum educational standards are relatively high, where Negroes and foreign immigrants are relatively infrequent, and where females and children are an unusually small part of the work force, one would expect to find a relatively high degree of substitutability between skilled and unskilled labor and, consequently, a narrow skill margin.[34] And, as is generally known, the skill margin is higher in the south and lower in the far west than in any of the other parts of the United States.[35]

---

of the labor force; e.g. low (unskilled) wage areas tend to offer much employment in textiles, agricultural processing, personal service (domestic and otherwise), etc. Conversely, where the ratio is high, these industries tend to be unimportant users of manpower. In other words, interarea differences in unskilled wage rates are, to a considerable extent, associated with differences in the industrial composition of the labor force. (This point is similar to that of Simon Rottenberg, 'Note on economic progress and occupational distribution', *Rev. Econ. Stat.*, vol. 35 [May 1953], pp. 168–70.)

32. This association obviously holds only up to a certain level of education and proportion of employment in manufacturing.

33. See Donald Dewey, 'Negro employment in southern industry' *Jour. Pol. Econ.*, vol. 60 (August 1952), pp. 279–99.

34. In the far west, there is not an unusually high percentage of semiskilled employment. However, the other factors mentioned make for a high degree of substitutability between skilled and unskilled labor despite this fact.

35. W. S. Woytinsky and associates, op. cit., p. 470 and Appendix, table 115, p. 760; Colin Clark, *The conditions of economic progress*, 2nd edn (New York, 1951), pp. 461–6.

Now let us consider intercountry differences in skill margins. In principle, it should be possible to explain these differences in the same manner as in the case of regional differences in the United States. That is, countries with relatively high skill margins should be 'backward areas' and those with low margins should tend to be more 'advanced' countries. This contention is similar to Colin Clark's and would seem on the whole to be supported by the data he offers.[36] However, there are certain facts which, superficially at least, are incompatible with this theory; the most notable of these is the fact that, even when the south is excluded, the margin for skill in the United States is substantially higher than in almost any country in western Europe or Australia.[37]

The reason for this apparent conflict between theory and fact is that although the United States possesses the highest per capita income in the world, it has not had, at least until recently, as high *minimum* educational standards as most western countries. This is the obverse side of the fact that until the mid-1920s we accepted large numbers of uneducated immigrants (from southern and eastern Europe) and that we permitted our rural population – especially in the south – to fall well below the standards effective elsewhere in the country. These undereducated workers provided much of our unskilled labor prior to the Second World War, which resulted in a low elasticity of substitution between the skilled and unskilled parts of our labor force. Developments since 1941 have greatly increased the substitutability of unskilled for skilled labor,[38] and skill margins have descended toward the

36. Clark, op. cit., pp. 458 *et seq.*, especially the table, p. 460.

37. The case of Italy may also be one difficult to reconcile with our theory, which would imply that in Italy – at least in the southern part – skill differentials should be relatively high. J. T. Dunlop and M. Rothbaum, 'International comparisons of wage structures', *Internat. Lab. Rev.*, vol. 70 (April 1955), pp. 356–7, indicate that skill differentials in Italy are, and have been, less than in the United States and of the same order of magnitude (in 1952–53) as in France; but it is not clear whether these figures include southern Italy.

38. These developments include large-scale 'on-the-job' training programs during the Second World War, extensive technical training given by the armed services to draftees, reduction of employment discrimination against Negroes, etc. It should be noted that the increase in substitutability between skilled and unskilled labor is indirect; i.e. both kinds of labor have

levels prevailing in western Europe, although they remain somewhat higher.

Alternative Hypotheses

The theory of the skill margin that we have offered would appear quite dissimilar to that presented or implied in many other discussions. We have stressed economic factors, and have not assigned any role to union or government policies (in determining skill differentials) except via changes in SM. Obviously, it is possible that either union or government policy – or employer beneficence – *could* affect the skill margin, and in some cases it probably has. The pertinent question, however, concerns the importance of these cases.

We do not consider it likely that union or government policy has greatly affected either the long-run movement in the skill margin or the sharp decline since 1940. (There are some exceptions that will be noted.) This assertion flies in the face of much expert opinion, and the fact that a decline in skill margins has been often proclaimed as an objective of unions and/or governments – or has been implied by other policies they have attempted to follow.

If, however, union or government policy has been a cause of reduced skill margins, then it must have kept skilled rates below, or unskilled rates above, what otherwise would have been the case; i.e. what market conditions would have established. As there were shortages of both skilled and unskilled labor in practically all countries during the Second World War, it is entirely possible that the policies of the wage-fixing agencies did serve to reduce the skill margin during this period; the reverse is also possible.[39] Within the United States and a number of other countries, it seems unlikely that wartime policies exercised much influence toward *reducing* skill margins, as the relaxation of wage controls after the war did not result in any increase above wartime levels; in the United States, the margin declined still further.

---

become more interchangeable with semiskilled labor of different grades which are, in turn, substitutable for one another.

39. i.e. unskilled rates may have been kept further below market equilibrium than skilled.

However, there are countries (e.g. Denmark and Italy) where there was a widening of the skill margin after wartime controls were relaxed, suggesting that the controls may have worked toward narrowing the earning advantage of the skilled.[40] But, by the same token, the effect of government wage controls and/or union policy in the United States was to keep the skill margin from being reduced even more than it was.

As long as there is substantially full employment of all grades of labor it is difficult to test any hypothesis concerning the effect (over and above that of market forces) of union and/or government policy upon wage differentials. But the fact that the relatively overvalued grade of labor (as compared with market equilibrium) has not (*ex hypothesi*) experienced unemployment suggests that it has not been much overvalued. And the phenomenon of the 'wage glide'[41] clearly indicates that where wage rates are placed below market levels – either by government order or union policy – employers tend, in one way or another, to circumvent the rules by paying over the prescribed maxima. Hence, where union of government ceilings are not circumvented, there is reason to suspect that the prescribed maximum rates are not too far from market equilibrium.

Where there is persistent unemployment of the overvalued (or all) grades of labor, and the prescribed minimum rates are maintained, there is ample opportunity for union or government wage policies to alter relative wage rates. For example, it would seem entirely possible that, in the 1930s, the upsurge of industrial unionism in the United States tended to force up the wages of the

40. For the Danish case see Galenson, op. cit., pp. 178–80. Galenson's interpretation, however, differs from that suggested here. The Italian case is discussed in Dunlop and Rothbaum, op. cit., p. 357, especially n. 1.

41. The phenomenon of actual rates climbing above the union scale has occurred in Sweden, where it is called the 'wage glide'; cf. W. Galenson, *Comparative labor movements* (New York, 1952), p. 160, *et seq.* It has also occurred in Germany (see Clark Kerr, 'Wage structures and trade unionism', a paper read at the International Economic Association Round Table on Wage Determination, 4–14 September, 1954), and in England (B. C. Roberts, 'Trade union behavior and wage determination', a paper read at aforementioned Round Table on Wage Determination). In Denmark, where skilled workers have 'personal rates' – determined by individual bargaining – in addition to a union scale minimum, the same remarks would apply (Galenson, *The Danish system of labor relations*, op. cit., pp. 146–50).

unskilled and semiskilled relative to those of the skilled. It seems even more likely that in the same period government policy, by raising SM, narrowed skill margins (see p. 211). But the presence of large-scale unemployment tends to eliminate (for the 1930s) explanations running in terms of labor market competition. This is not the case for the 1940s and 1950s.

As this would suggest, we distrust the frequently advanced argument that one reason why skill margins have narrowed since 1939 is that unions have successfully demanded, or governments have imposed, 'equal cents per hour' wage increases for all workers. Taken literally, this argument is analogous to saying that the incidence of a tax is determined by the fiat of the levier, and is vulnerable to the same question, i.e. 'What if the buyer refuses to pay?' The fact that skilled wage rates have not risen more than they have since 1945 strongly suggests that employers did not choose to bid them up in the process of competing for skilled labor.

For the long-run trend, we would contend that unions have been successful in narrowing skill margins because employers have found it convenient to yield to union demands on this issue in exchange for concessions on other matters. For, after yielding to the union, the employer has still had many degrees of freedom regarding skill differentials, when he has needed them; i.e. he could pay over the union scale, create new jobs or job titles, etc.[42] In short, the economic developments discussed above have encouraged employers to do what unions wanted – or often said they wanted[43] – on the matter of skill margins. And had it been

42. For an illustration of how employers can use these 'degrees of freedom' see Clark Kerr and L. H. Fisher, 'Effect of environment and administration on job evaluation', *Harvard Bus. Rev.*, vol. 28 (May 1950), pp. 77–96.

43. Kerr, 'Wage structures and trade unionism', op. cit., argues that unions tend to increase, rather than reduce, the skill margin. This proposition is as plausible, *a priori*, as the more widely accepted opposite view. It would seem likely that the direction unionism gives to skill margins varies from one case to another. But whatever the 'true' effect of unionism *per se*, the pressure of other forces is likely to continue to narrow skill margins. Consequently, the independent effect of unionism, when it is working to narrow skill margins, will be obscured. But, contrariwise, when it operates to widen skill margins the effect of unionism is likely to be clearly visible. Thus I suspect that Kerr's hypothesis will appear to be supported by the 'evidence', whatever the true state of affairs.

otherwise, employers would have frustrated union policy by setting in motion a secular wage glide for skilled rates.[44]

Implications for Annual Labor Income

In the preceding sections we have developed a theory of hourly wage differentials. This theory obviously has a number of implications for the theory of annual labor income differentials. However, we can discuss only two of these implications here; these are rather simple and closely related to the main theme of this article.

The first of these implications refers to the cyclical pattern of labor–income skill differentials. It will be recalled that we were reluctant to assert the existence of a cyclical pattern in the (hourly) margin for skill (see pp. 214–5). At best, such a pattern would be expected only in the most pronounced fluctuations and, even there, the evidence is questionable – *vide* 1929–32. However, the case for a cyclical pattern in the skill differentials in annual earnings is better, although the evidence is scanty. Common observation, statistical evidence, and the implications of our model all agree that unskilled workers should be more subject to cyclical unemployment than skilled.[45] As the hourly earnings of the

44. One contrary possibility may be mentioned. If union pressure to raise unskilled rates should be sufficiently strong and, if attempts to substitute capital for labor (i.e. to mechanize) should lead to reductions in the demand for skilled labor, it is possible that union attempts to narrow skill margins might lead to a reduction in the demand for skilled labor, and thereby generate market pressure to reduce the skill margin. This assumes the operation of a mechanism analogous to Giffen's paradox. Whether this possibility is more than imaginary is impossible to say.

45. i.e. if real G.N.P. declines between t_0 and t_1, the increase (between t_0 and t_1) in the percentage of unskilled workers unemployed will be greater than the percentage of the skilled. The relevant facts from the U.S. 1940 Census are summarized by Horst Mendershausen, 'Changes in Income Distribution during the Great Depression', *Studies in Income and Wealth*, vol. VII, Nat. Bur. Econ. Research (New York, 1946), pp. 69–70.

This inference is in accord with 'the spirit' of our model because employers often, during a slack period, substitute skilled men for nonskilled (on nonskilled jobs) and discharge the nonskilled workers. That is, the employer raises hiring standards for nonskilled jobs. The employer gains – especially if he can pay the skilled worker the nonskilled rate – by having a pool of skilled labor to draw upon during future expansion. Similar

unskilled are lower than those of the skilled, it follows that the annual wage incomes of the 'low' (hourly) wage earners should decline more in a depression than those of the 'high' wage earners; i.e. annual wage incomes should become more unevenly distributed.

The available evidence supports this inference: Mendershausen[46] found that, during the Great Depression, the degree of (annual) income inequality (as measured by the coefficient of concentration) increased appreciably (from 1929 to 1933) among the urban recipients of 'lower' incomes. As the incomes of these urban families (the lower 50–70% of all recipient units) consist mostly of wages, the behavior of their distribution is a fairly clear reflection of the changing distribution of annual wage income – and it is so interpreted by Mendershausen. That is, Mendershausen interpreted this finding as tantamount to an indication that increased unemployment had caused an increase in the inequality of the distribution of annual wage receipts among wage earners.[47] This interpretation is supported by the further finding that, among American cities, the increase in the coefficient of concentration of annual income, among lower-income recipients (from 1929 to 1933), was positively associated with the increase in the percentage of unemployed workers during the same period.

If the inference is correct, the reverse of the depression behavior should have occurred during major (e.g. wartime) booms. And the findings, both of Kuznets and Goldsmith *et al.*, indicate that the inference is compatible with the events of the Second World War; i.e. they found that, during 1939–44, the share of annual wage receipts accruing to the upper 5% of recipient units declined.[48]

---

considerations apply in hiring new nonskilled workers; thus skilled workers, *ceteris paribus*, can get rehired more easily than nonskilled.

46. op. cit., pp. 61–8, esp. table 22.

47. op. cit., pp. 79–80. It is worth noting that among all income recipients, the coefficient of concentration diminished during 1929–33 – the reverse of what happened among the lower-income groups.

48. S. S. Kuznets, *Shares of upper income groups in income and savings*, N.B.E.R. (New York, 1953), ch. 2; S. Goldsmith, G. Jaszi, M. Kaitz, and M. Liebenberg, 'Size distribution of income since the mid-thirties', *Rev. Econ. Stat.*, vol. 36 (February 1954), pp. 16–17.

The second implication refers to the distributional behavior of wage income in the face of an increase in the work force which considerably exceeds the contemporaneous increase in aggregate labor demand. The effect that such an occurrence will have upon relative wage rates and the distribution of wage income depends, *ceteris paribus*, upon the distribution of the increased labor force between skilled and unskilled grades. It is possible, *a priori*, for such an increase in the labor force to be confined to skilled workers, to unskilled, or to any combination of the two. However, in practice, much interest attaches to the case where the increase occurs largely among unskilled workers; this was true of English economic development during the early nineteenth century (*circa* 1790–1830).

In cases such as this, our model would imply that the increased supply of unskilled labor should drive down the annual incomes of the unskilled, relative to those of the skilled, either by widening the per-hour margin for skill, or creating unemployment among the unskilled to a much greater degree than among the skilled. There is substantial authority for the view that this is precisely what happened in England during the first part of the nineteenth century. Thus, although his evidence is admittedly inconclusive, Ashton concludes that:

> There were, however, masses of unskilled or poorly skilled workers – seasonally employed agricultural workers and hand-loom weavers in particular – whose incomes were almost wholly absorbed in paying for the bare necessities of life, the prices of which, as we have seen, remained high. My guess would be that the number of those who were able to share in the benefits of economic progress was larger than the number of those who were shut out from these benefits and that it was steadily growing. But the existence of two groups within the working class needs to be recognized.[49]

This conclusion will, no doubt, suggest further speculations about the effect of economic development upon the distribution of wage income and the margin for skill. However, this is too large a subject to be explored here.

49. T. S. Ashton, 'The standard of life of the workers in England, 1790–1830', pp. 127–59, in *Capitalism and the historians*, F. A. Hayek, ed. (London, 1954), p. 159; this article was reprinted from the *Jour. Econ. Hist.*, suppl. 9, 1949. Also see Ashton's further remarks (to the same effect) in 'The treatment of capitalism by historians', in the same volume, p. 41.

11 H. A. Turner

Inflation and Wage Differentials in Great Britain

Turner, H. A. (1957) Inflation and wage differentials in Great Britain, from J. T. Dunlop (ed.), *The theory of wage determination* (Macmillan), pp. 123–35.

The relative antiquity of collective bargaining in Britain may give custom and convention a greater influence on the fixing of wages there than is general. What follows is an interpretation of British experience, particularly that of the period of full employment since 1940, but much of it may have an application to other 'high employment' economies of the western type. There seems to be a dual relation between the inflationary trend characteristic of such economies and the system of wage differentials. Attention has been largely concentrated upon the effects of inflation on relative wages. Wage relationships, however, may also play a more positive role in sustaining the inflation and determining its form.

Wage Relationship and the Pressure for Wage Increases

A prominent feature of recent British wage trends has been the influence of the 'coercive comparison'. A large part of the strikes currently classified as wage disputes turns out, on nearer investigation, not to consist of actions for wage increases as such, but of attempts to maintain a relationship the workers concerned regard as established by custom: some margin over, or partly with, another group of workers.[1] The current language and practice of British industrial conciliation is full of terms – 'due relativities', 'proper parities', 'customary differentials' – which embody this comparative concept. The very term 'fair wages' is given by the Resolution of Parliament which governs wages

1. I refer to a number of instances of such disputes in a paper, 'The effects of the present wage structure' (British Institute of Management, 1953).

under government contracts just the meaning that these wages are to be comparable with those under collective agreements in private industry. The principle is explicitly expressed in the formula regulating the pay of civil servants. It seems to have been the most important guide to arbitration awards.[2]

It might be thought that this insistence on the maintenance of 'established relatives' would lead to stability. And it is true that the extension of collective bargaining has been associated with a certain rigidity in wage relationships. There are important instances of wage differentials that remained unchanged, despite economic upheavals, for 30, 50, or even (in the textile industry) for 60 years. This is, generally speaking, since the scope of collective bargains in the trades concerned widened beyond that of individual firms.[3] While in cases where such an 'established relativity' can no longer be maintained, the change usually occurs, not as a gradual modification but as a sharp break, accompanied by obvious conflict. An interesting example of this occurred in 1951, when the government, because of a persistent shortage of policemen, gave them a very large increase in pay. Since 1920 wages in the fire service had been varied with those of the police. The refusal of the 1951 increase to firemen provoked their widespread and prolonged refusal to continue on duty.

The system of 'established relativities' is, however, by no means self-consistent. One major point of friction is between wages of time workers in the same industry or firm. At their initiation, collective agreements usually establish wage rates which will yield comparable earnings for piece-work and time-work. British collective agreements often specify that piece rates shall be arranged to yield earnings a fixed percentage above time rate.

The recurrent gap between piece-workers' and time-workers' earnings is an important factor in the prominence of the mining and engineering industries in British wage demands. The latter industry illustrates both another such friction and the rigidity associated with widely based collective bargaining. In most

2. See the writer's *Arbitration: a study of industrial experience* (Fabian Research Series, 1952).

3. Several such cases are analysed in the writer's 'Trade unions, differentials, and the levelling of Wages', *Manchester School of Economic and Social Studies* (September 1952), pp. 244–58.

British industries, 'industry-wide' collective agreements are the rule. In engineering the agreement was first devised in 1917 and provided for two classes of worker: apprenticed craftsmen and labourers. The growth of mass production has produced a great class of 'semi-skilled' workers: the unions and employers' organizations have so far found it impossible to adapt the traditional structure of standard rates to these operatives, so their wages continue to be bargained in individual establishments. Such local bargaining gives speedier results than industry-wide negotiations so that wages of mass production operatives have in some cases risen above those of skilled mechanics.[4]

Another source of friction is the alternative arrangements of wage differentials that are possible. The 'due relativity' between, for instance, the wage of a skilled worker and that of his less skilled assistant may be 'established' in terms of a proportionate difference or an absolute cash sum, and different occupations have contrasting (and long-standing) customs in this respect. Workers of these different occupations may be employed in the same industry, or even in the same establishment. Thus a substantial general increase in wages inevitably produces disparities in pay between workers of comparable skill. Thus smelters in the steel industry have a percentage differential over labourers, while mechanics' differentials have been fixed in cash; many wage demands have arisen from this anomaly.

A similar consequence may follow from the successful prosecution of a general wage demand by a combination of more and less skilled workers. Such general demands have been, almost invariably, for a common percentage or absolute increase in the different wage rates concerned. If the group secures a percentage advance, its lower-paid members may complain that the skilled workers' cash advantage has been unfairly increased: if the advance is uniform in cash, the skilled workers protest that their differential has been relatively diminished. Either type of demand thus entails a certain aftermath of discontent. The leading role of railwaymen in recent British wage demands, for instance, is partly attributable to the reduction of locomotive engineers' wage differentials by a series of standard cash advances.

4. See 'Earnings in engineering, 1926–1948', by K. G. J. C. Knowles and D. J. Robertson, *Bulletin, Oxford Institute of Statistics* (June 1951).

The industries which have played the leading part in recent British wage movements are those in which such frictions as the above are most acute. Railwaymen, for instance – though their agreed wage rates have moved in step with those of collective agreements generally – have suffered a steady comparative worsening in their earnings, because they enjoy neither the piece-work pay of other 'organized' industries nor the opportunities of local and individual bargaining offered by certain less 'organized' trades.[5]

These frictions between the comparative standards of particular groups of workers present themselves to union leaders as a recurring complex of sectional pressures for wage adjustments. But where any substantial groups of members is concerned, selective or discriminatory wage demands usually provoke discontent among those who do not profit by them, so that union leaders usually prefer in such cases to seek a general increase in wages. So these sectional frictions commonly express themselves, in a way determined by the necessities of collective action, as general wage demands.

Employment Levels and the Pressure for Wage Increases

The preceding argument is that, given a general situation of high employment, the British system and techniques of collective wage regulation permit particular groups of workers to increase their wages faster than the generality. Other workers then demand wage increases to restore 'established relativities'. The unions' tendency is to convert such sectional wage demands into general demands. General wage increases, however, are only palliative,

5. Miss G. Evans, of the Economic Research Section of Manchester University, has just completed an analysis of the post-war movement of agreed wage rates industry by industry. Comparing this with the movement of earnings, and allowing for the effect of overtime, the extent to which average wages actually paid exceed the centrally agreed wage rates appears to vary from nil to about 20%. This variation does not appear to be related to the relative profitability or labour shortage of different industries, but seems most pronounced in industries: (a) where piece rates are common and physical productivity has increased; (b) where opportunities for local bargaining are greatest.

and may themselves – by their effect on differentials – provoke renewed discontent.

This is not, of course, presented as the sole factor in continuing wage inflation. But it seems a persistent one, which may explain why wage demands continue to be pressed by unions when the factors usually put forward to justify them – increases in prices or profits – are not obvious. For instance, it does not seem that either of these factors sufficiently explains the failure of the rigid 'wage stop' imposed (by agreement between the T.U.C. and the government) in January 1950. Between that month and September 1950, when the 'wage stop' began to give way before persistent wage demands, the cost of living increased[6] only 1% and the profits currently declared by industrial companies did not reflect the onset of the Korean boom until near the end of the year.[7] But average earnings rose about 4%, and it is clear (since most centrally agreed wage rates were 'frozen') that considerable 'inequities' must have developed.[8]

Whatever the relative importance in stimulating wage demands of changes in prices, profits, and wage relationships, the effect of the last factor does seem especially precise. First, changes in the relative wages of associated groups of workers seem immediately and acutely perceived (especially if an accustomed 'relativity' has existed between them) by the workers themselves. Second, to any trade union, an increase in the wage rates of an associated union's members is an instant commentary on its own leaders' efficiency. High employment has strengthened the comparative principle in wage fixing for four reasons. First, by strengthening the unions themselves. High employment is accompanied by increasing union membership. Where (as in Britain) the union's own structure cuts across the boundaries of different occupations and industries, the result is to widen the area of interwage comparisons and to multi-

6. A. T. Peacock and W. J. L. Ryan, in 'Wages and inflation: influences on the timing of claims', *Manchester Guardian* (15 May, 1952), suggest a rise of 5 points in the British index of retail prices to be required to generate a wage demand.

7. Estimated from *Financial Times* monthly analysis, 'Trend of industrial profits'.

8. A more detailed commentary is given in Turner, *Arbitration: a study of industrial experience.*

ply the number of points on which each group of workers rests its particular standard of 'fair wages'. British trade unionism has, of course, a mixed structure of 'horizontal' craft and general labour unions and of 'vertical' industrial unions, so that few unions confine themselves to one industry, and few industries are organized by one union alone.

The second effect of high employment is usually to increase the area and effectiveness of collective bargaining, because employers become more willing to accept its restraints. Since any widely based collective agreement is usually founded on the wage relationships existing at its initiation, the effect is commonly to set, formalize, and make explicit 'relativities' which may before have been merely conventional or even indeterminate.

Thirdly, the government's desire to avoid the disturbance of prosperity by industrial conflicts – and particularly its more recent assumption of the responsibility to maintain full employment – has driven it to encourage the orderly regulation of wage questions. This it does by establishing conciliation services, arbitration tribunals, legal wage boards, and the like. It has been noted that such institutions lean heavily upon interwage comparisons and upon 'established relativities' to form their decisions.

The fourth reason is that, while a departure from 'established relativities' may be resented by workers, when unemployment is widespread, those who do not gain an increase may accept the fact for fear of losing their jobs. But such departures are often remembered as injustices, and the collective memory which the unions represent is longer than that of individuals. When the fear of unemployment dwindles, not only is insistence upon 'the maintenance of relativities' strengthened, but some groups may try to reassert a former status. A major example of this concerns the increase in wages of London printers which initiated the collapse of the official 'wage stop' of 1950. This was granted after a dispute (involving a major stoppage of work) originating from an event of 1922. In that year's wage conflicts the rates of provincial printers were cut more than those in London, so that a previously established wage differential was widened. The provincial printers accepted the situation until after the Second World War. They then tried to re-establish the pre-1922 margin. The London printers reacted to their final success by demanding the restoration of the post-1922 differential.[9]

The history of British collective bargaining suggests in any case certain long-term trends. Once collective bargaining has become established in a particular sector of employment, its scope tends to widen so that the whole of the industry concerned is, in effect, regulated by collective contracts, even if all the employers are not formally party to them. There is a similar tendency for regulation of wages to become established in industries where the trade unions are not strong enough to enforce it themselves. Here, particularly, the aid of the state has been enlisted. The effect of the current British national arbitration system, for instance, is virtually to make legal enforcement of agreed wage rates available to any union that desires it, while the system of legal wage boards (originally designed to ensure minimum standards in certain badly organized trades) has in effect become a widely used device for 'organized' employers and workers to impose the terms of collective contracts upon the unorganized.

There is thus a trend to the centralization of collective bargaining. Industry-wide agreements tend to replace local or occupational contracts. Even where the various employers in an industry are not formally party to a single agreement, the trade generally will follow the lead set (as in the printing, steel, and cotton industries) by a particular sectional agreement, or even (as in chemicals) by the wage contracts of a particular firm.

Associated with these trends is a certain uniformity in the results of collective regulation. This uniformity is first and most prominently marked in wage increases, which are added to the diverse existing wage rates. But there then follows a gradual process of standardization, in which general minimum wage rates are established, a number of minor wage differences (like variations in wage rates between localities) are eliminated, and finally the minimum wage rates approximate also to maxima.[10] In

9. See 'Report of a Court of Inquiry into ... a dispute between the London Master Printers' Association and the London Society of Compositors', Ministry of Labour (October 1950).

10. This conclusion I particularly base on a study (as yet unpublished) of collective bargaining in the United Kingdom cotton industry over the past century.

Britain, the phenomenon of uniform general wage increases has been recurrent under industry-wide contracts, although outside the public services and monopolistic industries only a few trades have yet reached the last stage of collective bargaining, in which a structure of standard wage rates absolutely determines the earnings of employees.

These trends appear to reflect both the effects of internal solidarity in employers' and workers' organizations and their desire to prevent 'unfair competition' by the unorganized or less disciplined. But this long-term development has been irregular. The London printers' example illustrates how the system of 'established relativities' may break up in the presence of rising unemployment, but tends to reform when employment is high. As it reforms, its diverse internal frictions help to incite a general pressure for wage advances. At the same time its elaboration has ensured that the advances secured in certain leading industries shall be imitated throughout the economy.

At what level does unemployment cease to be a barrier to this tendency? Certainly, at some point considerably short of full employment. Thus in 1952–3 there was a fall in British industrial employment which was partly concealed by widespread partial employment and by the dismissal of 'marginal' workers who did not register as unemployed, but which probably amounted to some 4 or 5%.[11] Industrial profits fell sharply and the cost-of-living ceased to rise. However, the rhythm of wage demands (and increases) apparently continued without significant abatement. While in the cotton industry, where recorded unemployment alone amounted to some 30%, the unions not only presented to the employers a demand for a general wage increase but also persisted to the point of partial success. It seems that the cotton unions were more fearful of their members' wage rates falling behind those of other industries than of the less determinate effect of a wage increase on employment. So long as any important group of workers was in a position to press home wage demands (and any significant unemployment, of course, is likely to be uneven in its incidence), a similar choice would confront other unions. One has no means of determining exactly the critical degree or

11. See H. A. Turner, 'Measuring unemployment', *Journal of the Royal Statistical Society* (part I, 1955), pp. 28–50.

general unemployment at which sectional wage demands would become effective and most other unions induced to follow suit. But if a guess will serve to illustrate the point, one might say that once employment comes within, say, 6 or 7% of 'full', a general and persistent pressure for wage increases will develop. Average wages might, of course, start to rise well before that point.

Restraints on Wage Increases

The process of successive wage cycles has, however, the appearance of a steady and controlled march rather than a runaway stampede. One reason for this is that the protracted rituals of contemporary collective bargaining combine with the elaborate system of dependent comparisons it creates to impose certain restraints upon wage movements.

In Britain the presentation of wage demands has assumed a certain annual or biennial rhythm, corresponding to the unions' habit of periodic representative conferences. Their settlement has acquired an equal formality. Most demands are stalled until settlements are reached in the leading industries. These involve lengthy negotiations with the employers (who are aware of their trades' strategic position), and commonly involve arbitration procedure and government intervention. This intervention is compelled by the need to forestall a breach of industrial peace, not that of economic moderation. But its effect is to give an implicit approval to the settlement it secures. The general wage advance follows.

A second restraint is imposed by what seems an extension of the comparative principle into time. In each cycle of wage increases, since their pattern became settled during the Second World War, the average weekly wage rate seems to have increased by much the same amount. It seems that unions are not prepared to accept much less – or employers to concede much more – than they did in the previous cycle.

The movement has, nevertheless, an inexorable quality. The official 'wage stop' of 1950, for instance, achieved no more than a temporary halt, and the wage cycle which terminated it was followed so shortly by a second round of wage increases as to cancel its effect. One might say that the trend of collective bargaining's recent development is to give wage earners as a whole what many salaried employees have enjoyed for a long time as individuals – a periodic increase of pay.

It is curious, however, that each successive general increase in wage rates has resembled its predecessors, not in proportionate but in absolute terms, so that the pace of the movement shows a relative diminution. In so far as prices follow wages, this means, of course, that the inflationary effect of wage advances tends also to diminish. The British economy, indeed, seems very near the point at which productivity (increasing at a proportionate rate) will overhaul the advance of wages.

This tendency for the effect of the wage pressure to diminish might be attributed to a reduction of the 'frictions' in wage relationships, following from the gradual standardization and simplification of the wages structure as collective bargaining extends and improves its techniques. However, it seems also probable that the repeated general advances of wage rates have established a certain expectation, among organized workers, upon their leaders' future performance. The arithmetic progression of wage advances may be connected with another phenomenon of the recent period – the tendency of the successive general increases in wage rates to be uniform in terms of cash.

Narrowing of Wage Differentials

A most notable feature of this time has been a diminution of relative differences in wages. This 'narrowing' has been very general: we shall discuss it mainly in relation to differentials for skill and responsibility among manual workers as its most prominent and typical case. This demonstrates also the factors operating upon local and inter-industry differentials. Sex differentials and the differential between wages and salaries (i.e. for non-manual labour) have been subject to the same general force, but in these cases its working has been modified by special circumstances which would involve more detailed discussion than is possible here.

This narrowing has been attributed to the spread of popular education and to technical change. These things have certainly contributed to the reduction of particular differentials. But there is no obvious correlation between the rate of technical and educational progress and the general movement of differentials. Relative skill differentials, for instance, were pretty constant in Britain during the latter nineteenth century and up to the First World War. They then declined sharply, but were partly restored in the inter-war period. The narrowing, however, was resumed with the coming of the Second World War and has continued to the present day.[12] There is, therefore, a certain inverse connexion between the general level of employment and that of relative differentials. So the narrowing has also been attributed to the greater fluctuation of employment among unskilled workers and the general high employment of recent years. But the relative scarcities of skilled and unskilled labour do not seem greatly affected by general fluctuations in employment. We have had, for instance, many recent cases of local unemployment caused by a shortage of skilled labour.

There are, in any case, certain employments where – although they have been quite as subject to changes in technique and in the general levels of education and employment as others – occupational differentials have suffered very little diminution. Some other explanation than these three factors is therefore required.

In Britain the narrowing of differentials has been associated with periods of rapidly rising wages, and particularly with the growth of mass trades unionism (as opposed to the exclusive 'labour aristocracies' which preceded it). As mentioned above, trade unions prefer to demand equal wage advances for all their members: mass trade unionism has, on the whole, chosen to demand increases which are equal in absolute terms. The general preference for such 'flat-rate' increases has been the first cause of the narrowing.

This preference has been strongest in certain industries (like building and woodworking) where the organization of workers was once confined to exclusive craft unions, and where apprenticeship is still a necessary qualification for entry to skilled jobs. While unskilled labour remained unorganized, these craft unions were able to maintain their members' relative differentials. When

12. For a statistical analysis see K. G. J. C. Knowles and D. J. Robertson, 'Differences between the wages of skilled and unskilled workers, 1880–1950', *Bulletin, Oxford Institute of Statistics* (April 1951), pp. 109–27.

the mass unions appeared, however, the craft unions were generally driven to combine with them in bargaining with employers. The choice of flat-rate wage demands by these combinations seems to have been largely dictated by the numerical preponderance of the less skilled workers.

The preference for flat-rate advances has been almost exclusive among certain one-time craft unions that later opened their ranks to unapprenticed workers. These unions have been competing with general labour unions for membership among the unskilled. A union of this type dominates the alliance of British engineering operatives; every wage demand of this combination from its formation in 1917 until 1952 was for a uniform cash advance.

This form of wage demand has therefore been selected by the major unions because it is most attractive to the mass of less-skilled, lower-paid workers. But certain unions have usually presented percentage wage demands, or (like the steel workers) maintained relative differentials by other devices. These unions have not experienced the general compulsion to canvass the allegiance of the less skilled. They were formed and dominated by the most skilled workers, but did not exclude unskilled labour. On the contrary, the skilled workers sometimes (as in certain of the cotton unions) compelled their assistants to join, thus continuing, in effect, to determine the latter's wages, and excluding general labour unions from their industry. On the other hand, such unions have not interested themselves in expanding into other employments: they are, therefore, not compelled by a need to maintain some parity between members in different industries – as are the great craft and general labour unions. But these exceptional unions have no apprenticeship system, and entry to the better paid jobs is by promotion from the less skilled workers. In these cases it seems that the lower paid have been reconciled (or, at least, divided in their opposition) to the maintenance of abnormal differentials by the chance of ultimately enjoying them.

Some unions have generally preferred the 'percentage' form of wage demand because they wish mainly to recruit higher-paid employees. But the general direction of unionism's advance has been towards the lower-paid mass. The average effect of wage demands has thus been somewhat to increase differentials in cash terms, but far from enough to maintain them relatively. In the last year or two a certain reaction against flat-rate demands has set in. This may be explained by a growing consciousness of their effect, the accumulated resentment of skilled men, and (with the slowing down of the unions' expansion) the diminution of the pressure of interunion competition for the lower-paid workers' allegiance. However, this reaction has so far been mainly expressed by a reversion to percentage demands which halt the narrowing but do not reverse it.

It may be that this policy has not been unacceptable to employers. Skilled labour does not readily change its occupation, and is slow to train. The growth within individual industries of combination among employers (and of private and public monopoly) may have concentrated competition for labour upon unskilled workers who are not yet committed to particular trades. While labour shortage has obliged industry to compete with the home for such workers, it is quite possible that a narrowing of differentials would have occurred without the modern unionization of the less skilled.

But that is speculative. In general, employers have accepted the form of union demands, and confined themselves to bargaining about the amount of the general advances. Thus the industries where relative skill differentials have been abnormally maintained are ones where employers are strongly disciplined and where the unions' insistence on the system of recruiting skilled workers by promotion (as opposed to apprenticeship) absolutely prohibits their movement between firms. This renders competitive bidding for skilled labour not only restricted, but useless. These industries have suffered by the relatively low wage they offer unskilled labour. Nevertheless, the employers have generally preferred to accept the situation rather than provoke disputes about differentials.[13] The main factors, therefore, remain the policy of unions and the attitudes of workers.

13. It does not in any case seem that the greater freedom to pay wages above the collectively agreed rates of employers in less disciplined industries has offset the effects of union wage policies. Knowles and Robertson ('Earnings in engineering, 1926–1948') suggest occupational relative earnings to have followed broadly the trend of relative wage rates. Inter-industry differentials have also been affected by the predominance of flat-rate claims, and here Miss Evans's study suggests that the narrowing in

The broad argument here has been that the growth of collective organization that has accompanied high employment has imposed on British wage movements a particular pattern of repeated (almost regular) cycles of wage advances, which have also so far involved a reduction in most relative wage differentials. This pattern reflects very largely the working and internal necessities of the institutions now concerned in the fixing of wages, and amounts to an implicit wage policy.

The pattern has not so far shown itself amenable to direct state action: the unsuccessful 'wage stop' of 1950, for instance, represented a governmental attempt to limit wage increases in a selective fashion. The government might disrupt it by monetary policy, but only if it were prepared to accept a politically uncomfortable degree of unemployment.

Such significant modifications to this pattern as have occurred have been of two kinds. First, those arising from the uneven tenure of collective regulation and its imperfect techniques, and from the exceptional institutional arrangements of certain trades. Second, from the few economic changes which have been sufficiently drastic to practise the system of 'established relativities'. Only two major examples of this occur to the writer. On the one hand, the violent 1952 recession in the cotton trade so delayed the cotton workers' participation in the contemporary wage cycles as, in effect, to reduce their relative wage rates substantially. On the other, the rapid post-war expansion of the vehicle industry made the employers there reluctant to accept the discipline of the engineering employers' association. Wages in the biggest motor-car factories were thus bargained on the spot, producing high relative wages.[14]

Most recent economic developments appear, therefore, to have taken the system of 'established relativities' as given, so that adaptation must otherwise proceed by changes in the employment distribution. The economy's tolerance of the wage pattern

relative wage rates is reflected (though not to the full extent) in relative earnings.

14. See Knowles and Robertson, 'Earnings in engineering, 1926–1948'. It is interesting, however, that the individual motor-car producers have now adopted a system of regulating wage advances by reference to engineering collective agreements that virtually 'freezes' the wage differential.

may, then, be partly attributable to the fact that, given a generally high level of employment, few economic changes involve such particular shortages or surpluses of labour as to disrupt it. The evidence, in any case, suggests that the distribution of labour between industries is less affected by differences in wages than by employment opportunities.

Part Seven **Unemployment**

Before the Second World War economists concerned themselves with the causes and possible cures of cyclical unemployment. In the post-war period economists have been preoccupied with the relationship between unemployment and the increase rate of the general level of prices. It is possible that increasing the general level of unemployment may bring about price level stability, but this may cause a disproportionate rise in the level of unemployment in particular occupations, industries, or regions (Northern Ireland, Scotland, and the north-east coast have tended to suffer from the effects of 'stop–go'). In the U.S.A. structural unemployment has been associated with the tendency of the economy to experience price rises while there has been considerable unemployment, and fears have also been expressed that automation might increase the amount of structural unemployment. The possibilities of structural unemployment weaken the impact of Keynesian aggregate demand policies and raise the problem of new policies: Lipsey's article examines the relationship between the two types of unemployment and sketches a theory of structural unemployment.

12 R. G. Lipsey

Structural and Deficient-Demand Unemployment Reconsidered

Excerpts from Lipsey, R. G. (1965) Structural and deficient-demand unemployment reconsidered, in A. M. Ross (ed.), *Employment policy and the labour market* (University of California Press), pp. 210–18 and 243–55.

The intention in this paper is to re-examine the controversy between the two competing explanations for higher rates of unemployment in the United States: the structuralist and the deficient-aggregate-demand theories. [The first part] attempts to define various types of unemployment in a way which is operationally meaningful, [while the remainder] presents a preliminary report on the question of whether or not it is possible to build a formal theory of structural unemployment which will yield predictions precise enough so that a test does become possible.

The Nature of the Problem

Consider the problem of reducing unemployment. Almost everyone would prefer less unemployment to more unemployment *ceteris paribus*. Problems arise, however, when the objective of reducing unemployment conflicts with other objectives such as maintaining a stable level of prices and a satisfactory balance of payments. The problems that concern us can be illustrated by considering only two policy variables: the level of unemployment (U) and the general level of prices (P). The argument can, of course, be generalized to include as many policy goals as is desired. [. . .]

In fig. 1 we plot the percentage of the labor force unemployed (U) against the percentage rate of change of prices ($\dot{P}$). It is necessary to show both the actual relation existing between these two variables and the nature of the policy makers' preferences. The RR curve shows combinations of U and $\dot{P}$ which can be attained by varying the level of aggregate demand; generally, the

245

higher the level of aggregate demand is, the lower will be the level of unemployment, but the higher will be the rate of price inflation.[1]

The preferences of the policy maker can be of two genera types. First, he can say that there is some maximum rate of inflation he is prepared to tolerate, in which case $\dot{P}$ enters his preference functions as a constraint. [. . .] Two such constraints

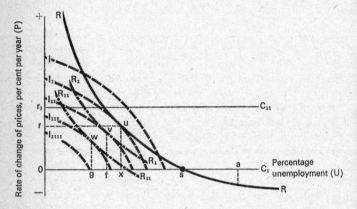

Figure 1

are illustrated by the lines $r_1 C_{11}$ and OC_1 in fig. 1, the lines indicating that inflations in excess of $Or\,1$ per cent per year in the case of C_{11} and zero per cent per year in the case of C_1 would not be tolerated. Second, the policy maker can say that there is some rate at which he is prepared to trade an increase in the rate of inflation in return for a reduction in unemployment. An example of the second type of 'policy makers' preference function' is

1. The RR curve is derived from a Phillips curve which relates the rate of change of money wages to the level of unemployment plus an additional relation: ($\dot{P} = f(\dot{W})$). Even if the Phillips curve does not *closely* describe the experience of a particular economy, it is generally agreed that periods of very high aggregate demand tend to be periods of low unemployment and rapid rates of inflation, while periods of low aggregate demand tend to be periods of high unemployment and low rates of inflation. If prices are completely inflexible downward, the RR curve coincides with the U-axis to the right of s.

illustrated in fig. 1 by the set of concave indifference curves, the ordering of which is such that more preferred positions are attained as one moves 'southwest' (i.e. reducing both U and $\dot{P}$). We shall carry out our analysis assuming the policy makers' preferences to be of the general form illustrated by our indifference map, but the whole analysis is easily amended to cover other types of preference functions, including the special case of the constraint C' which indicates that no positive rate of inflation will be tolerated.[2]

The point u at which an indifference curve is tangential to the RR curve indicates the point at which aggregate-demand policy should be aimed, given the policy makers' own trade-off rates between U and $\dot{P}$. If unemployment is higher than Os (say it is Oa), then aggregative measures can reduce unemployment without incurring any inflation; if unemployment lies between Os and Ox, then aggregative measures can be used to reduce unemployment at a cost in inflationary terms which is acceptable to the policy maker. We shall call Or the *acceptable rate of inflation* (always remembering that Or could be zero). The phrase 'acceptable rate of inflation' thus stands for the maximum rate of inflation which, according to the policy makers' own scale of preferences, it is worth incurring in order to reduce unemployment.

Now consider reducing the level of unemployment below Ox. It would not be rational to try to do this by increasing aggregate demand, but it might be possible to do so by shifting the RR curve.[3] There are many measures which might serve to shift the RR curve to the left. This is not the place to consider these in detail, but they would include structural measures which had the

2. Some interesting problems arise when a number of individual decision makers have different preference functions, but for our purposes we assume this political problem to be solved, so that those actually making the decisions have a consistent ordering of the various states.

3. The RR curve might shift automatically after high demand had been maintained for some time. If equilibrating adjustments which tend to equalize unemployment rates in various markets operate with a substantial distributed time-lag, then the minimum level of over-all unemployment compatible with some given rate of inflation might fall over time. In practice, this might be an important problem, but for simplicity in exposition we shall assume the RR curve to be the long-run one which reflects the relation between $\dot{P}$ and U after time has been allowed for normal adjustment mechanisms to work.

effect of, for example, (1) reducing inequalities in excess demand (and hence in unemployment rates) between various labor markets, and (2) reducing the time taken in changing the supply of labor into the form in which it was being demanded. Generally, policy measures designed to shift the RR curve will have a cost. (Whenever costless measures are discovered, they should be introduced, whatever the state of the economy and whatever the precise nature of the policy makers' trade-off rates.) We could conceive of making a cost-benefit analysis of the various measures for shifting the RR curve, the costs being those of the scheme and the benefits being the discounted value of the increase in output which occurred as a result of the scheme.[4] All measures which yield a net return on standard cost-benefit analysis would shift the RR curve. If we assume that such measures shift the curve to R_1R_1, it would be possible to reduce unemployment from Ox to Of by measures which paid in the above defined sense. Of course, it would be possible to shift the RR curve still further to the left, and it is doubtful that the point would ever be reached at which some further shifting of the curve would not be possible. We could, for example, use jet transports to move all workers and their families between areas in order to reduce transitional unemployment; we could retrain workers with obsolete skills even when they had only a few months of working life remaining; we could have government placement officers in all factories arranging new jobs for workers the moment they gave or were given notice.

There may be some reductions in unemployment which one would wish to effect even though they showed a loss on a calculation of the monetary costs and benefits. These structural measures which would be desirable on social grounds in spite of showing a net monetary loss[5] would shift the RR curve further to the left

4. For example, re-education schemes for forty-year-old workers whose skills had been rendered technologically obsolete might pay if the cost of these schemes were set against the increased output available from the re-educated workers; on a similar calculation re-education schemes for fifty-five-year-old workers might not pay.

5. For example, I would favor retraining older workers even though the costs exceeded the total possible output of these workers over the remainder of their working lives. This would seem to be a small cost to pay in order to offset the threat of being rendered technologically unemployable at some unforeseeable stage of one's working life.

– say, to $R_{11}R_{11}$ – which would reduce unemployment by a further amount, fg.

Now what can we say about these various levels of unemployment which we have distinguished? Taking present unemployment to be Oa, we can say that the amount ax is deficient-demand unemployment in the sense that this much unemployment could be removed by raising aggregate demand without creating unacceptable conflicts with other goals of policy. The amount xg can be called structural unemployment in the sense that it can be removed by structural cures, some of which pay for themselves on an analysis of the money costs and money benefits and some of which are justified because the nonpecuniary social benefits are judged to justify the net money cost of the schemes. The amount Og can be referred to as frictional unemployment in the sense that we do not wish to remove it on grounds of an assessment of either the monetary or the social benefits of doing so; the persistence of this amount of unemployment is thus consistent with our notion of full employment and we may define Og as full employment.

It is interesting to note the extent to which value judgments enter into the determination of these various points. The point s is objectively determined and independent of the decision takers' preferences. The location of the point u, on the other hand, involves preferences as well as the objective RR curve. Thus, if by deficient-demand unemployment we mean unemployment which can be removed by raising aggregate demand without encountering *unacceptable* conflicts with other goals of policy, our definition necessarily involves preferences, since we must know what constitutes an 'unacceptable conflict'. The R_1R_1 curve is determined objectively but the point v is determined both by this curve and by the subjective preference function. Finally the $R_{11}R_{11}$ curve is itself influenced by subjective valuations of nonmonetary social advantages. Thus the full-employment point w has a two-fold subjective element in its determination, the location of both the indifference curve and the $R_{11}R_{11}$ curve being influenced by the value judgments of the decision taker.

Our categories also point up the fact that structural and frictional unemployment shade into each other with no clear boundary separating them. Much of what is called structural unemployment merely consists of frictional unemployment operating with an unacceptably long time-lag. In the extreme case the time-lag becomes infinite, so that the displaced worker never finds another job; but this is rare, relative to the cases in which the transition to a new job takes a very long time but is accomplished eventually. Thus, in a very real sense, structural unemployment is that part of frictional unemployment which is not acceptable either because there would be a net money gain in removing it or because the social gains of removing it are judged to outweigh the *net* money cost of so doing.

We have defined full employment as occurring when measured U is Og. It is worth while noting the effect of defining full employment as occurring when unacceptable rates of inflation are experienced, i.e. at Ox in fig. 1. (This was done, for example, in the *Annual Report of the Council of Economic Advisers* in 1962.) This makes all unemployment deficient-demand unemployment by definition in the sense that, whatever its causes, full employment can always be restored solely by increasing aggregate demand. Any structural change which shifts the RR curve to the right merely raises the level of U at which full employment is defined to occur. Clearly, there is nothing to be gained by this defining away of the problem, and it is thus necessary to define the goal of full employment which is similar, if not identical, to the one adopted here.

It should also be noted that our classification is based on cures rather than on causes. From the policy point of view, this seems to be the most interesting basis for classification, but it is worth remembering that a classification based on the causes of the unemployment might not produce identical measurements of the relative importance of deficient-demand and structural unemployment.

Policy disagreements

When the unemployment problem is analysed in these terms, several important sources of disagreement are revealed. We can disagree over the factual questions of the location of the RR and the R_1R_1 curves, and we can disagree over the value judgments necessary to locate both the $R_{11}R_{11}$ curve and the indifference map which orders various combinations of U and P.

These disagreements can affect the location of each of the points that we have distinguished. Consider, for example, the location of the important point u. If we are very worried about inflation, our utility function will be such that x will move close to s, so that, for a given total level of unemployment, less will be deficient-demand and more will be structural. The second possible disagreement concerns the location of the RR curve. Structuralists believe that the ratio of structural unemployment to total unemployment is high, while deficient-demand theorists believe that it is low. Almost everyone seems to agree that in the United States in the mid-1960s the point x is located below 5% and above, say, 2%. From this it follows that the pursuit of correct lines of policy does not require further information on the dispute between structuralists and deficient-demand theorists. Since few, if any, structuralists deny that an increase in aggregate demand would reduce unemployment somewhat,[6] the rational policy in the present situation would clearly be to increase aggregate demand progressively until unacceptable degrees of inflation were encountered. Once this deficient-demand unemployment had been eliminated, we could see how much structural unemployment remained and take steps to remove it.[7] If the structuralists are correct, unacceptable rates of inflation might be encountered around, say, $4\frac{1}{2}$–$4\frac{3}{4}$% U, while, if the deficient-demand theorists are correct, it might be possible to get U down to, say, $3\frac{1}{2}$ or even 3% before $\dot{P}$ became unacceptably large.

Thus in a perfect world, in which policy makers acted rationally, we would behave *as if* we were deficient-demand theorists and increase aggregate demand until the limit set by acceptable price rises was reached; we would then all behave as structuralists and consider how the remaining unemployment could be removed.

The worst that could happen if we followed this policy is that we might overshoot the mark and experience rates of inflation one

6. See, e.g., C. Killingsworth, in *The nation's manpower revolution*, U.S. Senate, Committee on Labor and Public Welfare, part 5 (1963), p. 1479.

7. It is generally accepted that, once everything possible has been done with the tool of aggregate demand, some unacceptable structural unemployment will remain (see e.g., *Annual report of the council of economic advisers* [1964], appendix A, p. 168).

or two percentage points above the acceptable level for a short time until demand could be lowered to the desired level. Of course, there can be no finality about value judgments, but I should regard anyone who opposed this policy because of fear of inflation as having either an insufficiently thought-out position or a set of value judgments that were definitely perverse judged by any common standard. The *possibility* of incurring a once-for-all rise in the price level of one or two percentage points cannot be regarded as a high price to pay in order to discover by how much unemployment can be reduced by using the relatively simple tools of fiscal policy.

There is one other, possibly more serious, disagreement over current policy: if the decision makers refuse to follow the rational policy of raising aggregate demand until the unacceptable rate of inflation is reached, can unemployment be reduced by applying *only* structural cures? Here there is more disagreement, but again the only rational policy would be to find out by experiment. We would all agree that, unless their costs were extremely high, little could be lost by trying structuralist cures in a situation of 5% unemployment, even though we might disagree about how much could be gained from such policies in this situation.

Reasons for considering the problem

Why, then, consider the problem at all, if a rational anti-unemployment policy could be pursued without further knowledge? Four reasons deserve mention.

1. There is a general belief that there exists a strong body of evidence which conflicts with the structuralist position. I do not believe that this is so, and since our view of the behavior of the economy is at issue, it seems important for the sake of general knowledge that we know the cause of the recent high levels of unemployment. Even if we all agree that the rational policy is to raise aggregate demand until the limit of usefulness of this tool is reached, it does not follow that we know the cause of the present unemployment. It would seem important on many counts that we try to understand the recent causes of high unemployment rates.

2. If the deficient-demand theorists are correct, the present bout of unemployment can be regarded as an isolated phenomenon and not as part of a general trend. If the structuralists are

correct, we must look forward to a long-term trend for the free market to produce high unemployment and we must look for long-term solutions requiring persistent and active government intervention. Also, other industrial economies can look forward to repeating the American experience within twenty years or so and they would be well advised to consider long-term solutions before the problem actually arises. Clearly, the whole western world has a considerable interest and stake in the outcome of the debate. This leads us directly to our next point.

3. The issue of structuralist versus deficient-aggregate-demand theories will arise at other times and at other places. It seems important, therefore, that an effective method of testing between these two theories should be developed, so that the procedure will be ready when the debate breaks out again.

4. From the point of view of designing anti-unemployment policies it might be useful to try to guess in advance how much structural unemployment would remain after the aggregate-demand tool had done all it could. This is of some importance, since there are such very long lags between the perception of a problem by economists, the designing of appropriate cures, and the actual enactment of the measures sufficient for the cure. [. . .]

The Theory of Structural Unemployment

In this section I intend to do no more than present some notes on the key characteristics of a model which might handle the problem of structural unemployment.[8]

A model of cyclical fluctuations

Consider a model which displays continuous fluctuations in the level of income and employment. These cycles may be generated by any one of a number of well-known processes. There might be

8. This paper is a preliminary report on a continuing study. The next phase in the study is the construction of a model which will be adequate to handle the problems of structural change and demand fluctuation. In the meantime this presentation provides an analysis of some of the relevant problems so far as I am able to handle them with verbal tools. I am acutely aware that it suffers from some of the defects of vagueness which I have been so ready to criticize in the works of others. Nonetheless, I hope the ideas mentioned here may be of some small interest to others working in the field.

an inventory cycle, or some form of a multiplier–accelerator process, or merely random shocks impinging on a set of relations which would otherwise produce a static equilibrium situation.

To this oscillating model let us add a floor and a ceiling of the type originally introduced into such models by J. R. Hicks. We shall assume that on most (but not necessarily all) upswings the economy is bounding off the ceiling. On the other hand, it is not necessary that the floor should be operative on most downswings; cases can be analysed in which the upturn occurs of its own accord and in which the upturn occurs because an unstable downward spiral encounters a floor.

The behavior of such a model is determined by a combination of aggregate-demand and structural factors. If both ceilings and floors are operative, then the period of the cycle is explained by aggregate-demand factors, but the amplitude of the oscillations and, thus, the mean values around which the fluctuations occur are determined by structural factors (the location of the ceilings and the floors).

The behavior of such an elementary model is illustrated in fig. 2. We have chosen to plot the course of unemployment rather than the course of income, and so in our figure the *ceiling* on income becomes a *floor* on unemployment. We assume that the line SS shows a time series for the level of unemployment corresponding to the point u in fig. 1, i.e. the level of unemployment below which inflationary pressures become unacceptable. We further assume that the policy makers' preference function is unchanged, so that the upward drift of the SS line indicates a rightward shift of the RR curve in fig. 1. We shall analyse the reasons for such a shift later. In the meantime we can assume by way of an example that a proportion of the labor force finds itself displaced by new machines each period and that some of these persons cannot or will not make the adjustments necessary to find new employment (retraining, reducing their supply price, and so on).

The ceiling to the upswing is not a simple constraint that is suddenly reached. Instead it is a range over which the RR curve in fig. 1 becomes progressively steeper, so that further increments in demand are more and more dissipated through increases in prices and are less and less effective in increasing employment and real output. The ceiling begins to be felt as soon as a bottle-neck in labor or capital is met in any sector; it becomes more and more constraining as further increases in output produce more and more bottlenecks.

Any increase in structural maladjustments of any sort raises the floor on unemployment. Since the floor is not a single con-straint level, it is possible for unemployment to fall below the level indicated by SS, but such periods will be times of heavy

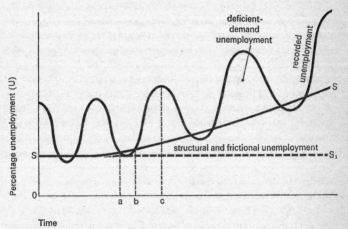

Figure 2

inflationary pressure and, unless the monetary authorities take steps to prevent it, the general excess demand will be eventually removed through the price rises that it causes.

As the level of structural unemployment rises, then, as illus-trated, each successive boom encounters heavy inflationary pres-sures at higher over-all levels of unemployment. Unemployment will not fall to as low a level as in previous booms, because increments in demand will begin to dissipate themselves, mainly in price increases, sooner than in previous booms (i.e. at progres-sively higher levels of U). This mechanism should be sufficient to ensure that the minimum level of U will rise from boom to boom as SS rises. A complete model, however, would include a reaction function for the central authorities, and as soon as unemploy-ment fell below SS (i.e. unacceptable rates of inflation were encountered), the central authorities could be expected to adopt deflationary policies which would dampen the upswing and help to reverse its direction.[9]

Structural unemployment

Now, with even so simple a model, we are able to start a consideration of the competing explanations of the rising rate of unemployment.

The model tested by Knowles and Kalachek is illustrated in fig. 3. The economy is envisioned as encountering a stable structural floor to unemployment until sometime around 1957 or 1958 when there was a once-and-for-all structural change which placed the actual unemployment rate well below the *SS* line. Actual unemployment is then envisioned as rising to reach its new floor (and possibly to oscillate above this floor, although this is never stated). Clearly, the predictions which follow from adding such an assumed structural change to our model are: (*a*) that bottlenecks and shortages will be manifest in many places in the economy; (*b*) that the pace of inflation will show a sudden step increase; and (*c*) that the price increases will eventually reduce aggregate demand sufficiently so that unemployment will rise (at least) to the level indicated by *SS* after its step increase.

It would seem that this version of the structural hypothesis is quite easily refuted as an explanation of the course of unemployment in the United States since 1958, because both inflationary pressures and labor bottlenecks were observed to diminish rather than increase. This is the version of the structural theory that has been given most attention in the past, and a large number of its predictions have been refuted. One of the few things about which we can be relatively certain in this whole debate is that this version is as close to being absolutely refuted as any probabilistic hypothesis could ever be.

9. If we have a rigid ceiling to unemployment that is independent of the floor, then the rise in structural problems would narrow the amplitude of the fluctuations and raise the mean level of U without raising its maximum level. This would be a rather unsatisfactory model, and we would want the maximum level of U to rise as the minimum level rose. This could be done either by making the ceiling in some way dependent on the floor, or by making the slump a self-correcting one which reversed itself without the benefit of a ceiling on U.

There is, however, a second version of this structural theory which deserves more serious attention. This version is illustrated by fig. 2. The version says that for various reasons the *SS* curve has been moving upward through time (i.e. the *RR* curve of fig. 1 has been shifting to the right). This theory requires that the bottle-necks and inflationary pressures which Knowles and Kalachek looked for occurred, not in the period 1958–60, but in 1955–57,

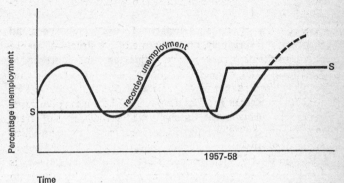

Figure 3

which was the last period in any way resembling a boom. If structural problems had been increasing sufficiently to be signifi-cant, this would have to be evidenced by inflationary pressures at a higher level of unemployment and a lower level of aggregate demand than in previous booms or, if unemployment fell to levels comparable with previous booms, it would be evidenced by significantly greater inflationary pressure than in previous booms.[10] Thus the time interval *a–b* in fig. 2 would correspond to the period 1955–57 and the interval *b–c* to, say, 1958–60.

10. Although this hypothesis deserves precise formulation and careful testing, it is worth noting in passing that there are bits of evidence which seem to fit in with this theory. Professor Gordon seemed to find some (albeit inconclusive) evidence of a structural shift in unemployment around this period. Also, this is the period which has produced an inflation most similar to that expected by cost-push theorists (rising prices in the face of apparently weak aggregate-demand forces) rather than being cost-push induced; such an inflation could be induced by structural bottlenecks occurring at a higher level of over-all *U* than in previous cycles.

The course of events after period *a–b* in this theory is complicated by *the important fact* that structural changes (which cause the *SS* curve to slope upward) may also affect the level of aggregate demand. Up to now we have been assuming aggregate demand to be fluctuating for reasons unrelated to the structure of floors and ceilings. It is quite possible, however, that a rise in structural unemployment (during, say, period *b–c*) would induce reductions in aggregate demand which would intensify the depression in the period *c–d*.

The relation between structural change and aggregate demand depends, not surprisingly, on the nature of the structural change under consideration. Since we are, at this stage, only concerned to reveal possibilities, we shall take one type of change as an illustration. Consider a change which replaces two unskilled workers by one skilled worker at $1\frac{1}{2}$ times the pay plus the same capital costs. If prices are held constant, the change redistributes incomes from wages to profits. It also redistributes incomes from the unskilled to the skilled. If prices are reduced in proportion to the saving in costs, then the only income redistribution within the industry is between unskilled and skilled workers. In this case there will also be an income redistribution between industries, the direction of which will depend on the price elasticity of demand for the goods in question.

In equilibrium, the effect on aggregate demand will depend on the savings propensities of the various groups. If profit earners and skilled workers have a higher marginal propensity to save than unskilled workers, aggregate demand will be lowered by the change. Also there may be some dynamic effects if the lag in the relation between spending and the receipt of income differs as between the groups. If those receiving extra income have a longer lag in their consumption functions than those losing income, there is an initial reduction in income caused by the fact that the losers cut their spending before the gainers increase theirs.[11]

Thus we conclude (*a*) that a structural shift can permanently

11. If, for example, we assume that consumption out of wages this month depends on last month's wage bill, while consumption out of profits in each month of this year depends on total profits earned last year, then a once-for-all structural change of this sort can set up a damped cyclical process of which the first phase is a downswing. Of course, if we add an accelerator to the process, the swings can be made to be of any magnitude.

affect the level of aggregate demand associated with a particular level of income by redistributing income between groups with different savings propensities, and (b) that a structural shift can set up cyclical swings in aggregate demand and income by redistributing income between groups with different lags in their consumption function.

Thus even if we were able to distinguish between deficient-demand and structural unemployment during time period b–c (i.e. we could locate the SS curve), we should find a higher-than-usual level of deficient-demand unemployment, but we might misinterpret the situation unless we realized that the decline in aggregate demand was itself the direct consequence of the structural changes in the economy.

Now the most important question which we have to ask is this: can we distinguish between situations in which rising average unemployment is owing to a structural change in the floor (to unemployment), so that the SS curve is as shown by the solid line in fig. 2, and situations in which rising unemployment is owing to a declining average level of aggregate demand, so that the SS curve in fig. 2 is the dotted line SS'?

Whether or not we can distinguish between these two situations by studying the structure of the unemployed[12] depends on the behavior of employers in laying off workers in the face of declining demand and in the face of those technological changes which are a possible cause of structural unemployment.

We can now introduce the following hypotheses:

1. When demand falls, workers are laid off according to any set of qualifications in proportions conforming to those desired in production. This means that the structure of the new increment of unemployed will show the same characteristics as the structure of the employed. This also means that a rise in demand will re-employ the unemployed in proportions (classified by any set of characteristics) which are the same as those displayed by those already employed.

2. When unemployment develops because of technological changes in the nature of production, the optimal structure of

12. By the phrase 'the structure of the unemployed' we shall understand the distribution of the unemployed according to any relevant classification (age, education, skills, etc.).

characteristics of the employed is established by releasing unwanted workers.

These two hypotheses ensure that the structure of the new demand for labor which will result from a rise in aggregate demand can be inferred by studying the structure of those now employed. Any mismatching of the characteristics of the unemployed with those of the employed indicates potential structural problems. Further, an increase in structural unemployment will cause an increasing difference between the structures of the unemployed and the employed. Thus, these two assumptions are sufficient to make sense of all the 'tests' of structural theories which have concentrated on the characteristics of the unemployed.

Unfortunately, the first hypothesis is categorically refuted. It has long been a commonplace among deficient-demand theorists to point out that a lack of agreement between the characteristics of the unemployed and the employed does not necessarily indicate potential structural problems. It is pointed out that when aggregate demand falls, the resulting unemployment hits particular groups (e.g. unskilled blue-collar workers) hardest. Thus, the characteristics of the unemployed do not match the proportions in which factors are actually required in the production process. Thus, when demand recovers, the unemployed are taken back in proportions which reflect the way they were dismissed and not the way they are required in actual production. This behavior, which represents a sort of private unemployment insurance for sheltered groups, means that one must take care in judging the adequacy of the available supply of labor by comparing the characteristics of the employed with the characteristics of the unemployed. This point has been made against the structuralists, and the procedure has been adopted of comparing the mix of characteristics of the unemployed at comparable stages of each cycle and asserting that, if there had been a rise in structural unemployment, this mix would be observed to change significantly. *But there is absolutely no reason to believe that this is so*. Indeed, the argument used against the structuralists is a double-edged sword. There is no reason why structural unemployment should not give rise to the same characteristic mix among the unemployed as would occur with deficient-demand unemployment. The only difference would be that with structural unemployment the mix of the *employed* would represent the mix at which new labor would be taken on as production increased, while this is not so with deficient-demand unemployment.

We now amend hypothesis 1 as follows:

1a. When demand falls, workers are not maintained in the proportions in which they are optimally required at full-capacity production; specifically, the ratio of skilled and nonoperatives to unskilled and operatives is raised as demand temporarily falls off. This means that the structure of the unemployed will be different from the structure of the employed.

1b. When demand recovers, workers will be rehired in the proportions in which they were laid off, so that the original structure of the employed will be re-established when full-capacity production again occurs.

Now if we take assumptions 1a and 1b combined with hypothesis 2, we find that we cannot distinguish between a rise in unemployment with technological causes and one with deficient-demand causes until the upswing occurs. Indeed, if there is some deficient-demand unemployment as well as some structural unemployment (as is almost certain to be the case), we will not be able to tell anything until full capacity of plant and equipment is reached. Once this level is reached, further increments in demand for labor will show a sharp break in its structure of characteristics from previous increments in demand. The structure of further increments in demand will change to being at least that displayed by the structure of the employed. Indeed, there may even be a more marked shift as new capacity using the very latest processes is installed, which will require a structure of labor more at variance with the structure of characteristics of the unemployed than the *average* requirement of all existing plants.

A further prediction of the theory which employs assumptions 1a, 1b, and 2 in a situation with some structural and some deficient-demand unemployment is that bottlenecks and inflationary pressure will set in at a higher level of unemployment than before. If this theory does correctly describe the facts, it follows that studies of the characteristics of the unemployed are quite irrelevant to the theories which the authors thought they were testing. (I would not, of course, rule out the possibility that further theorizing could develop some predictions about the structure of unemployment; I am only saying we do not have them now.)

Thus it follows that, as long as we all agree that there is some deficient-demand unemployment in the economy now, we can tell nothing from the structure of either the existing unemployed or those newly employed. Thus Heller is not correct in saying that the behavior of unemployment in the early upswing of the present cycle is inconsistent with the structural theory. (Heller would be correct only if someone held the extreme theory that there was *no* deficient-demand unemployment in the early 1960s.)

Structural unemployment and the price system

Last, we must ask: What if structural problems do occur before unemployment falls to the level desired? Can we not rely on the self-regulating mechanisms of a free market economy to remove these structural problems? These questions pose a host of problems which deserve serious and detailed consideration, but which cannot be dealt with here. We shall content ourselves with mentioning one or two problems.

If it were correct that structural problems would all be solved in a reasonable amount of time by the workings of our free market economy, given only a high enough level of aggregate demand, then the whole controversy that we have been considering would be of little practical interest. This is a position taken by some.

Let us ask whether, if there is a structural problem, the price system should not be able to remove it by suitable changes in relative wages. Clearly, there is nothing in economic theory that would lead us to expect relative wage changes generally to raise the aggregate demand for labor. Thus we should only expect, at best, that these changes could even out the incidence of unemployment, leaving the government free to decide on the appropriate general level of unemployment and to obtain this through policies affecting aggregate demand. Clearly, this is conceivable. What we need if this is to be the case are (this does not pretend to be an exhaustive list): perfectly flexible relative prices; no free-market equilibrium-factor price below the starvation wage or whatever conventional minimum above starvation is agreed, or else a well-behaved production function with isoquants asymptotic to all axes; sufficient knowledge so that the techniques necessary to combine all factors in all conceivable proportions are currently known (or discoverable at little cost); a process of innovation which is rapidly responsive to relative factor prices and not subject to considerable inertia or to fads, fashions, or cumulative behavior on the part of scientists and others.

Clearly, whether or not these conditions exist is an empirical question; they cannot be proved to be the only possible state of the world. Let us, by way of example, consider some other possible states.

1. Production functions might be such that the range of substitutability would not be great enough to provide full employment of all factors at widely acceptable prices.

2. If there existed unused supplies of one of the factors, would it not pay to invent processes which would utilize the cheap, readily available factors? The answer is: it might do so, but not necessarily. Inventive talent is an expensive and scarce resource and will be used where it shows the greatest probability of return. This does not necessarily consist in inventing ways of using the surplus labor. It is an open question what would happen to the course of inventions in, say, ten years' time, if the relative price of unskilled labor were allowed to fall as long as there existed an excess supply. If current trends in inventions are showing promise of reducing all inputs (but using factors in a proportion different from that in which they are available), it is not clear that a cheapening of unskilled labour would lead immediately to a whole new pattern of inventions. (Are we sure that, if we move in the direction of a much higher proportion of unskilled labor, current work in theoretical science will prove as readily useful?)[13]

If each successive invention uses more of some factors and less

13. Presumably it would be possible to invent techniques to use the limited talents of educationally subnormal persons. This is not done, because it would not repay the cost of making such inventions. Similarly it is quite conceivable that a time would come when it would not pay to invest considerable scientific talent to invent processes which could utilize persons with I.Qs. below, say, 105 even if these persons were free factors. We can hope that such a day will not soon come, but we cannot rule it out as being logically contradictory.

of others, there will be a body of techniques from which one can choose as relative prices change. If each successive invention is absolutely more efficient in the sense that it economizes on all factor inputs, then the range of possible substitutability may be too small to ensure full employment of all factors.

This brief discussion suggests that we must keep an open mind on this critical issue. There is little doubt that the price system could be used to reduce the impact of structural problems.[14] It is quite another thing, however, to assert that the price system could solve all, or even the majority, of structural problems over an acceptable span of time.

Conclusion

We may now summarize the results of this preliminary study of the theoretical problems of structural unemployment.

1. A theory that predicts the existence of adequate aggregate demand combined with high unemployment rates because the economy is currently bumping against serious constraints on the supplies of certain kinds of labor is pretty definitely refuted.

2. A variant of the structural theory which predicts that the economy is not now bumping against the constraints because real excess demand has been reduced by inflation caused by the excess demand which occurred when the constraints were operative in the past has yet to be conclusively refuted.

3. Various ways in which structural changes could affect unemployment have been studied, and it is concluded that the theories which predict that there is at present some higher level of structural unemployment *plus* some deficient-demand employment are the most serious contenders theoretically and the most difficult to test empirically. In particular, it has been argued that the theory that there has been a rise in structural unemployment does *not* necessarily predict that there will be a significant change in any index of the structure of unemployed workers (classified by any characteristic in which we are interested). Further predictions of this theory in relation to reductions in unemployment have been tentatively explored.

14. Eckstein, op. cit., presents some impressive evidence about the lack of use currently made of the price system as an equilibrating mechanism in labor markets.

4. In general, the problem of testing between the two sets of theories seems to be more difficult than has sometimes been thought. Sufficiently discriminating tests cannot be carried out until we have theoretical specifications of the theories which are precise enough to generate clear test statements. I have tried to sketch out here the beginnings of an attack on these problems.

Part Eight **Full Employment and Inflation**

The part played by wages in the inflationary process is still the subject of debate. Lipsey's lucid article considers the possibility that money-wage increases may be dependent upon the demand for labour, Hines' article is notable for its serious attempt to estimate the effects of trade-union pressure for wage increases as evinced through changes in membership, and Lydall's article is the forerunner of many on wage drift and the problems posed by inter-sectoral variations in wage movements. A more comprehensive examination of inflation will be found in the forthcoming Penguin Modern Economics Readings volume entitled *Inflation*, edited by J. R. Ball and Peter Doyle.

13 R. G. Lipsey

Can There Be a Valid Theory of Wages?

Lipsey, R. G. (1962) Can there be a valid theory of wages? *Adv. Sci.*, **19**, 105–12.

I have been asked in this paper to explain to the non-economist what I, as an economist, do and why. In a nutshell I can say that, as a practitioner in the field of economic science, I search for stable patterns of human behaviour in the economic sphere. Such behaviour patterns provide the basis for making the testable predictions without which there can be no science. In some cases we search the data directly to discover stable behaviour patterns which we suspect, for one reason or another, to exist; in other cases we *postulate* them, then *deduce* what their consequences would be, and only then search the data to see if these consequences can be observed.

The view that economics can be a discipline which deals *in a scientific manner* with human behaviour is not one which is universally accepted. Indeed some of the strongest opponents of this view are to be found amongst professional economists in government, business, and universities. What I wish to do here is to consider in general the major arguments advanced for the view that economic *science* is impossible, then to show how I would go about meeting these objections in the context of one particular practical problem, the determination of the general level of money wages.

The subject matter of economics is the ordinary person; and the ordinary person is very sensitive about his image of himself. The idea of laws – especially the eighteenth- and nineteenth-century idea of laws which grind forward inexorably with mechanical accuracy – applying to himself seems to rob the ordinary person of those facets which he regards as distinguishing him from the animal.

Human beings, it is argued, have 'free will'; they are capable of changing their behaviour in quite unpredictable ways. Consider trying to predict such a simple thing as when an individual will board a bus or an underground train on his journey home from work. Whether he leaves early or late will depend on a vast number of things, things which have happened to him from without, so to speak, such as how much work is put into his IN tray and how many friends stop to chat with him during the day; and things which have happened from within, such as his own state of mind and body. Even if we could know and sum up all these influences, the individual could confound our predictions by an utterly capricious change of mind – *an exercise of free will*. Similarly, for such things as the wage bargain, the outcome depends on a vast number of factors – who the arbitrator is, who the union negotiator is, many facets of the climate of opinion, accidental occurrences, and on top of all this it can be influenced by utterly capricious acts on the part of the negotiators. Surely, it is argued, such occurrences cannot be subject to stable behaviour patterns which can be used for prediction. Sometimes economists content themselves with listing all of the factors which might influence the outcome of some phenomenon; but such 'theory' does not get us very far and is often discouraging in that it paints a picture of an impossibly complex world in which simple stable patterns of behaviour appear to be most unlikely.

When contrasting the social and the natural sciences the general public and the professional economist usually look to classical physics and astronomy as models of science. Here the contrast is heightened by the nineteenth-century view of the physical world as a machine grinding forward with precision and inevitability. But even when a more subtle view is taken of these sciences, the great success of the impersonal scientific method in the study of the physical universe leads to gloom and often even defeatism on the part of the economists. Few economists who do look to science for guidance know much about chemistry and even fewer know anything about biology and other sciences which have problems much more akin to those of the Social Sciences but which have enjoyed undoubted success nonetheless.

Here then is the picture which seems to present itself: chaos and unpredictability in human affairs – in the simple case of the decision to go home, and in the economic case of, say, wage determination; this is contrasted with an orderly mechanical view of the physical world.

But there are certain general considerations which must make us mistrust this dichotomy between natural and social sciences. Although individual behaviour is very difficult to predict, group behaviour often shows remarkable constancy. Set people to measure the length of a room, and one person's errors are virtually impossible to predict; but ask many to do it and, by drawing a frequency distribution of the actual errors, you produce one of the most remarkable and beautiful of all constants, the normal curve of error. We can in fact predict with amazing accuracy how *the group* will make errors. You cannot predict when one person will begin his journey home, but *en masse* this behaviour is wonderfully constant. The unpredictability of the individual is reduced to the regular graph of loads carried on public transport from hour to hour. On a normal day such charts can be used to predict with a high degree of accuracy how many people will travel from place to place at any time of the day. Also if you make a change, say, raise fares for journeys commenced between 5.15 and 5.45, you will reduce total travel in this half-hour period, and such a change will be clearly observable on the graphs. Here we have a stable change in the human behaviour attributable to the *cause of the alteration in fares* (although of course John Jones, or any other single individual, may sometimes travel between 5.15 and 5.45 and sometimes travel outside of this period for reasons almost impossible to predict).

Now this should make us wonder if the same considerations might not apply to the wage bargain and other economic events. But in these cases we find not only individual behaviour which is difficult to predict, but also changing institutional circumstances so that, even if wage negotiations should show stable reactions to things like the level of unemployment in, say, the 1890s, we would hardly expect it to show the same reactions in the 1930s, let alone the 1950s. Surely the rise of unions and employers' organizations, the change in the level of negotiations (from the plant to the nation-wide bargain) and the increasing concern of government through such means as compulsory arbitration must mean that wages react to given circumstances in a very different way now than they did in the past. Thus, it is argued, each historical period is unique and we cannot hope to get a theory applying to more than a few years at a time.

Now these are powerful arguments for the unpredictability of human behaviour in economics but, on the other hand, we do have general knowledge showing that we can get somewhere with a scientific enquiry into at least some sphere of human behaviour. How then should we proceed? Clearly the answer to our particular question about the possibility of finding stable, hence predictable patterns of human behaviour in the economic sphere must be sought from empirical data. *A priori* arguments have been inconclusive; we cannot rule out stable behaviour in general because we have already found it in some cases, but we do not know how much we shall find and where we shall find it. We therefore frame the working hypotheses that group human behaviour shows stable patterns and that these patterns do not change in response to institutional variations. We then test this hypothesis against the data and abandon it only when forced to do so by the data.

Let me now try to illustrate all of this by making reference to the work that has been going on in the last few years, and in which I have played some small part, on the determination of the level of money wage rates. The general theory is that the level of demand for labour is an important determinant of wage changes.[1] More specifically it can be argued that, when there is positive excess demand for labour,[2] wage rates will rise, the larger the excess demand the faster the wage rise; and when there is excess supply wages will fall, the larger the excess supply the faster the fall in wages. Now the level of unemployment (i.e. the percentage of the labour force unemployed) is a reasonably good guide to the level of excess demand for labour, unemployment, and excess demand varying inversely with each other.[3] We may thus look, to

1. To the non-economist to whom this may seem an obvious platitude it must be pointed out that this was not the prevailing view a few years ago and that it is still not accepted by many economists.

2. Excess demand for labour is defined as: demand for labour *minus* supply of labour; negative excess demand is often called excess supply.

3. For a theoretical consideration of the precise relation see my 'The relation between the level of unemployment and the rate of change of un-

test our theory, for a relation between the level of unemployment (U) and the rate of change of money wage rates ($\dot{W}$). The theory recognizes that many other factors affect the wage bargain but cuts through all of these to assert that demand is a most important factor and that we can get a long way be relating wages explicitly only to demand and by summing up the effects of all other factors in an error term, ϵ.

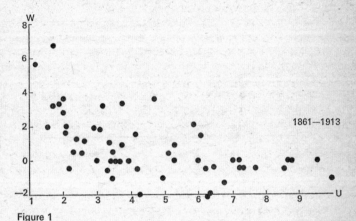

Figure 1

A casual glance at the time series for these two variables suggests that there is some relation. Now, in order to investigate this further, we can draw a scatter diagram plotting U on the horizontal axis and $\dot{W}$ on the vertical one, where each dot represents the figures for unemployment and the change in wages for one particular year from 1861 to 1913 (fig. 1). Now this graph is indeed very disappointing; there seems to be some sort of a vague relation but it does not seem to be a very strong one.

At this stage mental attitudes become critical. If we believe in the arguments against constant human behaviour patterns, we say, 'just as I thought', and we give up. Many people have in fact looked at a scatter diagram containing more or less the information given in fig. 1 and then given up. But, if we believe that

employment in the U.K., 1861–1957: a further analysis', *Economica*, (February 1960), section II (1). Since, even when there is large excess demand, labourers do change jobs, unemployment always exceeds zero.

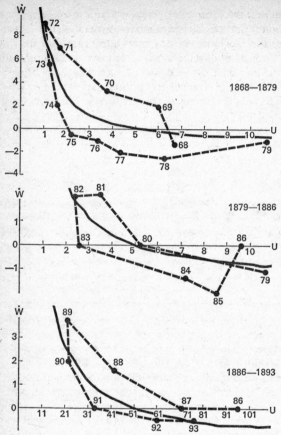

Figure 2

there is a stability to be found, then we go back to the data and we try again.

We might then reason somewhat as follows: the near chaos is only apparent, there *must* be some order here. But there is not much order in what I see, so I must have left out some critical bit of information. Well, in fig. 1 all points appear the same, but of course, they actually occur in a time sequence. Let us try dating the points and observe the sequence in which they occur. When we do this we observe the most remarkable phenomenon. The points form very clear loops, three of these loops being illustrated in fig. 2. It will be seen that, on the upswing of a trade cycle when U is falling, $\dot{W}$ is high, while on the downswing when U is rising $\dot{W}$ is low.

We now fit a curve to all the points for the years 1861–1913.[4] This curve, which is shown in fig. 2, describes the average relationships between $\dot{W}$ and U. When we relate each loop to this curve we find the following:

(1) Each complete loop corresponds to one trade cycle. (Over the nineteenth century these cycles occurred very regularly, each cycle lasting about eight to ten years.)

(2) The rising part of each loop lies above the curve of average relationship and the falling part of each loop lies below it. This indicates that, for any level of demand for labour, the wages rose faster when unemployment was falling (i.e. on the upswing of a cycle) and slower when unemployment was rising (i.e. on the downswing of a cycle). Now our original chaos has resolved into truly remarkable order!

Professor Phillips of the London School of Economics was the man who originally discovered this phenomenon of the loops.[5] He put forward a theory to account for the loops which, in my opinion, was incorrect.[6] But this does not matter; the important breakthrough was the discovery of order where before there seemed to be only chaos. The next stage is, of course, to advance a theory explaining this order; this Phillips also did. After that the new theory must be tested and, if it is refuted, this means that new knowledge (the observations which refuted the theory) has been brought to light. A new theory must then be put forward which explains the original phenomenon, but which is also consistent with the newly discovered observations which refuted the earlier theory.

4. There are clear theoretical reasons for using a curve and not a straight line (see Lipsey, op. cit., section II [1]).

5. A. W. Phillips, 'The relation between unemployment, and the rate of change of money wage rates in the United Kingdom, 1861–1957', *Economica* (November 1958).

6. One cannot be dogmatic on so difficult a subject as yet; but see my 'A test of some hypotheses concerning the relation between the rate of change of money wages and the rate of change of unemployment' [unpublished paper, mimeographed for private circulation].

The stage at which we now find ourselves is as follows: the observations seem to conform with our theory that the rate of change of money wages is related to the level of the excess demand for labour. We also have discovered the phenomenon of the loops, a relation between the rate of change of wages and the *rate of change* of unemployment. In this case I cannot as yet report to you a really satisfactory theory to explain this phenomenon. But now let us return to the theory of the relation between $\dot{W}$ and U.

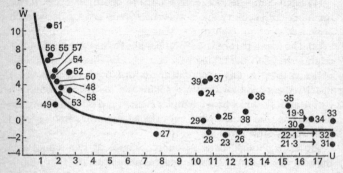

Figure 3

We have found that, in the period before the First World War, the rate of change of money wages was indeed related to the level of unemployment (with the proviso that the relation was different when unemployment was rising from what it is when it was falling). The next step is to discover how this remarkable relation has behaved over time. In fig. 3 we draw the curve describing the average relation between $\dot{W}$ and U as it existed in the nineteenth century and we then draw in the points indicating the actual post-First-World-War observations.

Immediately after the First World War we observe what looks like near chaos again. Wages shoot up by more than 25% per annum in 1918 and 1919 and then fall in 1921 and 1922 by almost the same amount. These movements appear to be unrelated to changes in unemployment. In fact they reflect two things:

   (1) a tying of wages to the price level which seemed a good thing from the point of view of the unions when prices were steadily rising during the war;

(2) a violent set of fluctuations in the level of retail prices due mainly to even more violent fluctuations in primary prices throughout the world.

Then, after the immediate post-war chaos, things settle down again – but unfortunately they settle down at a very high level of unemployment. It will be noted that the points for the last half of the 1920s lie reasonably close to the curve.

Now this was the period in which England had gone back on the gold standard at what was then an overvalued rate of exchange. This meant that it was necessary to force down the British price level before a balance between exports and imports could be obtained. In the event, wages and prices fell very slowly and the gold standard was abandoned before the necessary reduction in the price level was accomplished.

The prevailing view then and now about the failure of the gold standard experiment in the 1920s was that it was frustrated by institutional changes occurring about the time of the First World War. In the nineteenth century, it was argued, wages would have fallen rapidly in the face of such heavy unemployment and, once the reduction in wage costs had been effected, prices would soon have followed. But around the time of the First World War all of this was changed because of changes in institutions. The rise of really effective unions made wages very inflexible downwards and this policy of forcing down wages and prices, which would have worked in the nineteenth century, was frustrated by the changes. Clearly, and this was the important general inference, every historical period is unique and the experience of one period is no guide to that of another.

No one had bothered to lay out the data – although it was readily available at the time – and do an analysis such as I have just reported, so it was easy enough to hold this view. However, when Phillips did his analysis he found that the outcome of the disastrous experiment of the 1920s could have been predicted with considerable accuracy on the basis of the nineteenth-century experience. Phillips comments as follows on his analysis:[7]

The decision to check demand in an attempt to force the price level down in order to restore the gold standard at the pre-war parity of

7. Phillips, op. cit., pp. 294–5.

sterling prevented the recovery of business activity and unemployment remained fairly steady between 9·7 and 12·5% from 1925 to 1929. The average level of unemployment during these five years was 10·94% and the average rate of change of wage rates was –0·60% per year. The rate of change of wage rates calculated from the curve fitted to the 1861–1913 data for a level of unemployment of 10·94% is –0·56% per year, in close agreement with the average observed value. Thus the evidence does not support the view, which is sometimes expressed, that the policy of forcing the price level down failed because of increased resistance to downward movements of wage rates. The actual results obtained, given the levels of unemployment which were held, could have been predicted fairly accurately from a study of the pre-war data, if anyone had felt inclined to carry out the necessary analysis.

This again is a case in which mental attitude is critical. If one believes the general *a priori* arguments about changes in institutions, one never seeks to compare different periods and one accepts quite uncritically the interpretation of the 1920s based on *changing* behaviour patterns. If, on the other hand, one accepts the working hypothesis which I suggested, 'Institutional variations do not upset stable behavioural patterns', then one does seek to predict the 1920s using the data for the nineteenth century; in this case the results would be satisfactory; even, however, if they are not then one has discovered, by refuting the hypothesis, the direction and magnitude of the actual effects of institutional changes.

Now let us move on to consider two other time periods; that of the Great Depression in the 1930s and the period following the Second World War. In the very depths of the Great Depression, the years 1930–32, unemployment was 16%, 21%, and 22%, and the change in wage rates was approximately that predicted by the pre-First-World-War relation. Then from 1932 to 1939 unemployment fell every year (with the exception of 1938), but, even by the outbreak of the Second World War, unemployment had not fallen below the figure of 10%, which signalled the depths of a severe depression in the nineteenth century. During this period of recovery, wage rates rose in spite of the very high average levels of unemployment. An inspection of the figures shows that although movements in $\dot{W}$ do not appear random in relation to U, the relation is very different from those experienced previously.

Here then our simple theory that there is a unique and stable relation between $\dot{W}$ and U has been refuted by observations over the whole recovery period of the Great Depression. What then are we to think? First, we might look for some simple explanation which saves the theory of a unique relation between $\dot{W}$ and excess demand. I have in fact tried to do this in my earlier article, putting forward the hypothesis that the rise in the average level of wages was caused by wage rises in certain sectors in which unemployment was very low. Since wages rise faster when U is low than they fall when U is high it follows that if unemployment is very unevenly distributed (as it was in the 1930s) $\dot{W}$ can be rising for the whole economy even though the average level of U is quite high. This theory preserved a unique stable relation between $\dot{W}$ and U for each sector of the economy while abandoning it (as the evidence had shown it must be abandoned) for the whole economy. Unfortunately, careful tests[8] showed this theory not to be in conformity with the evidence. Apparently more radical departures are necessary.

Next one should notice that the late 1930s constitute the only set of observations that we have of the recovery of the economy from so severe a depression. It is always possible that the behaviour of the economy is radically different in such a depression than it would be otherwise. Theories of this sort would require another depression as severe as that of the thirties to be tested. Fortunately we will probably never get another chance to do such testing.

All that one can say at the moment is that the 1930s constitute a refutation of the simple hypothesis and provide a challenge for explanation by some other hypothesis. One can take refuge in the 'principle' of historical uniqueness and dismiss the thirties as a unique period never to be repeated and forget explanation. On the other hand one can try to find an explanation which preserves the general theory which does so well in most periods but which accommodates the 1930s as a special case. Such a theory is bound to have testable implications other than the ones that we already know. My own theory of sectorial inequalities was one of this sort and it was refuted by testing some of its other implications; it is along the lines of developing another theory of this sort that I am now working.

8. See my article already referred to [p. 275, fn. 6].

Now let us glance briefly at the figures for the 1950s. It will be seen that they lie pretty close to, but generally above, the curve fitted to the nineteenth-century data.[9] What are we to make of these observations? First there is quite clearly (and statistical analysis confirms this) a relation between $\dot{W}$ and U. The general hypothesis that there is such a relation continues to conform to the facts. Second, the observations definitely lie above the curve fitted to the nineteenth-century data, so that the simple hypothesis of a unique and stable relation is refuted.[10] Here at last we may have found the influence of changing institutions. Increased union power may mean that, for any given level of demand for labour, wages are now pushed up faster than previously. The shift in the relation (the average $\dot{W}$ over the period was 5·2% while the average predicted from the curve is 3·2%) would then be a measure of the quantitative importance of institutional shifts. Should this hypothesis of changing union strength pass other tests and be accepted (in the tentative sense in which any hypothesis is ever accepted), then we would have to abandon our original hypothesis that institutional changes had no effects on the

9. A plot of the crude unemployment figures as they are currently reported lies pretty well on the curve! It is generally agreed however that the definition of U has altered. The plotted figures for the post-war period have been corrected in an effort to make them comparable with those of the pre-war period. The corrections made are those that were suggested by G. Routh, an expert on the statistical data (see G. Routh, 'The relation between unemployment and the rate of change of money wage rates in the United Kingdom: a comment', Economica [November 1959]). Recently Professor Phillips has suggested to me that Routh's arguments about the changing definitions of U are incorrect and that U as measured in the nineteenth century is comparable with U as measured in the period following the Second World War. Should Phillips prove to be correct, then a reinterpretation of the evidence will be necessary.

10. This statement is not quite accurate. The observations show what actually happened to $\dot{W}$ and U. These occurrences are the result of a large number of *behavioural relations* between variables such as $\dot{W}$ and U. The *fitted relation* shown in the diagram is a *predicting relation* which predicts $\dot{W}$ from U, given all other associated changes which occur in the economy. It is just possible that the *predicting relation* has shifted without any change in the basic *behavioural relation* (showing the direct influence of U on $\dot{W}$. Indeed contemplation of the effects of known changes in the economy on the fitted relation between $\dot{W}$ and U shows this to be a distinct possibility.

relationship. But how much better to abandon the hypothesis after it has been carefully tested and how much better to have some *quantitative* idea of the amount by which these institutional changes have affected the behaviour of the system; how much better all this is than the position in which we find ourselves if we do not conduct the experiment at all on the grounds that institutional changes *must surely have upset the relationship*.

But another interpretation is possible. During the twentieth century cost-of-living adjustments have become important in wage determination. During the period following the Second World War the cost of living has been rising continuously. It is just possible that the same relation as existed earlier between $\dot{W}$ and U still holds but that the upward deviation of all the points represents the added influence of cost-of-living adjustments. There is, for example, little doubt that the extreme deviations in 1951 and 1952 were associated with the cost-of-living changes which were consequent on the Korean War. Clearly the various possible hypotheses have to be formulated carefully and tested comparatively before we can assess the significance of this shift. This is one of the tasks on which I am at present engaged.

This has been a very, very brief report on a series of hypotheses and empirical investigations in the field of aggregate wage determination.[11] I have been trying mainly to strike a note of hope for the scientific study of events in the economic sphere. But it is most important to note also the very severe handicaps under which economics does function as contrasted to the natural sciences. Some of the most severe problems are associated with the data. It is often necessary to formulate and test a theory in the face of no more than ten or twenty observations. The theory on which I have been reporting can be tested against observations over the last one hundred years, but this is rare. Few series go back this far, some start after the First World War, some in the 1930s, many not until after the Second World War and, in many cases, we have no observations at all. In the course of my work it has sometimes become necessary to test the theories by testing

11. The report has necessarily been on a somewhat intuitive level. The actual investigations have used more precise theoretical and statistical tools.

their implications about the data for individual industries;[12] here it is often not possible to get annual observations before 1945, and where a series can be pushed back into the inter-war period, a really major effort is required to do so. This poverty of data is often a discouraging thing, but on the other hand it seems to me that it should be a great cause for hope as to the future of our science beyond our own lifetimes. Economists too often forget the myriads of observations carefully collected over *centuries* which preceded the development of the Ptolemaic cosmology, to say nothing of the revolutions of Copernicus, Kepler, Galileo, and Newton. That economics has managed so much on the basis of a few observations collected over a few score of years should be a cause for great encouragement. For those of us who do not accept the defeatist arguments about the uniqueness of each historical period the prospect of future economists having at their disposal even a small fraction of the data available to Renaissance cosmologists is a most heartening thing. In the meantime, however, we stumble along with our desperately imperfect sets of observations.

Another data problem is that connected with the absence of controlled experiments in economics. Some economists have felt that, because of the impossibility of controlled experiments, economics could not be an empirical science. It is a mystery how this view could have been held in the presence of the obvious counter example of the science of astronomy. Controlled experiments obviously give tremendous advantages: they allow one to manufacture relevant evidence at will and they present the evidence in such a way that it is usually easily interpreted. The absence of controlled experiments means that we must wait for the passing of time to throw up evidence relevant to our hypotheses and on occasions we must wait a very long time indeed. Also it is often necessary to treat our data with elaborate statistical techniques in order to interpret it correctly; too many things are happening at once for our evidence to be easily and straightforwardly interpreted.[13]

12. See, for example, R. G. Lipsey and M. D. Steuer, 'The relation between profits and wages', *Economica*, (May 1961).

13. Having enough real difficulties with data there is no need, as is so often done, to invent non-existent difficulties. It has been argued to me, for

One is left, at the end of all this, with a feeling of the possibility of a truly scientific study of human behaviour in the economic sphere and with an attitude of optimism about the long-term development of such a science. In the past, economists both amateur and professional, have (1) taken too much to heart the difficulties of predicting individual behaviour and forgotten the remarkable group stability in many human fields; (2) been very discouraged by contrasting social sciences with an outdated, nineteenth-century view of physics, when a look at other sciences, or even a more critical look at physics and astronomy, would have given more cause for optimism; (3) been too easily convinced, *a priori*, that every historical sequence is unique. When in fact we take a look in a sphere most affected by these defeatist arguments we find evidence of simple behaviour patterns, remarkably stable over, what in economics, is a very long period of time, and, when complete stability has not been maintained, we find what looks like a reasonable chance of developing and extending our theories to cover these more complex patterns of behaviour.

---

instance, by several eminent economists that the whole of the theorizing and testing which I have reported is worthless because the wrong variable is employed. The theory uses *wage rates* which are the standard rates agreed at the union–management bargain; it is argued that *wage earnings*, which are the actual amounts earned allowing for bonuses, overtime, short-time, etc., should be used instead. To argue in this way is to ignore the facts that an empirical relation has been discovered between wage *rates* and unemployment, that a theory of the dependence of *rates* on unemployment has been put forward, and that this theory has passed tests other than the ones reported here. It also ignores the fact that, although *a priori* reasoning can suggest many reasons why rates and earnings might not move together, they do in fact stay, over any long period of time, remarkably close together, so that any theory which explains one will go a long way towards explaining the other. To dismiss a successful theory on the grounds that something else might have been made the subject of the theory is typical of the *a priori* and cavalier manner in which empirical evidence has been dismissed by so many economists.

14 A. G. Hines

Trade Unions and Wage Inflation in the United Kingdom
1893–1961

Excerpt from A. G. Hines (1964) Trade unions and wage inflation in the
United Kingdom 1893–1961. *Rev. Econ. Stud.*, **31**, 221–51.

In the past eight years there has been extensive empirical investigation of the process of wage inflation in the United Kingdom.
Brown (1955), Phillips (1958), and Lipsey (1960) have argued
that there is a significant relationship between the rate of change
of money wage rates (ΔW)[1] and the rate of change and level of
unemployment $(\Delta U$ and $U)$. Dow (1956), Dicks-Mireaux and Dow
(1959), Klein and Ball (1959), Dicks-Mireaux (1961), and Lipsey
and Steuer (1961) have investigated the relationship between
wages, prices, profits, and productivity. Those contributors who
have explicitly considered the possible influence of trade unions
on wages have either dismissed it as being unimportant or have
used somewhat unsatisfactory indexes to measure the impact of
the unions. They have thus reinforced the widely held view that
trade unions cannot affect wages independently of the state of
excess demand in the economy. In this context, the level and the
rate of change of unemployment have usually been taken as an
index of excess demand.[2]

This paper will attempt to show that, contrary to the prevailing
view, trade unions do affect the rate of change of wages *independently* of the demand for labour. Specifically, it will be shown
that one measure of trade union pushfulness, namely the rate
of change of the percentage of the labour force unionized (ΔT),
a measure which is uncorrelated with the demand for labour,
makes a statistically significant contribution to the explanation
of the total variation in wage rates. Indeed, in the inter-war and
post-war years, it is the most powerful of all the explanatory

1. For the precise definition of this and other variables see the appendix.
2. For a different but closely related index see Dicks-Mireaux and Dow
(1959).

variables. It is concluded that the rejection of trade union push-fulness as an explanation of the rate of change of money wages is not justified by the evidence.

This paper is divided into three parts. Part 1 presents evidence of a very close statistical relationship between the rate of change of unionization and the rate of change of money wage rates and advances and attempts to justify the hypothesis that unionization is the causal factor in the observed relationship. Part 2 deals with possible objections to our interpretation of the role of the union variable. Part 3 contains a model of the simultaneous determination of the rate of change of money wage rates, the rate of change of prices, and the rate of change of unionization.

Part 1

The view is widely held that trade unions cannot influence wage rates independently of the state of demand for labour. This is certainly the impression gained from a general survey of the literature. However, only a handful of contributors have attempted any systematic analysis of the relationship between movements in wage rates and trade union pushfulness. It might therefore be instructive to begin with a review of these latter contributions.

(a) In a discussion of theories of inflation, Lipsey (1963) points out that any meaningful explanation of the rate of change of money wages in terms of a cost-push-via-the-unions hypothesis requires a theory of variations in the strength of the cost push. He then examines the hypothesis that pushing is related to union strength, appropriate indexes of union strength being the percentage of the labour force unionized or the size of union funds. This hypothesis he considers to be 'slightly less crude' than one which says that unions always push upwards on wages with a uniform pressure. Lipsey then says: 'It seems to the present writer that all acceptable indexes of union strength would show a secular increase over the last hundred years. All of these, then, would produce the prediction of an ever faster rate of increase of wage rates and the price level.' Such a prediction, he says, is refuted by an inspection of the time series of ΔW and ΔP.

Presumably his argument runs as follows. ΔW and ΔP (ΔP is the rate of change of prices) are trendless variables exhibiting wide fluctuations. Any satisfactory index of union strength would produce a trend dominant time series. Clearly, the correlation between any two such series must be insignificant.

Since Lipsey's argument is supposed to refute the hypothesis $\Delta W = f(T)$, it depends crucially on the time series of the percentage of the labour force unionized showing a secular increase.

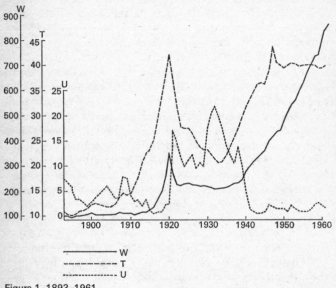

Figure 1 1893–1961

By this he presumably means that T is so dominated by its trend value, which is assumed to be positive, that not only is there a good fit between T and time, but also that variations in T around its line of trend are distributed at random. In consequence the degree of unionization (T) would not correlate well with ΔW, a trendless series exhibiting wide fluctuations. Reference to figs. 1 and 2 shows that Lipsey's argument is not correct. The T series is not dominated by its trend value. Moreover, T has a marked positive trend in one period only, namely the period 1893–1912. In the inter-war years, the trend is negative; in the post-war period it is not significantly different from zero; and, in these two later periods, the fit between T and time is very poor.

We have not found much relationship between T and the year to year variations in wage rates. But this is due to reasons which are different from those advanced by Lipsey. We shall put forward the view that it is the activity of unions, reflected in the rate of change of their membership, rather than the size of unions which influence year to year changes in wage rates. However, it

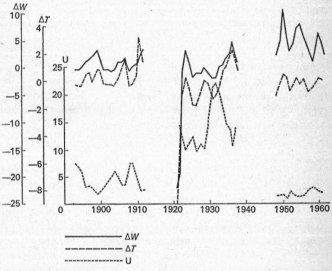

Figure 2 1893–1961

will be shown that when one considers the period 1921–61, excluding the war years, the *level* of unionization does make a significant contribution to the explanation of ΔW.

Lipsey did not consider the possibility that the rate of change of unionization as distinct from the level itself could influence wage rates. Nevertheless his statement concerning the behaviour of the level would, if it were correct, provide, by implication, a refutation of the rate of change hypothesis. If the T series is dominated by its trend value to such an extent as to falsify the level hypothesis, its rate of change would, except for random

287

fluctuations, be a constant (or a smooth positive function of time) and hence could not be expected to correlate with the rate of change of wages – a trend free variable with non-random fluctuations.

(b) in their analysis of wage inflation in the United Kingdom in the period 1946–57, Dicks-Mireaux and Dow (1959) considered 'whether trade unions exerted an independent influence upon wage settlements'. To facilitate this investigation, they constructed an index of trade union pushfulness which aims at measuring changes in the attitude of unions additional to their reaction to such objective factors as price changes and the state of excess demand for labour.

Their index measures pushfulness on a five point scale. The ratings are purely subjective. For example, they (the ratings) show 'that in the war period 1939–1945, trade unions were, for patriotic reasons, fairly restrained in their demands; that this disappeared in the first years of peace; that appeals for wage-restraint were effective in the years 1948–1950; and that in subsequent years, restraint gradually gave place to positive pushfulness'. An index with totally subjective ratings does not appear to be altogether satisfactory expecially since an objective index such as the degree of unionization and its rate of change is available.[3]

(c) Klein and Ball (1959) constructed an index to measure the impact of the political factor on the wage bargain. This factor is said to account for the independent pressure that the unions bring to bear on wage rates. The index takes on the value of zero before 1952 and a value of unity thereafter, in accordance with the supposition that the unions approach the wage bargain differently under a Conservative government than under a Labour government. They find that the coefficient of this dummy variable is significant.

However, the evidence to be presented here suggests that these constructed variables are perhaps not sufficiently sensitive to

3. Their findings on the importance of 'pushfulness' are inconclusive. The inclusion of 'pushfulness' in an equation explaining ΔW led to an 'apparent' gain in the explained variance. However, the statistical significance of the result could not be assessed since transformation of the variables did not remove autocorrelation in the residuals, loc. cit., p. 16.

account for all of the considerable annual variation in the strength of the independent pressure which the unions bring to bear on the rate of change of money wages.

The relation between unionization and wage rates

An inspection of the time series shown in figs. 1 and 2 and of the scatter diagrams of figs. 3–5 indicates that there is a close statistical relationship between unionization and the rate of change of money wages. The view to be advanced here is that unionization is the causal variable in the observed relationship. In other words, we shall hypothesize that the observed variation in money wage rates can be explained in terms of trade union pushfulness – the index of push being the level and/or the rate of change of the percentage of the labour force that is unionized. Three variants of this hypothesis were considered, namely,

(i) $\Delta W_t = a_1 + b_1 T_t,$

(ii) $\Delta W_t = a_2 + b_2 \Delta T_t,$

(iii) $\Delta W_t = a_3 + b_3 \Delta T_t + c_3 T_t.$

Separate calculations were done for three sub-periods (the two world wars providing breaks in the data), for the inter-war and post Second World War years pooled, and for all the years taken together, excluding war years. No attempt was made to test for the time stability of the parameters. The results are given in table 1, page 293.

Let us examine the hypothesis and the results in some detail.

(1) Consider the relationship between the rate of change of money wage rates and the rate of change of unionization. We hypothesize that the latter is an index of trade union pushfulness. When unions are being aggressive they simultaneously increase their membership and bid up wage rates.

Suppose that when their membership increases unions feel stronger and become more intransigent in the wage bargain. Suppose further that, as union activity on the shop floor increases, the workers become more militant so that employers are left in no doubt that were strike action to be taken, it would effectively close down the business. Employers would then be more willing to concede wage increases. In such circumstances, union officials would regard a successful membership drive as a necessary accompaniment of success in the wage bargain. Therefore, when a union puts in a wage claim it would seek immediately *before*

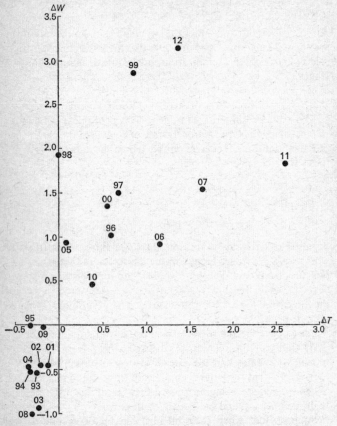

Figure 3 1893–1912

and *during* the period of negotiation to increase its bargaining power by increasing the proportion of the labour force over which it has direct control. Since it will be shown that the rate of change of unionization is uncorrelated with the demand for labour, ΔT may be taken to be an index of cost push. It reflects the intensity

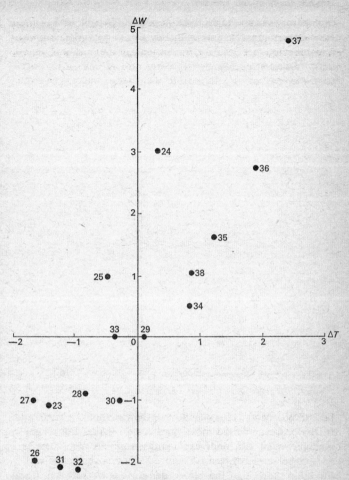

Figure 4 1921–38. (The years 1921 and 1922 have been excluded as they are years of very large negative ΔWs and ΔTs and they could not be included without making the scales unmanageable.)

of union activity which simultaneously manifests itself in wage claims and in the attitude to bargaining.

The results obtained in table 1 are compatible with this hypothesis. The rate of change of unionization is an important explanatory variable in each sub-period and overall. In the period 1893–1912, it removed approximately 50% of the variance in wage rates. Previous studies have shown that, in the inter-war period, most variables, except, perhaps, the rate of change of prices, correlate very poorly with the rate of change of wages. Yet, in this

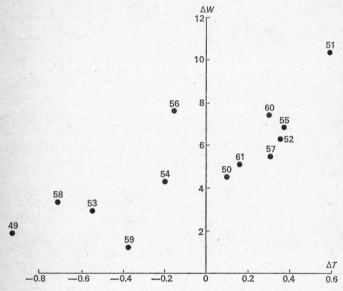

Figure 5 1949–61

period, ΔT accounts for over 90% of the variations in wage rates. In the post-war period most variables do badly. For example, unemployment is a poor explanatory variable. Yet, there is a 63% correlation between ΔT and ΔW. Moreover, section (i) of the table shows that the zero order correlation between T and ΔW is very poor.[4] This result is consistent with the hypothesis that the *rate of change* of unionization rather than the *level* of unionization is the index of union pushfulness. It is the activity of the unions rather than their size which influences year to year movements in wage rates.

4. Although there is a 55% correlation between the two variables in the period 1921–38, the regression coefficient has the wrong sign.

(2) Surprise might be occasioned by the fact that money wage rates are so sensitive to such small variations in union membership. This is particularly so in the post-war period. In these years, the variations in T have been very small relative to the variations which were observed in the nineteenth century and in the inter-war years and relative to the variations in wage rates. Indeed,

Table 1

		1893–1912	1921–38	1949–61	1921–38 and 1949–61	1893–1912, 1921–38, and 1949–61
(i) $\Delta W_t = a_1 + b_1 T_t$	r^2	0·1041	0·5532	0·0208	0·0603	0·0276
		(0·0046)	(0·4973)	(0)	(0)	(0)
	a_1	−1·6504	25·0319	−37·0114	−6·2155	−0·9762
	b_1	0·1874	−1·1914	1·1687	0·2075	0·0758
		(0·1795)	(0·2951)	(2·5422)	(0·3124)	(0·1132)
(ii) $\Delta W_t = a_2 + b_2 \Delta T_t$	r^2	0·4798	0·9125	0·6297	0·7682	0·6671
		(0·4220)	(0·9016)	(0·7522)	(0·6463)	
	a^2	0·2515	0·0982	5·3915	2·4234	1·3450
	b^2	0·9808	2·4876	4·2193	2·7628	2·3854
		(0·2407)	(0·0609)	(0·9754)	(0·2721)	(0·2355)
iii) $\Delta W_t = a_3 + b_3 \Delta T_t + c_3 T_t$	R^2	0·4843	0·9126	0·6750	0·9069	0·8240
		(0·3933)	(0·8951)	(0·5775)	(0·8969)	(0·8130)
	a_3	0·8080	0·7567	−64·2058	−7·3570	−3·2656
	b_3	1·0425	2·4540	4·3165	2·9224	2·7022
		(0·2713)	(0·2854)	(0·8436)	(0·1733)	(0·1782)
	c_3	−0·0463	−0·0268	1·7318	0·3107	0·1872
		(0·1115)	(0·1756)	(1·2869)	(0·0454)	(0·0304)
Durbin–Watson statistic		1·35†	1·59*	3·13*	1·57*	1·21

Correlation coefficients corrected for degrees of freedom and standard errors on the regression coefficients are shown in parenthesis.

* Indicates that the test showed no autocorrelation at the 1% probability level.

† Indicates that the test was inconclusive. For other values the term showed positive autocorrelation.

fig. 1 together with fig. 6 suggest what a 10% increase in unionization when the average level of unionization in 20% of the labour force has much less effect on wage rates than a 1% increase when the average level is 40%. Thus in fig. 6 and in table 1 we observe an increase in the *slope* of the function which relates ΔW to ΔT

in the post Second World War period. This observation is compatible with the following explanations:

(a) It could be the case that the higher the level of unionization, the more difficult it is to increase it any further. As membership increases there is a diminishing response to a given intensity of recruiting effort. This being so, a 1% increase in unionization when the average level is 40% of the labour force is indicative of more militancy than an increase of 10% when the average level is 20% of the labour force; and greater militancy is associated with greater pressure on the wage rate.[5]

(b) Suppose that there is a 5% increase in unionization in some sector. Let this increase correspond to a 1% increase in aggregate unionization. Suppose that this results in a 7% increase in wage rates in that sector. Let this be a leading sector both in terms of its size and in its position in the annual 'queue' and suppose that the bargaining environment is such that wage settlements in some such sector are taken to be the average increase for the whole economy in that year. In such circumstances, unions in sectors further back in the 'queue' can obtain wage adjustments which are based on the increase obtained in the leading sector. We would then observe a 1–2% increase in aggregate unionization associated with, say, a 5% increase in the aggregate wage index.

Thus, if a few leading sectors determine wages and other sectors follow, union activity in the leading sectors will determine

5. We may demonstrate this proposition thus. Let pushfulness be a latent variable which cannot be observed directly. Let the rate of change of unionization be an index of pushfulness and suppose that there is an upper limit to the proportion of the labour force that can be unionized. We can then write

$$\Delta T = f(Z)\{A - T\} \tag{1}$$

where Z is true pushfulness and A is the upper limit to unionization. Taking a linear form of equation (1):

$$Z = \frac{\Delta T}{\lambda(A - T)} \qquad \lambda < 0 \tag{2}$$

Now suppose that

$$\Delta W = g(Z) = a + \beta Z \qquad \beta > 0 \tag{3}$$

Then

$$\Delta W = a + \frac{\beta}{\lambda(A - T)}T \tag{4}$$

Thus a given ΔT is indicative of more militancy and hence more influence on wage rates the higher is the level of unionization.

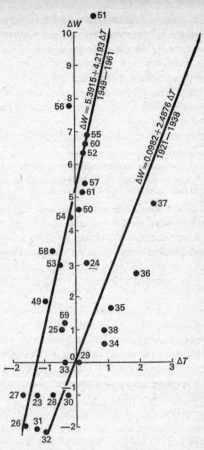

Figure 6 1921–38, 1949–61. (The years 1921 and 1922 have been excluded as they are years of very large negative ΔWs and ΔTs and they could not be included without making the scales unmanageable.)

movements in aggregate wage rates independently of the behaviour of union membership in the following sectors.

(3) Fig. 6 is a scatter diagram of ΔW and ΔT for the years 1921–61 excluding war years. It shows an upward shift in the post Second World War period. These latter observations differ from the former by a constant, but with some change in the size

of the 'b' coefficient. The shift reflects the steep rise in wage rates and the absence of negative ΔWs in the period since 1938. In consequence, when the data are pooled, and the regression repeated, we would expect a considerable reduction in the r^2. Surprisingly, this does not happen. The r^2 is 0·6671. However, if 1921 and 1922, the years of large negative rates of change of wages and unionization, are excluded, the r^2 reduces to 0·1459, which is the kind of result we would expect. It therefore seemed necessary to include a variable to account for the observed shift in the *constant term*.[6]

General equilibrium considerations would lead us to expect that a certain level of wage rates corresponds to a given long run configuration of such factors as the level of unemployment, the degree of unionization, the level of prices, and so on. Thus, on the assumption that variations around the average are not too violent, a lower average wage rate would correspond to a 20% level of unionization than would correspond to an average level of 40% unionization. Similarly, different equilibrium levels of the wage rate would correspond to different average levels of unemployment. This being so, substantial shifts in one of these variables would generate shifts in the level of wage rates which would be sufficient to cause a shift in the 'a' coefficient in the function relating ΔW and ΔT. The hypothesis put forward here is that the steep rise in wage rates and the consequent shift in the relationship between ΔW and ΔT can be explained by the upward shift in the *level* of unionization which has occurred over the same period.[7]

6. It must not be inferred from this that the high r^2 on ΔW and ΔT for the inter-war years is due solely to the inclusion of 1921 and 1922. For the period 1923–38 the r^2 is 0·7781. For the period 1926–38 it is 0·8884.

7. Let
$$W^* = W^*(T, U, \ldots) \tag{1}$$
where W^* is the equilibrium money wage rate and U is the level of unemployment. Equation (1) states that the *strength* of the unions, which is measured by the *level* of unionization, is one of the variables which determines the equilibrium *level* of wages and hence the factor distribution of incomes.

Suppose
$$\Delta W = \mu(W^* - W) \tag{2}$$
where μ depends on the *pushfulness* of the unions. Since our index of pushfulness is the rate of change of unionization, $\mu = \mu(\Delta T)$. Thus,
$$\Delta W = \mu(\Delta T)\{W^*(T, U, \ldots) - W\} \tag{3}$$

If unionization is fluctuating about a fairly constant level, T itself does not correlate with W. Suppose, however, that there is a marked increase in unionization, say an increase from 25 to 45% of the labour force. (This is the sort of increase that occurred between 1938 and 1947.) Let this increase reflect the new organization of some particular group or sector in the economy. It seems plausible to suppose that an immediate effect of the successful unionization of some sector is an increase in wage rates in that sector.[8] Given wages in the rest of the economy, this would result in a once and for all increase in the general level of rates. It could therefore provide an explanation of the shift which is shown in fig. 6.

The result of the test of this hypothesis is shown in section (iii) of table 1. The coefficient on the level of unionization is insignificant when in each sub-period it is used with ΔT as an explanatory variable. However, when the data are pooled, the situation changes. In the regression involving all the years since 1893 excluding the war years, the coefficient of the level of unionization is much larger than its standard error. However, the residuals from the fitted equation are positively autocorrelated. This is probably due to the exclusion of the level of unemployment which is, in the period 1893–1912, an important determinant of the rate of change of money wage rates. When this earlier period is excluded, and the inter-war and post-war years taken together, the T variable is significant. The coefficient is much larger than its standard error and the residuals are not autocorrelated. This result is even more marked when the years 1921 and 1922 are excluded from the analysis.[9]

Hence, $\qquad\qquad \Delta W = f(\Delta T, T, W, U, \ldots)$ $\qquad$ (4)

Rewrite (4) as $\qquad \Delta W = (a + bT) + c\Delta T$ $\qquad$ (5)

where the constant term represents all the terms in (4) except ΔT and T. It is easily seen that shifts in the level of unionization can cause shifts in the relationship between ΔW and ΔT.

8. Evidence documented in the United States indicates that when an industry is unionized wages rise by 15–25%. A summary of these findings is contained in A. Rees, *The economics of trade unions* (Cambridge University Press, 1962).

9. For the period 1923–38 and 1949–61 we have

$$\Delta W_t = 2\cdot3906 + 1\cdot7154\Delta T_t$$
$$(0\cdot4871)$$
$$r^2 \Delta W \Delta T = 0\cdot1909$$

Experiments were carried out with other shift variables such as the level of unemployment and dummy variables.[10] None did as well as (or better than) the degree of unionization. We therefore conclude that the data are consistent with the hypothesis that the marked increases of unionization has been responsible for the steep rise in the level of wage rates in the period since the Second World War, and for the consequent shift in the constant term in the function which relates ΔW to ΔT.

(4) Consider the equation

$$\dot{W}_t = a + b\dot{T}_t + cT_t \qquad (1)$$

in which $\dot{W}$ and T are the limiting values of ΔW and ΔT respectively. If the level of unionization does not alter, $bT = 0$; and, ignoring the constant term, the equation suggests that wages would, in equilibrium, increase at the constant rate cT ($c > 0$) indefinitely. Thus, a given degree of unionization would, *cet. par.*, imply a constant upward pressure on wage rates. Moreover, a marked increase in the level of unionization would increase the equilibrium rate of inflation. But, we might expect ΔW to be zero when T has settled down to some constant level. A similar result might be expected to follow an increase in the level of unionization which was due to the organization of some hitherto ununionized group of workers. Since this new organization reflects

---

When the level of unionization is added as an explanatory variable the fitted equation is

$$\Delta W_t = -7\cdot1469 + 1\cdot7587\Delta T_t + 0\cdot3083T_t$$
$$\qquad\qquad\qquad (0\cdot2973)\quad\ (0\cdot0429)$$
$$\bar{R}^2\Delta W.\Delta TT = 0\cdot8035 \qquad d.\ \text{statistic} = 1\cdot42*$$

10. When the level of unemployment is used as a shift variable, the results are as follows:

(a) 1921–38 *and* 1949–61
$$\Delta W_t = 5\cdot5119 + 2\cdot4524\Delta T_t - 0\cdot3626U_t$$
$$\qquad\qquad (0\cdot1817)\qquad (0\cdot0573)$$
$$\bar{R}^2\Delta W.\Delta TU = 0\cdot8938 \qquad d.\ \text{statistic} = 1\cdot84*$$

(b) 1923–38 *and* 1949–61
$$\Delta W_t = 5\cdot5365 + 1\cdot5688\Delta T_t - 0\cdot3504U_t$$
$$\qquad\qquad (0\cdot2973)\qquad (0\cdot0429)$$
$$\bar{R}^2\Delta W.\Delta TU = 0\cdot7856 \qquad d.\ \text{statistic} = 1\cdot61*$$

* Indicates that the test showed no autocorrelation at the 1% probability level.

increased militancy on the part of the unions, we would expect it to be associated with a sequence of positive ΔWs which should, over time, dwindle to zero.

We may obtain the desired result by letting the constant term in equation (1) represent other forces in the system such as the level of demand which, when T is constant, exert their influence in such a way as to generate a constant equilibrium wage rate.

To this end, let

$$a = f(W) = \beta W, \ \beta < 0, \ [W = F(\text{Demand} \ldots)] \qquad (2)$$

Substituting into (1) with $bT = 0$, we obtain

$$\dot{W}_t = \beta W_t + cT \qquad (3)$$

which is a first order nonhomogeneous linear differential equation in which cT is the constant term. Its solution is

$$W_t = ae^{\beta t} - \frac{c}{\beta} T \qquad (4)$$

Introducing the initial condition

$$t = 0 \qquad W(0) = W_0,$$

$$W_t = \left(W_0 + \frac{c}{\beta} T\right) e^{\beta t} - \frac{c}{\beta} T \qquad (5)$$

If $\beta < 0$, then, as $t \to \infty$, $W_t \to -\frac{c}{\beta} T$. Since $-\frac{c}{\beta} T$ is a constant, W will tend to a constant and hence $\dot{W} \to 0$. Thus, if there is a big increase in the level of unionization and if unionization remains constant thereafter, we should observe a sequence of positive ΔWs which will tend asymptotically to zero, the speed of convergence depending on $|\beta|$.

(5) It should be observed that these rationalizations of the relationship between ΔW and ΔT and between ΔW and T have further testable implications and that in this sense they constitute 'satisfactory' explanations. For example, we could discover whether the marked increase in unionization which began in the late 1930s and continued through the war into the early 1950s was the result of increased membership in industries that were already organized or the result of the new organization of particular groups or sectors in the economy. In the case of ΔW and

ΔT we could ascertain whether unions engaged in wage negotiations do in fact run membership campaigns. Other implications of our theory could be tested by an investigation of the relationship between aggregate ΔT and ΔW and ΔW and ΔT in different sectors.

Part 2

Factors determining the rate of change of unionization

Many hypotheses could be advanced concerning the determination of the rate of change of unionization. In this section we consider some of those which would, if they were true, constitute a refutation of our interpretation of the role of the union variable. The model of part 3 includes variables which we consider to be relevant to the explanation of ΔT.

(1) One could hypothesize that pushing is explained by the level and/or the rate of change of economic activity. (This is probably the most widely held view about the relationship between union activity and changes in wage rates.) One would then expect to find a high correlation between ΔT and some cyclical variable such as the level and/or the rate of change of unemployment which can be used as an index of activity. One would expect this because, so the argument would run, unions can push wages up only when demand conditions are favourable, i.e. in circumstances in which wages would in any case be rising. Moreover, changes in union membership might not even be associated with militancy. For example, if a given proportion of newly hired workers automatically join the unions, there would be an inverse relationship between ΔT and unemployment. Thus $\Delta W = f_1(U)$ and $\Delta T = f_2(U)$. Hence, we observe a relationship between ΔT and ΔW.

This hypothesis was tested by fitting to the data by ordinary least squares, the equation $\Delta T_t = a + bU_{t-\alpha} + c\Delta U_{t-\beta}$.[11] The

11. Phillips (1958) used a non-linear transformation of the level of unemployment in his analysis of the relationship between ΔW and U in the period 1861–1957. In our period, 1893–1961, standard tests, e.g. the Durbin–Watson statistic, do not provide a warrant for such a transformation either in the equation relating ΔW to U or in that relating ΔT to U. Note, however, that the results obtained are not significantly affected by replacing U with U^{-1}.

best fit to the data was obtained by assuming that the relationship holds with zero time-lag. The results are shown in table 2.[12]

Table 2

$\Delta T_t = a + bU_t + c\Delta U_t$

	1893–1912	1921–38	1949–61	1921–38 and 1949–61	1893–1912 1921–38, and 1949–61
R^2	0·3288	0·1349	0·0396	0·0818	0·1343
$\bar{R}^2$	(0·2103)	(0)	(0)	(0)	(0·0802)
b	−0·2754	−0·1216	−0·2075	−0·0804	−0·1031
	(0·0961)	(0·1531)	(0·2829)	(0·0592)	(0·0419)
c	−0·0021	0·0494	−0·0015	−0·0084	−0·0077
	(0·0076)	(0·0355)	(0·0045)	(0·0123)	(0·0084)

This evidence seems to refute the hypothesis that our index of pushfulness can be explained by unemployment. The level of unemployment makes a significant contribution to the explanation of the variance in the rate of change of unionization in one period only, namely the period 1893–1912.

Since there are reasons for thinking that unemployment is not an altogether satisfactory index of demand, two other indexes were tried. These are the Dicks-Mireaux–Dow index of excess demand and the deviation of the index of industrial production from a straight line trend. In neither case did the results differ materially from those obtained when the level of unemployment is used.[13] It seems unlikely that any other index of activity would alter these results.

It might be the case that the view which is being discussed relates the level of unemployment to the *level* of unionization.

12. The rate of change of unemployment is included on the grounds that for any level of U, unions are more pushful when U is rising and less pushful when U is falling. However, if the theory is that ΔT adjusts passively to changes in the level of unemployment, ΔU should be excluded from the equation.

13. The uncorrected r^2 for ΔT and the Dicks-Mireaux and Dow index for the post-war years is 0·0300; that between ΔT and the deviation of the index of production from a straight line trend is 0·0012.

However, our index of pushfulness is the *rate of change* and not the level of unionization. In any case, the correlation between T and U is very poor.[14]

(2) This paper advances the hypothesis that unionization is the causal variable in the observed relationship between ΔW and ΔT. However, it could be argued that the causal relation runs from ΔW to ΔT rather than the other way round. ΔW is determined by such factors as the level of unemployment. However, we may observe an association between ΔW and ΔT for at least one of two reasons. Workers *mistakenly* ascribe changes in wages to union activity, so that if wages rise they join the unions and pay the dues as a reward for services which they believe the unions have rendered. Alternatively, joining a union means paying the dues. The requisite expenditure may be a marginal item in the workers' budget. Thus, when wages rise for whatever reason, some workers can afford to meet the cost of union membership.

An attempt to test this hypothesis poses a serious problem. There are two conflicting theories which are consistent with the observed relationship. There is therefore a problem of identification. We may attempt to discriminate between the theories in at least two ways. Firstly, we may test other implications of the theories thus obtaining indirect checks on them.[15] Secondly, we may ascertain whether the theories imply anything about the lags in the adjustment of the dependent variable to the causal variable. For example, the pushfulness hypothesis is compatible with either a zero or a positive lag in the adjustment of ΔW to ΔT.[16] The alternative hypothesis implies the existence of a lag in

14. The zero order correlation coefficient between T and U is as follows:

1893–1912:	$r^2 = 0.0081$
1921–38:	$r^2 = 0.0576$
1949–61:	$r^2 = 0.1348$
1921–38 and 1949–61:	$r^2 = 0.7516*$
1893–1912, 1921–38, and 1949–61:	$r^2 = 0.0161$

* This high correlation is spurious. A scatter diagram shows that it is obtained by linking two clusters of points in each of which T and U are uncorrelated.

15. Such an inquiry is beyond the scope of the present paper.

16. Peacock and Ryan found a mean lag of four months between the filing and the settlement of wage claims (see 'Wage claims and the pace of in-

the adjustment of unionization to movements in wage rates. This being so, we might usefully postulate $\Delta W_t = f_1(\Delta T_{t-\alpha})$ as well as $\Delta T_t = f_2(\Delta W_{t-\alpha})$ and see what happens.

Two tests were carried out; one with $\alpha =$ one year, the other with $\alpha =$ six months. Six-month time-lags were obtained by centring the rates of change of the variables in the manner indicated in appendix (i). Shorter lags could not be introduced because data on trade union membership is available on an annual basis only. The results are shown in table 3, page 316. They show that the introduction of a six-month time-lag in the effect of unionization on wage rates yields results very similar to those generated by correlating both variables spot on. On the other hand, whether a six- or a twelve-month lag is hypothesized in the theory which makes the rate of change of unionization depend on the rate of change of money wages, the results are very poor.

(3) It could be urged that even if it were the case that unions push wage rates up quite independently of market forces, this is not so important as it appears to be. The important variable, particularly from the policy point of view, is earnings, not wage rates. Suppose that earnings rise because of the pressure of demand in factor and product markets. Unions may then press for and obtain upward adjustments in basic rates.[17] This hypothesis may be looked at in two ways.

(a) Suppose unions attempt to adjust basic rates to changes in earnings quite independently of the behaviour of their membership. We would then have to explain away the observed correlation between ΔW and ΔT. One could argue that it is changes in the demand for labour which cause both earnings and union membership to vary. Unions then adjust basic rates. This implies that we are to observe changes in unionization preceding changes in wage rates. Therefore the interpretation of the observed relationship between ΔW_t and $\Delta T_{t-\alpha}$ given in (2) would be wrong.

---

flation', *Economic Journal* [1953]. A similar finding is reported by B. Swift in the *Journal of the Royal Statistical Society*, series A, part 2 (1963). The pushfulness hypothesis says that a membership drive gets under way somewhere between the decision to make a wage claim and the settlement of that claim. It probably reaches a climax round about the date of the settlement.

17. I am indebted to Mr R. J. Ball for pointing out this argument to me.

However, we have already seen that there is virtually no correlation between the rate of change of unionization and the indexes of demand which we have tried. Therefore this view is untenable. (b) If the rate of change of unionization is taken to be an index of militancy and hence an index of pressure on wage rates, then the view being discussed would assert that when earnings rise, workers respond favourably to a membership campaign in order that the unions might put up basic rates. This does not appear to be very plausible.

Despite these reservations, the data were examined to see what lead-lag relationship, if any, existed between the rate of change of wage rates and the rate of change of earnings, on the one hand, and between the rate of change of unionization and the rate of change of earnings, on the other. In both cases, the best results were obtained by assuming that the relationship holds with a zero time-lag. Indeed, in the case of the rate of change of earnings and the rate of change of unionization, there is a slight tendency for the latter to lead the former.

(4) It could be argued that the correlation between ΔT and ΔW is due solely to the definition of the trade union variable.[18] T, the percentage of the labour force unionized, is defined as $T = \dfrac{100T^*}{L}$, where L is the labour force and T^* is trade union membership.

Suppose it were known that some changes in the labour force could be generated by changes in money wage rates. For example, married women may enter the labour market when wages were rising and conversely. Suppose further that the absolute level of trade union membership was constant. Then, if the labour force were to change in this way, we would necessarily observe variations in the T variable as it is defined. In such circumstances, any correlation between ΔT and ΔW would be due wholly to the correlation between the rate of change of wages and the rate of change of the labour force (ΔL). This hypothesis is easily refuted.

The assertion is that $L = F(W)$, $F' > 0$. But we know that given T^*, T is inversely related to L. Thus, we would have $T = \phi(W)$, $\phi' < 0$, which is contrary to what we observe.

18. This was pointed out to me by Dr J. K. Whitaker.

Part 3

The model to be estimated in this section consists of three equations.

$$\Delta W_t = a_0 + a_1 \Delta T_t + a_2 T_t + a_3 \Delta P_{t-\alpha} + a_4 U_t + u \quad (1)$$
$$a_1 > 0 \qquad a_2 > 0 \qquad 0 < a_3 \leqslant 1 \qquad a_4 < 0$$

$\alpha = 6$ months[19]

$$\Delta P_t = b_0 + b_1 \Delta W_t + b_2 \Delta M_{t-\beta} + b_3 \Delta X_t + v \quad (2)$$
$$b_1 > 0 \qquad b_2 > 0 \qquad b_3 \gtreqless 0$$

$\beta = 7$ months

$$\Delta T_t = c_0 + c_1 T_{t-\lambda} + c_2 \Delta P_{t-\mu} + c_3 D_{t-\gamma} + \epsilon \quad (3)$$
$$c_1 < 0 \qquad c_2 > 0 \qquad c_3 > 0$$

$\lambda = 1$ year $\qquad \mu = \gamma = 6$ months

ΔM is the rate of change of import prices; ΔX is the rate of change of productivity; u, v, and ϵ are random disturbance terms.

(a) We might usefully set up the familiar neo-classical model of the labour market to facilitate a comparison between equation (1) and wage equations which have been estimated in recent years.

$$N^D = f(w/p \,|\, X), \quad \text{(i)}$$
$$N^S = g(w/p \,|\, Z), \quad \text{(ii)}$$
$$N^D = N^S, \quad \text{(iii)}$$

X and Z are vectors of exogenous variables.

Recent work has employed the dynamic adjustment function

$$\Delta(w/p) = \lambda \left(\frac{N^D - N^S}{N^S} \right) = \lambda h(w/p \,|\, X, Z) \quad \text{(iv)}$$

The crucial assumption made, for example by Phillips and Lipsey, is that we can use the percentage of the labour force which is unemployed as a proxy variable for excess demand; i.e.

$$\lambda h(w/p \,|\, X, Z) = \phi(U) \quad \text{(v)}$$

19. Peacock and Ryan, *Economic Journal* (1953), found the lag on the price variable in the wage equation to be between three and six months and the lag on the wage variable in the price equation to be between zero and three months.

where ϕ is a monotonic decreasing function. The form of the function is such that when

$$\left(\frac{N^D - N^S}{N^S}\right) = 0 \qquad U = a_0 \qquad a_0 > 0$$

and when $\left(\dfrac{N^D - N^S}{N^S}\right) \to \infty \qquad U \to 0$

Equation (4) can therefore be written as

$$\Delta(w/p) = \phi(U) \tag{vi}$$

Using a Klein linearization,

$$\Delta(w/p) = \alpha\Delta W - \beta\Delta P \tag{vii}$$

Given this linearization, ΔW is then estimated as a function of the level of unemployment and past price changes.

Since the model implies that all factors influencing excess demand except past price changes are adequately reflected in the level of unemployment, it could be argued that the inclusion of a variable to represent trade union pushfulness would be unnecessary. Thus, Lipsey (1960) states that union induced shifts in the supply curve of labour would generate observations on the function which relates the rate of change of wage rates to the level of unemployment. All this is another way of saying $\Delta W = f_1(U)$ and $U = f_2(\Delta T)$. We have already seen that this is not the case.

Moreover, the model has certain undesirable equilibrium properties. Suppose union induced shifts in the supply curve generate excess demand for labour at the current wage rate. If the resulting wage change is equilibrating, in the new equilibrium, a higher wage rate is associated with a lower volume of employment; and given the stock of capital and abstracting from technical progress, there will be a lower level of output. This is clearly contrary to what we would expect to observe. It is well known that at this level of aggregation, the demand and supply functions are not independent of each other. Thus, when wage rates increase because of union induced shifts in the supply curve, factor incomes alter and, if relative shares are unaffected and the authorities pursue a policy of monetary ease, the demand curve for labour alters. Thus, different levels and rates of change of wages are compatible with an unchanged level of unemployment. In other words, a correct specification of equation (vi) is

$$\Delta(w/p) = \phi(U, | X, Z) \qquad \text{(viii)}$$

if changes in Z induce changes in X on the demand side, a higher level of wages could be consistent with an unchanged level of unemployment.

A similar result is obtained in a Keynesian type model in which the supply of labour is assumed to be a function of an institutionally determined money wage rate. In this model, the level of employment is determined by the real wage rate. This is exactly what happens in the neo-classical model. However, in the Keynesian model, to determine the level of employment we must solve the whole system (and not just the subset of equations which characterize the labour market and which in the neo-classical model are sufficient to determine the real wage rate and hence the level of employment). On certain assumptions, particularly about the behaviour of the money supply, it is easily shown that a given level of employment is consistent with different levels of the money wage rate.

Our theory about the role of the union variable is consistent with a lag of 0–4 months in the adjustment of wage rates to changes in unionization. On inspection of the data it was found that a zero time-lag was the more appropriate. The argument for the lags assumed by the other variables is given by Dicks-Mireaux and Dow (1959). Wages are adjusted annually in each industry. The changes made in any one month are assumed to depend on the change in the cost of living since the last settlement and the current level of unemployment. The change in wages in any one year is therefore a weighted average of the settlement made in each month. Assuming equal weights, we obtain a six-month time-lag on the price variable and a zero time-lag on the level of unemployment.

(b) Equation (2) is of the same form as that estimated by Klein and Ball (1959) and by Dicks-Mireaux (1961), and is discussed fully by them. Note, however, that we do not form any *a priori* expectation about the sign of the coefficient of the rate of change of productivity. Some very plausible hypotheses predict a negative coefficient; others predict a positive coefficient.

(c) Consider next the variable which appears in equation (3).

(i) *The level of unionization:* This variable is included because of the argument in part 2 which implies that the rate of change of unionization is a decreasing function of the level of unionization.[20]

It should be noticed that since $\Delta T_t = T_t - T_{t-1}$, we cannot have ΔT_t dependent on T_t, since to do so would be to admit an element of spurious correlation. Since $T_t = \sum_{i=0}^{t} \Delta T_i$, if we had $T_t = f\left(\sum_{i=0}^{t} T_t\right)$, we would be correlating ΔT_t with an expression which contained ΔT_t among its constituent elements. To avoid this we must have $\Delta T_t = f\left(\sum_{i=0}^{t-1} \Delta T_i\right)$, i.e. $\Delta T_t = f(T_{t-1})$.

(ii) *The rate of change of prices:* This variable is included on the grounds that changes in the cost of living between wage settlements are a factor which influences the militancy of the unions and are therefore reflected in the rate of change of union membership. The lag of six months is institutionally determined like the lag on the price variable in the wage equation.

(iii) *The level of profits:* Kaldor (1959) advanced the hypothesis that the prosperity of industry could provide an explanation of union pushfulness. He argues thus:

On this alternative theory . . . (alternative to a demand pull theory), the rise in money wages depends on the bargaining strength of labour; and, bargaining strength, in turn, is closely related to the prosperity of industry which determines both the eagerness of labour unions to demand higher wages and the ability of employers to grant them.[21]

Kaldor considers that profits are a good index of the prosperity of industry.[22] Since the rate of change of unionization is our

20. This is implied in equation (2), fn. (5), p. (294).

21. Kaldor (1959), p. 293.

22. The relationship is not completely specified. For example, he does not say whether it is the level or the rate of change of profits which is important; he does not specify the appropriate time-lags; he does not say whether the profit variable is to be expressed in real or in money terms. On these and allied points see Lipsey and Steuer (1961). We have used deflated profits and, having experimented with the data, decided that the level of real profits with a six-month time-lag is the appropriate variable.

index of pushfulness, we may interpret his hypothesis as saying that $\Delta W = f(\Delta T)$ and $\Delta T = f(D_{t-\alpha})$.

The estimated model

The model was fitted to annual data for the period since 1921 excluding war years. Estimates were not made for each sub-period. In each sub-period the observations are too few in relation to the number of variables. The period 1893–1913 was excluded because of the difficulty of obtaining satisfactory data for some of the series that enter into the price equation. However, single-stage least squares estimates of the equations explaining the rate of change of money wages and the rate of change of unionization were made for each sub-period and overall. These estimates are to be found in the appendix.

The equations were estimated first by ordinary least squares then by Theil's two-rounds method. The latter method makes allowance for the fact that each equation belongs to an inter-dependent system. It therefore avoids the bias which usually arises when each equation is separately estimated.[23] However, the former method is useful when one wants to experiment with different explanatory variables, alternative functional forms, and alternative specification of the lags. The estimates derived from both procedures are as follows.

Single-stage least squares

$$\Delta W_t = 0{\cdot}7445 + 1{\cdot}5114\Delta T_t + 0{\cdot}0639T_t + 0{\cdot}6199\Delta P_t$$
$$(0{\cdot}5116) \qquad (0{\cdot}1470) \qquad (0{\cdot}2334)$$
$$-0{\cdot}0409\Delta P_{t-1} - 0{\cdot}1243U_t \qquad \text{(1.a)}'$$
$$(0{\cdot}1049) \qquad (0{\cdot}1565)$$

$\bar{R}^2 = 0{\cdot}9141 : d.$ statistic $= 1{\cdot}24\dagger$

23. As an example, suppose equations (1) and (2) reduced to

$$\Delta W_t = \alpha\Delta P_{t-\lambda} + \mu$$
$$\Delta P_t = \beta\Delta W_{t-\mu} + \nu$$

Since we are using annual data, if $\mu + \lambda$ is less than one year, neither the determined price change and the determinant price change nor the determinant wage change and determined wage change are independent. Single-stage least squares will therefore yield asymptotically biased estimates of the parameters. On this and on associated points see Dicks-Mireaux (1961).

$$\Delta W_t = 1 \cdot 1588 + 1 \cdot 9604 \Delta T + 0 \cdot 0700 T_t + 0 \cdot 3865 \Delta P_{t-\frac{1}{2}}$$
$$\quad (0 \cdot 3398) \quad (0 \cdot 1235) \quad (0 \cdot 1183)$$
$$- 0 \cdot 1596 U_t$$
$$(0 \cdot 1351) \tag{1.b$'$}$$

$\bar{R}^2 = 0 \cdot 9197$: d. statistic $= 1 \cdot 17$†

$$\Delta P_t = -0 \cdot 2344 + 0 \cdot 5857 \Delta W_t + 0 \cdot 0844 \Delta M_{t-\frac{1}{2}}$$
$$\quad (0 \cdot 0820) \quad (0 \cdot 0443)$$
$$- 0 \cdot 0042 \Delta X_t$$
$$(0 \cdot 1789) \tag{2.0$'$}$$

$\bar{R}^2 = 0 \cdot 8963$: d. statistic $= 1 \cdot 21$†

$$\Delta T_t = 1 \cdot 7109 - 0 \cdot 1131 T_{t-1} + 0 \cdot 4265 \Delta P_t - 0 \cdot 0680 \Delta P_{t-1}$$
$$\quad (0 \cdot 0218) \quad (0 \cdot 0364) \quad (0 \cdot 0419)$$
$$+ 0 \cdot 0118 D_{t-\frac{1}{2}}$$
$$(0 \cdot 0127) \tag{3.a$'$}$$

$\bar{R}^2 = 0 \cdot 8762$: d. statistic $= 1 \cdot 64$†

$$\Delta T_t = 4 \cdot 1159 - 0 \cdot 0881 T_{t-1} + 0 \cdot 3239 \Delta P_{t-\frac{1}{2}} - 0 \cdot 0161 D_{t-\frac{1}{2}} \tag{3.b$'$}$$
$$\quad (0 \cdot 0357) \quad (0 \cdot 0414) \quad (0 \cdot 0207)$$

$\bar{R}^2 = 0 \cdot 6684$: d. statistic $= 1 \cdot 57$*

Two-stage least squares

$$\Delta W_t = -1 \cdot 9740 + 1 \cdot 5945 \Delta T_t + 0 \cdot 1282 T_t + 0 \cdot 6804 \Delta P_t$$
$$\quad (0 \cdot 2418) \quad (0 \cdot 0409) \quad (0 \cdot 1129)$$
$$- 0 \cdot 0812 \Delta P_{t-1} - 0 \cdot 0441 U_t$$
$$(0 \cdot 0276) \quad (0 \cdot 0370) \tag{1}$$

$\bar{R}^2 = 0 \cdot 9953$: d. statistic $= 1 \cdot 32$†

$$\Delta P_t = 0 \cdot 7797 + 0 \cdot 6924 \Delta W_t + 0 \cdot 0396 \Delta M_{t-\frac{1}{2}} + 0 \cdot 1346 \Delta X_t$$
$$\quad (0 \cdot 0348) \quad (0 \cdot 0173) \quad (0 \cdot 0725)$$
$$\tag{2}$$

$\bar{R}^2 = 0 \cdot 9834$: d. statistic $= 0 \cdot 98$†

$$\Delta T_t = 1 \cdot 4014 - 0 \cdot 1145 T_{t-1} + 0 \cdot 4664 \Delta P_t - 0 \cdot 0978 \Delta P_{t-1}$$
$$\quad (0 \cdot 0083) \quad (0 \cdot 0148) \quad (0 \cdot 0129)$$
$$+ 0 \cdot 0149 D_{t-\frac{1}{2}}$$
$$(0 \cdot 0048) \tag{3}$$

$\bar{R}^2 = 0 \cdot 9843$: d. statistic $= 1 \cdot 31$†

* Indicates that the test showed no autocorrelation at the 1% probability level.

† Indicates that the test was inconclusive.

Matrices of the zero order correlation for each equation in the simultaneous system are given in the appendix.

In the wage equation of the simultaneous system, the postulated lag of three to six months in the adjustment of wage changes to price changes is approximated by ΔP_t and ΔP_{t-1}. Similarly, the nought to three months lag in the adjustment of prices to wage changes is approximated by ΔW_t. The price variable appears with a six-month time-lag in some of the equations which were estimated by single-stage least squares. A comparison of the results shows that in some cases there are noticeable differences in the regression coefficients which were obtained by the two methods of estimation.

We now comment on the results obtained in the jointly estimated model observing that any assessment of the significance of the regression coefficients must be very cautious since at the 1% significance level the test for autocorrelation in the residuals yielded inconclusive results in two of the three equations in the model.

The wage equation. (i) The coefficients on the union variables are firm. A unit change in unionization is associated with a $1\frac{1}{2}\%$ change in the annual percentage rate of change of money wage rates.

(ii) The effect of an autonomous change in price is approximately two-thirds of the price change. This together with the coefficient on the rate of change of wages in the price equation ensures that the wage–price spiral is of the damped variety. The relevant price variable is ΔP_t. The lagged price variable, ΔP_{t-1}, has the wrong sign.

(iii) The level of unemployment does not appear to be an important factor in the determination of the rate of change of wage rates over the sample period. The coefficient on this variable is not significant at the 5% probability level. Contrary to what is generally thought to be the case, this result is actually confirmed by Lipsey (1960). His study is comparable to our own since it employs annual data and covers our sample period. He fitted an equation to the data for the period 1923–39 and 1948–57 which gave the following results:

$$\Delta W = 0 \cdot 74 + 0 \cdot 43 U^{-1} + 11 \cdot 18 U^{-4} + 0 \cdot 034 \Delta U + 0 \cdot 69 \Delta P$$
$$\quad\quad\quad\quad (2 \cdot 10) \quad\quad (6 \cdot 00) \quad\quad (0 \cdot 012) \quad\quad (0 \cdot 08)$$
$$\bar{R}^2 = 0 \cdot 91$$

The residuals were found to be uncorrelated at the 5% probability level. The proportion of the variance in W which is explained is quite large. However, the coefficients on U^{-1} and U^{-4} are less than twice their standard errors. The coefficient on ΔU has the wrong sign. In fact, the only significant variable is ΔP. We are thus left with an equation which in effect reads $\Delta W = f(\Delta P)$.

Klein and Ball (1959) obtained significant coefficients for the unemployment variable. However, their analysis is confined to the post-war period and employs quarterly data. We are precluded from fitting our model to quarterly observations because data on trade union membership is available on an annual basis only. However, our wage equation was fitted to the data for the period 1949–61 by ordinary least squares. The level of unemployment did not appear to be an important determining factor.

The price equation. It should be noted that for the period 1893–1912 we found, as did Phillips and Lipsey, that the level of unemployment made a significant contribution to the explanation of the variance in wage rates.

(i) A given change in wages has an immediate effect on prices which is approximately 70% of the wage change.

(ii) The coefficient on the rate of change of import prices lagged six months shows that, on average, 4% of a given change in import prices is reflected in the index of retail prices.

(iii) Since the coefficient on ΔX_t is positive, it would appear as if the effect of changes in productivity on prices is inflationary. However, the coefficient is insignificant at the 5% probability level.

The role of productivity in models such as this is still the subject of debate. It seems unlikely that this matter will be cleared up in models in which ΔX_t and U_t are assumed to be independent of each other and of ΔW.

(iv) The residuals from the fitted equation were correlated with the level of unemployment as a rough test of whether demand impinges directly on prices as well as indirectly via costs. There is no evidence of a direct relationship of this kind, the r^2 between the residuals and U is 0·0027.

The unionization equation. (i) A given change in the level of unionization lagged one year reduces the current rate of change of unionization by 11% of the change in the level of unionization.

(ii) The rate of change of prices has an immediate effect on ΔT which is approximately 50% of the change in ΔP. The coefficient on ΔP_{t-1} has the wrong sign.

(iii) The level of profit lagged six months is a significant explanatory variable. However, its effect seems to be very small. A given change in the level of profits results in a change in the index of pushfulness which is 10% of the change in profits.

Conclusions

It has been shown that an index of trade union pushfulness, namely the rate of change of unionization, is closely associated with the rate of change of money wage rates and that this index cannot be explained by the level and/or the rate of change of the demand for labour. This result is not upset in the jointly estimated model of part 3. Our hypothesis that the rate of change of unionization is the index of the causal variable in the observed relationship is therefore consistent with the data at this level of aggregation. Moreover, excess demand as measured by the level of unemployment does not appear to have made a significant contribution to the explanation of the variance in wage rates over the period 1921–61.

What is now required is an analysis of the data at a lower level of aggregation. For one thing, some of the implications of our hypothesis about the role of the union variable can only be tested in disaggregated studies. For another, it is important to know how the rate of change of unionization, the level of unemployment, and the rate of change of money wage rates are related to each other in a particular sector and in all other sectors. For example, the aggregate relationship between ΔW and ΔT and the lack of correlation between U and ΔT are consistent with either of two conflicting hypotheses. Suppose wage rates were to rise in some sector. Let it be each union's policy to prevent any widening of inter-industry wage differentials. Then this wage change would make unions in other sectors more militant, and if they successfully negotiate wage adjustments, a rise in aggregate ΔW and ΔT would be observed. Now, all this would be compatible with either an increase in demand for labour in the sector where the wage rise originated or with an increase in union militancy which was independent of demand conditions.

Appendix

The alignment problem[24]

For simplicity, consider a linear regression of Y on X which employs annual data. In each year, we have only one observation on each variable. The problem is to align the corresponding values of Y and X in such a way as to avoid the introduction of implicit time-lags. If, for example, the Xs are centred at mid-year, the Ys must be transformed in such a way that they are also centred at mid-year.

Suppose we are correlating the rates of change of the variables. Then we must find the most efficient way of evaluating the derivatives consistent with the condition set out in the preceding paragraph. The analysis of the text proceeded thus. If both the Xs and the Ys were centred at mid-June, the derivatives were evaluated by the first-central difference method, i.e. $\frac{dY}{dt} = \frac{\frac{1}{2}(Y_{t+1} - Y_{t-1})}{Y_t}$ which leaves the variables centred at mid-June. If the Ys were June-centred but the Xs were end-December figures, $\frac{dX}{dt}$ was calculated either by taking the absolute rate of change, i.e. $\frac{dX}{dt} = X_t - X_{t-1}$, or by taking $\frac{dX}{dt} = \frac{X_t - X_{t-1}}{X_t}$.[25] Both methods have the effect of centring the Xs at mid-June.

24. This problem is also discussed by W. G. Bowen and R. A. Berry in 'Unemployment conditions and movements of the money wage level', *Review of Economics and Statistics* (May 1963).

25. The case of the rate of change of unemployment is an exception. This variable was deliberately centred at 31 December to introduce a six-months time-lag into the relationship between it and the rate of change of wages as suggested by Phillips (1958).

Definition of variables

ΔW_t: 1893–1920 $= \dfrac{\frac{1}{2}(W_{t+1} - W_{t-1})}{W_t} \cdot 100$

   $=$ the percentage rate of change of an index of money wage rates

ΔW_t: 1921–61 $= \left(\dfrac{W_t}{W_{t-1}} - 1 \right) \cdot 100$

   $=$ the percentage rate of change of an index of money wage rates

T_t: 1893–1961 $= \dfrac{\left(\dfrac{T^*}{L} \cdot 100 \right)_t + \left(\dfrac{T^*}{L} \cdot 100 \right)_{t-1}}{2}$

   $=$ the percentage of the *labour force* unionized

ΔT_t: 1893–1961 $= T_t - T_{t-1}$

   $=$ the rate of change of the percentage of the *labour force* unionized

U: percentage of the labour force unemployed

ΔU_t: 1893–1961 $= \dfrac{\frac{1}{2}(U_{t+1} - U_{t-1})}{U_t} \cdot 100$

   $=$ the rate of change of the percentage of the labour force unemployed

ΔP_t: 1893–1961 $= \dfrac{\frac{1}{2}(P_{t+1} - P_{t-1})}{P_t} \cdot 100$

   $=$ the percentage rate of change of the retail price index

$\Delta M_{t-\frac{1}{2}}$: 1921–61 $= \left(\dfrac{M_t}{M_{t-1}} - 1 \right) \cdot 100$

   $=$ the percentage rate of change of an index of import prices

ΔX_t: 1921–61 $= \dfrac{\frac{1}{2}(M_{t+1} - M_{t-1})}{M_t} \cdot 100$

   $=$ the percentage rate of change of an index of productivity per man year

$D_{t-\frac{1}{2}}$: 1921–61 $= \dfrac{D_t + D_{t-1}}{2}$

   $=$ the level of money profits deflated by the index of retail prices

Table 3

		1893–1912	1921–38	1949–61	1921–38 and 1909–61	1893–1912, 1921–38 and 1949–61
$\Delta W_t, \Delta_t$	r^2	0·4798 (0·4220)	0·9125 (0·9016)	0·6297 (0·5624)	0·7682 (0·7522)	0·6671 (0·6463)
	b_1	0·9808 (0·2407)	2·4876 (0·0609)	4·2193 (0·9754)	2·7628 (0·0721)	2·3854 (0·2355)
$\Delta W_{t+\frac{1}{2}}, \Delta T_t$	r^2	0·2005 (0·1117)	0·9159 (0·9054)	0·4632 (0·3656)	0·7607 (0·7442)	0·6431 (0·6285)
	b_2	0·9790 (0·4608)	2·2356 (0·1599)	2·5381 (0·8237)	2·4685 (0·2515)	2·1467 (0·2256)
$\Delta W_{t+1}, \Delta T_t$	r^2	0·2129 (0·1255)	0·7064 (0·6697)	0·0573 (0)	0·5485 (0·5173)	0·4245 (0·4010)
	b_3	0·6482 (0·2941)	1·5853 (0·2608)	1·2353 (1·5122)	1·7854 (0·3063)	1·4786 (0·2436)
$\Delta T_t, \Delta W_{t-\frac{1}{2}}$	r^2	0·0606 (0)	0·1816 (0·0793)	0·3827 (0·2705)	0·2093 (0·1547)	0·1712 (0·1374)
	b_4	0·0590 (0·0549)	0·1838 (0·0986)	0·1591 (0·0610)	0·1622 (0·0587)	0·1436 (0·0455)
$\Delta T_t, \Delta W_{t-1}$	r^2	0·1394 (0·0438)	0·1144 (0·0037)	0·0169 (0)	0·1393 (0·0799)	0·1162 (0·0801)
	b_5	0·2923 (0·1712)	0·1290 (0·0918)	0·0242 (0·0557)	0·1187 (0·0561)	0·1172 (0·0480)

	1893–1912	1921–38	1949–61	1921–38 and 1949–61	1893–1912, 1921–38, and 1949–61
$\Delta W_{t+\frac{1}{2}} = a_6 + b_6\Delta T_t + c_6 T_t R^2$	0·2037 (0·0632)	0·9171 (0·9006)	0·4790 (0·3227)	0·9091 (0·8994)	0·7980 (0·7855)
a_6	1·2147	1·9732	35·1839	−6·5473	−2·3751
b_6	1·0596 (0·5645)	2·1435 (0·2733)	2·4978 (0·8543)	2·6166 (0·1616)	2·4391 (0·1803)
c_6	−0·0605 (0·2320)	−0·0734 (0·1681)	−0·7182 (1·3031)	0·2884 (0·0421)	0·1728 (0·0308)

Matrices of zero order correlations in the jointly estimated system

		ΔW_t	ΔT_t	T_t	ΔP_t	ΔP_{t-1}	U_t
ΔW_t	r^2		0·8394	0·0669	0·9762	0·3388	0·3601
	b		2·8750	0·2075	1·3368	0·7590	−0·5534
ΔT_t	r^2			0·0191	0·7728	0·1563	0·0701
	b			−0·0353	0·3790	0·1643	−0·0778
T_t	r^2				0·0991	0·2450	0·7510
	b				0·5309	0·8046	−0·9962
ΔP	r^2					0·4496	0·3911
	b					0·6463	−0·4263
ΔP_{t-1}	r^2						0·3205
	b						−0·8005
U_t							

		ΔT_t	T_{t-1}	ΔP_t	ΔP_{t-1}	$D_{t-\frac{1}{2}}$
ΔT_t	r^2		0·0977	0·7728	0·1563	0·0226
	b		−0·0778	0·3790	0·1643	−0·0193
T_{t-1}	r^2			0·0180	0·1058	0·4603
	b			0·0775	0·5433	1·3149
ΔP_t	r^2				0·4496	0·0211
	b				0·6463	0·0432
ΔP_{t-1}	r^2					0·2242
	b					1·5328
$D_{t-\frac{1}{2}}$						

		ΔP_t	ΔW_t	$\Delta M_{t-\frac{1}{2}}$	ΔX_t
ΔP_t	r^2		0·9762	0·6707	0·1218
	b		0·7303	−0·3361	0·8564
ΔW_t	r^2			0·5990	0·1819
	b			0·4297	−1·4157
$\Delta M_{t-\frac{1}{2}}$	r^2				0·0221
	b				−0·0076
ΔX_t					

Single-stage estimates of the wage equation

1893–1912
$$\Delta W_t = 1.8445 + 0.5260\Delta T_t + 0.0696\Delta P_{t-\frac{1}{2}} - 0.3171 U_t$$
$$\qquad\qquad (0.2591) \qquad\quad (0.0854) \qquad\qquad (0.1245)$$

$\bar{R}^2 = 0.5761$: d. statistic $= 1.35$†

1921–38
$$\Delta W_t = 1.0190 + 1.9981\Delta T_t + 0.2899\Delta P_{t-\frac{1}{2}} - 0.0483 U_t$$
$$\qquad\qquad (0.3035) \qquad\quad (0.1507) \qquad\qquad (0.1306)$$

$\bar{R}^2 = 0.9137$: d. statistic $= 1.04$†

1949–61
$$\Delta W_t = 5.5443 + 3.2215\Delta T_t + 0.4029\Delta P_{t-\frac{1}{2}} - 0.9678 U_t$$
$$\qquad\qquad (0.7905) \qquad\quad (0.1847) \qquad\qquad (0.6984)$$

$\bar{R}^2 = 0.7653$: d. statistic $= 2.89$*

1921–38 and 1949–61
$$\Delta W_t = 1.1588 +$$
$$\qquad 1.9604\Delta T_t + 0.0700 T_t + 0.3865\Delta P_{t-\frac{1}{2}} - 0.1596 U_t$$
$$\qquad (0.3398) \qquad (0.1235) \qquad (0.1183) \qquad\qquad (0.1351)$$

$\bar{R}^2 = 0.9197$: d. statistic $= 1.17$†

1893–1912, 1921–38, and 1949–61
$$\Delta W_t = -1.3383 +$$
$$\qquad 1.9073\Delta T_t + 0.1280 T_t + 0.3442\Delta P_{t-\frac{1}{2}} - 0.0990 U_t$$
$$\qquad (0.2389) \qquad (0.0320) \qquad (0.1040) \qquad\qquad (0.0527)$$

$\bar{R}^2 = 0.8708$: d. statistic $= 1.29$†

Single-stage estimates of the unionization equation

1893–1912
$$\Delta T_t = -1.5636 - 0.2235 T_{t-1} + 0.0401\Delta P_{t-} + 0.1039 D_{t-\frac{1}{2}}$$
$$\qquad\qquad\quad (0.1935) \qquad\quad (0.0831) \qquad\quad (0.0482)$$

$\bar{R}^2 = 0.2684$: d. statistic $= 1.58$*

1921–38
$$\Delta T_t = 7.2845 - 0.2649 T_{t-1} + 0.1919\Delta P_{t-\frac{1}{2}} - 0.0065 D_{t-\frac{1}{2}}$$
$$\qquad\qquad\quad (0.1193) \qquad\quad (0.1006) \qquad\quad (0.0339)$$

$\bar{R}^2 = 0.7948$: d. statistic $= 1.22$†

1949–61
$$\Delta T_t = 30.5150 - 0.7938 T_{t-1} + 0.0608\Delta P_{t-\frac{1}{2}} + 0.0095 D_{t-\frac{1}{2}}$$
$$\qquad\qquad\quad (0.3416) \qquad\quad (0.0428) \qquad\quad (0.0096)$$

$\bar{R}^2 = 0.5168$: d. statistic $= 2.70$*

1921–38 and 1949–61

$$\Delta T_t = 4{\cdot}1159 - 0{\cdot}0881T_{t-1} + 0{\cdot}3239\Delta P_{t-\frac{1}{2}} - 0{\cdot}0161D_{t-\frac{1}{2}}$$
$$\phantom{\Delta T_t = 4{\cdot}1159} (0{\cdot}0357) (0{\cdot}0414) (0{\cdot}0207)$$

$\bar{R}^2 = 0{\cdot}6684$: d. statistic $= 1{\cdot}57*$

1893–1912, 1921–38, and 1949–61

$$\Delta T_t = 0{\cdot}9316 - 0{\cdot}1009T_{t-1} + 0{\cdot}2887\Delta P_{t-\frac{1}{2}} + 0{\cdot}0148D_{t-\frac{1}{2}}$$
$$\phantom{\Delta T_t = 0{\cdot}9316} (0{\cdot}0268) (0{\cdot}0364) (0{\cdot}0109)$$

$\bar{R}^2 = 0{\cdot}6175$: d. statistic $= 1{\cdot}63*$

References

BROWN, A. J. (1955). *The Great Inflation, 1939–1951*, Oxford University Press.

DICKS-MIREAUX, L. A. (1961). 'The inter-relationship between cost and price changes, 1949–1959', *Oxford Economic Papers*, October.

DICKS-MIREAUX, L. A. and DOW, J. C. (1959). 'The determinants of wage inflation in the United Kingdom, 1946–56', *Journal of the Royal Statistical Society*. Series A (General), vol. 122, part 2.

DOW, J. C. and DICKS-MIREAUX, L. A. (1958). 'Excess demand for labour', *Oxford Economic Papers*.

DOW, J. C. (1956). 'Analysis of the generation of price inflation', *Oxford Economic Papers*.

DURBIN, J. and WATSON, G. S. (1951). 'Testing for serial correlation in least squares regression', *Biometrica*, vol. 38, parts 1 and 2.

JOHNSTON, J. (1963). *Econometric Methods*, McGraw-Hill.

KALDOR, N. (1959). 'Economic growth and the problem of inflation', part 2, *Economica*, November.

KLEIN, L. R. and BALL, J. R. (1959). 'Some econometrics of the determination of the absolute level of wages and prices', *Economic Journal*, September.

KLEIN, L. R. *et al.* (1961). *An Econometric Model of the United Kingdom*, Blackwell, Oxford.

LIPSEY, R. G. (1960). 'The relation between unemployment and the rate of change of money wage rates in the United Kingdom, 1862–1957. A further study', *Economica*, February.

LIPSEY, R. G. (1963). *An Introduction to Positive Economics. Appendix to Chapter 33*, Weidenfeld and Nicolson.

LIPSEY, R. G. and STEUER, M. D. (1961). 'The relation between profits and wage rates', *Economica*, May.

PHILLIPS, A. W. (1958). 'The relation between unemployment and the rate of change of money rates in the United Kingdom', *Economica*, November.

15 H. F. Lydall

Inflation and the Earnings Gap

Lydall, H. F. (1958) Inflation and the earnings gap. *Bull. Oxford Inst. Stats.*, **20**, 285–304.

The current debate amongst economists about the causes of inflation is of obvious practical as well as theoretical importance. If one believes that excess demand is the cause of the persistent rise in prices, then the measures adopted in the past two years may be justified. This is clearly the point of view of the Cohen Council. On the other hand, if the inflation is mainly due to a rise in costs, restriction of demand may not achieve the aim of reducing prices but may merely result in cutting output and the rate of economic growth. This, in the opinion of many economists, is the great danger implicit in the continuation of present policies.

The discussion of these issues is often confused by the fact that the argument is proceeding at two levels. On the first level, the question is whether fluctuations in demand affect prices, *even when cost conditions are unchanged*. In other words, it is a question of whether excess demand causes a profit inflation. If one accepts the traditional conception of a smoothly rising supply curve and a reasonably perfect market, this automatically follows. But once it is recognized that, at least in manufacturing and service industries, the characteristic arrangement is for prices to be 'administered' at 'full cost', it is clear that the old concept of a rising supply curve is inappropriate. The supply curve for the output of the full-cost firm is horizontal up to the point of maximum capacity – after which it becomes vertical. The vertical part is, in practice, generally non-operative since, when output at the full-cost price is not sufficient to meet demand, orders are usually allowed to pile up and customers have to wait for delivery. In this situation an increase in demand for the products of full-cost industries will simply result in greater output at the same price level up to the point of maximum capacity. 'Excess' demand only exists when orders are increasing faster than output and the stock of unfilled orders is growing. When demand is high, profits will, of course, be high; but this is simply the result of maintaining a constant overhead and profit margin over a larger output. The existence of an overhead element in costs means that profits will fluctuate more than in proportion to output.

If we lived in a closed economy and all our enterprises – including farming – operated on the full-cost principle, there would be no influence from the demand side on the gap between prices and labour costs. Where demand clearly does have an influence on this gap is in agriculture, and more especially on the price of imports of food and raw materials. It is only too obvious that it was excess demand which caused the enormous rise in world commodity prices in 1950–1; and it is equally obvious that it is the decline in world demand, relative to output, which is responsible for the fall in these prices at the present time. To that extent, those who believe in the power of demand are justified: if we want to cut the prices of primary products we can always do so by reducing demand in the advanced industrialized countries. It should not be forgotten, however, that, since in the short run both the demand for and supply of primary products is very inelastic, the effect of cutting back the demand for these products is to induce an extremely sharp fall in the incomes of primary producers. The economic and political consequences of such a policy may, therefore, be somewhat risky, to say the least.

But there is a second, and more difficult, level at which the discussion of the effects of demand on prices is proceeding. This is the level of *derived* demand. High demand, it is said, is responsible not only for raising prices directly, thereby increasing profits, but also for raising the prices of the factors of production – expecially of labour. Here attention is drawn to the persistent upward trend of wage costs over the past two decades; and it is argued that this, in itself, is *prima facie* evidence that we have been suffering from excess demand.

It is possible to think of assumptions on which the 'excess demand' explanation of the rise in wages would be justified. But the adherents of this view have so far done little to explain the mechanism through which a rise in wage costs per unit of output

321

is actually brought about. One might expect that some attempt would be made to establish an empirical relation between changes in demand and changes in unit wage costs. It is, indeed, customary in this connexion to refer to the statistics of employment vacancies and to compare them with the number of unemployed; but no one has yet shown that a clear relationship exists between 'excess demand for labour', as measured in this way, and the rate of increase in unit wage costs.[1]

In recent months a new argument has been developed to give empirical support to the 'demand' theory of wages. The argument has been used by several economists, notably Professors Robbins and Paish and Mr B. C. Roberts.[2] It has also been employed by the Cohen Council and the British Employers' Confederation.[3] Perhaps the best statement of the theory is that which occurs in the *First Report* of the Cohen Council.[4] It runs as follows:

Another important feature of the period . . . has been the tendency for average earnings to rise faster than weekly wage rates. The reasons for this are complex, but there seems no reason to doubt that one of them is the tendency of some employers, in time of high demand, to attract labour by bidding up its price above the figure embodied in national agreements and awards. Here too, as we should expect, the extent of the gap seems to vary with the intensity of demand.

Professor Paish puts the matter this way:

If the general level of wage rates had been forced up by trade union pressure, it is difficult to see why actual weekly earnings, which are largely within the control of employers, should have risen faster than wage rates; whereas if they have been forced up by the competition of employers for scarce labour this development is quite intelligible.[5]

1. A useful index of 'excess demand for labour' has been compiled by J. C. R. Dow and L. A. Dicks-Mireaux (see 'The excess demand for labour. A study in conditions in Great Britain, 1946–56', *Oxford Economic Papers* [February 1958]). The authors do not, however, attempt to relate their index to the rise in wage costs.

2. Professor Robbins in the *Financial Times*, 28 August 1957; Professor Paish in the *District Bank Review*, March 1958; Mr Roberts in *The London and Cambridge Economic Bulletin*, September 1957.

3. *First Report of the Council on Prices, Productivity and Incomes* (1958), para. 82, and 1957 *Report* of the British Employers' Confederation (quoted in *The Times*, 5 March 1958).

4. loc. cit.   5. op. cit., p. 10.

He adds that it was 'for this reason' that between 1946 and 1951, while wage rates rose by only 24%, weekly earnings rose by 43%.

Professor Robbins, who argues the case most forcefully, believes that if our inflation were wage-induced, wage rates would rise faster than earnings, rather than the other way round.[6]

The attention which has thus been drawn to the relative movements of earnings and wage rates is welcome. For it is a very striking phenomenon and challenges an explanation. But I believe that the interpretation placed on it by the above-quoted authors may well be mistaken; that a widening of the earnings gap may be not so much a sign of *inflation*, at least in the sense of a rise in prices, as of potential *deflation*. There is, of course, a difficulty in the ambiguity of these terms. 'Inflation' may mean an increase in money incomes, in the money supply, or in the general price level; and some people even use the term to mean a government deficit. The problem with which we are concerned is the stability of the general price level and I shall use the word inflation to mean a rise in this.

If this is what we are after, then the important question is, not whether wage rates or earnings rise, but whether they rise faster than output. What I propose to show below is that a widening of the earnings gap generally indicates that output is increasing, and indeed that output is increasing *faster* than the earnings gap itself. Although it is undoubtedly true that the earnings gap widens when demand increases, and *vice versa*, this is in a sense a 'spurious correlation'. Increasing demand results in increasing output – provided the productive capacity to meet the demand exists – and increasing output entails an increase in the earnings gap. Hence, it is not simply demand as such that causes the widening of the gap but the translation of demand into output. It is not primarily a process of 'bidding up' wages but of paying more for more work; and since the extra wage cost is smaller than the extra output produced, the net effect is likely to be deflationary rather than the reverse.

6. loc. cit.

The Relation between Earnings and Wage Rates

A gap between earnings and wage rates can be caused by one or more of the following influences: first, shifts in the composition of the labour force by age and sex; secondly, changes in the relative importance of different industries and occupations; thirdly, changes in the hours of work; fourthly, changes in piecework earnings resulting from increasing output per worker; and fifthly, changes in individual or group payments made by employers beyond the rates approved under national agreements.[7]

Now it is obvious that, if there is any 'bidding up' of the price of labour by competition between employers for scarce labour, its impact on earnings will be made through the last of these components. Nobody knows how much of the earnings margin can be attributed to such extra payments, although there is a good deal of talk amongst employers about 'temptation' and 'bribery' rates. My own view is that much of this is merely an enforced adaptation of individual firms' rates to changes in the earnings situation amongst their immediate competitors. I shall elaborate this idea below. But one thing is certain, namely, that only a part of the earnings margin can be attributed to this cause. Penrice's figures for 1948–55 show that the influence of shifts in the sex and age composition of the labour force and of changes in the importance of different industries in this period was small, and about half the earnings gap was caused by changes in the number of hours worked. The other half has to be divided between the effect of changes in piecework earnings and in the 'above-rate' payments. I now propose to show that piecework earnings are likely to account for a substantial part of this.

Let us start by considering the conditions under which piecework earnings fluctuate. Such fluctuations may be the result of (1) a change in the piece rate or (2) a change in output per pieceworker. Changes in piece *rates* may either be the consequence of changes in the basic wage rate, following some national or regional agreement, or of changes in the specific rate applicable to a particular job. Changes in nationally or regionally agreed rates presumably enter into the Ministry of Labour's wage-rate

7. See G. Penrice, 'Earnings and wage rates, 1948–55' *London and Cambridge Economic Bulletin* (December 1955).

index. Hence, changes in the margin between piecework earnings and the official wage rate (other than those caused by overtime payments or special merit rates) must be due either to a change in the rates for specific jobs or to a change in output per worker.

Changes in individual job rates will usually be the consequence of a change in the product or the process of production. Such changes are especially likely to occur when there is a change in the machinery or equipment provided. They will, therefore, be discontinuous. In general, it may be expected that the rate for a new job – or new process – will be set at a level which will yield the pieceworker not less than the weekly earnings received on the previous job. The business of fixing piece rates is, however, a very tricky one. When a new job is first introduced the worker will be unfamiliar with it, the new tools may not be fully adapted to their purpose, and the supply of parts or components may still need some adjustment. In all these – and perhaps other – ways there will be room for improvement. Once the price for the job is fixed, it will be possible for the worker – or group of workers in the case of a gang piecework system – to develop more efficient ways of doing the job. There are often important improvements in technique that can be introduced in this manner on the initiative of the workers themselves; and it is, of course, one of the main purposes of a piecework system to stimulate such improvements. But increased output per worker may also be the result of a general improvement in factory organization, better co-ordination of processes, more careful planning of the sequence of operations, a smoother supply of components, and so on. Many of these improvements, both in the worker's own technique and in the wider organization, are likely to be induced by increased pressure of demand; so that, if the job prices are already fixed, increased demand will automatically result in higher piecework earnings. Thus a connection can be established between fluctuations in demand, in output, and in piecework earnings.

But, it may be objected, there is no logical reason why piecework earnings per worker should fluctuate with total output. Would it not be more rational for an employer to ensure that his pieceworkers are always fully employed and working to the maximum of their willingness? When he needs to vary his total output – because of a change in demand – he can do so by

325

varying the *number* of pieceworkers he employs, not their average output. The answer to this is that conditions in the labour market and in the structure of industrial organization are not such as to make this type of adjustment possible in all circumstances. Labour, as a factor of production, is not perfectly divisible, nor are the complex processes within industry completely adjustable. Much labour is, within limits, an overhead cost, which must be spread over larger or smaller outputs according to the state of demand.

Moreover, when the economy has been operating for some years near to the full employment ceiling, many employers are afraid to adjust themselves to a slight recession of demand by sacking part of their staff, in case they should find it impossible to replace them when demand recovers.[8]

We have seen that, so far as pieceworkers are concerned, a direct relation is likely to exist between output and earnings. Let us now consider some examples of the form which this relation may take in particular cases. Consider, first, the case of a firm in which *all* the operatives are on piecework and their *entire* earnings are in this form. The former assumption is unlikely to be true of any actual firm, but the latter assumption is true of pieceworkers in some firms in, for example, the textile industry. Let us assume that the workers in this firm are paid 1*s* a piece. Then, if they produce on the average 100 pieces a week, their average weekly earnings will be £5. Now suppose that, without any change in the equipment or in the number of hours worked the number of pieces produced per worker goes up to 120 a week. Then earnings will be £6 per worker. Since wage rates as such are assumed not to have changed, there will be a 'gap' or 'margin'

8. The 'overhead' character of much office and supervisory labour is well known; but the same tendency is growing amongst manual workers, partly perhaps as a result of the increasingly complex internal organization of large firms and partly because of trade union resistance to redundancy. Whatever the reasons, it is a striking fact that in recent years fluctuations in output – both upwards and downwards – have always been greater than fluctuations in employment. Two important corollaries flow from this relationship: first, that it is unlikely that output per worker can be increased by deflating demand; and secondly, that the unemployment figures do not accurately measure the degree of under-employment of total resources. At the present time, for example, the degree of under-utilization of productive capacity is perhaps four or five times as great as the 2% of recorded unemployment.

between earnings and wage rates, or more strictly a gap between the relative change in earnings and in wage rates. Earnings have increased by 20%, wage rates not at all; and the earnings gap has therefore widened by 20% of the initial earnings figure.

It should be noted that, in this example, the increase in earnings is exactly equal to the increase in output and is entirely caused by it. Moreover, since output and wage earnings have moved *pari passu*, wage cost per unit of output has remained constant. If the firm is assumed to fix its prices on the 'full cost' principle, i.e. on the basis of direct costs of labour and raw materials, there will be no reason from the wage cost side why prices should rise. Hence the widening of the earnings margin, in this case, will not be associated with a rise in prices.[9]

Next, let us take the case of a firm in which all workers are on piecework, but only part of their earnings are related to output. Of these two assumptions, the former is again unrealistic but the latter is to be found in many industries. For example, in the engineering industry it is the standard rule that part of a piece-worker's earnings is calculated on a time basis (i.e. according to the number of hours he is at work) while the other part varies with his output, The relative proportions of these two parts varies from worker to worker, from week to week, from firm to firm, and from one wage settlement to another, but a typical situation would be one in which two-thirds of a pieceworker's weekly earnings were time-based and one-third earned from piecework. Let us assume that this situation existed in our factory in the initial position, with each worker receiving 66s. 8d. from time work and 33s. 4d. from piecework, £5 in all. This means that, if the workers are producing 100 pieces each, the rate is 4d. per piece. What is now the effect of an increase of output to 120 pieces per week? Piecework earnings rise by 20%; but total earnings rise by only $6\frac{2}{3}$%. Since, as before, the wage rate has

9. If prices are fixed by 'supply and demand' there is equally no reason why they should rise as a consequence of a change in output and earnings of this sort, since the proportionate increase in wage incomes is equal to the proportionate increase in output, and there is no reason why the proportionate increase in non-wage incomes should be any higher. It might well be lower; and, if allowance is made for a rising marginal propensity to save, and for the influence of direct taxation, the net effort on the balance of demand and supply is likely to be mildly deflationary.

remained unchanged, the earnings gap will have widened by $6\frac{2}{3}\%$.

In this example the rise in output is *three times as great* as the increase in the earnings gap and, since wage costs per unit have actually fallen, there is no reason to expect that prices will be raised (unless the increased demand for raw materials raises raw material costs very substantially). If prices are kept constant (and raw material prices are unchanged) the effect of the increased output will be to raise total incomes in the same proportion as total output; but since wage incomes will have risen by only one-third of the rate of increase of total incomes, non-wage incomes – especially profits – will have risen much faster. In this situation the marginal propensity to save is likely to be high, and a substantial part of the additional output will be available for investment. It is clear, therefore, that a rise in the earnings margin which comes about in this way is not necessarily a sign of inflation or of a shift of resources from investment to consumption, but could well be a sign of exactly the opposite tendencies.

If all workers in all industries were pieceworkers and if the earnings of all of them were related partly to their hours of work and partly to their output – as in the example just considered – then the initial effect of any general increase in output (without any change in hours worked) would be deflationary, in the sense in which I have used the word above. But this situation would not be, except in a very special case, a stable one. For the increase in the earnings of each worker would depend on two things: first, the proportion of his peace earnings to his time earnings at the beginning of the period; and secondly, the increase in his output – and hence in his piece earnings – during the period. In any actual situation these two ratios will be different for different workers, so that the effect of a general increase in output will be to raise the earnings of some workers more than others.[10]

Repercussions of Increases in Piecework Earnings

Before we proceed, it is desirable to remove one of the simplifying assumptions made so far. This is the assumption that *all* the

10. In a limiting case there might be two groups of workers, one of which derived all its income from piecework and the other group none (cf. J. R. Hicks, 'The instability of wages', *Three Banks Review* [September, 1956]).

wage-earners in a given firm or industry are pieceworkers. It is, of course, an unrealistic assumption, since there are always some 'overhead' jobs that need to be done in any firm, such as maintenance and repair of machinery, toolmaking, transport, storage, and sweeping up. There are also some processes in most firms which cannot easily be put on a piecework basis, such as experimental and development work, the operation of machines which require specially skilled attention, or where the machine paces the job. Then, of course, within any industry there are usually some firms which do not have a piecework system but pay their workers solely on a time basis.

According to figures collected by the Ministry of Labour about 40% of all workers in manufacturing are on some system of payment by results (not including good time-keeping bonuses, merit payments, profit sharing, or co-partnership). The proportion increases very markedly with the size of the establishment (see table 1), mainly because the proportion of establishments operating a piecework system increases with size. In establishments with 10 or fewer wage-earning employees only about one in ten have any sort of piecework system, while, at the other extreme,

Table 1

Piecework in Manufacturing, October 1957

Size of establishment (number of wage-earners)	Establishments with systems of piecework as percentage of all establishments in the group	Workers employed on piecework as percentage of all workers in the group	Workers employed on piecework as percentage of all workers in piecework establishments
1–10	11	7	50
11–24	23	12	50
25–99	42	23	51
100–499	66	38	55
500–999	80	47	58
1,000 and over	88	56	64
All	38*	41	58

* Since establishments employing up to 10 were under-represented in the sample, this figure is not a reliable estimate of the proportion of all manufacturing establishments operating a piecework system.

Source: *Ministry of Labour Gazette*, April 1958, p. 128.

amongst establishments employing 1,000 wage-earners or over nearly nine out of ten have a piecework system. It is interesting to note that in firms which have a piecework system only half or a little more of the wage-earners employed are paid wholly or partly on piecework. (The rise in this percentage in the larger size groups shown in column 3 of table 1 is probably partly an effect of the increasing proportion of establishments operating piecework systems *within* each size range shown.) The proportion of establishments operating piecework systems varies in different industries. In gas, water, and electricity it is negligible; in motor repairing and garages less than 5%; and in printing less than 10%. On the other hand, in cotton textiles it is nearly 90%; in metal manufacture nearly two-thirds (with 100% in sheet steel); and in clothing over 60%. In manufacturing industry as a whole the proportion is about 44% for establishments employing 11 or more wage-earners, but, as we have seen, only 11% or less for the smaller establishments. The weighted average for all establishments, irrespective of size, would be about 20%, but this is heavily influenced by the multitude of very small firms, which are of little consequence in terms of output or employment.

Now the question arises: What is the effect on non-pieceworkers employed in pieceworking firms of a rise in the earnings of the pieceworkers? And further, what is the effect on the workers in non-pieceworking firms of a rise in the earnings of pieceworkers (and perhaps also of timeworkers) in pieceworking firms within the same industry? No comprehensive or statistical evidence exists for answering these questions; and we are therefore obliged to consider them in the light of general principles, together with such fragmentary evidence as can be collected from those with a knowledge of industry. I think it will be generally agreed that a rise in the earnings of one group of workers within a firm, which is not entirely attributable to their working 'harder' or for longer hours, will set up tensions, or disequilibria, within the firm. If pieceworkers' hourly earnings are rising because of a general increase in output, then sooner or later the management of the firm will be obliged to concede some increase in earnings to other workers in the same firm whose wages are time-based. This is sometimes arranged quite simply by giving the timeworkers a 'lieu' rate, which is related to the average piecework earnings of the pieceworkers. Where such a system does not exist the management may have to resort to other methods of maintaining the differentials, for example, by merit rates, special departmental rates, and so forth.

The problem as it presents itself *within* pieceworking firms is capable of fairly ready solution along these lines. Since the increased earnings of the pieceworkers are the result of a rise in output per worker, the firm can usually afford to add to the earnings of the non-pieceworkers in the same proportion and still make greater profits. More heartburning is caused, however, over the discrepancies which emerge between earnings in different firms in the same industry. There are, it is true, very wide and unexpected differences between firms within the same industry in the average level of their workers' earnings.[11] Nevertheless, it seems reasonable to believe that if, within a certain industry and in a certain area, hourly earnings in firm A go up, sooner or later pressures will be exerted to push up earnings in firms B, C, and D. The mechanism may be very imperfect and there may be substantial time-lags. But I would argue that a rise in piecework earnings in firm A will set up a *tendency* for earnings to rise in non-piecework firms within firm A's orbit of influence in the labour market.

This is a point which needs more detailed consideration. It is well known that many employers have been obliged in recent years to pay their workers rates above the nationally agreed rates. On one interpretation the existence of these 'bribery' rates is a living testimony to the fact of excess demand for labour. But this is not a necessary conclusion. It may be that these extra payments simply reflect the fact that earnings in some firms have got out of line with earnings in other firms in which piecework systems operate; that, in other words, they are not a symptom of a 'bidding up' of the price of labour but of a readjustment of rates within an industry in which temporary disequilibria have arisen. It is difficult to believe that 'bidding up' of the price of labour is generally a sensible policy for firms to pursue, even when there is tightness in the labour market, since the marginal cost of labour obtained in this way is very high. Oligopoly – which is the

11. cf. T. P. Hill and K. G. J. C. Knowles, 'The variability of engineering earnings' (May 1956).

typical situation – makes the cost even greater.[12] But if, for reasons beyond an individual firm's control, earnings per worker increase, as they do under the piecework system with rising output, then the other firms in that market area must sooner or later adjust themselves to the new situation or face increasing labour unrest.

From a theoretical standpoint this view of the labour market is based on the belief that the supply curve of labour to an individual firm is kinked. The left-hand portion is an almost horizontal line, whose position is determined by the earnings of labour in alternative occupations, whilst the right-hand portion rises sharply in reflection of the oligopolistic situation in the labour market. The position of the kink – or the price of labour, in the sense of the average earnings for a normal week – will be influenced partly by collective bargaining over wage rates and partly by the effect on piecework earnings of the level of output. When there is a rise in the nationally agreed rate, non-union firms are obliged – under conditions of near-full employment – to give approximately the same increase to their workers; similarly, when earnings rise in piecework firms, timeworking firms will sooner or later have to conform. The price of labour in money terms has a ratchet, maintained by trade union and other resistances, which prevents employers from cutting rates except by prolonged and bitter struggles. I cannot, therefore, believe that employers will voluntarily push that ratchet up, although I grant that it may be difficult in practice to distinguish between the process of pushing up the ratchet and of re-establishing an appropriate relationship to a wage-level which has already been lifted up by other forces.

Irrespective of the view one takes of the significance of 'bribery' rates, I think it is obvious that an increase in hourly earnings in piecework firms, as a consequence of increasing output, will gradually spread its effects through the industries to which those firms belong. And these effects are most likely to take the form of special increases in rates in non-piecework firms, beyond the national agreements. Indeed this is inevitable; for the problem is one of re-establishing 'relativities' between two groups of firms

12. cf. G. C. Archibald, 'The factor gap and the level of wages', *Economic Record* (November 1954).

in the same labour market. A change in the national rate would do nothing to correct this disequilibrium; therefore, individual firms must necessarily bring themselves into line by individual action.

Within the national economy we may broadly distinguish two sectors, which I shall call the piecework sector and the non-piecework sector. More conveniently they may be referred to as sector A and sector B. Sector A consists of those industries in which an appreciable proportion of the workers are on piecework. It is not possible to draw a strict line of division; but it seems reasonable to regard any industry in which 25% or more of the workers are on piecework as likely to be subject to their influence, while industries in which 10% or less are on piecework are unlikely to be affected by changes in piecework earnings. Industries with between 10 and 25% of pieceworkers are intermediate; but it happens that there are not very many of them. Industries which contain 25% or more pieceworkers include most of manufacturing, mining, and – from the service trades – laundries and dry-cleaning. Those with less than 10% of pieceworkers include certain manufacturing industries which handle bulk commodities by continuous processes – such as grain milling, oil refining, and cement and others which are closely associated with retailing – such as garages, bakers, and meat and milk products. Apart from these, the bulk of sector B consists of public utilities and service trades, such as gas, electricity, and water, transport, distribution, banking and insurance, public administration, the professions, and a wide variety of other services. It also includes agriculture. Altogether about half of our total manpower is in sector A and half in sector B, and the two sectors are of approximately equal importance in their contribution to the national income.

Now I wish to suggest that, within sector A, increases in piecework earnings, resulting from increased output, spread their effects amongst timeworkers predominantly by forcing up the special rates and bonuses paid by individual firms. These help to raise the level of earnings, but they have no direct influence on the national index of wage rates. Hence they contribute to the creation of the earnings gap. So far as sector B is concerned, however, the effects of increases in earnings in sector A are communicated mainly through changes in official wage rates. Thus, for example, if in a particular town hourly earnings in some engineering factories go up, as a result of increases in piecework earnings, this will tend to cause *earnings* in other (timeworking) engineering factories to rise, by means of individual increases in rates given within those factories. But the repercussions of this general increase in earnings in engineering will also begin to spread to the workers in the sector B industries in the town. For example, the bus workers will become discontented; and sooner or later, if the discontent is national in its scope, there will be a demand for a revision of bus workers' wage *rates*. If this demand is not met there will be increasing tension within the trade union movement leading eventually to strikes. If it is met, the official wage rate index will go up.

We may regard the development of wages under full employment (and even perhaps with somewhat less than full employment) as conforming broadly to the following simplified model. Let us assume for the moment that there have been no changes in prices and that hours of work are fixed. Then the first step away from an original 'equilibrium' will be caused by an increase in output per worker in sector A. This causes piecework earnings in sector A to rise, followed by the 'lieu' rates of timeworkers in piecework firms in sector A, followed again by the special 'bribery' rates in other (non-piecework) firms in sector A. Now earnings in sector A as a whole have gone ahead of earnings in sector B. But earnings in sector B can only be increased in an orderly way by increasing wage rates in sector B's industries. So the wage rates of the busmen, the railwaymen, the shop workers, the agricultural workers, and the civil servants are gradually pushed up. But this in turn causes further repercussions in sector A itself. The workers in engineering, etc., argue that their increased earnings are the result of greater productivity. They know that profits in their industry are booming. The newspapers tell them that various groups of workers in sector B are getting increases in their agreed *rates*. So they also demand that their rates shall go up; and a new round of repercussions may begin[13]

I now propose to examine the workings of a model of this sort.

13. Workers in sector A may also be anxious to consolidate their position by securing an increase in their basic timework rates, which can less easily be reduced in times of depression.

On some assumptions the model will produce an inflationary trend, on other assumptions a deflationary one. What will chiefly interest us will be the possibilities of achieving price stability or, at the most, a 1 or 2% annual rate of increase in prices. Given the structure of the model, the outcome depends on the values of the following parameters:

(1) The proportions of the national income generated in sectors A and B respectively, in the initial position.

(2) The rate of increase of productivity (output per worker) in each sector.

(3) The 'piecework effect' of an increase in productivity in sector A on average earnings in sector A, i.e. the percentage increase in average earnings in sector A which results from a given percentage increase in productivity in this sector.

(4) The 'earnings effect' of an increase in earnings in sector A on the level of wage rates in sector B, i.e. the percentage increase in wage rates in sector B resulting from a given percentage increase in earnings in sector A.

(5) The effect on wage rates in sector A of an increase in wage rates in sector B.

Empirical information about the values of these parameters is of variable quality. We have already given a rough estimate of (1), and we can make reasonable guesses about some of the others. About one which is of crucial importance – number (3) – we have some partial information, which it will now be useful to consider.

The Strength of the 'Piecework Effect' in Sector A

There are no available figures of earnings, wage rates and productivity in the piecework sector as such, but some approximate indication of the 'piecework effect' of output on the earnings gap may be obtained by considering the situation in manufacturing. Most of manufacturing is in sector A; and for manufacturing industry as a whole we have official estimates of wage rates, earnings, and output per worker. In table 2 I have assembled the relevant data. The first two columns show the annual percentage changes in wage rates and earnings; and column (3) gives the gross earnings gap. For simplicity this has been computed by subtracting column (2) from column (1) instead of by dividing the ratio of earnings in two consecutive years by the ratio of wage rates. But the result is effectively the same. The fourth column shows the

Table 2

Productivity and the Earnings Gap in Manufacturing
(percentage changes on previous year)

Year	Wage rates (1)	Earnings per worker (2)	Gross earnings gap (3)	Output per worker (4)	Hours per week (5)	Net earnings gap (6)	Adjusted output per worker (7)
1949	3·4	4·0	0·6	5·7	0·3	0·1	5·4
1950	1·8	4·8	3·0	5·9	1·0	1·5	4·9
1951	9·4	9·3	−0·1	2·4	0·4	−0·8	2·0
1952	8·5	8·3	−0·2	−3·1	−0·7	0·8	−2·4
1953	4·6	6·3	1·7	4·9	1·0	0·2	3·9
1954	4·2	6·6	2·4	7·0	0·9	1·1	6·1
1955	6·5	8·9	2·4	8·5	0·3	1·9	8·2
1956	7·9	7·5	−0·4	−1·9	−0·8	0·7	−1·1
1957	5·0	5·1	0·1	1·4	−0·3	0·6	1·7

(1) Ministry of Labour index of weekly wage rates in manufacturing.

(2) Average of April and October weekly earnings of all manual workers in manufacturing.

(3) Column (2) minus column (1).

(4) Index of production for manufacturing divided by index of average number of wage earners employed in manufacturing. The latter figure is based on estimates given in the National Income Blue Book for the years prior to 1957. In 1957 it was assumed that the number employed was the same as in 1956.

(5) Average of April and October weekly hours of all manual workers in manufacturing.

(6) Column (3) minus 1½ times column (5).

(7) Column (4) minus column (5).

percentage changes in output per wage earner and the fifth column the changes in average weekly hours. Adjustments have next been made to the gross earnings gap and to the output changes in order to exclude the effects of changes in hours of work. From the changes in gross earnings I have subtracted one-and-a-half times the changes in hours, to allow for overtime rates, while from the changes in output I have subtracted simply the changes in hours. These operations give us, in columns (6) and (7), the net earnings gap and changes in output per worker adjusted for changes in hours.

Now, according to our previous reasoning about the effect of changes in output on earnings in sector A, we should expect to find a fairly close relation between changes in productivity and changes in the net earnings gap. In order that we may study this relation more closely the figures from columns (6) and (7) of table 2 are plotted against one another in [a chart]. The points

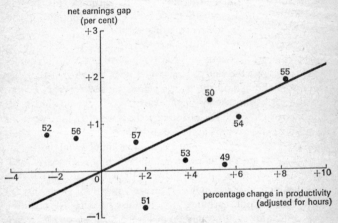

Productivity and the earnings gap in manufacturing

are somewhat scattered; but they are broadly consistent with the hypothesis that the net earnings gap varies directly with productivity. On the assumption that the 'true' relation is a straight line passing through the origin, I have drawn in a line which seems to give a reasonable fit to the points. The slope of this line is 0·22 and it implies that for every 5% increase in productivity there will be an increase of 1·1% in the net earnings gap. This, I believe, is a rough measure of the piecework effect of changes in output on changes in hourly earnings in sector A.

Is this a plausible interpretation of the data? We ought, perhaps, to offer some explanation of the failure of particular years to lie close to the line. This may easily be the result of inadequacies in the underlying figures, or to the lack of correspondence between sector A as defined in the model and the manufacturing sector which has had to be used in the test. There may also be individual peculiarities in particular years which would account for their deviation from the line. The net earnings gap includes all the effects other than the effect of changes in hours. It will, therefore, be influenced by changes in the composition of the labour force by age, sex, occupation, or industry. It will also contain any independent effects of the 'excess demand' for labour. As we have already noted, changes in the composition of the labour force have had little effect on the earnings gap. It only remains to consider whether 'excess demand' for labour can claim to be responsible for part of the gap.

If 'excess demand' for labour is to be given credit for causing part of the earnings gap, we should expect to find that the points which lie above the line in [the chart] refer to years of high demand for labour, and the points below the line to years of low demand for labour. According to the index of demand for labour compiled by Dow and Dicks-Mireaux the years of greatest demand in our period were 1951 and 1955, and the year of lowest demand was 1952. 1953 and 1954 were years of rising demand; 1952 and 1956 were years of falling demand. When we compare these indications with the position of the points on our chart we get no real support for the view that excess demand for labour causes an increase in the earnings gap. It must be admitted that the years 1952 and 1956 occupy an awkward position on any hypothesis. In these two years both the demand for labour and output per worker employed in manufacturing declined. Yet the net earnings gap widened. It is worth noting, however, that the *gross* earnings gap did fall slightly in these years. It is the adjustment for average hours worked that converts a negative *gross* earnings gap into a positive *net* earnings gap. A similar difficulty occurs in the case of 1951, where the net earnings gap fell, despite an increase in productivity and in the demand for labour.

The Working of the Model

We are now in a position to study the behaviour of our model. We shall assume throughout this discussion (1) that hours of work remain unchanged, (2) that the economy is self-sufficient,

(3) that all goods and services are priced at 'full cost', and (4) that there is no trade in intermediate goods between sectors A and B, so that the final prices of each sector's output depend entirely on unit wage costs within that sector.

We shall use the following notation and definitions:

a = basic timework earnings per worker in sector A;

b = piecework and related earnings (including above-rate payments and 'lieu' bonuses) per worker in sector A;

$c = a + b$ = total earnings per worker in sector A;

d = total earnings per worker (all from timework) in sector B;

w_t = percentage change in average time rates of all workers in year t compared with year $t-1$;

e_t = percentage change in total earnings per worker in sector A in year t compared with year $t-1$;

k = proportionate effect of an increase in earnings in sector A in one year on the increase in time rates in both sectors in the following year;

p' = percentage increase in output per worker in sector A;

p'''' = percentage increase in output per worker in sector B;

n' = number of workers employed in sector A;

n'' = number of workers employed in sector B.

Thus we have the following relations:

$$c = a + b$$

$$\frac{a_t}{a_{t-1}} = \frac{d_t}{d_{t-1}} = 1 + \frac{w_t}{100}$$

$$\frac{w_t}{100} = k \cdot \frac{e_{t-1}}{100} = k\left(\frac{c_{t-1}}{c_{t-2}} - 1\right)$$

$$\frac{b_t}{b_{t-1}} = 1 + \frac{p'}{100}$$

Let us consider, first, how the model develops under the following conditions:

(1) In the initial position average earnings per worker and the number employed in sector A are equal to average earnings and the number employed in sector B ($c = d$, $n' = n''$).

(2) The number employed in each sector remains constant.

(3) $k = 1$.

(4) $p' = 5$.

(5) $\frac{a}{b} = 4$. This is based on the assumption that, since the net earnings gap appears to increase by about one-fifth of any increase in productivity in sector A, the proportion of earnings in sector A which vary directly with output must be about one-fifth. We shall see later that this is not true within the framework of this model.

The effect of these assumptions on the model is shown in table 3. It will be seen that the initial effect of the 5% increase in productivity in sector A is to produce an earnings gap $(e - w)$ of

Table 3

Model of the Relations between Wage Rates, Earnings, and Productivity in Two Sectors

Year	Sector A Time earnings an'	Piece earnings bn'	Total earnings cn'	Sector B Total earnings dn''	Percentage change in c e	Percentage change in a and d w
1	400·0	100·0	500·0	500·0	—	—
2	400·0	105·0	505·0	500·0	1·00	—
3	404·0	110·3	514·3	505·0	1·83	1·00
4	411·4	115·8	527·2	514·3	2·51	1·83
5	421·7	121·6	543·3	527·2	3·06	2·51
6	434·6	127·6	562·3	543·3	3·49	3·06
7	449·8	134·0	583·8	562·3	3·83	3·49
8	467·0	140·7	607·7	583·8	4·10	3·83
9	486·2	147·8	633·9	607·7	4·31	4·10
10	507·1	155·1	662·3	633·9	4·47	4·31

1%. Gradually, however, the feeding back of the effects of the rise in c into the level of wage rates, with a time-lag of one year, causes the earnings gap to diminish. By year 10 the earnings gap has fallen to 0·16%; and it is obvious that it will continue to diminish with the further passage of time. In other words, the effect of a constant rise of 5% per annum in productivity in sector A (within the framework of this model) is to produce a series of increases in earnings in both sectors which are convergent towards the same figure of 5%. That this is an equilibrium level can be seen if we consider the situation which would arise if wage rates were to increase in any year by exactly 5%. Then total earnings in that year would also rise by 5%, and wage rates in the following year would continue to increase by the same figure.

What will be the effect of these changes in wage rates and earnings on the price level? The answer depends on the course of changes in productivity. In sector A, on our assumption of a constant rate of increase in productivity of 5%, wage costs per unit will at first be falling (approximately by the margin between 5% and e). Eventually, when e itself reaches 5%, there will be stability of wage costs in sector A. The position in sector B depends on the rate of increase of productivity in that sector. If, for example, we assume a value $p'' = 2$, then wage costs per unit in sector B will be falling for the first four years, but thereafter they will be rising at a steadily increasing rate. When w reaches 5%, wage costs per unit in sector B will be rising by nearly 3% per annum. At this point the average wage cost for the output of both sectors will be increasing at a rate of nearly $1\frac{1}{2}\%$ per annum; and, on the assumption that prices are fixed at full cost, the average price level will also be rising at this rate.

The above model gives us a picture of an economy which is expanding smoothly and without too much instability of prices. There may however be a danger that the rise in prices will cause a secondary reaction on wage rates; and if this happens the situation will obviously become less satisfactory. Let us then consider what are the requirements of a situation in which average prices do not rise. If we stick to our assumptions about the relative proportions of the two sectors, of the relative weights of time and piece earnings within sector A, and of the rates of growth of productivity in each sector, we can then consider the effect of varying k. It is not difficult to discover an appropriate figure for this proportion, which will keep the average price level stable. The requirements of the problem are met if wage rates increase by $3\frac{1}{3}\%$ per annum, and total earnings in sector A by $3\frac{2}{3}\%$ per annum. Average wage costs per unit are then increasing by $3\frac{1}{2}\%$ which is equal to the increase in average productivity. An increase of $3\frac{1}{3}\%$ in the timework earnings in sector A, together with 5% on piecework earnings, gives the required rate of increase of total sector A earnings of $3\frac{2}{3}\%$. Since $3\frac{1}{3}$ stands in the ratio of $\frac{10}{11}$ to $3\frac{2}{3}$, it follows that, in order to maintain price stability, wage rates in each year should rise by ten-elevenths of the average percentage increase in earnings in sector A in the previous year, i.e. $k = \frac{10}{11}$. This is not a very restrictive condition; and it does not seem beyond the bounds of practical industrial and political statesmanship that a relation of this sort should be established. It should be noted that, under these conditions, average prices in sector A will be falling by nearly $1\frac{1}{3}\%$ per annum, while average prices in sector B are rising to the same degree.

One puzzling feature of the examples discussed above is that they do not, in fact, yield an earnings gap as large as that which emerged from our earlier analysis of the historical figures. When productivity in sector A is increasing by 5%, we should expect it to produce an earnings gap – from the piecework effects alone – of about 1%. But the first variant of our model shows a steadily falling – and ultimately vanishing – earnings gap, while the second variant produces an ultimate equilibrium gap of only $\frac{1}{3}\%$. The explanation of this is that our model carries back, through the rise of wage rates in sector A, the effects of the initial earnings rise in that sector. It is, however, quite possible to adapt the model so as to produce the required earnings gap. For this purpose an adjustment must be made to the proportion of time and piece earnings in sector A. The original assumption – that piece earnings amounted to only 20% of the total in sector A – was somewhat unrealistic, in face of such facts as are known about conditions in sector A. In engineering, for example, the proportion of piecework earnings to total earnings of pieceworkers appears to be in the region of one-third; in textiles it is probably much higher.

If we assume that time and piece earnings are equal – in the initial position – in sector A, then an ultimate equilibrium of wage rates, earnings, and prices will be produced if wage rates rise by 3% per annum, earnings in sector A by 4% (as a result of 3% in time earnings and 5% in piecework earnings), and overall productivity by $3\frac{1}{2}\%$, as before. In this case we have the desired earnings gap of 1%. Prices in sector A will fall by nearly 1% per annum, and rise in sector B by a similar amount. In order to maintain the equilibrium, however, wage rates in each year must not rise by more than three-quarters of the percentage rise in sector A earnings in the previous year.

The Policy Implications of the Model

Are the conditions postulated by this model unrealistic, or over-optimistic? I do not think so. A great deal obviously hinges on the rate of increase of productivity in the two sectors and on the relation between changes in earnings in sector A and the consequent increases in general wage rates. It should not be impossible to achieve the assumed rates of increase of productivity. Such rates are desirable for other reasons than those considered here. An average rate of $3\frac{1}{2}\%$ per annum for the whole economy is certainly greater than the average rate achieved in this country in the past ten years, but for much of that time investment has been at a lower level than we have wanted it to be. To maintain this rate of growth year after year would require an annual net investment of perhaps 12–14% of net national income per annum; but this is not beyond our means or, apparently, our willingness to save under present conditions.

On the other crucial question – the relation between general wage rates and earnings in sector A – there would need to be negotiations with the trade unions. It is the popular view in some quarters – especially amongst those economists who attribute the whole inflationary process to an excess of demand – that no good can come of attempts to co-operate with the trade unions in a national wages policy. Yet, as can be seen in table 2, both wage rates and earnings rose comparatively little in 1949 and 1950, when the trade unions were working with the government in the interests of price stability. In those years the average standard of living in this country was much lower than it is now, and the pent-up demand from the war years was still pressing upon us. How much more easy it should be today to arrive at a working arrangement with the trade unions, provided the government could show that it had a policy designed to expand production and increase the standard of living all round! To ask for a moderate degree of wage restraint, when real incomes are rising by $3\frac{1}{2}\%$ per annum, is a very different matter from asking for a wage standstill, when production and real incomes are almost completely stagnant – as they are today.

Assuming that agreement on a policy of this sort can be reached, within the framework of an expanding economy, there would still be certain problems of adjustment which would require attention. The last variant of the model implies that average earnings per worker in sector A would be increasing by 4% per annum, while earnings per worker in sector B would be increasing by only 3% per annum. After a time this disparity would lead to difficulties, especially if it were required to shift workers from sector A to sector B, as is likely to be the case. As a means to overcoming this difficulty it might be possible to secure a consolidation from time to time of part of the rise in piecework earnings in sector A into the timework part of total earnings in that sector, in place of part of the normal annual increase in wage rates in that sector. There may also be other and better ways of achieving the same object.

Another possible line of approach is to try to reduce the importance of piecework in our industrial system. There are doubtless things to be said both in favour of and against piecework as a means of encouraging efficient work. But little or no attention has been paid to its economic implications. One suggestion which might well be considered, in any event, is that the proportion of piece earnings in the total earnings of pieceworkers in each industry should be kept down to less than half, or even to no more than a third. This, in itself, would strengthen the forces making for price stability.[14]

In addition to the general problem of maintaining a correct relation between average earnings in sector A and sector B, we shall continue to be faced by the well-known problem of adjusting differentials between occupations. But this is a problem which will fall into the second rank, provided the major problem of maintaining the momentum of economic progress can be solved. The rational adjustment of differentials would be made much easier if detailed statistics were collected of the number of vacancies and the number of applicants for jobs in each occupational group.

The consideration of the questions raised in this paper has a direct relevance to our current economic problems. At this time – in the summer of 1958 – the British economy probably has an excess output capacity of at least 10% in manufacturing, and per-

14. It is interesting to note that several large firms 'in this country have recently abandoned piecework on the grounds that it is less efficient than timework for their purpose. This follows a similar trend in the United States. It is a trend which is likely to be further stimulated by automation.

haps 7 or 8% in total. This is the natural result of the policy of holding back output over the past three years, despite the rising wave of investment in industry. We are, therefore, in the very favourable position of now being able to make use of this extra capacity to increase both investment and consumption. Far from suffering from 'excess' demand, we have too little demand; and potential output is going to waste.

The continued rise in wage rates in this period has been partly the consequence of the price inflation injected into our system in 1950-1 (which has been further extended by the removal of subsidies and the lifting of rent control) and partly the result of a breakdown of confidence between the trade unions and the government. It is certainly not the result of excess demand, since, as already said, output in this period has risen hardly at all, while output capacity has been growing steadily.

There has, of course, been 'full employment', but it is noteworthy that in the past three years available manpower has risen much less, on the average, than in previous post-war years. There are some indications that registered unemployment covers only part of the total unemployed – many of whom are married women who do not bother to register at the labour exchanges. There is also a good deal of disguised unemployment, since firms which are working below capacity often prefer to keep their full complement of workers rather than run the risk of being unable to re-employ them when demand recovers.

In this situation an expansion of output in the first year by, say, 7% in manufacturing and 3% elsewhere would give an increase in the real national product of about 5%. We could allow wage rates in the first year to rise by 3%, and earnings per worker in manufacturing by 5%, and still keep the rise in wage costs within the rise in productivity (which would be somewhat less than 5% if total manpower employed were increased).

This, it seems to me, is the obvious way to approach our internal economic problem. The real difficulty of such a policy lies, not so much in the complex interrelations of wages, earnings, and prices, as in the repercussions of a rising home income on our balance of payments. There need not be, according to this model, any worsening of our competitiveness in world markets in terms of prices, but the inevitable effect of an increase in British home production and real income is that more food and raw materials will be purchased from abroad. The problem is to ensure that the increased imports are matched by increased exports. But that is another story, which cannot be adequately discussed as a footnote to the present article.

Part Nine Labour's Share in the National Income

Ever since Ricardo, economists have been intrigued by the determinants of the functional distribution of income and in particular of labour's share, which may or may not be stable since the statistics may be imperfect. Yet it is with this subject that we broach the major effects of trade unions. Relative wages may be altered by unions, but only by causing a redistribution of a stable labour share: Kaldor's essay surveys many of the important theories and introduces his own explanation.

16 N. Kaldor

Alternative Theories of Distribution

Kaldor, N. (1955–56) Alternative theories of distribution. *Rev. Econ. Studies*, **23**, 83–100.

According to the Preface of Ricardo's Principles, the discovery of the laws which regulate distributive shares is the 'principal problem in Political Economy'. The purpose of this paper is to present a bird's eye view of the various theoretical attempts, since Ricardo, at solving this 'principal problem'. Though all attempts at classification in such a vast field are necessarily to some extent arbitrary, and subjective to the writer, in terms of broad classification, one should, I think, distinguish between four main strands of thought, some of which contain important sub-groups. The first of these is the Ricardian, or classical, theory, the second the Marxian, the third the neo-classical or marginalist theory, and the fourth the Keynesian. The inclusion of a separate 'Keynesian' theory in this context may cause surprise. An attempt will be made to show however that the specifically Keynesian apparatus of thought could be applied to the problem of distribution, rather than to the problem of the general level of production; that there is evidence that in its early stages, Keynes' own thinking tended to develop in this direction – only to be diverted from it with the discovery (made some time between the publication of the *Treatise on money* and the *General theory*) that inflationary and deflationary tendencies could best be analysed in terms of the resulting changes in output and employment, rather than in their effects on prices.

The compression of a whole army of distinguished writers, and schools of thought, between Ricardo and Keynes (Marx aside) under the term of neo-classical or marginalist theory is harder to justify. For apart from the marginalists proper, the group would have to include such 'non-marginalists' or quasi-marginalists (from the point of view of distribution theory) as the Walrasians and the neo-Walrasians,[1] as well as the imperfect competitionists, who though marginalist, do not necessarily hold with the principle of Marginal Productivity. But as I shall hope to show, there are important aspects which all these theories have in common,[2] and which justifies bringing them under one broad umbrella.

Ricardo prefaced his statement by a reference to the historical fact that 'in different stages of society the proportions of the whole produce of the earth which will be allotted to each of these (three) classes under the names of rent, profit, and wages will be essentially *different*'.[3] Today, a writer on the problem of distribution would almost be inclined to say the opposite – that 'in different stages of (capitalist) society the proportions of the national income allotted to wages, profits, etc., are *essentially similar*'. The famous 'historical constancy' of the share of wages in the national income – and the similarity of these shares in different capitalist economics, such as the U.S. and U.K. – was of course an unsuspected feature of capitalism in Ricardo's day. But to the extent that recent empirical research tends to contradict Ricardo's assumption about the variability of relative shares, it makes the question of what determines these shares, more, rather than less, intriguing. In fact no hypothesis as regards the forces determining distributive shares could be intellectually satisfying unless it succeeds in accounting for the relative stability of these shares in the advanced capitalist economies over the last 100 years or so, despite the phenomenal changes in the techniques of production, in the accumulation of capital relative to labour and in real income per head.

1. By the term 'neo-Walrasians' I mean the American 'linear programming' and 'activity analysis' schools, as well as the general equilibrium model of von Neumann (*Review of Economic Studies* [1945–6], vol. 13 [1] whose technique shows certain affinities with Walras even though their basic assumptions (in particular that of the 'circularity' of the production process) are quite different. From the point of view of distribution theory, however, the approach only yields a solution (in the shape of an equilibrium interest rate) on the assumption of constant real wages (due to an infinitely elastic supply curve of labour); it shows therefore more affinity with the classical models than with the neo-classical theories.

2. With the possible exception of the 'neo-Walrasian' group referred to above.

3. Preface (my italics).

Ricardo's concern in the problem of distribution was not due, or not only due, to the interest in the question of distributive shares *per se*, but to the belief that the theory of distribution holds the key to an understanding of the whole mechanism of the economic system – of the forces governing the rate of progress, of the ultimate incidence of taxation, of the effects of protection, and so on. It was through 'the laws which regulate distributive shares' that he was hoping to build what in present-day parlance we would call 'a simple macro-economic model'.[4] In this respect, if no other, the Ricardian and the 'Keynesian' theories are analogous.[5] With the neo-classical or marginalist theories, on the other hand, the problem of distribution is merely one aspect of the general pricing process; it has no particular theoretical significance apart from the importance of the question *per se*. Nor do these theories yield a 'macro-economic model' of the kind that exhibits the reaction-mechanism of the system through the choice of a strictly limited number of dependent and independent variables.

The Ricardian Theory

Ricardo's theory was based on two separate principles which we may term the 'marginal principle' and the 'surplus principle' respectively. The 'marginal principle' serves to explain the share of rent, and the 'surplus principle' the division of the residue between wages and profits. To explain the Ricardian model, we must first divide the economy into two broad branches, agriculture and industry, and then show how, on Ricardo's assumptions, the forces operating in agriculture serve to determine distribution in industry.

4. 'Political Economy,' he told Malthus, 'you think is an enquiry into the nature and causes of wealth – I think it should rather be called an enquiry into the laws which determine the division of the produce of industry amongst the classes who concur in its formation. No laws can be laid down respecting quantity, but a tolerably correct one can be laid down respecting proportions. Every day I am more satisfied that the former enquiry is vain and delusive, and the latter only the true objects of the science.' (Letter dated 9 October 1820, *Works* [Sraffa edition], vol. 8, pp. 278–9.)

5. And so of course is the Marxian: but then the Marxian theory is really only a simplified version of Ricardo, clothed in a different garb.

The agricultural side of the picture can be exhibited in terms of a simple diagram (fig. 1), where Oy measures quantities of 'corn' (standing for all agricultural produce) and Ox the amount of labour employed in agriculture. At a given state of knowledge and in a given natural environment the curve P–Ap represents the product per unit of labour and the curve P–Mp the marginal

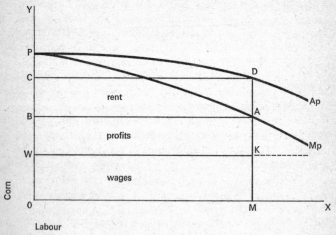

Figure 1

product of labour. The existence of these two *separate* curves is a consequence of a declining tendency in the averge product curve – i.e. of the assumption of diminishing returns. Corn-output is thus uniquely determined when the quantity of labour is given:[6] for any given working force, OM, total output is represented by the rectangle $OCDM$. Rent is the difference between the product of labour on 'marginal' land and the product on average land, or (allowing for the intensive, as well as the extensive, margin) the difference between average and marginal labour productivity which depends on the elasticity of the P–Ap curve, i.e. the extent to which diminishing returns operate.

6. This abstracts from variations in output per head due to the use of more or less fixed capital relative to labour – otherwise the curves could not be uniquely drawn, relative to a given state of technical knowledge. As between fixed capital and labour therefore the model assumes 'fixed coefficients'; as between labour and land, variable coefficients.

The marginal product of labour (or, in classical parlance, the 'produce-minus-rent') is not however equal to the wage, but to the sum of wages and profits. The rate of wages is determined quite independently of marginal productivity by the supply price of labour which Ricardo assumed to be constant in terms of corn. In modern parlance, the Ricardian hypothesis implies an infinitely elastic supply curve of labour at the given supply price, OW.[7] The demand for labour is not determined however by the $P–Mp$ curve, but by the accumulation of capital which determines how many labourers can find employment at the wage rate OW. Hence the equilibrium position is not indicated by the point of intersection between the $P–Mp$ curve and the supply curve of labour, but by the aggregate demand for labour in terms of corn – the 'wages fund'.[8] As capital accumulates, the labour force will grow, so that any addition to the total wage fund, through capital accumulation – the *agricultural* wages fund is indicated

7. The basis of this assumption is the Malthusian theory of population, according to which numbers will increase (indefinitely) when wages are above, and decrease (indefinitely) when they are below, the 'subsistence level'. In Ricardo's hands this doctrine had lost its sharp focus on a biologically determined quantum of subsistence to which the supply price of labour must be tied; he emphasized that habits of restraint engendered in a civilized environment can permanently secure for labour higher standards of living than the bare minimum for survival. Yet he retained the important operative principle that in any given social and cultural environment there is a '*natural* rate of wages' at which alone population could remain stationary and from which wages can only deviate temporarily. The hypothesis of an infinitely elastic supply curve of labour thus did not necessarily imply that this supply price must be equal to the bare minimum of subsistence. Yet this assumption was inconsistent with another (implied) feature of his model discussed below, that wages are not only *fixed* in terms of 'corn' but are entirely (or almost entirely) *spent* on corn.

8. Total wages depend on – and are 'paid out of' – capital simply because production takes time, and the labourers (unlike the landlords) not being in the position to afford to wait, have their wages 'advanced' to them by the capitalists. This is true of fixed as well as circulating capital, but since with the former, the turnover period is relatively long, only a small part of annual wages is paid out of fixed capital; the amount of circulating capital was therefore treated as the proper 'wages fund'. Despite his analysis of the effect of changes in wages on the amount of fixed capital used relative to labour, i.e. on the proportions of fixed and circulating capital employed in production (Professor Hayek's celebrated 'Ricardo effect') for the purpose of his distribution theory, this ratio should be taken as given, irrespective of the rate of profit.

by the area $OWKM$ – will tend to be a horizontal addition (pushing the vertical line KM to the right) and not a vertical one (pushing the horizontal line WK upwards).[9]

For any given M, profits are thus a residue, arising from the difference between the marginal product of labour and the rate of wages. The resulting ratio, $\dfrac{\text{profits}}{\text{wages}}$, determines the rate of profit % on the capital employed; it is moreover *equal* to that ratio, on the assumption that the capital is turned over once a year so that the capital employed is equal to the annual wages-bill. (This latter proposition however is merely a simplification, and not an essential part of the story.)

In a state of equilibrium, the money rate of profit % earned on capital must be the same in industry and in agriculture, otherwise capital would move from one form of employment to the other. But it is the peculiarity of agriculture that the money rate of profit in that industry cannot diverge from the rate of profit measured in terms of that industry's own product, i.e. the corn-rate of profit. This is because in agriculture both the input (the wage outlay) and the output consist of the same commodity, 'corn'. In manufacturing industry, on the other hand, input and output consist of heterogeneous commodities – the cost per man is fixed in corn, while the product per man, in a given state of technical knowledge, is fixed in terms of manufactured goods. Hence the only way equality in the rate of profit in money terms can be attained as between the two branches is through the prices of industrial goods becoming dearer or cheaper in terms of agricultural pro-

9. The feature which the modern mind may find most difficult to swallow is not that capital accumulation should lead to a rise in population but that the reaction should be taken as something so swift as to ignore the intervening stage, where the increase in the wages fund should raise the rate of wages rather than the numbers employed. The adjustment of population to changes in the demand for labour would normally be treated as a slow long-run effect whereas changes in the demand for labour (caused by capital accumulation) may be swift or sudden. Ricardo however conceived the economy as one which proceeds at a more or less steady rate of growth in time, with the accumulation of capital going on at a (more or less constant) rate; while he conceded that *changes* in the rate of capital accumulation will temporarily raise or lower wages, he assumed that the rate of population growth itself is adapted to a certain rate of capital accumulation which had been going on for some time.

ducts. The money rate of profit in manufacturing industry therefore depends on the corn-rate of profit in agriculture,[10] the latter, on the other hand, is entirely a matter of the margin of cultivation, which in turn is a reflection (in a closed economy and in a given state of technical knowledge) of the extent of capital accumulation. Thus 'diminishing fertility of the soil', as James Mill put it, 'is the great and ultimately only necessary cause of a fall in profit'.

To make the whole structure logically consistent it is necessary to suppose, not only that wages are fixed in terms of 'corn' but that they are entirely spent on 'corn', for otherwise any change in the relation between industrial and agricultural prices will alter real wages (in terms of commodities in general) so that the size of the 'surplus', and the rate of profit on capital generally, is no longer derivable from the 'corn rate of profit' – the relationship between the product of labour and the cost of labour working on marginal land. Assuming that ('corn') agricultural products are wage-goods and manufactured products are non-wage goods (i.e. ignoring that *some* agricultural products are consumed by capitalists, and *some* non-agricultural products by wage-earners), the whole corn-output (the area $OCDM$ in the diagram) can be taken as the annual wages fund, of which $OWKM$ is employed in agriculture and $WCDK$ in the rest of the economy. Any increase in $OWKM$ (caused, e.g. by protection to agriculture) must necessarily lower the rate of profit (which is the source of all accumulation) and thus slow down the rate of growth.[11] Similarly all taxes, other than those levied on land, must ultimately fall on and be paid out of, profits, and thus slow down the rate of accumulation. Taxation and agricultural protection thus tend to accelerate the tendency (which is in any case inevitable – unless *continued* technical progress manages to shift the $P–Ap$ and

10. The analytical basis for this conclusion, given above, was never, as Sraffa remarks, stated by Ricardo in any of his extant letters and papers though there is evidence from Malthus's remarks that he must have formulated it either in a lost paper on the Profits of Capital or in conversation (cf. *Works*, vol. 1, Introduction, p. xxxi).

11. The evil of agricultural protection is thus not only that real income is reduced through the transfer of labour to less productive employments but also that owing to the reduction in the rate of profit, industrial prices fall in terms of agricultural prices; income is thus transferred from the classes which use their wealth productively to classes which use it unproductively.

P–Mp curves to the right sufficiently to suspend altogether the operation of the law of diminishing returns) to that ultimate state of gloom, the stationary state, where accumulation ceases simply because 'profits are so low as not to afford (the capitalists more than) an adequate compensation for their trouble and the risk which they must necessarily encounter in employing their capital productively'.[12]

The Marxian Theory

The Marxian theory is essentially an adaptation of Ricardo's 'surplus theory'. The main analytical differences are: (1) that Marx paid no attention to (and did not believe in) the law of diminishing returns, and hence made no analytical distinction between rent and profits; (2) that Marx regarded the supply price of labour (the 'cost of reproduction' of labour) as being fixed, not in terms of 'corn', but of commodities in general. Hence he regarded the share of profits (including rent) in output as determined simply by the surplus of the production per unit of labour over the supply price (or cost) of labour – or the surplus of production to the consumption necessary for production.[13]

There are important differences also as between Marx and Ricardo in two other respects. The first of these concerns the reasons for wages being tied to the subsistence level. In Marx's theory this is ensured through the fact that at any one time the supply of labour – the number of workers seeking wage-employment – tends to exceed the demand for labour. The existence of an unemployed fringe – the 'reserve army' of labour – prevents wages from rising above the minimum that must be paid to enable the labourers to perform the work. Marx assumed that as capitalist enterprise progresses at the expense of pre-capitalistic enterprise more labourers are released through the disappearance of the non-capitalist or handi-craft units than are absorbed in the capitalist sector, owing to the difference in productivity per head

12. Ricardo, *Principles*, p. 122 (Sraffa edition).

13. Ricardo himself abandoned in the *Principles* the idea that wages *consist* of corn (to the exclusion of manufactures) but whether he also abandoned the idea that the agricultural surplus is critical to the whole distribution process through the fixity of wages in terms of *corn only* is not clear (cf. Sraffa, op. cit., pp. xxxii–xxxiii).

between the two sectors. As long as the growth of capitalist enterprise is at the cost of a shrinkage of pre-capitalist enterprise the increase in the supply of wage labour will thus tend to run ahead of the increase in the demand for wage labour.

Sooner or later, however, the demand for labour resulting from accumulation by capitalist enterprise will run ahead of the increase in supply; at that stage labour becomes scarce, wages rise, profits are wiped out, and capitalism is faced with a 'crisis'. (The crisis in itself slows down the rate of accumulation and reduces the demand for labour at any given state of accumulation by increasing the 'organic composition of capital', so that the 'reserve army' will sooner or later be recreated.)

The second important difference relates to the motives behind capital accumulation. For Ricardo this was simply to be explained by the lure of a high rate of profit. Capitalists accumulate voluntarily so long as the rate of profit exceeds the minimum 'necessary compensation' for the risks and trouble encountered in the productive employment of capital. For Marx, however, accumulation by capitalist enterprise is not a matter of choice but a necessity, due to competition among the capitalists themselves. This in turn was explained by the existence of economies of large scale production (together with the implicit assumption that the amount of capital employed by any particular capitalist is governed by his own accumulation). Given the fact that the larger the scale of operations the more efficient the business, each capitalist is forced to increase the size of his business through the re-investment of his profits if he is not to fall behind in the competitive struggle.

It is only at a later stage, when the increasing concentration of production in the hands of the more successful enterprises removed the competitive necessity for accumulation – the stage of 'monopoly capitalism' – that in the Marxian scheme there is room for economic crises, not on account of an excessive increase in the demand for labour following on accumulation but on account of an insufficiency of effective demand – the failure of markets resulting from the inability of the capitalists either to spend or to invest the full amount of profits (which Marx called the problem of 'realizing surplus value').

Marx has also taken over from Ricardo, and the classical

economists generally, the idea of a falling rate of profit with the progressive accumulation of capital. But whereas with the classicists this was firmly grounded on the law of diminishing returns, Marx, having discarded that law, had no firm base for it. His own explanation is based on the assumed increase in the ratio of fixed to circulating capital (in Marxian terminology, 'constant' to 'variable' capital) with the progress of capitalism; but as several authors have pointed out,[14] the law of the falling rate of profit cannot really be derived from the law of the 'increasing organic composition' of capital. Since Marx assumes that the supply price of labour remains unchanged in terms of commodities when the organic composition of capital, and hence output per head, rises, there is no more reason to assume that an increase in 'organic composition' will yield a lower rate of profit than a higher rate. For even if output per man were assumed to increase more slowly than ('constant' plus 'variable') capital per man, the 'surplus value' per man (the excess of output per man over the costs of reproduction of labour) will necessarily increase faster than output per man, and may thus secure a rising rate of profit even if there is diminishing productivity to successive additions to fixed capital per unit of labour.

While some of Marx's predictions – such as the increasing concentration of production in the hands of large enterprises – proved accurate, his most important thesis, the steady worsening of the living conditions of the working classes – 'the immiseration of the proletariat'[15] – has been contradicted by experience, in both the 'competitive' and 'monopoly' stages of capitalism. On the Marxian model the share of wages in output must necessarily fall with every increase in output per head. The theory can only allow for a rise of wages in terms of commodities as a result of

14. cf., in particular, Joan Robinson, *An essay in Marxian economics*, pp. 75–82.

15. It is not clear, in terms of Marx's own theoretical model, why such a progressive immiseration should take place – since the costs of reproduction of labour appear to set an *absolute* limit to the extent to which labour can be exploited. Some parts of *Das Kapital* could however be construed as suggesting that wages can be driven below the (long run), reproduction cost of labour, at the cost of a (long run) shrinkage in the labour force: and with the increasing organic composition of capital, and the rise of monopolies, the demand for labour may show an equally declining tendency.

the collective organization of the working classes which forces the capitalists to reduce the degree of exploitation and to surrender to the workers some of the 'surplus value'.[16] This hypothesis however will only yield a constant share of wages on the extremely far-fetched assumption that the rate of increase in the bargaining strength of labour, due to the growth of collective organization, precisely keeps pace with the rate of increase in output per head.

The Neo-Classical Theories

Marginal productivity

While Marx's theory thus derives from Ricardo's surplus principle, neo-classical value and distribution theory derives from another part of the Ricardian model: the 'marginal principle' introduced for the explanation of rent (which explains why both Marx and Marshall are able to claim Ricardo as their precursor). The difference between Ricardo and the neo-classics is (1) that whereas Ricardo employed the 'principle of substitution' (or rather, the principle of 'limited substitutability' – which is the basic assumption underlying all 'marginal' analysis) only as regards the use of labour relative to land, in neo-classical theory this doctrine was formalized and generalized, and assumed to hold true of any factor, in relation to any other;[17] (2) whereas

16. Marx himself would have conceived a reduction in the 'degree of exploitation' in terms of a reduction in the length of the working day rather than a rise in real wages per day. In fact both have occurred side by side.

17. As well as of any particular commodity in the sphere of consumption. The utility theory of value is really Ricardian rent-theory applied to consumption demand. In fact, as Walras has shown, limited substitutability in consumption might in itself be sufficient to determine distributive shares, provided that the proportions in which the different factors are used are different in different industries. His solution of the problem of distribution, based on 'fixed coefficients' of production (intended only as a first approximation), is subject however to various snags since the solution of his equations may yield negative prices for the factors as well as positive ones and it cannot be determined beforehand whether this will be the case or not. If the solution of the equations yields negative prices the factors in question have to be excluded as 'free goods'; and the operation (if necessary) successive repeated until only factors with positive prices are left. Also, it is necessary to suppose that the number of different 'factors' is no greater than the number of different 'products' otherwise the solution is indeterminate.

Ricardo employed the principle for showing that a 'fixed' factor will earn a surplus, determined by the gap between the average and marginal product of the variable factor, neo-classical theory concentrated on the reverse aspect – i.e. that any factor variable in supply will obtain a remuneration which, under competitive conditions, must correspond to its marginal product. Thus if the total supply of *all* factors (and not only land) is being taken as given, independently of price, and all are assumed to be limited substitutes to one another, the share-out of the whole produce can be regarded as being determined by the marginal rates of substitution between them. Thus in terms of our diagram, if we assumed that along Ox we measure the quantity of any particular factor of production, x, the quantities of all the others being taken as fixed, $P–Mp$ will exhibit the marginal productivity function of the variable factor. If the actual employment of that factor is taken to be M, AM will represent its demand price per unit, and the rectangle $OBAM$ its share in the total produce. Since this principle could be applied to any factor, it must be true of all (including, as Walras and Wicksell have shown, the factors owned by the entrepreneur himself) hence the rectangle $BCDA$ must be sufficient, and only just sufficient, for remunerating all other factors, but x on the basis of their respective marginal productivities. This, as Wicksteed has shown,[18] requires the assumption that the production function will be homogeneous of the first degree for all variables taken together – an assumption which he himself regarded as little more than a tautology, if 'factors of production' are appropriately defined.[19] From the point of view of the theory, however, the *appropriate* definition of factors

18. *The co-ordination of the laws of distribution* (1894).

19. ibid., p. 53 'We must regard every kind and quality of labour that can be distinguished from other kinds and qualities as a separate factor; and in the same way, every kind of land will be taken as a separate factor. Still more important is it to insist that instead of speaking of so many £s worth of capital we shall speak of so many ploughs, so many tons of manure, and so many horses or footpounds of power. Each of these may be scheduled in its own unit.' Under these conditions it is true to say that 'doubling all factors will double the product', but since these 'factors' are indivisible in varying degrees, it does not mean that the production-function is a linear and homogeneous one in relation to incremental variations of output. Also a change in output may be associated with the introduction of *new* factors of production.

involves the elimination of intermediate products and their conversion into 'ultimate' or 'original' factors, since only on this definition can one assume the properties of divisibility and variability of coefficients. When factors are thus defined, the assumption of constant returns to scale is by no means a tautology; it is a restrictive assumption, which may be regarded, however, as being co-extensive with other restrictive assumptions implied by the theory – i.e. the universal rule of perfect competition, and the absence of external economies and diseconomies.

The basic difficulty with the whole approach does not lie, however, in this so-called 'adding-up problem' but in the very meaning of 'capital' as a factor of production.[20] Whilst land can be measured in acres-per-year and labour in man-hours, capital (as distinct from 'capital goods') cannot be measured in terms of physical units.[21] To evaluate the marginal product of labour it is necessary to isolate two situations containing identical 'capital' but two different quantities of labour, or identical amounts of labour and two differing quantities of 'capital', in precise numerical relationship.[22]

Marshall, without going into the matter in any detail, had shown in several passages that he was dimly aware of this; and in carefully re-defining marginal productivity so as to mean 'marginal *net* productivity' (*net* after deduction of all associated expenses on other 'factors') he shied away from the task of putting forward a general theory of distribution altogether.[23]

20. For a general equilibrium system, capital goods cannot be regarded as factors of production *per se* (in the manner suggested by Wicksteed) otherwise the same things are simultaneously treated as the parameters and the unknowns of the system.

21. Measurement in terms of value (as so many £s of 'capital') already assumes a certain rate of interest, on the basis of which services accruing in differing periods in the future, or costs incurred at differing dates in the past, are brought to a measure of equivalence.

22. The product of the 'marginal shepherd' is the difference, in terms of numbers of sheep, between 10 shepherds using 10 crooks and 11 shepherds using 11 slightly inferior crooks, the term 'slightly inferior' being taken to mean that the 11 crooks in the one case represent precisely the same amount of 'capital' as the 10 crooks in the other case (cf. also Robertson, 'Wage grumbles', in *Economic fragments* [1931]).

23. 'The doctrine that the earnings of a worker tend to be equal to the net product of his work, has by itself no real meaning; since in order to

In fact, in so far as we can speak of a 'Marshallian' theory of distribution at all, it is in the sense of a 'short period' theory, which regards profits as the 'quasi-rents' earned on the use of capital goods of various kinds, the supply of which can be treated as given for the time being, as a heritage of the past. The doctrine of the 'quasi-rent' assimilates capital as a factor of production to Ricardian land: the separate *kinds* of capital goods being treated as so many different kinds of 'land'. Here the problem of the measurement of capital as a factor of production does not arise: since, strictly speaking, no kind of change or reorganization in the stock of intermediate products is permitted in connexion with a change in the level or composition of production. It was this aspect of Marshall which, consciously or sub-consciously, provided the 'model' for most of the post-Marshallian Cambridge theorizing. Prices are equal to, or determined by, marginal prime costs; profits are determined by the difference between marginal and average prime costs; prime costs, for the system as a whole, are labour costs (since raw-material costs, for a closed economy at any rate, disappear if all branches of industry are taken together); ultimately therefore the division of output between profits and wages is a matter depending on the existence of diminishing returns to labour, as more labour is used in conjunction with a *given* capital equipment; and is determined by the elasticity of labour's average productivity curve which fixes the share of quasi-rents.

Marshall himself would have disagreed with the use of the quasi-rent doctrine as a distribution theory, holding that distributive shares in the short period are determined by long-period forces.[24] Clearly even if one were to hold strictly to the assumption that 'profit margins' are the outcome of short-period profit-maximization, this 'short-period' approach does not really get us

---

estimate the net product, we have to take for granted all the expenses of production of the commodity on which he works, other than his own wages.' Similarly, the doctrine that the marginal efficiency of capital will tend to equal the rate of interest 'cannot be made into a theory of interest, any more than a theory of wages, without reasoning in a circle' (cf. *Principles*, 8th edn, book 6, ch. 1, paras. 7–8).

24. cf., in particular, *Principles*, 8th edn, book 5, ch. 5, para. 6, and book 6, ch. 8, para. 4.

anywhere: for the extent to which diminishing returns operate for labour in conjunction with the capital equipment available today is itself a function of the price-relationships which have ruled in the past because these have determined the quantities of each of the kinds of equipment available. The theory does not therefore really amount to more than saying that the prices of today are derived from the prices of yesterday – a proposition which is the more true and the more trivial the shorter the 'day' it conceived to be, in terms of chronological time.

For the true neo-classical attempt to solve the general problem of distribution we must go to Wicksell, who thought that by integrating the Austrian approach to capital with Walrasian equilibrium theory he could provide a general solution, treating capital as a two-dimensional quantity, the product of time and labour. The 'time' in this case is the investment period or waiting period separating the application of 'original' factors from the emergence of the final product, and the marginal productivity of capital the added product resulting from an extension of 'time'. This attempt, again, came to grief (as Wicksell himself came near to acknowledging late in life[25]) (i) owing to the impossibility of measuring that period in terms of an 'average' of some kind;[26] (ii) owing to the impossibility of combining the investment periods of different 'original' factors in a single measure.[27]

In fact the whole approach which regards the share of wages and of profits in output as being determined by the marginal rate of substitution between capital and labour – with its corollary, that the constancy of relative shares is evidence of a unity-elasticity of substitution between capital and labour[28] – is hardly

25. cf. the concluding passage of his posthumous contribution to the Wieser Festschrift (*Die Wirtschaftstheorie der Gegenwart* [1928], vol. 3, pp. 208–9); also his analysis of Akerman's problem, reprinted in *Lectures*, vol. 1, p. 270.

26. Since, owing to compound interest, the weights to be used in the calculation of the average will themselves be dependent on the rate of interest.

27. For a more extended treatment of my articles on capital theory in *Econometrica* (April 1937 and May 1938); also Joan Robinson, 'The production function in the theory of capital', *Review of Economic Studies*, vol. 21 (1953–4) p. 81, and *Comment*, by D. G. Champernowne, ibid., p. 112.

28. Cf. Hicks, *The theory of wages* (1932), ch. 6, passim.

acceptable to present-day economists. Its inadequacy becomes evident as soon as it is realized that the 'marginal rate of substitution' between capital and labour – as distinct from the marginal rate of substitution between labour and land – can only be determined once the rate of profit and the rate of wages are already known. The same technical alternatives might yield very different 'marginal rates of substitution' according as the ratio of profits to wages is one thing or another. The theory asserts, in effect, that the rate of interest in the capital market (and the associated wage rate in the labour market) is determined by the condition that at any lower interest rate (and higher wage rate) capital would be invested in such 'labour-saving' forms as would provide insufficient employment to the available labour; whilst at any higher rate, capital would be invested in forms that offered more places of employment than could be filled with the available labour.

Quite apart from all conceptual difficulties, the theory focuses attention on a relatively unimportant feature of a growing economy. For accumulation does not take the form of 'deepening' the structure of capital (at a given state of knowledge) but rather in keeping pace with technical progress and the growth in the labour force. It is difficult to swallow a theory which says, in effect, that wages and profits are what they are for otherwise there would be too much deepening or too little deepening (the capital/output ratios would be either too large or too small) to be consistent with simultaneous equilibrium in the savings-investment market and in the labour market.

The 'degree of monopoly' theories of distribution

Monopoly profit was always regarded as a distinct form of revenue in neo-classical theory, though not one of any great quantitative importance since the mass of commodities was thought of as being produced under competitive conditions. But the modern theories of imperfect competition emphasized that monopoly profit is not an isolated feature. Profits in general contain an *element* of monopoly revenue – an element that is best defined as the excess of the actual profit margin in output over what the profit margin would have been under perfectly competitive conditions. Under Marshallian 'short-period' assumptions the perfectly competitive profit margin is given by the excess of marginal cost over average prime costs. The additional monopoly element is indicated by the excess of price over marginal cost. The former, as we have seen, is a derivative of the elasticity of labour's productivity curve where capital equipment of all kinds is treated as given. The latter is a derivative of the elasticity of demand facing the individual firm. The novel feature of imperfect competition theories is to have shown that the increase of profit margins due to this element of monopoly need not imply a corresponding excess in the rates of profit on capital over the competitive rate; through the generation of excess capacity (i.e. the tendency of demand curves to become 'tangential' to the cost curves) the latter may approach a 'competitive' or 'normal' rate (as a result of the consequential rise in the capital/output ratio) even if the former is above the competitive level.

Kalecki[29] built on this a simplified theory of distribution, where the share of profits in output is shown to be determined by the elasticity of demand alone. This was based on the hypothesis that in the short period, labour and capital equipment are largely 'limitational' and not 'substitutional' factors, with the result that the short-period prime cost-curve is a reverse L-shaped one (prime costs being constant up to full capacity output). In that case marginal costs are equal to average prime costs; the ratio of price to prime costs (and hence, in a closed economy, the ratio of gross profits to wages) is thus entirely accounted for by the elasticity of the firm's demand curve.

On closer inspection, however, the elasticity of the demand curve facing the individual firm turned out to be no less of a broken reed than its counterpart, the elasticity of substitution between factors. There is no evidence that firms in imperfect markets set their prices by reference to the elasticity of their sales-function, or that short-period pricing is the outcome of any deliberate attempt to maximize profits by reference to an independent revenue and a cost function. Indeed the very notion of a demand curve for the products of a single firm is illegitimate

29. The original version appeared in *Econometrica* (April 1938). Subsequent versions appeared in *Essays in the theory of economic fluctuations* (1938), ch. 1, *Studies in economic dynamics* (1943), ch. 1, and *Theory of dynamic economics* (1954), part 1.

if the prices charged by different firms cannot be assumed to be independent of each other.[30]

In the later versions of his theory Kalecki abandoned the link between the 'degree of monopoly' and the elasticity of demand, and was content with a purely tautological approach according to which the ratio of price to prime costs is *defined* simply as the 'degree of monopoly'. Propositions based on implicit definitions of this kind make of course no assertion about reality and possess no explanatory value. Unless the 'degree of monopoly' can be defined in terms of market relationships of some kind (as, for example, in terms of the 'cross-elasticities' of demand for the products of the different firms)[31] and an attempt is made to demonstrate how these market relationships determine the relation between prices and costs, the theory does not provide a hypothesis which could be affirmed or refuted.

There is no need, of course, to follow Kalecki in the attempt to lend spurious precision to the doctrine through implicit theorizing – a vice which afflicts all theories which we grouped together as 'neo-classical' in varying degrees. Fundamentally, the proposition that the distribution of income between wages and profits depends on market structures, on the strength or weakness of the forces of competition, is not a tautological one; it asserts *something* about reality (which may in principle be proved false) even if that 'something' cannot be given a logically precise formulation. Just as the positive content of the marginal productivity theory can be summed up by the statement that the rate of profit on capital (and the margin of profit in output) is governed by the need to prevent the capital/output ratio from being either too large or too small, the positive content of the 'degree of monopoly' theory can be summed up in the sentence that 'profit margins are what they are because the forces of competition pre-

30. The theory of the 'kinked' demand curve is in fact no more than a recognition of the fact that the demand curve of the firm (in the sense required for the purpose of deriving price from the postulate of profit maximization) is non-existent. Since the position of the 'kink' *depends* on the price, it cannot *determine* the price; it thus leaves the profit margin completely undetermined.

31. The 'cross-elasticities' of demand indicate the degree of interdependence of the markets of different firms and are thus inversely related to monopoly power in the usual sense of the word.

vent them from being higher than they are and are not powerful enough to make them lower than they are'. Unfortunately neither of these statements gets us very far.

Dissatisfaction with the tautological character and the formalism of the 'marginal revenue-equals-marginal cost' type of price theory led to the formulation of the 'full cost' theories of pricing,[32] according to which producers in imperfect markets set their prices independently of the character of demand, and solely on the basis of their long run costs of production (including the 'normal' rate of profit on their own capital). If these theories asserted no more than that prices in manufacturing industry are *not* determined by the criterion of short-run profit-maximization, and that profit margins can be fairly insensitive to short-period variations in demand[33] (the impact effect of changes in demand being on the rate of production, rather than on prices), they would provide a healthy antidote to a great deal of facile theorizing. When, however, they go beyond this and assert that prices

32. cf. Hall and Hitch, *Oxford Economic Papers* (1939); P. M. S. Andrews, *Manufacturing business* (1949).

33. This, I believe, was the intention of the original Hall–Hitch article (cf. Marshall, *Principles*, book 6, ch. 8, para. 4); 'We see then that there is no general tendency of profits on the turnover to equality; but there may be, and as a matter of fact there is, in each trade and in every branch of each trade, a more or less definite rate of profits on the turnover which is regarded as a "fair" or normal rate. Of course these rates are always changing in consequence of changes in the methods of trade; which are generally begun by individuals who desire to do a larger trade at a lower rate of profit on the turnover than has been customary, but at a larger rate of profit per annum on their capital. If however there happens to be no great change of this kind going on, the traditions of the trade that a certain rate of profit on the turnover should be charged for a particular class of work are of great practical service to those in the trade. Such traditions are the outcome of much experience tending to show that, if that rate is charged, a proper allowance will be made for all the costs (supplementary as well as prime) incurred for that particular purpose, and in addition the normal rate of profits per annum in that class of business will be afforded. If they charge a price which gives much less than this rate of profit on the turnover they can hardly prosper; and if they charge much more they are in danger of losing their custom, since others can afford to undersell them. This is the 'fair' rate of profit on the turnover, which an honest man is expected to charge for making goods to order, when no price has been agreed on beforehand; and it is the rate which a court of law will allow in case a dispute should arise between buyer and seller' (cf. also Kahn, *Economic Journal* [1952], p. 119).

are determined quite independently of demand, they in effect destroy existing price theory without putting anything else in its place. Quite apart from the fact that a 'full cost' theory is quite unable to explain why some firms should be more successful in earning profits than others, the level of the 'normal profit' on which the full cost calculations are supposed to be based is left quite undetermined. The very fact that these full cost theories should have received such widespread and serious consideration as an alternative explanation of the pricing process is an indication of the sad state of vagueness and confusion into which the neo-classical value theory had fallen.

The Keynesian Theory

Keynes, as far as I know, was never interested in the problem of distribution as such. One may nevertheless christen a particular theory of distribution as 'Keynesian' if it can be shown to be an application of the specifically Keynesian apparatus of thought and if evidence can be adduced that at some stage in the development of his ideas, Keynes came near to formulating such a theory.[34]

34. I am referring to the well-known passage on profits being likened to a 'widow's cruse' in the *Treatise on money* vol. 1, p. 139. 'If entrepreneurs choose to spend a portion of their profits on consumption (and there is, of course, nothing to prevent them from doing this) the effect is to *increase* the profit on the sale of liquid consumption goods by an amount exactly equal to the amount of profits which have been thus expended . . . Thus however much of their profits entrepreneurs spend on consumption, the increment of wealth belonging to entrepreneurs remain the same as before. Thus profits, as a source of capital increment for entrepreneurs, are a widow's cruse which remains undepleted however much of them may be devoted to riotous living. When on the other hand, entrepreneurs are making losses, and seek to recoup their losses by curtailing their normal expenditure on consumption, i.e., by saving more, the cruse becomes a Danaid jar which can never be filled up; for the effect of this reduced expenditure is to inflict on the producers of consumption-goods a loss of an equal amount. Thus the diminution of their wealth, as a class is as great, in spite of their savings, as it was before.' This passage, I think, contains the true seed of the ideas developed in the *General theory* – as well as showing the length of the road that had to be traversed before arriving at the conceptual framework presented in the latter work. The fact that 'profits', 'savings', etc., were all defined here in a special sense that was later discarded, and that the argument specifically refers to expenditure on consumption goods, rather than entrepreneurial expenditure in general, should not blind us to the fact that here Keynes

The principle of the multiplier (which in some way was anticipated in the *Treatise* but without a clear view of its implications) could be alternatively applied to a determination of the relation between prices and wages, if the level of output and employment is taken as given, or the determination of the level of employment, if distribution (i.e. the relation between prices and wages) is taken as given. The reason why the multiplier-analysis has not been developed as a distribution theory is precisely because it was invented for the purpose of an employment theory – to explain why an economic system can remain in equilibrium in a state of under-employment (or of a general under-utilization of resources), where the classical properties of scarcity-economics are inapplicable. And its use for the one appears to exclude its use for the other.[35] If we assume that the balance of savings and investment is brought about through variations in the relationship of prices and costs, we are not only bereft of a principle for explaining variations in output and employment, but the whole idea of separate 'aggregate' demand and supply functions – the principle of 'effective demand' – falls to the ground; we are back to Say's law, where output as a whole is limited by available resources, and a fall in effective demand for one kind of commodity (in real terms) generates compensating increases in effective demand (again in real terms) for others. Yet these two uses of the multiplier principle are not as incompatible as would appear at first sight: the Keynesian technique, as I hope to show, can be used for both purposes, provided the one is conceived as a short-run theory and the other as a long-run theory – or rather, the one is used in the framework of a static model, and the other in the framework of a dynamic growth model.[36]

---

regards entrepreneurial incomes as being the resultant of their expenditure decisions, rather than the other way round – which is perhaps the most important difference between 'Keynesian' and 'pre-Keynesian' habits of thought.

35. Although this application of Keynesian theory has been implicit in several discussions of the problem of inflation (cf. e.g., A. J. Brown, *The great inflation* [Macmillan, 1955]).

36. I first thought of using the multiplier technique for purposes of a distribution theory when I attempted the ultimate incidence of profits taxation under full employment conditions in a paper prepared for the Royal Commission on Taxation in 1951. The further development of these ideas,

We shall assume, to begin with, a state of full employment (we shall show later the conditions under which a state of full employment will *result* from our model) so that total output or income (Y) is given. Income may be divided into two broad categories, wages and profits (W and P), where the wage-category comprises not only manual labour but salaries as well, and profits the income of property owners generally, and not only of entrepreneurs; the important difference between them being in the marginal propensities to consume (or save), wage-earners' marginal savings being small in relation to those of capitalists.[37]

Writing S_w and S_p for aggregate savings out of wages and profits, we have the following income identities:

$$Y \equiv W + P$$
$$I \equiv S$$
$$S \equiv S_w + S_p$$

Taking investment as given, and assuming simple proportional saving functions $S_w = s_w W$ and $S_p = s_p P$, we obtain:

$$I = s_p P + s_w W = s_p P + s_w (Y - P) = (s_p - s_w)P + s_w Y$$

Whence

$$\frac{I}{Y} = (s_p - s_w)\frac{P}{Y} + s_w \tag{1}$$

---

and particularly their relationship to a dynamic theory of growth, owes a great deal to discussions with Mrs Robinson, whose [...] book, *The accumulation of capital*, contains a systematic exploration of this field. I should also like to mention here that I owe a great deal of stimulus to a paper by Kalecki, 'A theory of profits' (*Economic Journal*, June–September 1942) whose approach is in some ways reminiscent of the 'widow's cruse' of Keynes' *Treatise* even though Kalecki uses the technique, not for an explanation of the share of profits in output, but for showing why the *level* of output and its fluctuations is peculiarly dependent on entrepreneurial behaviour. (In doing so, he uses the restrictive assumption that savings are entirely supplied out of profits.) I have also been helped by Mr Harry Johnson and Mr Robin Marris, both in the working out of the formulae and in general discussion.

37. This may be assumed independently of any skewness in the distribution of property, simply as a consequence of the fact that the bulk of profits accrues in the form of company profits and a high proportion of companies' marginal profits is put to reserve.

and

$$\frac{P}{Y} = \frac{1}{s_p - s_w} \cdot \frac{I}{Y} - \frac{s_w}{s_p - s_w} \tag{2}$$

Thus, given the wage-earners' and the capitalists' propensities to save, the share of profits in income depends simply on the ratio of investment to output.

The interpretative value of the model (as distinct from the formal validity of the equations, or identities) depends on the 'Keynesian' hypothesis that investment, or rather, the ratio of investment to output, can be treated as an independent variable, invariant with respect to changes in the two savings propensities s_p and s_w. (We shall see later that this assumption can only be true within certain limits, and outside those limits the theory ceases to hold.) This, together with the assumption of 'full employment', also implies that the level of prices in relation to the level of money wages is determined by demand: a rise in investment, and thus in total demand, will raise prices and profit margins, and thus reduce real consumption, whilst a fall in investment, and thus in total demand, causes a fall in prices (relatively to the wage level) and thereby generates a compensating rise in real consumption. Assuming flexible prices (or rather flexible profit margins) the system is thus stable at full employment.

The model operates only if the two savings propensities differ and the marginal propensity to save from profits exceeds that from wages, i.e. if:

$$s_p \neq s_w$$

and

$$s_p > s_w$$

The latter is the stability condition. For if $s_p < s_w$, a fall in prices would cause a fall in demand and thus generate a further fall in prices, and equally, a rise in prices would be cumulative. The degree of stability of the system depends on the *difference* of the marginal propensities, i.e. on $\dfrac{1}{s_p - s_w}$, which may be defined as the 'coefficient of sensitivity of income distribution', since it indicates the change in the share of profits in income which follows upon a change in the share of investment in output.

If the difference between the marginal propensities is small, the coefficient will be large, and small changes in $\frac{I}{Y}$ (the investment/output relationship) will cause relatively large changes in income distribution $\frac{P}{Y}$; and vice versa.

In the limiting case where $s_w = 0$, the amount of profits is equal to the sum of investment and capitalist consumption, i.e.:

$$P = \frac{1}{s_p} I$$

This is the assumption implicit in Keynes' parable about the widow's cruse – where a rise in entrepreneurial consumption raises their total profit by an *identical* amount – and of Mr Kalecki's theory of profits which can be paraphrased by saying that 'capitalists earn what they spend, and workers spend what they earn'.

This model (i.e. the 'special case' where $s_w = 0$) in a sense is the precise opposite of the Ricardian (or Marxian) one – here wages (not profits) are a residue, profits being governed by the propensity to invest and the capitalists' propensity to consume, which represent a kind of 'prior charge' on the national output. Whereas in the Ricardian model the ultimate incidence of all taxes (other than taxes on rent) fall on profits, here the incidence of all taxes, taxes on income and profits as well as on commodities, falls on wages.[38] Assuming however that $\frac{I}{Y}$ and s_p remain constant over time, the share of wages will also remain constant – i.e. real wages will increase automatically, year by year, with the increase in output per man.

If s_w is positive the picture is more complicated. Total profits

38. The ultimate incidence of taxes can only fall on profits (on this model) in so far as they increase s_p, the propensity to save out of *net* income after tax. Income and profits taxes, through the 'double taxation' of savings, have of course the opposite effect: they reduce s_p, and thereby make the share of *net* profits in income larger than it would be in the absence of taxation. On the other hand, discriminatory taxes on dividend distribution, or dividend limitation, by keeping down both dividends and capital gains, have the effect of raising s_p. (All this applies, of course, on the assumption that the Government *spends* the proceeds of the tax – i.e. that it aims at a balanced budget. Taxes which go to augment the budget surplus will lower the share of profits in much the same way as an increase in workers' savings.)

will be reduced by the amount of workers' savings, S_w; on the other hand, the sensitivity of profits to changes in the level of investment will be greater, total profits rising (or falling) by a greater amount than the change in investment, owing to the consequential reduction (or increase) in workers' savings.[39]

The critical assumption is that the investment/output ratio is an independent variable. Following Harrod, we can describe the determinants of the investment/output ratio in terms of the rate of growth of output capacity (G) and the capital/output ratio, v:

$$\frac{I}{Y} = Gv \qquad (3)$$

In a state of continuous full employment G must be equal to the rate of growth of the 'full employment ceiling', i.e. the sum of the rate of technical progress and the growth in working population (Harrod's 'natural rate of growth'). For Harrod's second equation:

$$\frac{I}{Y} = s$$

we can now substitute equation (1) above:

$$\frac{I}{Y} = (s_p - s_w)\frac{P}{Y} + s_w$$

Hence the 'warranted' and the 'natural' rates of growth are not independent of one another; if profit margins are flexible, the former will adjust itself to the latter through a consequential change in $\frac{P}{Y}$.

This does not mean that there will be an *inherent* tendency to

39. Thus if $s_p = 50\%$, $s_w = 10\%$, $\frac{I}{Y} = 20\%$, $\frac{P}{Y}$ will be 15%; but a rise in $\frac{I}{Y}$ to 21% would raise $\frac{P}{Y}$ to 17·5%. If, on the other hand $s_w = 0$, with $s_p = 50\%$, $\frac{P}{Y}$ would become 40%, but an increase in $\frac{I}{Y}$ to 21% would only increase $\frac{P}{Y}$ to 42%. The above formulae assume that average and marginal propensities are identical. Introducing constant terms in the consumption functions alters the relationship between $\frac{P}{Y}$ and $\frac{I}{Y}$ and would reduce the *elasticity* of $\frac{P}{Y}$ with respect to changes in $\frac{I}{Y}$.

a smooth rate of growth in a capitalist economy, only that the causes of cyclical movements lie elsewhere – not in the lack of an adjustment mechanism between s and Gv. As I have attempted to demonstrate elsewhere,[40] the causes of cyclical movements should be sought in a disharmony between the entrepreneurs' *desired* growth rate (as influenced by the degree of optimism and the volatility of expectations), which governs the rate of increase of output capacity (let us call it G') and the natural growth rate (dependent on technical progress and the growth of the working population), which governs the rate of growth in output. It is the excess of G' over G – not the excess of s over Gv – which causes periodic breakdowns in the investment process through the growth in output capacity outrunning the growth in production.[41]

Problems of the trade cycle, however, lie outside the scope of this paper; and having described a model which shows the distribution of income to be determined by the Keynesian investment-savings mechanism, we must now examine its limitations. The model, as I emphasized earlier, shows the share of profits $\frac{P}{Y}$, the rate of profit on investment $\frac{P}{vY}$, and the real wage rate $\frac{W}{L}$[42], as functions of $\frac{I}{Y}$, which in turn is determined independently of $\frac{P}{Y}$ or $\frac{W}{L}$. There are four different reasons why this may not be true, or be true only within a certain range.

(1) The first is that the real wage cannot fall below a certain subsistence minimum. Hence $\frac{P}{Y}$ can only attain its indicated

40. *Economic Journal* (March 1954), pp. 53–71.

41. $\frac{I}{Y}$ will therefore tend to equal $G'v$, not Gv. It may be assumed that taking very long periods G' is largely governed by G but over shorter periods the two are quite distinct, moreover G itself is not independent of G', since technical progress and population growth are both stimulated by the degree of pressure on the 'full employment ceiling', which depends on G'. The elasticity of response of G to G' is not infinite however: hence the greater G', the greater will be G (the *actual* trend-rate of growth of the economy over successive cycles) but the greater also the ratio $\frac{G'}{G}$ which measures the strength of cyclical forces.

42. Where L = labour force.

value, if the resulting real wage exceeds this minimum rate, w'. Hence the model is subject to the restriction $\frac{W}{L} \geqslant w'$, which we may write in the form:

$$\frac{P}{Y} \leqslant \frac{Y - w'L}{Y} \tag{4}$$

(2) The second is that the indicated share of profits cannot be below the level which yields the minimum rate of profit necessary to induce capitalists to invest their capital, and which we may call the 'risk premium rate', r. Hence the restriction:

$$\frac{P}{vY} \geqslant r \tag{5}$$

(3) The third is that apart from a minimum rate of profit on capital there may be a certain minimum rate of profit on turnover – due to imperfections of competition, collusive agreements between traders, etc., and which we may call m, the 'degree of monopoly' rate. Hence the restriction:

$$\frac{P}{Y} \geqslant m \tag{6}$$

It is clear that equations (5) and (6) describe *alternative* restrictions, of which the higher will apply.

(4) The fourth is that the capital/output ratio, v, should not in itself be influenced by the rate of profit, for if it is, the investment/output ratio Gv will itself be dependent on the rate of profit. A certain degree of dependence follows inevitably from the consideration, mentioned earlier, that the value of particular capital goods in terms of final consumption goods will vary with the rate of profit,[43] so that, even with a *given technique*, v will not be independent of $\frac{P}{Y}$. (We shall ignore this point.) There is the further complication that the relation $\frac{P}{Y}$ may affect v through making more or less 'labour-saving' techniques profitable. In other words, at any given wage–price relationship, the producers

43. cf. p. 354, above. In fact the whole of the Keynesian and post-Keynesian analysis dodges the problem of the measurement of capital.

will adopt the technique which maximizes the rate of profit on capital, $\frac{P}{vY}$; this will affect (at a given G) $\frac{I}{Y}$, and hence $\frac{P}{Y}$. Hence any rise in $\frac{P}{Y}$ will reduce v, and thus $\frac{I}{Y}$, and conversely, any rise in $\frac{I}{Y}$ will raise $\frac{P}{Y}$. If the sensitiveness of v to $\frac{P}{Y}$ is great, $\frac{P}{Y}$ can no longer be regarded as being determined by the equations of the model; the *technical* relation between v and $\frac{P}{Y}$ will then govern $\frac{P}{Y}$ whereas the savings equation (equation (2) above) will determine $\frac{I}{Y}$ and thus (given G) the value of v.[44] To exclude this we have to assume that v is invariant to $\frac{P}{Y}$,[45] i.e.:

$$v = \bar{v} \qquad (7)$$

If equation (4) is unsatisfied, we are back at the Ricardian (or Marxian) model. $\frac{Y}{I}$ will suffer a shrinkage, and will no longer correspond to Gv, but to, say, αv where $\alpha < G$. Hence the system will not produce full employment; output will be limited by the available capital, and not by labour; at the same time the classical and not the Keynesian, reaction-mechanism will be in operation: the size of the 'surplus' available for investment determining investment, not investment savings. It is possible, however, that owing to technical inventions, etc., and starting from a position

44. This is where the 'marginal productivity' principle would come in, but it should be emphasized that under the conditions of our model where savings are treated, not as a constant, but as a function of income distribution, $\frac{P}{Y}$, the sensitiveness of v to changes in $\frac{P}{Y}$ would have to be very large to overshadow the influence of G and of s_p and of s_w on $\frac{P}{Y}$. Assuming that it is large, it is further necessary to suppose that the value of $\frac{P}{Y}$ as dictated by this technical relationship falls within the maximum and minimum values indicated by equations (4)–(6).

45. This assumption does not necessarily mean that there are 'fixed coefficients' as between capital equipment and labour – only that technical innovations (which are also assumed to be 'neutral' in their effects) are far more influential on the chosen v than price relationships.

of excess labour and underemployment (i.e. an elastic total supply of labour), the size of the surplus will grow; hence $\frac{I}{Y}$ and α will grow; and hence α might rise above G (the rate of growth of the 'full employment ceiling', given the technical progress and the growth of population) so that in time the excess labour becomes absorbed and full employment is reached. When this happens (which we may call the stage of *developed* capitalism) wages will rise above the subsistence level, and the properties of the system will then follow our model.

If equations (5) and (6) are unsatisfied, the full employment assumption breaks down, and so will the process of growth; the economy will relapse into a state of stagnation. The interesting conclusion which emerges from these equations is that this may be the result of several distinct causes. 'Investment opportunities' may be low because G' is low relatively to G, i.e. the entrepreneurs' expectations are involatile, and/or they are pessimistic; hence they expect a lower level of demand for the future than corresponds to potential demand, governed by G. On the other hand, 'liquidity preference' may be too high, or the risks associated with investment too great, leading to an excessive r. (This is perhaps the factor on which Keynes himself set greatest store as a cause of unemployment and stagnation.) Finally, lack of competition may cause 'over-saving' through excessive profit margins; this again will cause stagnation, unless there is sufficient compensating increase in v (through the generation of 'excess capacity' under conditions of rigid profit margins but relatively free entry) to push up Gv, and hence $\frac{I}{Y}$.

If, however, equations (2)–(6) are all satisfied, there will be an inherent tendency to growth and an inherent tendency to full employment. Indeed the two are closely linked to each other. Apart from the case of a developing economy in the immature stage of capitalism (where equation (4) does not hold, but where $\gamma < G$), a tendency to continued economic growth will only exist when the system is only stable at full employment equilibrium – i.e. when $G' \geqslant G$.

This is a possible interpretation of the long-term situation in the 'successful' capitalist economies of western Europe and North America. If G' exceeds G, the investment/output ratio $\frac{I}{Y}$ will not be steady in time, even if the *trend* level of this ratio is constant. There will be periodic breakdowns in the investment process, due to the growth in output capacity outrunning the possible growth in output; when that happens, not only investment, but total output will fall, and output will be (temporarily) limited by effective demand, and not by the scarcity of resources. This is contrary to the mechanics of our model, but several reasons can be adduced to show why the system will not be flexible enough to ensure full employment in the short period.

(1) First, even if 'profit margins' are assumed to be fully flexible, in a downward; as well as an upward, direction, the very fact that investment goods and consumer goods are produced by different industries, with limited mobility between them, will mean that profit margins in the consumption goods industries will not fall below the level that ensures full utilization of resources in the consumption goods industries. A *compensating* increase in consumption goods production (following upon a fall in the production of investment goods) can only occur as a result of a transfer of resources from the other industries, lured by the profit opportunities there.

(2) Second, and more important, profit-margins are likely to be inflexible in a downward direction in the short period (Marshall's 'fear of spoiling the market') even if they are flexible in the long period, or even if they possess short period flexibility in an upward direction.[46]

This applies of course not only to profit margins but to real wages as well, which in the short period may be equally inflexible in a downward direction at the *attained* level, thus compressing $\frac{I}{Y}$, or rather preventing an *increase* in $\frac{I}{Y}$ following upon a rise in the entrepreneurs' desired rate of expansion G'. Hence in the short period the shares of profits and wages tend to be inflexible for two different reasons – the downward inflexibility of $\frac{P}{Y}$ and the downward inflexibility of $\frac{W}{L}$ – which thus tend to reinforce

46. cf. the quotation from Marshall [p. 367, fn. 33].

the long-period stability of these shares, due to constancy of $\frac{I}{Y}$, resulting from the long period constancy of Gv and $G'v$.[47]

We have seen how the various 'models' of distribution, the Ricardo–Marxian, the Keynesian, and the Kaleckian, are related to each other. I am not sure where 'marginal productivity' comes in in all this – except that in so far as it has any importance it does through an extreme sensitivity of v to changes in $\frac{P}{Y}$.

47. This operates through the wage–price spiral that would follow on a reduction in real wages; the prevention of such a wage–price spiral by means of investment rationing of some kind, or a 'credit squeeze', is thus a manifestation of downward inflexibility of $\frac{W}{Y}$.

Further Reading

Classics

DOUGLAS, P. H. (1934) *The theory of wages* (Macmillan, New York).

DUNLOP, J. T. (1950) *Wage determination under trade unions* (2nd edn., Macmillan, New York and London).

HICKS, J. R. (1963) *The theory of wages* (2nd edn. Macmillan, London).

MARSHALL, A. (1920) *Principles of economics* (8th edn. Macmillan, London).

MARSHALL, A. (1899) *Economics of industry* (Macmillan, London).

ROSS, A. M. (1948) *The theory of union wage policy* (University of California Press).

ROWE, J. W. F. (1928) *Wages in practice and theory* (Routledge).

Textbooks

CARTER, A. M. (1959) *The theory of wages and employment* (Irwin).

LESTER, R. A. (1964) *Economics of labour* (2nd edn. Macmillan, London).

PHELPS BROWN, E. H. (1962) *The economics of labour* (Yale University Press).

REDER, M. W. (1957) *Labour in a growing economy* (Wiley).

REYNOLDS, L. G. (1964) *Labour economics and labour relations* (4th edn. Prentice Hall).

ROBERTSON, D. J. (1961) *The economics of wages and the distribution of income* (Macmillan, London).

Specialist reading

BECKER, G. S. (1964) *Human capital* (Columbia University Press).

BOWEN, W. G. (1960) *The wage-price issue* (Princeton University Press).

DOW, J. AND DICKS-MIREAUX, L. (1959) Determinants of wage inflation *Journ. Roy. Stat. Soc.*, series A, **122**, 145–74.

ECKSTEIN, O. AND WILSON, T. A. (1962) Determination of money wages in American industry. *Quart. Journ. Econ.*, **76**, 379–414.

FELLNER, W., *et al.* (1964) *Rising prices* (Organization for Economic Co-operation and Development).

LEWIS, H. G. (1963) *Unionism and relative wages in the United States* (University of Chicago Press).

LONG, C. D. (1961) *The labour force under changing income and employment* (Princeton University.)

MCCORD WRIGHT, D. (1951) *The impact of the union* (Harcourt).

PHELPS BROWN, E. H. AND BROWNE, M. H. (1962) Earnings in the industries of the United Kingdom, 1948–1959, *Econ. Journ.*, **2**, 517–49.

PHELPS BROWN, E. H. AND HART, P. E. (1952) Share of wages in the national income. *Econ. Journ.*, **62**, 253–77.

PHILLIPS, A. W. (1958) Relation between employment and the rate of change of money wage rates in the United Kingdom, 1867–1957. *Economica*, **27**, 283–99.

REES, A. (1962) *Economics of trade unions* (Cambridge University Press).

REYNOLDS, L. G. AND TAFT, C. (1956) *The evolution of wage structure* (Yale University Press).

ROSS, A. M. (ed., 1965) *Employment policy in the labour market* (University of California Press).

ROUTH, G. (1965) *Occupation and pay in Great Britain* (Cambridge University Press).

SALTER, W. E. G. (1966) *Productivity and technical change* (2nd edn. Cambridge University Press).

SLICHTER, S. H. (1941) *Union policies and industrial management* (Brookings Institution, Washington D.C.).

SLICHTER, S. H., HEALY, J. J. AND LIVERNASH, E. R. (1960) *The impact of collective bargaining on management* (Brookings Institution, Washington D.C.).

STEIN, J. L. (1958), The predictive accuracy of the marginal productivity theory of wages. *Rev. Econ. Stud.*, **25**, 182–9.

STEVENS, C. M. (1963) *Strategy and collective bargaining negotiation* (McGraw-Hill).

TURNER, H. A. (1952) Trade unions, differentials and the levelling of wages. *Manchester School*, **20**, 227–82.

TURNER, H. A. (1962) *Trade union growth, structure and policy* (Allen & Unwin).

WEBB, S. AND B. (1902) *Industrial democracy* (2nd edn. Longman).

WOLFF, P. DE. (1965) *Wages and labour mobility* (Organization for Economic Co-operation and Development).

Acknowledgements

Permission to reproduce the material published in this volume is acknowledged from the following sources:

Reading no. 1: Richard A. Lester and the American Economic Association.

Reading no. 2: Fritz Machlup and the American Economic Association.

Readings no. 3 and 6: Reprinted from the *Industrial and Labor Relations Review*, 9, pp. 183–99, and vol. 13, pp. 349–62.

Reading no. 4: Gary S. Becker and the Royal Economic Society.

Reading no 5: H. A. Turner (who has developed and refined the analysis contained in this article in his book *Trade union growth, structure and policy*, published by Allen & Unwin) and *Political Quarterly*.

Reading no. 7: Paul A. Weinstein and the American Economic Association.

Reading no. 8: Carl M. Stevens and the Harvard University Press.

Reading no. 9: W. B. Reddaway and Lloyds Bank Limited.

Reading no. 10: M. W. Reder and the American Economic Association.

Reading no. 11: H. A. Turner, Macmillan & Co. Ltd, St Martin's Press Inc., and the Macmillan Company of Canada Ltd.

Reading no. 12: Richard G. Lipsey and the University of California Press.

Reading no. 13: Richard G. Lipsey and the British Association for the Advancement of Science (this article was the Lister Lecture delivered at the Norwich meeting of the British Association for the Advancement of Science).

Reading no. 14: A. G. Hines and the *Review of Economic Studies*.

Reading no. 15: H. F. Lydall and Basil Blackwell.

Reading no. 16: N. Kaldor and the Review of Economic Studies.

Author Index

Author Index

Author Index

Subject Index

Subject Index

Subject Index

Penguin Modern Economics

Other titles available in this series are:

Economics of Education: 1
Ed. M. Blaug

The quality of the labour force and the methods of training it have
recently attracted the attention of economists. The education system
is an important factor in economic growth, the degree of mobility of
labour and the distribution of income. These important issues are
considered in this volume of articles. A second volume, also edited
by Professor Blaug, will examine the internal efficiency of schools,
and the relations between the costs of education and methods of
financing these costs. These Readings will be widely welcomed by
educationists, sociologists and political scientists as well as
economists. X56

Managerial Economics
Ed. G. P. E. Clarkson

The growth, range and complexity of problems facing the modern
corporation mean that many managers must acquire new skills.
Managerial economics deals with the process of decision-making
within the firm. It uses the economist's concepts of utility and
maximizing of profit to analyse, with mathematical and statistical
techniques, a wide range of problems of finance, marketing, and
production. X57

Public Enterprise
Ed. R. Turvey

The public sector as a consumer of resources and a producer of
goods and services is apparent. But the methods of ensuring
efficiency in public corporations are not obvious. Public enterprises
may aim at social as well as commercial ends in conjunction with a
private sector which is all too often imperfect in structure and
behaviour. This volume of Readings is deliberately selective and
provocative in an area where there is much confusion and
disagreement. X59

Regional Analysis

Ed. L. Needleman

Appalachia, Northern Ireland and Mezzogiorno are witnesses to the uneven geography of economic development. Indeed, they may seem part of an 'underdeveloped' world. The application of the tools of economic analysis to regional problems has only just begun: the editor offers here a full range of regional work on one of the most interesting and exciting areas of economic inquiry. X60

Transport

Ed. Denys Munby

'There is no escape from transport.' 'Almost every transport decision is a public issue.' These two challenging statements form the prelude to a collection of articles devoted to the economics of transport. The quality of the analysis and prescriptions is dictated by Dupuit's article and proceeds through Lewis, Vickrey, Walters, Meyer, and Foster. All demonstrate the important contribution economists can make to the analysis of transport problems and the formulation of appropriate policies. X58

Modern Economics

J. Pen

In 1936 Keynes published his famous *General Theory of Employment, Interest and Money* and the science of economics has never been the same. Gone is the comfortable 'classical' belief in a self-adjusting balance between supply and demand: moreover, allied to Keynesian theory, the growth of exact quantitative economics has tended to produce a distinct 'modern economics'. A silent revolution has occurred.

It is widely held that Keynesian theories can only be comprehended by the expert, and this in itself delays the application of modern ideas, since every citizen, when he shops, works, or votes, is a practising economist. Professor Pen, the well-known Dutch economist, challenges this assumption in this Pelican, in which he sets out to explain to the non-expert the meaning of Keynes's ideas and the findings of modern statistical methods.

His book provides a clear (and frequently humorous and hard-hitting) introduction to modern theories regarding international trade, national budgets, the function of money, inflation and deflation, wages, economic growth, and many other economic topics in daily discussion. A710/5s

Economic Philosophy

Joan Robinson

This exceptionally stimulating book begins by showing how the basic human need for a morality on which the conscience can work has led to the necessity for a philosophy of economics in any society. It is stressed that economic values and money values are not identical, and it is the task of the economist to justify the image of Mammon to man – 'not to tell us what to do, but show why what we are doing anyway is in accord with proper principles'. The relations between science and ideology over the last two hundred years are traced from Adam Smith, through Marx and Keynes, to the dichotomy that exists in current economic thinking and the pressing fundamental problems which must now be faced.

'It would be difficult to think of a better book than this is placed in the hands of the reader who thinks that economics is simply a matter of statistics, and who needs to be convinced of its intellectual interest and excitement.' Samuel Brittan in the *Observer*. A653/3s 6d

For copyright reasons this edition is not for sale in the U.S.A.

A History of British Trade Unionism

Henry Pelling

Today trade unionism plays a more important part in the nation's economy than ever before, and its problems of internal reform and its relations with the government and the public are constantly under discussion. But its present structure can only be understood in relation to its long history. And, indeed, its history in Britain is also the first chapter in the history of trade unionism all over the world.

In this, the first comprehensive book on the subject for thirty-five years, Henry Pelling, a Fellow of Queen's College, Oxford, and author of *The Origin of the Labour Party*, leads the reader through a vivid story of struggle and development covering more than four centuries: from the medieval guilds, and early craftsmen's and labourers' associations to the dramatic growth of trade unionism in Britain in the nineteenth and twentieth centuries. Most important, he traces the course of two significant issues: first, the shift in power from the craft unions to the amalgamated unions, and finally in our time to the giant general unions. And, secondly, the changing relationships of the labour and political functions of the unions from the early nineteenth century through the Labour Representation Committee to the block vote and the 1959 Labour Party Conference. Trade unions are an essential part of our society and we must understand them if we are to understand Britain today. A616/5s

The Social Psychology of Industry

J. A. C. Brown

In recent years it is becoming increasingly apparent that the classical approach to industrial psychology is inadequate. This approach regarded the worker primarily as a machine to be studied by the techniques of physiological psychology, and as an isolated individual whose aptitudes caused him to be suited or unsuited for a given job. The results obtained by such an approach are not necessarily wrong but, as Elton Mayo demonstrated conclusively more than twenty years ago, they are bound to be incomplete because the 'isolated' human being is a fiction. Since each individual is a member of society, and each worker a member of a working group, the attitudes of these groups are bound to play a large part in influencing his behaviour both as citizen and worker.

This book makes no attempt to replace other textbooks on industrial psychology; it should rather be regarded as an attempt to supply the reader with an understanding of the social background of industry. Believing that if we begin with the wrong assumptions no amount of accurate research can produce the correct answers, the author has tried to discuss such fundamental questions as: what is human nature? what causes men to work? what is morale? and what influence has the nature of industrial work upon the mental health of the individual worker and his community? A296/4s 6d